FROM SCHLEMIEL TO SABRA

PERSPECTIVES ON ISRAEL STUDIES

S. Ilan Troen, Natan Aridan, Donna Divine, David Ellenson, Arieh Saposnik, and Jonathan Sarna, *editors*

Sponsored by the Ben-Gurion Research Institute for the Study of Israel and Zionism of the Ben-Gurion University of the Negev and the Schusterman Center for Israel Studies of Brandeis University

FROM SCHLEMIEL TO SABRA

Zionist Masculinity and Palestinian Hebrew Literature

Philip Hollander

INDIANA UNIVERSITY PRESS

This book is a publication of

Indiana University Press
Office of Scholarly Publishing
Herman B Wells Library 350
1320 East 10th Street
Bloomington, Indiana 47405 USA

iupress.indiana.edu

© 2019 by Philip Hollander

Manufactured in the United States of America

Library of Congress Cataloging-in-Publication Data

Names: Hollander, Philip, author.
Title: From schlemiel to sabra : Zionist masculinity and Palestinian Hebrew literature / Philip Hollander.
Description: Bloomington, Indiana : Indiana University Press, [2019] | Series: Perspectives on Israel studies | Includes bibliographical references and index.
Identifiers: LCCN 2019013211 (print) | LCCN 2019014981 (ebook) | ISBN 9780253042095 (ebook) | ISBN 9780253042057 (hardback : alk. paper) | ISBN 9780253042064 (pbk. : alk. paper)
Subjects: LCSH: Israeli literature—History and criticism. | Masculinity in literature. | Schlemiels in literature. | Sabras. | Zionism in literature. | Agnon, Shmuel Yosef, 1887-1970—Criticism and interpretation. | Brenner, Joseph ?Hayyim, 1881-1921—Criticism and interpretation. | Arieli, L. A., 1886-1943—Criticism and interpretation. | Reuveni, A., 1886-1971—Criticism and interpretation.
Classification: LCC PJ5020 (ebook) | LCC PJ5020 .H64 2019 (print) | DDC 892.409/353—dc23
LC record available at https://lccn.loc.gov/2019013211

ISBN 978-0-253-04205-7 (hdbk.)
ISBN 978-0-253-04206-4 (pbk.)
ISBN 978-0-253-04209-5 (web PDF)

1 2 3 4 5   24 23 22 21 20 19

For my father, Dr. Joshua Hollander z"l

CONTENTS

ACKNOWLEDGMENTS

THIS BOOK REPRESENTS MORE THAN TWENTY-FIVE YEARS OF research into early twentieth-century Hebrew literature and Israeli culture. It began with a course on early twentieth-century Hebrew literature taught by Nili Gold, who opened my eyes to the literature's riches and the scholar's ability to reveal them. It was subsequently conceptualized, researched, and written in the waters of the Mediterranean, Jerusalem, New York, Princeton, New Orleans, and Madison.

After graduating college, I immigrated to Israel. While my subsequent military service on Israeli naval ship *Ma'oz* might seem far from academic questions, it influenced this book's ultimate shape. It immersed me in Hebrew culture to the point where Hebrew became the dominant language of my unconscious, and it developed my thought on masculinity and relations between men. My thanks go to my former shipmates. Special thanks, however, go to Michah Cohen z"l, Asaf Guy, and Ran Ziv. Asaf and Ran provided me with a brotherhood of the mind, and Michah presented his belief that paternity trumped military accomplishment in the mark of a man. I still remember when he fearlessly delivered his newborn child into my arms.

Dan Miron's example and mentorship dominated my graduate training at Hebrew University and Columbia University. My current understanding of early twentieth-century Hebrew literature bears the mark of his research and teaching. A hands-off mentor, he encouraged me to write my dissertation on Levi Aryeh Arieli's fiction and drama; he left me free to develop an independent approach to it. Nonetheless, he knew when to intervene and supplied important encouragement in his unique laconic way. I am grateful to other teachers who contributed to my scholarly development too. At the beginning of my graduate studies, Ezra Fleischer z"l, Matti Huss, Pinchas Mandel, and Yigal Schwartz gave me the confidence to believe that I could complete a doctorate and contribute to Hebrew literary scholarship. In New York, Yael Feldman, Nili Gold, and Hannan Hever further developed my understanding of Hebrew literature, Michael Stanislawski deepened my understanding of its historical context, and David Roskies collaborated with Dan Miron to provide me with the resources necessary to study Hebrew literature alongside its Yiddish counterpart. I am also grateful for the community of friends and colleagues who enlightened and encouraged me during my graduate training. I am particularly indebted to Jill Aizenstein, Jennifer Altman, Vicki As-Shifris, Beverly Bailis, Marc Caplan, Nehama Edinger, Naomi Kadar z"l, Rebecca Kobrin, Barbara Landress, Rebecca Margolis, Marc Miller, Eddie Portnoy, Alyssa Quint, Miryam Segal, Andrea Siegel, Magda Teter, Scott Ury, Katja Vehlow, and Kalman Weiser.

As the breadth of my research expanded, I refined my ideas about Modern Hebrew literature and Israeli culture through teaching at Princeton University, Rutgers University, Tulane University, and University of Wisconsin–Madison. Thanks to Mark Cohen, Nancy Sinkoff, Brian Horowitz, and Rachel Brenner for helping provide me with these opportunities; thanks to my students, first and foremost Michael Yaari, for their aid.

When writing a book, writers imagine a community of readers to whom they address their work. I, however, didn't need to tax my imagination. An actual scholarly community helped me develop my ideas. Through their research, lectures, conversation, and friendship, numerous colleagues have helped birth this book. In addition to aforementioned individuals who have followed this project from its infancy, I would like to thank Nancy Berg, Mikhal Dekel, Shai Ginburg, Rachel Harris, Todd Hasak-Lowy, Tamar Hess, Adriana Jacobs, Sheila Jelen, Stephen Katz, Dan Laor, Edna Nahshon, Moshe Naor, Shachar Pinsker, Michael Weingrad, Eric Zakim, and Wendy Zierler. One group and a few individuals deserve special thanks. The directors and fellow participants in the 2011 AAJR Early Career Faculty Workshop were the first to offer positive feedback on this project. Since he shared his dissertation research with me, Yaron Peleg has been an implicit interlocutor. I couldn't imagine a nicer guy with whom to disagree. While never formerly my teacher, through participation in my oral exams and my dissertation defense, Alan Mintz z"l guided me. Subsequently, he read my research, offered support, and treated me as a respected counterpart. Finally, since we first met, Gur Alroey has been an amazing sounding board, an intellectual guide to Pre-State Israel's history, and a true mensch.

My scholarly community does not end with those to whom I addressed my research. I found community and the material and emotional support that come with it at Princeton University, Tulane University, and University of Wisconsin–Madison. Following Hurricane Katrina, when I was exiled from New Orleans, Princeton University supplied me with an apartment, an office, and library access. These generous gifts enabled me to begin converting my dissertation into a broader study. Similarly, I am beholden to Tulane University. Colleagues in the Department of Germanic and Slavic Studies supplied me with emotional support following my return to New Orleans; the support of a Committee on Research Summer Fellowship and a Research Enhancement Fund Phase II Grant made critical research for this book possible. Since my arrival in Madison, its tight-knit academic community has proven welcoming. I am grateful to colleagues and friends across the disciplines who have helped make the University of Wisconsin–Madison what it is today. I am particularly indebted to those who worked with me in the Department of Hebrew and Semitic Studies and the Department of German and those who currently work alongside me in the Mosse/Weinstein Center for Jewish Studies and the Department of German, Nordic, and Slavic. Special thanks go to Sabine Gross, Judith Kornblatt, Pam Potter, and Patricia Rosenmeyer, senior colleagues who played pivotal roles in helping me advance my research. I would especially like to thank the University of Wisconsin–Madison German Program for funding production of the index for this book. Finally, support for this research was provided by the University of Wisconsin–Madison Office of the Vice Chancellor for Research and Graduate Education with funding from the Wisconsin Alumni Research Foundation. I would like to gratefully acknowledge multiple Wisconsin Alumni Research Foundation grants.

I am grateful to a group of people who have eased the way from manuscript to book. Sylvia Fuchs Fried, director of Brandeis University Press, provided generous aid. She spoke with me at length about my book prospectus, edited versions of it, and offered timely advice and encouragement. Ilan Troen and Arieh Saposnik, editors of Indiana University Press's Perspectives on Israel Studies book series, promptly read through my book proposal and sent my manuscript out for review. The three anonymous peer reviewers offered detailed advice for revision and improvement of the manuscript. Finally, Indiana University Press editors Dee Mortensen and Paige Rasmussen have guided me through the publication process.

Earlier versions of material from chapters 2, 3, and 4 appeared in the following publications: "The Role of Homosociality in Palestinian Hebrew Literature: A Case Study of Levi Aryeh Arieli's 'Wasteland,'" *Prooftexts* 29, no. 2 (2009): 273–304 (reprinted by permission of Indiana University Press); "Contested Zionist Masculinity and the Redemption of the Schlemiel in Levi Aryeh Arieli's 'Allah Karim!'" *Israel Studies* 17, no. 3 (Fall 2012): 92–118 (reprinted by permission of Indiana University Press); "Rereading 'Decadent'

Palestinian Hebrew Literature: The Intersection of Zionism, Masculinity, and Sexuality in Aharon Reuveni's 'Ad Yerushalayim,'" *AJS Review* 39, no. 1 (April 2015): 3–26 (reprinted by permission of Cambridge University Press). I thank the publishers for permission to reprint. I am also indebted to the Central Zionist Archives, the National Library of Israel, and Duke University Libraries and their staffs for assistance with images for the book. Special thanks to Yael Blau for permission to use images from the Agnon Archive.

As the Bible tells us, *aharon aharon haviv.* Exceptional thanks go to friends and family whose friendship and love precedes this book, as well as family members who entered this world during its birthing. I am particularly grateful to Dr. Richard Bernstein z"l, memory of whom never leaves me. Similarly, I am indebted to Rabbi Ben and Judy Hollander z"l, who opened their Jerusalem home and hearts to me. I hope to voice a small part of the positivity they brought to the world. Luckily, my beloved cousins Ilana Hanokh, Eli Hollander, Dvir Hollander, and Netanel Hollander and their families aid me in this enterprise. I am beholden to my freewheeling cosmopolitan aunt Paula Horwitz, who taught me to strive to realize one's personal vision, for her love and backing. The support of the California Hollanders has long been unflinching. Thanks to Henry, Katherine, Nate, Ruth, and Reuben. Since my birth, Susan Hollander has had my back. Thanks for keeping your eyes peeled, big sister. The ceaseless love and support of my mother, Sheila, and my father, Joshua z"l, never ceases to amaze me, and I strive to supply my sons with the same. Such a task proves surprisingly easy. Doobie and Nash provide me with empowering affection and love that push me to succeed in all my endeavors. Finally, my boundless love and thanks go to my wife, Juliet Page. Since we met, this book has dwelled with us. I hope you enjoy the empty nest.

NOTE ON TRANSLITERATION AND TRANSLATION

I HAVE FOLLOWED A MODIFIED FORM OF THE Library of Congress transliteration system for Hebrew throughout this book. I transliterate the Hebrew tzadi as "tz," rather than "ts," and I leave out most diacritical marks and dots. In cases where the convention is to transliterate the names of individuals or institutions differently from how my transliteration would suggest, I retain the conventional spelling of those names in the body of the text and transliterate them according to my system in the notes and bibliography. Thus, individual and institutional names are often spelled differently in various places in the book. Despite the potential confusion this might generate, it makes it easier for individuals who do not speak Hebrew to learn more about individuals and institutions that I refer to in the body of the text, and it allows Hebrew speakers to more easily locate the Hebrew sources in the footnotes and bibliography. On occasion, I have not followed the transliterative system set out above. In many of these cases, I have done this to match the transliteration of Hebrew writers' names to those employed by the online *Leksikon ha-sifrut ha-'Ivrit ha-hadashah* and the transliteration of Yiddish writers' names to those employed by the online edition of *The YIVO Encyclopedia of Jews in Eastern Europe*. Thus, one finds Amos Oz, Shmu'el Yosef Agnon, and Khone Shmeruk, rather than 'Amos 'Oz, Shmu'el Yosef 'Agnon, and Honeh Shmeruk, in the footnotes and bibliography.

Rather than employ both the Hebrew term *Eretz Yisra'el* (Land of Israel) and the term *Palestine* used by English speakers to refer to the same geographic area during the late Ottoman and British mandate periods, I have endeavored as much as possible to use the term *Palestine* to refer to the location where the literary works written prior to the establishment of the State of Israel, as discussed in this book, were composed. Thus, when this book discusses Palestinian Hebrew literature, it refers to the belles lettres composed by Jewish writers active in Palestine until 1948. Hebrew literature written by Palestinian Arabs emerged only after 1948. On a few occasions, Land of Israel appears in lieu of the Hebrew term.

When published translations of Hebrew literary works cited in the text are available, they have been employed and referenced in the footnotes. Occasionally, published translations have been slightly modified for accuracy or clarity. All other translations from Hebrew or Yiddish are my own.

FROM SCHLEMIEL TO SABRA

GENERAL INTRODUCTION

A Rhetoric of Empowerment

Zionism was an uneasy coalition of diverse dreams, and by definition it would
have been impossible for all those dreams to have been fulfilled. Today, some are
partially fulfilled, some forgotten, and some have turned into nightmares.

—Amos Oz, "A Monologue: Behind the Sound and Fury"

Masculinity, Early Twentieth-Century Hebrew Literature, and Palestinian Zionism

Modern Hebrew literature's relationship to Israeli history and culture is not
straightforward. On the one hand, Modern Hebrew literature is now synonymous with Israeli literature. On the other hand, it predates the State of
Israel's establishment by nearly two hundred years. Similarly, while contemporary Hebrew literature is almost exclusively composed within Israel's borders, Modern Hebrew–language literary centers once existed in
Germany, Austria, Russia, and the United States.[1] Finally, Modern Hebrew
literature's political character is perpetually changing. It has fervently supported, passionately questioned, vociferously opposed, and proven wholly
indifferent to Zionism and the Jewish state.

In the early twentieth century, when Palestinian Jewish settlement was
in its infancy, the uncertainty concerning Modern Hebrew literature's relationship to Zionism and Israeli history reached its apex. Consequently, it
has been interpreted in contradictory ways. Some view Modern Hebrew literature as an important contributor to the Palestinian Jewish community's
development, and others view Modern Hebrew literature as undermining
it. Thus, the influential Palestinian Zionist leader Yosef Aharonowitz (1877–
1937) argues that "the question of Palestinian [Hebrew] culture doesn't come
to add or subtract from the settlement question, rather it is the settlement
question's essence in its most poignant form."[2] In contrast, historian David
Biale sees a negative correlation between Zionism and Palestinian Hebrew
culture. He asserts that "a national revolution [has never] been accompanied

My name is Israel.
I am 20.

Good people died that I might be
born in a land called home.
I have heard the stories and seen the
graves.
But now we are here, and the land is
ours. Not all milk and honey, but ours.
We share a name, the land and I—
Israel. And we share a birthday.
Twenty years. For me, a long time.
For my people, who waited thousands
of years, almost nothing.
But we have made something of
that waiting.
Now the hills of rock are hills of
trees. Fifty million trees, Jerusalem
pines, planted one at a time.
Cities thrive where nothing thrived.
Orange trees bloom where nothing
bloomed.
An almost dead language is alive
again. We read the Dead Sea Scrolls as
easily as you read this magazine.
We mine copper where King Sol-
omon mined copper.
We make fresh water from the sea,

and we share what we have learned
with other nations.
We build airports and schools in
Asia, sell baby chickens and farm
equipment in Europe, and exchange
our students with even younger countries in Africa.
How do we go to so many places?
Easy. We have our own airline.
El Al Israel Airlines.
You don't know what El Al means?
It means "to the skies" in that almost
dead language.
It also means that our jets are wel-
come in 17 different nations.
Yes, we have everything now. Uni-
versities, symphony orchestras, great
museums, politicians, druggists, traffic
jams, a little air pollution—everything.
We are of the century, with all of the
strengths and weaknesses and prob-
lems of people everywhere.
We will survive.
Because, above all, we are here. Alive.
In a land called home.

The Airline of the People of Israel

Fig. 0.1 "My name is Israel. I am 20." This male figure embodies the sabra stereotype.
It serves to convey the positive rooted masculine character of Israeli men and their nation.
National Library of Israel. Marvin G. Goldman EL AL Collection.

by such a culture of pessimism in which a mythological idea of virile national revival coexisted improbably with a poetics of impotence."[3]

With the phrase "a poetics of impotence," Biale alludes to how masculinity bound Hebrew literature to Zionist discourse and succinctly introduces this book's focus: early twentieth-century Palestinian Hebrew
literature and drama employing this poetics. Many early twentieth-century
Zionists viewed Palestinian Jewish men's youthful vigor, physical strength,
and connection to the land as prerequisites for their participation in Zionist development. Palestinian Hebrew literary representations do not supply these gendered images. Instead, the belletristic works of Yosef Hayyim
Brenner (1881–1921), Levi Aryeh Arieli (1886–1943), Aharon Reuveni (1886–
1971), and Shmuel Yosef Agnon (1887–1970) appear to feature "ineffectual
[Jewish] male characters" who "sink irrevocably back into the pathological
degeneration . . . of the Diaspora" and prove incapable of pursuing erotic
relations with women.[4]

The view that Palestinian Hebrew belles lettres lacking vigorous,
physically powerful, and rooted protagonists prove inimical to Zionism

is grounded in the belief that realization of Zionist aims required *shlilat ha-golah*, or negation of the Diaspora. For the New Jewish Man (*ha-yehudi he-hadash*) to arise in Palestine, it was asserted, elements of diasporic Jewish masculinity, especially those evoked by the Yiddish term *schlemiel*, an awkward, clumsy person, a blunderer; a "born loser"; a "dope" or "drip" needed to be eradicated. Only this would enable the New Jewish Man, rugged and rooted in the land like the sabra cactus and externally prickly with a sweet interior like a sabra fruit, to emerge. Therefore, introduction of Diaspora Jewish male characteristics into the literary portrayal of Palestinian Jewish men ran counter to national rebirth.[5]

Even if we accept the sabra norm as a hegemonic pattern of practice that perpetuated patriarchy and shaped early state period culture, this preeminence was not seamlessly achieved when the first Zionist settlers arrived in Palestine. Hegemony is attained through force, culture, institutions, and persuasion, or some combination thereof. Pre-State Palestinian Zionists, however, lacked the institutions, the cultural unity, and the means of force necessary to advance a specific masculine form as "the most honored way of being a man" and demand that "all other men . . . position themselves in relationship to it." In fact, the Ottoman and mandatory periods constitute a liminal phase during which many aspects of embryonic Israeli culture, including masculinity, remained indeterminate.[6]

Rather than constituting a subject of consensus, culture proves to be a highly contested topic that people fight about; in the early twentieth century, there were ongoing debates within the Palestinian Jewish public sphere about Jewish nationalism's territorial dimension, its relationship to the Jewish past, its attitude to the Jewish body, and its view of what would enable national awakening. Consequently, different New Yishuv groups weighed in on these and other issues, proselytized for new adherents, and jockeyed for dominance of the Zionist public sphere. Sharing a widespread sense that individual Jews and the whole Jewish nation were in jeopardy, contemporary Palestinian Hebrew authors actively voiced their opinions about political and cultural issues and participated in this struggle for ascendancy.[7]

Like other groups debating their envisioned national community's future character, Palestinian Hebrew authors exploited masculinity as a vehicle for communication of their positions. Therefore, early twentieth-century Palestinian Hebrew literature's representation of "impotent" Jewish men and its refusal to promote the type of New Jewish Man represented by the sabra does not reflect authorial despair, or opposition to or ambivalence about Zionism. In fact, the rhetorical use of Jewish male impotence was common in East European Jewish politics and literature, where writers deployed it to advance masculine forms they considered most conducive to a better Jewish future. Similarly, Brenner, Arieli, Reuveni, and Agnon utilized seemingly anti-Zionist representations of masculinity to promote a distinct Zionist masculine form in line with their politic and cultural views. Furthermore, Modern Hebrew writers' presentation of the sabra ideal's limitations, as well as those of other gendered Zionist images, played an important role in their advancement of political action in line with their views. By drawing attention to the shortcomings of *opposing* Zionist ideological and cultural positions as well as non-Zionist ones, Hebrew literary texts were constructed to make their authors' views appear more attractive in public sphere debates.

Pivotal to the masculine model Brenner, Arieli, Reuveni, and Agnon promoted was a view of the relationship between diasporic and Palestinian Jewish culture divergent from the one held by the sabra model's supporters. In fact, diasporic Jewish life's ongoing influence on Jewish immigrants to Palestine and their descendants proved central to "Self-Evaluative masculinity." Like many Palestinian Zionists, these writers viewed complete severance of ties between Diaspora and Palestinian Jewries as unrealizable, and they worked to exploit this connection for social betterment. Through critical reexamination of diasporic experience's continuing impact on their lives, they asserted, Palestinian Zionists could prevent deleterious manifestations of this connection and repurpose diasporic experience's most vital elements for advancement of their nationalist aims. Moreover, promoting an agenda offering a positive and reassuring sense of continuity with the diasporic Jewish past could reassure their brethren and engage them.

Although these writers participated actively in early twentieth-century Palestinian political life, neither the masculine form grounded in self-examination and subsequent moral action their belletristic works conveyed nor the political program it supported found broad support. Instead, the sabra model and its associated political program, with their reticence to acknowledge the Diaspora's influence on Israeli culture and society, achieved widespread endorsement. In part, their success was due to their adherents' recognition of the divergent representations of gender and sexuality found in literary works promoting Self-Evaluative masculinity and its associated national program. Categorizing these literary works as decadent, they delegitimized them.

Contextualized readings of leading works by Self-Evaluative masculinity's proponents during the first two decades of the twentieth century, when these writers were at the height of their ideational confluence, challenge this characterization. First, they reveal how these writers deploy gendered representations and portray sexual relations to advance their national program. Second, they support a gradualist approach to Israeli society's development. Finally, they illuminate masculinity and nationalism's widespread contestation in Pre-State Palestinian Jewish society—something that has continued unabated into the state period.

Palestinian Hebrew Literature's Political Heritage

Early twentieth-century Palestinian Hebrew fiction's political character was not an aberration. From its inception in late eighteenth-century Germany, Modern Hebrew literature possessed a political dimension. When the Hebrew journal *ha-Me'asef* appeared, its progenitors established "a new venue for communication, a literary arena that had not existed before" and allowed new ideas to proliferate. Thus, Hebrew emerged as "a national tool" that allowed Jewish writers and commentators to process and clarify "various approaches to and comments and ideas upon which [the Jews' welfare] now depended." The rabbinic establishment lost power to those who could successfully navigate the expanding Hebrew public sphere. Consequently, Hebrew writers viewed their literature, broadly understood, as "a Jewish literary parliament," and themselves as individuals whose moral certitude and reasoned approach justified their assumption of a leadership role once held by divinely inspired biblical prophets.[8]

Despite Hebrew writers' desire to lead, the Hebrew literary republic only gradually matured and blossomed. Starting in the 1880s, however, the male scions of the traditional East European Jewish middle class, who had received a classical Jewish education and attained Hebrew literacy, joined its ranks. "A truly national reading public numbering in the hundreds of thousands" emerged.[9] Political upheaval, enlightenment, industrialization, urbanization, immigration, and social change, whose affects became increasingly felt, reduced extant Jewish communal structures' effectiveness and fractured individual Jews' sense of self. Consequently, Hebrew literature, newspapers, and periodicals drew in secularizing East

European Jewish men struggling to find footing within the modernizing world. They did this by providing them with information about the myriad changes these men were facing, guidance about how to respond to their unstable reality, and details about frameworks offering a sense of order and belonging.[10]

Born in the 1880s, Agnon, Arieli, Brenner, and Reuveni were profoundly affected by this vibrant public sphere. Like other members of their Hebrew literary generation, they grew up in an East European Jewish world that supported Hebrew dailies, specialized literary almanacs, literary journals, and book series edited by Hebrew belletristic writers that published belles lettres and literary criticism. Consequently, these writers-to-be frequently witnessed Jews looking for direction analyzing and discussing these materials in a way once reserved for Talmudic passages. They imbibed their Hebrew literary predecessors' sense that Hebrew literature constituted an important national cultural institution whose authors were leaders and guides. Therefore, when they decided to pursue literary careers, they chose both a creative life and "a national public mission for themselves and their society."[11]

East European Jewish Influence on Gender and Sexuality's Politicized Use in Palestine

By late in the first decade of the twentieth century, East European Hebrew writers' political ideas faced increasing opposition, their social status eroded, and the Hebrew public sphere contracted sharply.[12] Within Jewish national circles, political Zionism was attracting followers who had previously looked to the Asher Ginsburg–led Hebrew literary community for guidance. Simultaneously, a distinctive Jewish national public sphere, whose participants employed Yiddish, emerged and mounted an even more substantial challenge to Hebrew writers' political aspirations. Jewish political discussions were taking place in Yiddish and non-Jewish languages. Hebrew literature's pertinence was openly questioned by the Jewish masses and Jewish intellectuals interested in addressing them. Looking for ways to remain relevant, Hebrew writers took note of the strategic use of gender and sexuality within the broader East European public sphere and increasingly utilized them to advance their own political ideas.

Gender and sexuality's programmatic employment did not aid East European Hebrew writers in significantly expanding the political influence of their belletristic work. While Hebrew authors continued to write in Europe for decades, increasing political and cultural marginalization led most Hebrew writers to consider emigration. Nonetheless, Hebrew writers took East European tactics with them to Palestine where they had a greater political impact. Consequently, brief examination of the existential issues underpinning Jewish politics in the Russian Empire and the intertwined roles of gender and sexuality in its discourse sheds light on what motivated the composition of Palestinian Zionists' texts and their political utilization of gender and sexuality.[13]

Just as changes in individual and communal Jewish life had spurred the Hebrew public sphere's expansion decades earlier, Jewish communal institutions' increasing dysfunction and Jews' growing feelings of alienation, anonymity, and loneliness ignited the turn-of-the-century growth of a broad-based East European public sphere.[14] In this period, libraries, coffeehouses, literary societies, drama circles, theaters, musical groupings, and learned societies numbered among the important public sphere institutions where individuals began to come together to debate collective affairs and work to solve modernity's problems.

While such institutions fostered the emergence of new social groupings, they proved particularly well suited for the political mobilization of distinct ethnolinguistic communities. Thus, activists successfully utilized Yiddish, a language nearly all East European Jews understood, to create a distinctive Jewish national public sphere whose participants employed Yiddish and were interested in advancing the Jewish people's needs.

Yiddish newspapers' effective elucidation of East European Jewry's deficiencies and needs and political methods for addressing these deficiencies and for meeting these needs made them into the Jewish public sphere's central institution and the Yiddish journalists who performed this task into politically prominent figures. Modern Hebrew writers implicitly understood that their ability to incorporate stratagems utilized by Yiddish journalists for provision of a sense of order could increase the political impact of their belletristic works. Therefore, these approaches serve as precursors and parallels to fictional schemes utilized by Agnon, Arieli, Brenner, and Reuveni.[15]

Yiddish newspapers' increasingly prominent role in the public sphere derived from their ability to inform readers about urban life and provide them with a broad perspective on modern existence. Political motivation undergirded this activity. By eschewing portrayal of the city as enchanting and new and depicting it as a "dangerous modern jungle in which little was sacred," Yiddish journalists directed public sphere discussion to specific problems and political methods for their resolution and shaped how their readers understood modern life.[16]

Yiddish journalists' portrayal of the individual and collective Jewish encounter with modernity drew heavily on gendered representations. In fact, women's victimization by "forces of social abandon and moral decay" proved integral to descriptions of modernity's emasculating and feminizing effects and the implicit call for Jewish men to remasculinize themselves and their symbolically understood male nation.[17] Consequently, stories of Jewish women deceived or forced into prostitution recurred. They impelled readers to view traditional forms of Jewish masculinity as inadequate for combatting sexual exploitation; they created a negative perception of individual and collective Jewish male character. Similarly, urban tales of abandoned children and unidentified corpses hinted at insufficient paternal oversight. Finally, reports of widespread urban violence buttressed the negative perception of individual and collective Jewish male character by highlighting how Jewish men were just as vulnerable as women and children.[18]

Jewish male migrants to the city imbibed these descriptions and searched out ways to respond to modernity's "feminizing" effects. They found that close male friendships eased feelings of confusion and inability to cope and reinforced one's sense of masculine vigor. Therefore, when developing alternative frameworks intended to provide members with a sense of order and belonging, they turned to homosociality, the relations between men imbued with homoeroticism (sexual attraction to a member of the same sex) and voicing emotional ties.[19]

Homosociality's ability to encompass behaviors categorizable as both heterosexual or homosexual makes it a useful tool for establishing social boundaries, and Yiddish journalists' effective utilization of it helped them shape the Jewish masses' understanding of society and mobilize them for political action. In the early twentieth century, *homosexuality* did not exclusively refer to men's engagement in specific sexual acts with other men or their desire to perform such acts. The term served as a catch-all to allude to socially unacceptable ways for men to relate to one another. This broader and more ambiguous definition influenced how men interacted with one another and how they understood themselves as men. Thus, writers could depict actual homosocial relations, or homosocial relations within an individual's fantasy life, as homosexual to stigmatize such relations and their associated behaviors. In this way, journalists and authors representing homosexuality could dissuade men from maintaining or adopting such relationships and related behaviors and push them to behave in ways tied to specific political action plans considered acceptably masculine and heterosexual.[20]

Self-Evaluative Masculinity—Context, Origins, and Distinctiveness

Context

Between 1900 and 1914, approximately thirty-five thousand Jews immigrated to Palestine, and its Jewish population grew to eighty-five thousand. Many of these immigrants as well as internal Palestinian Jewish migrants found Jaffa's modern, secular, and entrepreneurial spirit attractive and settled there permanently or for extended periods. Free of the East European shtetl and the Old Yishuv's religious bonds and conservative Jewish customs, Jaffa's Jewish residents established political, social, cultural, and economic institutions recasting Jewish life in Zionist terms. Excited by this process, the growing ranks of immigrant Hebrew literati were drawn to it and the city of Tel Aviv developing on its outskirts.[21] These writers were well positioned to influence the city and the developing Zionist community's various institutions through formal institutional labor and voluntary organizational participation.

When Brenner, Arieli, Agnon, and Reuveni chose to enter the orbit of organized Zionist politics, however, they placed less emphasis on residence in Jaffa–Tel Aviv and looked to their belletristic writing as the most effective means through which they could influence Palestinian Jewish life. The young men found throughout Palestine who were striving to make Hebrew their primary language of life and culture constituted an important potential readership. Through strategic utilization of gender and sexuality in their literary work and its publication in appropriate venues, Brenner, Agnon, Arieli, and Reuveni strove to promote Self-Evaluative masculinity and its associated political program to the widest possible Palestinian audience. Therefore, they frequently chose not to publish in leading Hebrew literary journals in the Diaspora and they did not prioritize establishment of distinctly literary journals. Instead, they welcomed their literary work's publication alongside news of general party meetings and Zionist congresses, calls for Hebrew labor and discussion of settlement methods in Palestinian Hebrew labor movement papers and journals such as *ha-Po'el ha-tza'ir*

Fig. 0.2 Masthead and table of contents of the newspaper *ha-Po'el ha-tza'ir*, 1909. The contents, including Agnon's story "Be'erah shel Miryam" and Yosef Aharonowitz's article "Hekhal ha-kulturah ha-'Ivrit," reflect Hebrew literature's place alongside more overtly political essays and articles in early twentieth-century Palestinian Zionist newspapers and journals. Historical Jewish Press website—www.Jpress.org.il—founded by the National Library and Tel Aviv University.

(The young worker), *ha-Ahdut* (The unity), *ha-Adamah* (The earth), and *ha-Aretz veha-'avodah* (The land and labor).

When Agnon, Brenner, Arieli, and Reuveni turned to fiction and drama to promote Self-Evaluative masculinity, they consciously faced off against thinkers who considered other Zionist masculine forms more conducive to the New Yishuv's development. Evidence of these alternatives can be found in the contemporary Palestinian Hebrew press and earlier scholarship on Zionist masculinity. Thus, Zionist leader Max Nordau's call for a "Jewry of Muscle" has been cited as an important indication of transformed male bodies' importance to early twentieth-century Zionists.[22] Similarly, other scholars inspired by Yosef Trumpeldor's apocryphal statement "It is good to die for our country" have asserted that Zionism, like other national movements, promoted death in service of the nation as masculine behavior's apogee.[23] Hence, they argue that readiness for national martyrdom was the sine qua non for a Zionist masculinity that fostered Palestinian Jewish settlement. Still other scholars stress the significance of an agrarian ideal embodied by the charismatic early twentieth-century Zionist Aharon David Gordon (1856–1922) and put into practice on moshavim and kibbutzim throughout Israel. These scholars contend that male Palestinian Zionists who took a femininely gendered land's virginity and impregnated it with new life voiced their desire for the Land of Israel (Eretz Yisra'el); they underwent a process of rebirth and girded themselves with a healthy masculinity that enabled them to found the State of Israel. Finally, scholars have recently pointed to a more cosmopolitan Zionist masculinity that arose following the outbreak of World War I. Its advocates viewed it as ideal for Palestinian Jewish men acting simultaneously in divergent national and imperial contexts.[24]

These masculine models as well as the aforementioned sabra model illustrate masculinity's social construction and offer insight into how alternative masculine models arise and compete against one another within a developing society such as the New Yishuv. Some masculine forms prove more conducive to realization of specific or general societal needs than others, and perceived differences in societal needs contribute to why different masculinities are developed, how they are promoted for communal dominance, and which models achieve widespread support.[25] Ultimately, affinity, debate, peer pressure, and social imposition propel men to voluntarily or involuntarily adopt what will become a hegemonic form, but as was the case in the New Yishuv, this process can go on for decades.

Origins

At the heart of Agnon, Brenner, Arieli, and Reuveni's development and promotion of Self-Evaluative masculinity lay the schlemiel figure and its distinctly malevolent heritage. Emerging in late eighteenth-century German culture, it constitutes a modern incarnation of the medieval anti-Jewish image of the Wandering Jew cursed to wander the earth until Jesus's second coming as punishment for taunting him on the way to the crucifixion.[26] As such, it served as a repository for all the negative qualities associated with the Jew, and it voiced an antisemitic belief that the Jew could not transcend his flawed biological essence. Hence, all Jewish efforts to integrate into European society, including acculturation, assimilation, and conversion, or to develop a national community proved comical. Left unaddressed, the internalized perception of oneself as a schlemiel, in accordance with European discourse, constituted a psychological burden inhibiting Jewish men's ability to better their lives and the life of their people. By confronting the figure of the schlemiel and gradually introducing positive elements into its portrayal, however, Jewish writers reappropriated it and produced forms of modern Jewish identity, including the Self-Evaluative masculine model, that Jewish men found easier to identify with.

Reticent to accept their categorization as schlemiels doomed to failure, Jews initially developed a strategy of projection to psychologically liberate themselves from the schlemiel and its off-putting characteristics. Thus, late eighteenth-century German Jewish Enlightenment satires frequently featured a schlemiel-like Jewish Other whose deficiencies and missteps were intended to amuse readers and educate them to negative characteristics that German Jews needed to overcome to integrate into general German society.[27] With Jewish Enlightenment's rise in East Europe, its proponents projected the schlemiel image onto traditional-minded Jews and Hasidim who opposed the changes they advocated.

Reappropriation of the schlemiel began when lack of noticeable improvement in the Jewish condition led East European Jewish writers to question the Enlightenment project and the possibilities for Russian Jewish emancipation in the 1860s and 1870s. Thus, while *Kitser masoes Binyomin hashlishi* (The brief travels of Benjamin the Third, 1878) starts out as a biting social satire featuring a schlemiel protagonist whose characteristics must be transcended for Jewish progress, Sholem Yankev Abramovitsh (1835–1917) deconstructs the genre and presents a schlemiel characterized by more than

Fig. 0.3 "He who has the choice . . .": "With whom would it be best for me to travel?" As an airplane labeled *Achad Haam Luftmenschen* descends toward a crash, a Wandering Jew figure representative of the Jewish people considers advancement with one of the Jewish political parties symbolized by the various wagons. While the airplane and wagons convey more rapid movement toward a modern destination than walking, the airplane crash, the wagons' premodern character, and the use of the Wandering Jew figure place successful Jewish modernization into question. *Schlemiel*, no. 3, 1919, David M. Rubenstein Rare Book and Manuscript Library, Duke University.

Fig. 0.4 "The Crossing of the Red Sea: Herzl and Nordau": "Stop! The water is not yet standing like a wall." Russian Jewish Zionists figured like the Wandering Jew act to redeem the Jewish people against expressed wishes of Zionist leadership that wants them to wait for completion of diplomatic initiatives. *Schlemiel* no. 4, 1904, David M. Rubenstein Rare Book and Manuscript Library, Duke University.

vulnerability, ineffectualness, and embryonic victimhood. After forced mobilization into the Russian army, Benjamin refuses to condone his non-Jewish military superiors' dubious morality and reliance on brute force to get their way. He stubbornly insists that moral values transcend realpolitik. Even if his powerlessness prevents him from voicing a distinct moral vision, he resists and reveals a heroic dimension.[28] In this way, the schlemiel became a figure with whom Jews could positively identify.

While turn-of-the-century European Jewish writers developed more relatable and psychologically nuanced schlemiel figures, Self-Evaluative writers and their Zionist brethren still found it difficult to construct a positive modern Jewish identity around it. Seemingly lacking traditional masculine virtues such as "strength, courage, pride, [and] fortitude," the schlemiel did not act heroically to shape his environment. Instead, when he lacked control over his environment, he employed language to rename this environment and reinterpret events to fit his vision.[29]

Looking to convince their male readers that they could better turn-of-the-century Jews' lives by employing more than words to respond to the difficult conditions their people faced, Self-Evaluative Hebrew writers reworked the schlemiel figure to reveal his possession of the requisite masculinity to act in history. As Brenner asserted in his influential essay on Abramovitsh's fiction, "Ha'arakhat 'atzmenu bi-shloshat ha-kerakhim" (Self-Evaluation in three volumes, 1914), Jews' efforts to maintain their senses of self and self-worth in the face of external forces looking to deny them did not keep them beautiful within.[30] On the contrary, "limited self-awareness" and "total insensitivity to the incongruities of [their] situation" led to a state of affairs where the ugly and base nature of their external reality was reflected in their souls.[31] Consequently, he asserted the need for Jews to forgo a positive and stable sense of self. By beginning a process of "self-evaluation" grounded in critical appraisal of individual and collective character, Jewish men could tap into self-understanding and understanding of the surrounding world as resources for bettering turn-of-the-century Jews' lives. Thus, self-evaluation offered Jews a way to ascend from a "primitive" and purely biological condition and assume a cultured existence through ethical pursuit of individual and collective improvement.[32] By maintaining "limited self-awareness" and "total insensitivity to the incongruities of his situation," the schlemiel maintained his senses of self and self-worth in the face of external forces looking to deny them.[33] Yet, as Self-Evaluative writers asserted, this was too great a price to pay for a positive and stable sense of self. By forgoing it, accepting modern identity's instability, and critically evaluating both the positive and negative aspects of one's character, Jewish men could tap into self-understanding and understanding of the surrounding world as resources for bettering turn-of-the-century Jews' lives.

Perception of potential connections between the Jews' fate and their actions proved empowering. Extant Jewish and general norms and moral codes sometimes made it seem that it would be impossible for Jews to better their lives. Yet when the individual Jewish male pursued introspection, he could push aside these norms and morals, clarify his goals, and locate ways to effectively pursue them through improved understanding of his and his coreligionists' successes and failures. Introspection, taken up in tandem with efforts to better understand one's surroundings, prepared Jewish males to exploit opportunities to act, even when they required a transvaluation of values. Thus, introspection and efforts to better understand one's environment underlay the Self-Evaluative masculine ideal promoted by Agnon, Brenner, Arieli, and Reuveni. Regardless of their physical attributes or professions, all early twentieth-century Palestinian Jewish male immigrants could take up this ideal and positively redefine themselves through pursuit of their individual and collective goals.

Distinctiveness

Agnon, Brenner, Arieli, and Reuveni considered Self-Evaluative masculinity the Zionist masculine form best able to advance the New Yishuv's development, because it could aid in satisfaction of the New Yishuv's procreative, provisioning, and protective needs. They considered Self-Evaluative masculinity's ability to aid Palestinian Jewish men striving to meet the New Yishuv's procreative needs and shepherd its youth into adulthood particularly noteworthy. While diasporic Jewish culture had successfully advanced a masculine ideal that promoted paternal commitment, cultivation of youth, and social betterment for millennia, proponents of masculine forms grounded in a radical break with the diasporic past denied these forms' adherents a positive sense of continuity with this past and the confidence that could be derived from it. In contrast, Agnon, Brenner, Arieli, and Reuveni, who acknowledged the continuing impact of diasporic experience on Palestinian Jewish men's lives, critically reexamined this experience. Through their reevaluation of it, they communicated how Palestinian Jewish men could prevent Diaspora Jewish life's deleterious characteristics from finding further expression and repurpose its most vital elements through adherence to Self-Evaluative masculine standards. Adoption of these standards, they argued, would provide Palestinian Jewish men with an enriching sense of continuity with early Jewish masculine models, a feeling of connection to other Palestinian Jewish men adopting them, and confidence that these standard's widespread adoption would advance the New Yishuv's needs in an effective and sustainable way.

Overview of Subsequent Chapters

Although Agnon, Brenner, Arieli, and Reuveni were prominent early twentieth-century Palestinian Hebrew writers and Agnon and Brenner constitute Israeli cultural icons, they remain largely unknown outside of

Israel. Consequently, a brief biographical primer will present a short collective biography of their literary generation and more detailed biographical snippets about the four authors before delving into their literary work and its cultural significance.

Chapter 1 presents how Agnon utilized gendered representations in his preimmigration and early Palestinian writings (1903–13) to advocate social change, contemplate different approaches to it, and eventually promote Self-Evaluative masculinity as a viable means for Jewish social transformation. Agnon's Galician writings feature frequent portrayals of victimized Jewish women suffering at the hands of a morally suspect and neglectful Jewish society. Through these depictions, these texts exemplify how early twentieth-century Hebrew literature promotes the perception that Jewish society is feminized and in crisis and pushes readers to conclude that only remasculinization of Jewish men and their symbolically male nation can counter modernity's emasculating effects. Additional Galician texts display their author's thoughts about how to best remasculinize Jewish society and provide its men with a sense of belonging and order, and the appropriate role for the Hebrew writer in this process. Following his immigration to Palestine, Agnon concluded that adoption of Self-Evaluative masculinity offered the most viable solution to contemporary Jewish crisis and affiliated with other Palestinian Hebrew writers promoting it through literature.

More than Agnon, Brenner was concerned with how to best inculcate Self-Evaluative masculinity norms and get Palestinian Jewish men to engage in moral and socially productive activities. Ideally, the public sphere would foster shared values and stimulate common cause, but as chapter 2's analysis of his 1911 novel *mi-Kan umi-kan* (From here and from there) demonstrates, Brenner portrays the Palestinian Jewish public sphere as underdeveloped and holding the national community back from meeting its needs. Addressing the novel to Palestinian Jewish men struggling with feelings of uprootedness and isolation and a fear that they were inherently feminine and incapable of improvement, Brenner reassures them that this underdevelopment, rather than their essential character, was preventing them from improving their and their people's lives. To address this significant shortcoming, advance shared values and stimulate common cause, the novel exploits Jewish male shame and hints at the pleasure of engaging in long-term pursuit of collective aims alongside other Palestinian Jewish men. In this way, Brenner looked to nurture homosocial bonds that would compel Palestinian Jewish men to adopt Self-Evaluative masculine standards and behave in a socially productive manner.

Analysis of Arieli's *Allah Karim!* (God is full of mercy!) in chapter 3 points to how Self-Evaluative masculinity's proponents were actively involved in widely followed earlier twentieth-century debates about the Palestinian Jewish community's evolving character. No form of Zionist masculinity dominated the cultural landscape and discussion of divergent masculine forms' suitability for contemporary circumstances proved central to these deliberations. Employing a strategy popular in his cohort, Arieli exposes alternative masculine models' limitations in his 1912 drama to advertise Self-Evaluative masculinity's ability to best mobilize Jewish men for achievement of communal aims. Invented traditions constituted an important element in these persuasive efforts. Drawing on Jewish religious ceremonies and texts, Self-Evaluative masculinity's supporters stressed the homosocial pleasure one could derive from advancement of communal goals alongside other Jewish men committed to this ideal.

World War I's outbreak placed extant and emergent social bonds and social structures in question. Consequently, support for Self-Evaluative masculinity wavered. In response, as chapter 4's scrutiny of Arieli's novella *Yeshimon* (Wasteland, 1918–20) reveals, exponents of Self-Evaluative masculinity built on their early use of Jewish male shame and increasingly turned to "homosexual panic," or fear of having oneself and one's male relationships stigmatized as homosexual, to promote their preferred masculine form. Through its portrayal of a Jewish man's military service in the Ottoman military, "Wasteland" pillories bonds with non-Jewish and non-Zionist Jewish men and creates social pressure to oppose transnational masculinities as homosexual. Simultaneously, it classifies Self-Evaluative masculinity and the homosocial bonds linking its adherents as acceptably heterosexual. Thus, Self-Evaluative masculinity's proponents contributed to sexuality's increasingly prominent role in ongoing debates about Zionist masculinity.

Chapter 5 reveals how purportedly decadent depictions of Jewish gender and sexuality are deployed in Reuveni's *'Ad-Yerushalayim* (Till Jerusalem) for Self-Evaluative masculinity's advancement, how they clarify the role envisaged for Hebrew writers by its advocates, and what factors lie behind its eclipse. The trilogy stresses that Palestine's harsh conditions prevent East European Jewish male immigrants' radical transformation and instead reveal their individual weakness. Failure to address such weakness, however, could devastate a community. Consequently, the trilogy asserts that to overcome personal weakness and participate in the Palestinian Jewish community's gradual development Palestinian Jewish men need to acknowledge individual male weakness and unify around newly developed national norms intended to combat it. Introspection and the ability to concede one's limitations were talents that writers were capable of developing and the trilogy calls on writers to cultivate them and push their contemporaries to concede their individual flaws and embrace collective action's redemptive possibilities. Thus, for Reuveni, as for other members of his literary cohort, Hebrew authors employing Self-Evaluative aesthetics constituted Self-Evaluative masculinity's most effective practitioners.

Prominent Zionist masculine models, such as the sabra model, that elided Jewish male weakness and embraced the spirit of euphoria that emerged in the Palestinian Jewish community in the late 1910s stood in opposition to the Hebrew writer's idealization and the concomitant gradualism promoted by Self-Evaluative masculinity's proponents. Consequently, impatient advocates of these Zionist masculine models, who looked to delegitimize Self-Evaluative masculinity, portrayed depictions of individual weakness and immorality in *Till Jerusalem* and other related works as manifestations of decadent Jewish gender and sexuality. These assertions effectively neutralized Arieli and Reuveni's ability to promote Self-Evaluative masculinity, earned them decadent labels, and contributed to Self-Evaluative masculinity's declining cultural prominence over the course of the 1920s and 1930s.

Although Self-Evaluative masculinity did not achieve a hegemonic cultural position within the New Yishuv, the afterword explores what lesson can be drawn from its study, its legacy in subsequent Israeli culture and society, and its implications for subsequent research. First, it points to how sexuality's use for the advancement of masculine standards voicing a broader social vision was not limited to the literary work of those advocating Self-Evaluative masculinity. Second, the afterword briefly discusses how the cultural primacy achieved by sabra masculinity in the early state period was eroded and forced to compete with other masculinities, evocative of Self-Evaluative masculinity, that were more open to Diaspora life. Finally, it addresses implications of this exploration of Self-Evaluative masculinity for subsequent research in Modern Hebrew literature and Israel studies.

Notes

1. Glenda Abramson and Tudor Parfitt, eds., *The Great Transition: The Recovery of the Lost Centers of Modern Hebrew Literature* (Totowa, NJ: Rowman and Allenhald, 1985).

2. Yosef Aharonowitz, "Hekhal ha-kulturah ha-'Ivrit," *ha-Po'el ha-tza'ir*, July 1, 1909.

3. David Biale, *Eros and the Jews: From Biblical Israel to Contemporary America* (Berkeley: University of California Press, 1997), 200.

4. For earlier discussion of masculinity's centrality to the connection between Zionism and early twentieth-century Hebrew literature, see Mikha'el Gluzman, *ha-Guf ha-Tzioni: le'umiut, migdar u-miniut ba-sifrut ha-'Ivrit ha-hadashah* (Tel Aviv: ha-Kibutz ha-Me'uhad, 2007), 11; Biale, *Eros and the Jews*, 200. Besides Brenner, all these writers Hebraized their given names following immigration to Palestine. For purposes of clarity, I employ the authors' chosen names throughout the text. The given names of Agnon, Arieli, and Reuveni were Shmu'el Yosef Tshatshkes, Levi Aryeh Orlof, and Aharon Shimshelevich, respectively. Early in their literary careers, Agnon and Arieli employed their given names.

5. On negation of the Diaspora, see Anita Shapira, "Le'an halkhah shlilat ha-galut," in *Yehudim, Tzionim, ve-ma she-benehem* (Tel Aviv: 'Am 'Oved, 2007), 63–110. On the schlemiel's literary representation, see Ruth Wisse, *The Schlemiel as Modern Hero* (Chicago: University of Chicago Press, 1971); Sanford Pinsker, *The Schlemiel as Metaphor: Studies in Yiddish and American Jewish Fiction* (Carbondale: Southern Illinois University Press, 1991). On the relationship between antisemitic discourse and representations of diasporic Jewish men, see Sander Gilman, *Jewish Self-Hatred: Anti-Semitism and the Hidden Language of the Jews* (Baltimore: Johns Hopkins University Press, 1992), 107–38; John Efron, *Defenders of the Race: Jewish Doctors and Race Science in Fin-de-Siècle Europe* (New Haven, CT: Yale University Press, 1994); Mitchell Hart, *Social Science and the Politics of Modern Jewish Identity* (Stanford, CA: Stanford University Press, 2000). On Zionist masculinity's emergence in contradistinction to diasporic masculinity, see Hannah Naveh, "Migdar ve-hazon ha-gavriut ha-'Ivrit," in *Zeman Yehudi hadash: tarbut Yehudit be-'idan hiloni; mabat entziklopedi*, ed. Yirmiyahu Yovel (Jerusalem: Keter, 2007), 3:1117–23; and Oz Almog, *The Sabra: The Creation of the New Jew*, trans. Haim Watzman (Berkeley: University of California Press, 2000).

6. Almog, *The Sabra*, 3; Raewyn W. Connell and James Messerschmidt, "Hegemonic Masculinity: Rethinking the Concept," *Gender and Society* 19, no. 6 (2005): 832. On the idea of a liminal period when nascent Israeli values and beliefs were just beginning to coalesce in Pre-State Palestine, see Yael Zerubavel, *Recovered Roots: Collective Memory and the Making of Israeli National Tradition* (Chicago: University of Chicago Press, 1995), 33–36.

7. On culture as the object of vigorous debate, see Geoff Eley and Ronald Suny, "Introduction: From the Moment of Social History to the Work of Cultural Representation," in *Becoming National: A Reader*, ed. Geoff Eley and Ronald Suny (New York: Oxford University Press, 1996), 9. Dominance of the public sphere proves significant, because, as the theorist of nationalism Pheng Cheah explains, "the nation and the public sphere are mutually constitutive." Scott Ury, *Barricades and Banners: The Revolution of 1905 and the Transformation of Warsaw Jewry* (Stanford, CA: Stanford University Press, 2012), 174. The terms *New Yishuv* and *Old Yishuv* refer to Pre-State Palestine's pro-Zionist Jewish community and its non-Zionist Jewish religious community, respectively. On these terms and their historicity, see Yisra'el Bartal, "'Yishuv hadash' ve-'yishuv yashan'—ha-dimui veha-

metzi'ut," in *Galut ba-aretz: yishuv Eretz -Yisra'el be-terem Tzionut* (Jerusalem: ha-Sifriyah ha-Tzionit, 1995), 74–90. On the rhetoric of Jewish demise, see Arieh Saposnik, "Exorcising the 'Angel of National Death'—Nation and Individual Death (and Rebirth) in Zionist Palestine," *Jewish Quarterly Review* 95, no. 3 (2005): 557–78.

8. Dan Miron, *From Continuity to Contiguity: Towards a New Jewish Literary Thinking* (Stanford, CA: Stanford University Press, 2010), 57, 61, 58–69, 117; Craig Calhoun, "Introduction: Habermas and the Public Sphere," in *Habermas and the Public Sphere*, ed. Craig Calhoun (Cambridge, MA: MIT Press, 1992), 12. On *ha-Me'asef* and its context, see Shmuel Feiner, *The Jewish Enlightenment*, trans. Chaya Naor (Philadelphia: University of Pennsylvania Press, 2004). On the public sphere, see Jürgen Habermas, *The Structural Transformation of the Public Sphere: An Inquiry into a Category of Bourgeois Society*, trans. Thomas Burger (Cambridge, MA: MIT Press, 1996). For critique and further development of Habermas's foundational work, see Calhoun, *Habermas and the Public Sphere*; Eley and Suny, *Becoming National*.

9. Miron, *From Continuity to Contiguity*, 72.

10. For fuller discussion of Modern Hebrew literature's readership, see Dan Miron, *Bodedim be-mo'adam: le-deyoknah shel ha-republikah ha-sifrutit ha-'Ivrit bi-thilat ha-me'ah ha-'esrim* (Tel Aviv: 'Am 'Oved, 1987), 56–111. On these changes and the "Modern Jewish Revolution" they sparked, see Benjamin Harshav, *Language in Time of Revolution* (Berkeley: University of California Press, 1993), 3–80.

11. Miron, *Bodedim be-mo'adam*, 286; see also 285–87.

12. On Hebrew literature's changing position within Zionist politics, see Dan Miron, "me-Yotzrim ve-bonim li-vnei bli bayit," in *Im lo tihyeh Yerushalayim* (Tel Aviv: ha-Kibutz ha-Me'uhad, 1987), 9–89; on the Hebrew public sphere's turn-of-the-century contraction, see Miron, *Bodedim be-mo'adam*, 86–111.

13. Jonathan Frankel, *Prophecy and Politics: Socialism, Nationalism, and the Russian Jews, 1862–1917* (New York: Cambridge University Press, 1984), 366–452.

14. On the public sphere and East European Jewish life, see Jeffrey Veidlinger, *Jewish Public Culture in Later Imperial Russia* (Bloomington: Indiana University Press, 2009); Ury, *Barricades and Banners*; Eli Lederhandler, *Road to Modern Jewish Politics* (New York: Oxford University Press, 1989).

15. On newspapers' role in national consciousness's development, see Benedict Anderson, *Imagined Communities: Reflections on the Origins and Spread of Nationalism* (New York: Verso, 2006), 22–36; on fiction's role in national consciousness's construction, see Anderson, *Imagined Communities*, 22–36; Jonathan Culler, "Anderson and the Novel," in *Grounds of Comparison: Around the Work of Benedict Anderson*, ed. Pheng Cheah and Jonathan Culler (New York: Routledge, 2003), 29–52.

16. Ury, *Barricades and Banners*, 46.

17. Ury, *Barricades and Banners*, 61.

18. Ury, *Barricades and Banners*, 57–67, 85; for discussion of the rhetoric of feminization and remasculinization in Imperial Russian society and culture, see Laura Engelstein, *The Keys to Happiness: Sex and the Search for Modernity in Fin-de-Siècle Russia* (Ithaca, NY: Cornell University Press, 1992).

19. Scott Ury, "The Generation of 1905 and the Politics of Despair: Alienation, Friendship, Community," in *The Revolution of 1905 and Russia's Jews*, ed. Stefani Hoffman and Ezra Mendelsohn (Philadelphia: University of Pennsylvania Press, 2008), 96–110. The definition of homosociality introduced here follows Eve Sedgwick's parameters. Eve Sedgwick, *Between*

Men: English Literature and Male Homosocial Desire (New York: Columbia University Press, 1985), 1–5.

20. Stigmatizing depictions of homosocial relations frequently featured sadomasochistic behavior with sadomasochism understood as the interrelated derivation of pleasure from infliction of pain and the experiencing of pain. For fuller discussion of sadomasochism, see Jean Laplanche and Jean-Bertrand Pontalis, *The Language of Psycho-analysis*, trans. Donald Nicholson-Smith (New York: Norton, 1973), 401–4.On masculinity's centrality to national mobilization, see George Mosse, *The Image of Man* (New York: Oxford University Press, 1996), 107–32.

21. Even purportedly "diasporic" Hebrew writers explored potential integration into Palestine's increasingly rich literary environment. Thus, Uri Nisan Gnessin (1879–1913) and David Vogel (1891–1944) traveled there for extended visits in 1907 and 1929, respectively.

22. The term *Jewry of Muscle* comes from an eponymous speech delivered by Nordau (1849–1923). See Mendes-Flohr and Reinharz, *The Jew in the Modern World*, 434–35. For discussion of Muscle Jewry in Western Zionism, see Michael Berkowitz, *Zionist Culture and Western Jewry before the First World* War (Chapel Hill: University of North Carolina Press, 1996); on efforts to make Muscle Jewry a central aspect of Palestinian Zionist masculinity, see Todd Presner, *Muscular Judaism: The Jewish Body and the Politics of Regeneration* (New York: Routledge, 2007).

23. On Trumpeldor and his famed quote, see Zerubavel, *Recovered Roots*, 39–47, 84–95, and 147–77.

24. For general discussion of martyrdom as an important component of nationalism, see Benedict Anderson, *Imagined Communities*, 9–36. For scholars supporting Anderson's view in relationship to Zionist masculinity, see Mikhal Dekel, *The Universal Jew: Masculinity, Modernity, and the Zionist Movement* (Evanston, IL: Northwestern University Press, 2011), 198–224; Yael Feldman, *Glory and Agony: Isaac's Sacrifice and National Narrative* (Stanford, CA: Stanford University Press, 2010), 51–105; Yigal Schwartz, *The Zionist Paradox: Hebrew Literature and Israeli Identity*, trans. Michal Sapir (Waltham, MA: Brandeis University Press, 2014), 97–141; Boʿaz Neumann, *Land and Desire in Early Zionism,* trans. Haim Watzman (Waltham, MA: Brandeis University Press, 2011); Boʿaz Neumann, *Teshukat ha-halutzim* (Tel Aviv: ʿAm ʿOved, 2009), 34. On the Palestinian Sephardic proponents of "inclusivist Zionism," see Abigail Jacobson, *From Empire to Empire: Jerusalem between Ottoman and British Rule* (Syracuse, NY: Syracuse University Press, 2011), 82–116; Michelle Campos, *Ottoman Brothers: Muslims, Christians, and Jews in Early Twentieth Century Palestine* (Stanford, CA: Stanford University Press, 2011), 197–223.

25. For more on this approach to masculinity, see David Gilmore, *Manhood in the Making: Cultural Concepts of Masculinity* (New Haven, CT: Yale University Press, 1990), 1–29.

26. Dov Sadan, "Le-sugyah: Shlomiʾel," *Orlogin* 1 (1950): 198–202; Gilman, *Jewish Self-Hatred*, 107–14. Scholars reject Heinrich Heine's assertion that the schlemiel tradition dates back to the Hebrew Bible and stress the important role publication of Adelbert von Chamisso's "Peter Schlemihl's wundersame Geschichte" [Peter Schlemihl's miraculous story, 1814] played in its spread. Wisse, *Schlemiel as Modern Hero*, 125–26.

27. Gilman, *Jewish Self-Hatred*, 109.

28. Wisse, *Schlemiel as Modern Hero*, 30.

29. Wisse, *Schlemiel as Modern Hero*, 51, 54–55.

30. Yosef Hayyim Brenner, "Ha'arakhat 'atzmenu bi-shloshat ha-kerakhim," in *Ketavim* (Tel Aviv: ha-Kibutz ha-Me'uhad, 1978–85), 4:1294.

31. Brenner, "Ha'arakhat 'atzmenu bi-shloshat ha-kerakhim," 4:1294.

32. Brenner, "Ha'arakhat 'atzmenu bi-shloshat ha-kerakhim," 4:1225, 1284.

33. Wisse, *Schlemiel as Modern Hero*, 57, 53.

OF THEIR TIME AND THEIR PLACES

A Biographical Introduction to the Self-Evaluative Writers

Fast-Tracked to the Literary World:
A General View of the 1880s Generation

Born in the 1880s, Brenner, Reuveni, Arieli, and Agnon came of age in an East European world whose economic, social, and cultural foundation had been shaken. Nevertheless, contemplation of the future roles that religion and enlightenment, socialism and nationalism, liberalism and art would play in the lives of East European Jews catalyzed an intellectual and aesthetic ferment and a coterminous efflorescence of Modern Hebrew literature.

Regardless of its vitality, Modern Hebrew literature and journalism's active contemplation of change and presentation of alternative Jewish possibilities challenged Jewish religious authorities in the Austrian and Russian empires, and Hebrew writers encountered strong opposition through the 1880s and into the early 1890s. For example, traditionally minded communities marginalized prominent writers such as Avram Ber Gottlober (1811–99) by limiting their interactions with other Jews and forcing them to live on the outskirts of town. Similarly, as in the case of Moshe Leib Lilienblum (1843–1910), they pressured them to relocate due to their deviant views. Consequently, important turn-of-the-century Hebrew writers such as Mikhah Yosef Berdichevsky (1865–1921), Hayyim Nahman Bialik (1873–1934), and Mordechai Ze'ev Feierberg (1874–99) portrayed the interior lives of troubled young men caught between a traditional world that both attracted and repelled them and a cold and distant modern world they felt drawn to and excluded from. They effectively voiced the dramatic conflict between traditional Jewish forces and those pursuing modernizing paths at its apex.

By the fin de siècle, however, the Hebrew literary and journalistic world had expanded successfully. As a result, the Self-Evaluative writers were acculturated into a world where Modern Hebrew literature and journalism were playing increasingly important roles and Hebrew writers no longer viewed themselves as adrift between worlds.[1] Even if unresolved issues of Jewish identity continued to trouble them, a cultural space that modernizing Jews could call home now existed. This enabled members of the 1880s generation to follow paths trod by their predecessors and readily assume active roles in the Hebrew literary world. Thus, even Brenner, the oldest featured writer, whose father opposed his literary and political aspirations and pressured him to become a Talmudic scholar, received his yeshiva head's tacit consent to pursue his literary aspirations while studying in Pochep. This sped his literary evolution, and he published his earliest fiction before his twentieth birthday. Many of this generation's other writers also debuted at a young age and subsequently dedicated their lives to their craft and its development.

Individual Biographies: Creativity and National Mission Intertwined

Brenner and Agnon's lives most closely resemble the generational biography sketched out above. Born in Novy Mlini, in the Ukrainian district of Chernigov, in 1881, Brenner was initially shaped by his father Shlomo's expectations.[2] A lowly and impoverished primary school teacher, Shlomo saw his son's attainment of Talmudic erudition as a means to improve his and his son's social standing. Consequently, he pushed his son to learn. Starting from an extremely young age, Brenner enrolled in various Ukrainian and Belorussian yeshivas and acquired vast Talmudic knowledge. While an excellent and devoted student, Brenner began to surreptitiously read and write Modern Hebrew literature. Expelled from the Konotop yeshiva for this pursuit, Brenner sought out more welcoming environments; for the next few years, he successfully pursued Talmud study and his literary interests.

Brenner eventually lost faith, distanced himself from paternal expectations, and devoted himself exclusively to literature and his growing interest in politics. Seeking to expand his horizons and develop his literary career, Brenner spent time in Bialystok, Homel, and Warsaw between 1899 and 1902. Urban life allowed him to directly interact with other modernizing Jews and to acquire facility in Russian language. Soon, he was devouring Russian literature and getting his fiction published. His stylistically distinctive first collection *me-'Emek 'akur* (From a dirty valley, 1900) was favorably reviewed by critics.

After completing basic training, Brenner carved out time for writing during his mandatory military service, and he authored fiction that catapulted him to contemporary Hebrew literature's forefront. Between March and December 1903, his novel *ba-Horef* (In winter) was serialized in the journal *ha-Shiloah* and garnered rave reviews. Yet with the Russo-Japanese War's outbreak, Brenner's military duties looked ready to undermine his literary pursuits. Unprepared to abandon them or give up his life serving an autocratic state, he deserted.

Brenner traveled to England, where he assumed an increasingly important Hebrew cultural role. He continued to expand his horizons and produce important works such as his novel *mi-Saviv la-nekudah* (Around the point), but his editorial and publishing efforts proved even more impactful. Brenner founded the literary journal *ha-Me'orer* (The awakener). It served as Hebrew literature's primary literary journal after the 1905 Russian Revolution brought about Hebrew publishing's temporary cessation in the Russian Empire. Like the issues of *Revivim* (Rains) that Brenner later edited in Lvov, *ha-Me'orer* united the Hebrew literary community at a vulnerable time, while simultaneously bringing the 1880s generation and its new literary direction to Hebrew culture's forefront.

Brenner's 1909 arrival in Palestine proved significant for the development of Palestinian Hebrew culture.[3] Less prominent literary figures taking direction from the East European center previously dominated cultural life, but Brenner quickly employed his prestige and authority to push Palestinian Hebrew culture toward independence and a more engaged relationship with settlement efforts. Along the way, he emerged as the literary community's prime mover. Among the many whom Brenner influenced were Agnon, Arieli, and Reuveni, and he actively promoted their literary careers. Thus, irrespective of individual differences, these writers constitute a distinct literary group.[4]

Regardless of shared dedication to their literary craft's pursuit from a young age, several important biographical differences help account for Brenner and Agnon's divergent personalities and temperaments. Born in 1887 to an affluent bourgeois family in the small Galician city of Buczacz, Agnon grew up at a time and in an environment where his Hebrew literary aspiration never encountered strong parental or communal opposition.[5] Both Agnon's father and maternal grandfather had rabbinic ordination and hoped that Shmuel Yosef would follow their example. Yet when he started

Fig. 0.5 Group picture of Hebrew authors in Jaffa photographed by Avraham Suskind in 1910. From right to left: Shmuel Yosef Agnon, David Shimoni, Alexander Ziskind Rabinovich, and Yosef Hayyim Brenner. National Library of Israel. Agnon Archive. Courtesy of Yael Blau.

publishing in his youth, they took pride in his literary accomplishments and encouraged him to continue.

Austrian imperial rule's progressivism offered Buczacz's Jews an opportunity for economic and social advance denied Russian Jews. Agnon's father and grandfather exploited it and succeeded in business. Consequently, despite continued religious devotion, their economic success and greater social integration made them more open to the surrounding culture than Brenner's father. Thus, after Agnon completed a traditional Jewish primary school education, his father allowed him to study German language and personally tutored him in Talmud. Later, when not studying Talmud or learning about Hasidism, Agnon read German literature recommended to him by his mother. Unlike Brenner, whose father sent him out to achieve Talmudic erudition, Agnon remained in his bourgeois parents' comfortable home and independently developed his intellect. Consequently, he uninhibitedly read modern literature in the local study house and wrote Hebrew and Yiddish belles lettres.

After Agnon served as an editorial assistant at the Yiddish newspaper *Di Yiddishe Wecker* (The Jewish awakener), his life took a marked turn.

He accepted the invitation of Gershon Bader (1868–1953) to serve on the editorial board of the Hebrew paper *ha-'Et* (The epoch) in 1907. The position was Agnon's first paying job. More importantly, it placed him more firmly within the literary world that he wanted to inhabit. It allowed him to leave his parents' home and travel to a big city where he could directly interact with numerous other writers and expand his intellectual horizons. Unfortunately, Agnon's time in Lvov, a city with one hundred thousand inhabitants, proved short-lived. When the paper folded, Agnon went home.

Agnon immigrated to Palestine in 1907 for numerous reasons. Electoral fraud that silenced the voice of Galician Jewry alienated him, forced mobilization into the Austrian military disinterested him, and a desire to better the lives of world Jewry, including his Jewish brethren suffering across the nearby Russian border, motivated him. Yet just as importantly, Agnon looked for a way out of what he now perceived as a provincial backwater. He wanted to grow as a writer and make a name for himself. Rather than traveling to Hebrew literary centers in the Russian Empire, where he would have faced virulent antisemitism, Agnon immigrated to Palestine. It offered him a way to develop his literary talents and voice his political commitment without alienating his parents, whose Jewish millennial desire made it difficult for them to question his decision.

Agnon arrived in Palestine in 1908 and settled in Jaffa's Jewish quarter. A skilled networker, he quickly found clerical work. The new environment aided his literary development and output. Less than a year after his arrival, he gained wide critical acclaim following publication of his short story "Agunot" (Abandoned wives). Brenner, one of his earliest supporters, used his own limited funds to publish Agnon's novella *ve-Hayah he-'akov le-mishor* (And the crooked shall become straight, 1912). Agnon now regularly published in leading local and Diaspora platforms.

During his time in Jaffa and later Jerusalem, Agnon looked for his place in the Palestinian Jewish world. Experimentation in fiction and lifestyle typified this period. While testing out Scandinavian-influenced impressionism, Agnon abandoned religious proscription and custom and sampled various secular lifestyles. Although he later reassumed a religious lifestyle and obscured his strong connections to the contemporary milieu, Agnon's early Palestinian writings display clear connection to his time and place.

Agnon's October 1912 departure for Germany constitutes one of the primary reasons that critics separate him off from contemporary Palestinian Hebrew writers. Looking to further develop as a writer, Agnon accepted the invitation of the noted Zionist official and sociologist Arthur Ruppin (1876–1943) to travel with him to Germany. Agnon's time in Berlin and Frankfurt, his interactions with the crème de la crème of German Jewry, his acquisition of department store magnate Salman Schocken's patronage, and his twelve-year presence outside of the Palestinian cultural environment gave Agnon freedom to develop in directions likely unimaginable had he remained in Palestine and faced the same cultural demands that his counterparts worked to address.

In 1924, when Agnon returned to Palestine, where he resided for the remainder of his life, he was a mature writer with financial means. The environment still placed demands on Hebrew writers, but they were less extreme, and Agnon resisted normative pressure. He continued to develop in a unique direction, even if this initially limited his critical and popular success. Finally, with publication of his novel *Oreah natah lalun* (A guest for the night, 1939), Agnon again achieved critical and popular success in Palestine on his own terms. Ultimately, this success would extend beyond Israeli borders with Agnon's reception of the Nobel Prize for Literature in 1966.

It proves significant that the biographies of the final two authors whose works this book discusses diverge markedly from the generational biography sketched above. Arieli and Reuveni grew up in Zionist homes, where they were exposed to Modern Hebrew culture, but neither demonstrated Hebrew literary aspirations prior to moving to Palestine. Their literary careers must be understood in relationship to their Zionism and their efforts to find a place within Palestinian Jewish society. Interested in more than aesthetics, they strove to advance their political views through literature.

A grain merchant and estate manager and a weaving workshop owner, respectively, Arieli's father and mother had the financial resources necessary to successfully raise ten children in the small Ukrainian town of Shishak.[6] They, however, did not aspire to raise a Talmudic scholar. A committed Zionist who immigrated to Palestine in the 1920s, Kalman Orlof provided his son with a traditional Jewish education that afforded him the linguistic tools he later employed in his writing. Yet when his son turned thirteen, he sent him to Myrhorod, one of Poltava Oblast's major cities, to attain a secular education.

Levi Aryeh pursued external studies and supported himself through tutoring, but politics soon became his primary educational arena. Like many contemporary Russian Jewish youths, he took part in Labor

Zionist activities and was even wounded during Jewish self-defense efforts in Myrhorod. Drafted into the Russian military and stationed in Tula in 1907, Levi Aryeh continued his political involvement, a decision that catalyzed his immigration to Palestine. Outside of the Pale of Settlement, his ability to interact with Jewish political parties was limited. Consequently, he forged ties with the Russian Social Democratic Party and the Socialist Revolutionary Party. These ties soon led to his arrest. Arieli luckily escaped imprisonment and returned home. There, his family advised him to immigrate to Palestine, seeing it as a safe and cost-effective option.

Arieli lived in Palestine between 1908 and 1923. He initially worked as an agricultural laborer and a watchman, but neither these professions nor his coworkers engaged him. In contrast, the Zionist esprit de corps of the Hebrew literary community coalescing around Brenner proved attractive. With his first short story's publication in 1909, Arieli achieved full communal membership and the status bestowed on a leading Palestinian Hebrew author. Subsequent works, such as his drama *Allah Karim!* (God is full of mercy!, 1912) and his novella *Yeshimon* (Wasteland, 1918–20) cemented his literary reputation.

Arieli immigrated to the United States in 1923 for personal reasons.[7] Arieli married Bella Wager in 1911, and he fathered four children. He started teaching full time to support his family, but even after placing his writing on the backburner, he had trouble making ends meet. World War I, Ottoman military service's demands, and the uncertain postwar world made things more difficult. Then, disagreements concerning Arieli's literary pursuits combined with financial issues to sour his marriage. Immigration resolved Arieli's financial difficulties and distanced him from his wife. Through work as an American Hebrew educator, Arieli was finally able to support his family. Subsequently, he found personal happiness. He divorced his first wife, remarried, and carved out time to pursue his literary career. Until his premature death from a stroke in 1943, Arieli contributed to American Hebrew literature's development.

Like Arieli, Reuveni was raised in a Hebrew Zionist home.[8] His father, Tzvi Shimshelevich (1862–1953) was a dedicated Jewish nationalist, who wrote on Jewish issues in the Hebrew and Russian Jewish press. He was also a committed Hovevei Tzion (Lovers of Zion) member, an adherent of Bnei Moshe (Sons of Moshe), an elite fraternity under the leadership of Ahad Ha-Am (1856–1927), and following the movement's establishment, an active Zionist leader. Furthermore, he subscribed to various Hebrew newspapers; modernizing Jews, Jewish nationalists, and Hebrew-language devotees stopped by the Shimshelevich family home in Poltava to read his copies. Thus, Aharon imbibed Zionism and Hebrew culture from his youth.

While his brother Yitzhak Ben-Zvi (1884–1963) easily absorbed his father's teachings, Aharon proved reticent to follow in his father's footsteps. Instead, he ceased formal study at a young age. An autodidact, he gradually acquired a firm grounding in Jewish and general sources. He also attained fluency in Russian language, something that stimulated his attraction to socialist ideas. In fact, Reuveni reentered the Zionist fold only after reading the work of Zionist theoretician Ber Borochov (1881–1917), who convinced him that Zionist and socialist ideas could coexist. Yet in 1904, after Aharon briefly participated in the Po'alei Tzion (Zion Workers) party, his parents, who worried about his future, sent him to America to try his luck.

Reuveni spent less than two years in the United States, but he developed an interest in literature during his time here. Arriving in America without a support network or English-language competency, Reuveni, who lacked skilled training, encountered demeaning conditions, struggled with loneliness, and found his new environment alienating. Like other Russian-speaking Jewish intellectuals, especially those espousing leftist views, Reuveni soon found a modicum of community through consumption of American Yiddish culture.[9] At a time when Jewish socialism infused all its facets, including poetry, American Yiddish culture helped Reuveni find a sense of order and belonging. Thus, looking to contribute to this affirmative culture, he began writing Yiddish belles lettres.

Despite Reuveni's acclimatizing efforts, his heart remained in the Russian Empire. Consequently, following the outbreak of the 1905 Russian Revolution, he returned to it. He looked to participate in the sweeping changes the October Manifesto heralded, but his hopes were quickly dashed. When the police discovered weapons in the family home, hidden there by his brother Yitzhak for Jewish self-defense purposes, Reuveni was arrested and charged with illegal weapon possession. Finally tried in 1908, he was exiled to Siberia for life. Unwilling to serve out his sentence, he escaped. He wandered through Siberia for a year and eventually made it to the city of Irkutsk. After subsequent stops in Manchuria, Shanghai, and Hawaii, Reuveni eventually arrived in Palestine in 1910.

With his brother's assistance, Reuveni, a former Po'alei Tzion party member, found work in Jerusalem writing for its Hebrew paper *ha-Ahdut*.

Lacking requisite Hebrew language skills, he wrote his articles in Yiddish and had them translated. Reuveni completed his first stories in this period, and Brenner numbered among his first readers. Impressed with his Yiddish writing and its ability to capture Palestinian Jewish life's essence, Brenner strove to integrate him into a protean Hebrew literary community possessing few similar talents. Consequently, Brenner translated his stories into Hebrew, published them as separate books and in journals he edited, wrote criticism promoting them, and functioned as his literary agent. Thus, even before he wrote in Hebrew, Reuveni gained a reputation as a leading Palestinian Jewish writer and achieved a place within the Hebrew canon.

During his first decade in Palestine, Reuveni acquired the Hebrew linguistic skills necessary to write Hebrew fiction, but he composed his monumental trilogy *Till Jerusalem* in Yiddish and translated it into Hebrew with the assistance of leading Hebrew writers including Mordechai Temkin (1891–1960) and Rachel Blowstein (1890–1931). Although *Till Jerusalem* is widely considered a masterpiece, Brenner's early death robbed Reuveni of his fiction's primary proponent; after its publication, Reuveni became increasingly isolated and produced little new fiction. After extended critical neglect, Reuveni's literary work garnered renewed interest, just before his death, in the late 1960s.

Notes

1. For additional discussions of the lives of authors of this literary generation and their relationship to its art, see Dan Miron, *Bodedim be-mo'adam: li-deyoknah shel ha-republikah ha-sifrutit ha-'Ivrit bi-thilat ha-me'ah ha-'esrim* (Tel Aviv: 'Am 'Oved, 1987), 296–429; Shachar Pinsker, *Literary Passports: The Making of Modernist Hebrew Fiction in Europe* (Stanford, CA: Stanford University Press, 2011), 1–29; cf. Alan Mintz, *Banished from Their Father's Table: Loss of Faith and Hebrew Autobiography* (Bloomington: Indiana University Press, 1989), 3–24.

2. For the most definitive account of Brenner's life, see Anita Shapira, *Brenner: Sipur hayyim* (Tel Aviv: 'Am 'Oved, 2008).

3. Zohar Shavit, *ha-Hayyim ha-sifrutiyim be-Eretz Yisrael, 1910–1933* (Tel Aviv: ha-Kibutz ha-Me'uhad, 1982), 28–72.

4. These writers have been previously grouped together; see Gershon Shaked, *Ha-siporet ha-'Ivrit, 1880–1980* (Tel Aviv: ha-Kibutz ha-Me'uhad, 1988), 2:17–36.

5. For fuller discussion of Agnon's biography, see Arnold Band, *Nostalgia and Nightmare: A Study in the Fiction of S. Y. Agnon* (Berkeley: University of California Press, 1968), 1–28; Dan Laor, *Haye Agnon* (Jerusalem: Schocken, 1998).

6. Born Levi Aryeh Orlof, Arieli changed his name following immigration to Palestine. He penned works under the names Orlof and Arieli. Numerous critics refer to him as Arieli-Orlof, a name he never employed. He will be referred to by his chosen name. For further

biographical information, see Gila Ramraz-Ra'ukh, *L. A. Arieli (Orlof): hayyav ve-yetzirato* (Tel Aviv: Papirus, 1992), 9–53. For more on his place in contemporary Hebrew literature, see Shaked, *Ha-siporet ha-'Ivrit*, 2:117–28; Yig'al Shvartz, *Li-heyot ke-de li-heyot: Aharon Re'uveni—monografiyah* (Jerusalem: Hotza'at Magnes, 1993), 312–14; Pinsker, *Literary Passports*, 165–84.

7. On the issues behind Arieli's immigration, see Philip Hollander, "Between Decadence and Rebirth: The Fiction of Levi Aryeh Arieli" (PhD diss., Columbia University, 2004), 379–80.

8. For more on Reuveni's life, see Shvartz, *Li-heyot ke-de li-heyot*, 15–19, 46–47; Getzel Kressel, *Leksikon ha-sifrut ha-'Ivrit ba-dorot ha-ahronim* (Merhavyah: Sifriyat ha-Po'alim, 1967), 2:809–10; David Tidhar, *Entziklopedyah le-halutze ha-Yishuv u-vonav* (Tel Aviv: Sifriyat Rishonim, 1947–71), 3:1359–60, also available online at http://www.tidhar.tourolib.org; Aryeh Pilovsky, introduction to *Gezamlte dertzeylungen*, by Aharon Re'uveni (Jerusalem: Hotza'at Magnes, 1991), vii–viii.

9. Tony Michels, *A Fire in Their Hearts: Yiddish Socialists in New York* (Cambridge, MA: Harvard University Press, 2005), 69–124.

1

HOLDING OUT FOR A HERO
Crisis and the New Hebrew Man

In this life of anguish that isn't life, but rather a long dying, jealousy rules.
Oy, mommy, I've experienced great bitterness and the pain is so great!
The moon in the light of her sad face looked down from the sky like one reflecting,
and it seemed that she was appeasing and consoling me: "What my son?
What, O miserable wretch? A Jew shalt not, schlemiel, a Jew shalt not,
unfortunate, complain. He should hide his pain and
silently suffer the burden placed upon him!"

—S. Y. Abramovitsh, *Sefer ha-kavtzanim* (The book of beggars)

Agnon and the Compatibility of Aesthetics and Social Commitment

Midway through Agnon's posthumously published novel *Shira*, Byzantine historian Manfred Herbst and his wife, Henrietta, travel to the Jezreel Valley. Their journey and their late 1930s sojourn at the fictional kvutzah Kfar Ahino'am enrich their lives and revive their marriage.[1] Manfred's silent decision to take his wife's hand and press it fondly during their drive north from Jerusalem augurs well. Having left their daily routine behind, they see their lives with fresh eyes and successfully reconnect with the love and commitment that unite them. The ideological devotion and steadfast dedication of Kfar Ahino'am's young pioneers, including Manfred and Henrietta's daughter Zahara and her husband, Avraham-and-a-half, stimulate this process. Asked to lecture before the kvutzah members, Manfred rediscovers the joy that initially drew him to his field of academic study; Henrietta, who hears her husband lecture for the first time in years, takes pride in the charismatic man to whom she has linked her fate. Consequently, following the conclusion of Manfred's lecture, Henrietta "took his hand and clasped it to hers, not letting go until they got up."[2] Then, later that night, after an extended kiss, Manfred turns to Henrietta and tells her, "You please me more than any woman in the world."[3] This signals his intention to conclude his extramarital affair with the nurse Shira. At the moment of their son Gabriel's conception, it will be this love and the couple's commitment to each other that will animate them. Although Manfred does not work the Jezreel Valley's soil with shovel and hoe, mere proximity to agricultural labor and advancement of Zionist aims seems to transform his life.

Manfred's sojourn in Kfar Ahino'am distances him from Jerusalem and the young nurse Shira, whose domination of his thoughts and actions reflects a midlife crisis. Shira does not conform to any standard of feminine beauty. A "hard-bitten, mannish, unseductive, coldly imperious, neither young nor pretty" figure, she proves a stark contrast to Henrietta, a maternal and domestic ideal. Nonetheless, Shira entices Manfred.[4] In fact, the contrast underlies Manfred's attraction to her. She offers him an alternative to fulfillment of his husbandly, paternal, and intertwined scholarly and Zionist commitments. By starting a sadomasochistic relationship with her on the very day that Henrietta goes into labor and gives birth to the couple's third daughter, Manfred finds a way to access the Freudian child's "premoral realm of polymorphous perversity" long denied him.[5]

Following the Herbsts' return to Jerusalem, a desire for an answer to the question of whether Manfred will maintain his renewed commitment to Henrietta or continue his relationship with Shira draws in readers. One planned ending of the uncompleted novel has Manfred locating Shira in a leper colony and joining her there. Again distanced from the agrarian Zionism of Kfar Ahino'am, Manfred fails to conclude his relationship with Shira and pursue a healthy relationship with Henrietta.

The Hebrew meaning of Shira's name points to a potential allegorical reading of Manfred's relationship with her that helps make sense of this ending. Pursuit of Shira, or poetry, requires that one push past efforts to restrict it. Health and sickness, love and death—one must be ready to integrate every element of human experience into art to realize one's full potential. In contrast, national and familial commitment, as embodied by the kvutzah and Henrietta Herbst, require that individuals erect fences and leave opportunities and experiences unexplored. Understood in this way, Manfred's life points to an impasse preventing successful integration of art and social commitment.

Current research on Modern Hebrew literature, Zionism, and Israeli history shares a similar belief that art and social commitment cannot be addressed simultaneously. Thus, even as scholars point to early twentieth-century Palestinian developments' critical importance to understanding the State of Israel and its culture, those studying Modern Hebrew literature read it outside the context of Zionism, and those analyzing Zionism and Israeli history do not consider Palestinian Hebrew culture's role in their development.[6]

In contrast, through examination of early twentieth-century Palestinian Hebrew literature within its historic context, this chapter demonstrates how proponents of Self-Evaluative masculinity produced socially engaged art; further, it advocates for integrated study of Hebrew literature, Zionism, and Israeli history. These Hebrew authors remained connected to a tradition of prophetically inspired engaged writing and refused to consign Shira to the leper colony and join her there. Instead, they felt compelled to free her and introduce issues of individual and collective illness and imperfection to the public sphere. Rather than viewing such writing as a form of "infection," they saw it as an important means for stimulating discussion and communal response to issues impeding improvement of the Jewish people's condition. Readers expected that Hebrew literature would address contemporary issues, and that is what advocates of Self-Evaluative masculinity strove to do.

Prima facie Agnon's early twentieth-century Palestinian Hebrew writings, as well as subsequent works like *Shira*, exemplify his dedication to production of modernist masterpieces with limited political import. Comprehensive perusal of the stories Agnon wrote in Palestine from 1908 to 1912, when he departed for Germany, as well as his preimmigration writing, however, fails to bear this out. On the contrary, it points to the prominent role gender plays in advancement of Jewish nationalist positions in Agnon's oeuvre. Furthermore, it demonstrates how many of these works constitute part and parcel of broader efforts by Self-Evaluative masculinity's proponents to advance specific Zionist aims through incorporation of gendered representations into their fiction, a trend that even the most apolitical Hebrew writers found difficult to resist.[7]

Gendered representations in Agnon's preimmigration writing express his serious dissatisfaction with a flawed East European Jewish social reality; varied portrayals of Jewish masculinity featured therein illuminate his efforts to voice normative behavior capable of advancing social improvement and to find the best method to persuade his male readers to assume these behavioral norms.

Following his immigration to Palestine, Agnon interacted with other proponents of Self-Evaluative masculinity, identified with their ideas, and employed similar persuasive methods in his fiction. A shared sense of purpose developed through his personal interactions with Brenner in particular. Through examination of three "secular" tales from Agnon's first Palestinian period, this chapter shows how these stories utilize methods common to champions of Self-Evaluative masculinity to promote some of its most important aspects. Analysis of "Be'erah shel Miryam" (Miryam's well, 1909) points to these writers' rejection of Palestinian immigration as the ultimate solution to Jewish problems. Only creation of a masculine community whose members collectively adopt a self-critical norm and modify their behavior in accordance with it could resolve difficulties rooted in Jewish masculine failure. "Ahot" (Sister, 1910) develops this point by stressing Jewish masculinity's psychological component. Individual renunciation of attraction to feminine-tinged weakness could yield masculine health and benefit women and children incapable of such renunciation.

Finally, "Tishre" (Tishre, 1911) illustrates the importance that Self-Evaluative masculinity's supporters assigned to its promotion and adoption. Although Jewish continuity constituted the impetus behind the Palestinian Jewish community's development, the Yishuv's divergence from prior forms of Jewishness created an implicit sense of rebellion among its proponents.[8] Numerous young men, caught between a desire to remain loyal to the past and a desire to create something radically new, encountered a crisis of authority. This crisis manifested itself in paralysis, inability to pursue heterosexual relationships and marriage, and failure to effectively advance communal goals. Extrication from this crisis required interrogation of the past to find continuity within change, a process difficult to pursue in isolation. Hebrew writers needed to work on behalf of their Palestinian Jewish male brethren to cultivate productive homosocial relations capable of aiding their male community's collective working through of simultaneous feelings of loyalty to and estrangement from the Jewish past. Only such a collective working through would enable the instauration of shared masculine values capable of ensuring the Palestinian Jewish community's future. Failure to pursue such an agenda, these advocates asserted, would lead to alienation and an individual and collective sense of dispossession.

Masculinity, Social Criticism, and Issues of Authorial Responsibility in Agnon's Galician Writing

The literary craftsmanship in Agnon's preimmigration writings is well documented.[9] In contrast, the social engagement of his Buczacz writing has garnered little attention and its relationship to his socially engaged Palestinian fiction remains a scholarly lacuna. Consequently, "ha-Sarsur la-'arayot" (The pimp, 1905) and "ha-Igeret" (The letter, 1905) prove particularly illuminating.[10] These stories illustrate the role gender plays in Agnon's expression of serious dissatisfaction with a flawed social reality and his call to readers to act for social betterment. Furthermore, their analysis paves the way for discussion of his Palestinian fiction's socially engaged character.

Itche, protagonist in "The Pimp," previously worked as an elementary school teacher's assistant. In that capacity, he inculcated traditional East European Jewish values, but when extreme poverty leads him to abandon this work, his contribution to value transmission paradoxically grows. After becoming a pimp and marrying a former charge, the nouveau riche ascends to a position of honor within the Jewish community, a status confirmed by synagogue performance of the priestly blessing on Rosh Hashanah. The other Jewish attendees have no issue with this, because they fail to see a disconnection between Itche's de facto values and their own. This elevation disturbs only non-Jewish observers. Consequently, when they see Itche assume a leadership role, they laugh scornfully. To them, Itche's newfound status communicates his society's lack of moral principles and its passive acceptance of those failing to uphold proclaimed standards of masculine virtue.

Although Itche's wealth and his profession's perceived ties to sexual virility make him a potential vehicle for alternative masculine standards' transmission, his wife's barrenness alludes to the inability of the values he embodies to offer a viable Jewish future. Only a Jewish future grounded in masculine virtue will silence non-Jewish observers' righteously critical laughter.

God is notably absent from Agnon's Buczacz fiction, which never promotes repentance and rededication to God and his commandments as a way for East European Jewish men to reclaim their moral compass and act virtuously.[11] "The Letter" voices this absence and presses secular Hebrew writers to employ alternative means for virtue's instauration among Jewish men.

In its construction, "The Letter" closely resembles the monologue "Dos Tepl" (The pot, 1901) by Sholem Aleichem (1859–1916); it can be best understood through comparison with the Yiddish master's work.[12] In "The Pot," a Jewish woman goes to her town rabbi to ostensibly inquire about a pot's ritual cleanliness. While this is a fully plausible scenario, she already recognizes the pot's ritual impurity; her visit serves as a way for her to vent her anger at religious Jewish society and its leaders' failure to alleviate her suffering. Similarly, in "The Letter," an illiterate Jewish widow visits a Hebrew scribe purportedly to have him write her two eldest sons to request money. Yet she neither knows their exact whereabouts nor possesses the fee for letter-writing services. Instead, she comes to the male writer, who stands in for the emerging Jewish secular intelligentsia, to express her ire about traditional religious and secular Jewish men's betrayal.

The illiterate widow strove to raise her children as educated religious Jews, but gentiles murdered her husband, her first two sons emigrated and abandoned her, and she will soon need to have her talented youngest son leave his religious studies to apprentice for food and a future livelihood. Prepared to shift her allegiance to the secular intelligentsia, the widow, who embodies East European Jewry, demands that it meet her needs. As things currently stand, she does not see the secular intelligentsia as distinguishable from the men in her life. In the absence of faith, her eldest sons have no moral qualms about ignoring family obligations. Furthermore, her son Pinchas's work as a white slave trader recalls "The Pimp" and hints that secular Jewish men's propensity for exploitation equals that of traditional Jewish men. Not every member of Jewish society has benefited from the reforms advanced by secular activists. The widow desperately needs change. If the Hebrew writer wants to earn a readership, the text implies, he must think about more than aesthetic matters. He must transform Jewish masculinity so that Jewish men will work to alleviate a feminized Jewish people's suffering. Unprepared to undertake this, the Hebrew writer addressed by the widow is left speechless at story's end. His unresponsiveness makes him unworthy of reward, as his failure to receive payment for his transcription implies.[13]

"The Pimp" and "The Letter" employ gender to give readers a sense that East European Jewish society is in crisis. Modernity has emasculated and feminized it. Consequently, Jewish men need to remasculinize themselves and a symbolically male nation for the betterment of Jewish society and its members; "The Letter" points to Hebrew writers as those best able to instruct male readers how to do this.

Surveying Alternative Jewish Masculinities

Earlier Jewish sources presented different masculine forms for adoption; Agnon's Galician works show him considering many of them as he looked to identify a masculine form capable of assisting Jewish men in meeting their people's needs. For example, the Hebrew poem "Gibor katan" (Little hero, 1904) draws on a combination of traditional and Zionist elements related to the Lag ba-ʿomer holiday to earnestly portray a young boy who takes up bow and arrow to fight Satan. The narrator's mention of heaven's oversight indicates that the poem does more than just celebrate juvenile imagination. The hero's youth and employment of a weapon show him to be different than Jewish males who employ piety and erudition to bring salvation; this difference underlies the boy's "sublime power" and his ability to show his people redemptive "wonders."[14] Similarly, the Yiddish poem "Rebbe Yosef Dela Reyne" (1903) promotes an active male hero through a playful retelling of the eponymous hero's unsuccessful attempt to bring about salvation through imprisonment of the evil spirits Samael and Lilith.[15] Finally, Agnon's poem "Yerushalayim" (Jerusalem, 1904) contemplates the demands of such masculine heroism and considers national martyrdom as the apogee of masculine behavior. Like the speaker in Yehuda Halevi's poem "Tzion Halo Tish'ali" (Won't you ask after, O Zion), the obvious inspiration for Agnon's poem, the speaker states his readiness to sacrifice his life, his spirit, and his soul to realize the Jewish people's return to Zion.[16]

Despite Agnon's youthful engagement with masculine forms drawn from the Jewish tradition, he found them intangible and distant. Lacking religious faith, messianic pretensions, connection to a martial tradition, and readiness for martyrdom, Jewish men could not easily adapt earlier masculine forms possessing these characteristics for Jewish societal transformation. Consequently, Agnon soon pondered masculine models rooted in the surrounding non-Jewish world and considered whether he could modify them to help Jewish men meet their suffering people's tangible needs.

Centering on a father and his two sons, Agnon's story "Avram Leybush u-vanav" (Avram Leybush and his sons, 1905) addresses the issue of social continuity and contemplates imitation of non-Jewish masculine norms to achieve this goal.[17] A proponent of traditional East European Jewish values, Avram, like the widow in "The Letter," works to carry Judaism forward through cultivation of a son learned in the Talmud and punctilious in ritual

Fig. 1.1 Shmuel Yosef Agnon, Lvov, ca. 1908. National Library of Israel. Agnon Archive. Courtesy of Yael Blau.

commandments' performance. Yet circumstances push him to reevaluate his efforts and embrace a different type of masculinity.

Avram's son Yitzhak Me'ir initially appears to epitomize his father's values but soon displays an unsavory character. He possesses the critical acumen and genius characteristic of traditional East European Jewish society's Yeshiva Bochur masculine ideal as well as the physical appearance associated with it.[18] He is a "weak youth, thin and lean with long sidelocks that dragged slowly across his pale bloodless cheeks."[19] Yet perusal of secular texts and adoption of modern ideas precipitate his loss of faith. Yitzhak Me'ir's erudition, critical mind, and external appearance still hew to the ideal, but his inner character degenerates. Thus, even after ceasing to study and perform ritual commandments, he ignores his aging father's need for assistance with his business dealings.

Hirshkeh, Yitzhak's younger brother, contrasts with him markedly. Burly and robust, he lacks his brother's delicacy and critical acumen. An ignoramus like the neighboring peasants, Hirshkeh embarrasses Avram and Yitzhak. Nonetheless, his seemingly "non-Jewish" physicality enables him to aid his father with firewood sales and assorted odd jobs.

As the story concludes, Avram reevaluates his views of his sons. Yitzhak's lapsed religious observance will prevent a rich religious father-in-law from rewarding him with a large dowry that can help support his family. In contrast, Hirshkeh's humble efforts prove critical to his family's well-being. Sitting in the booth that Hirshkeh has skillfully erected in honor of the Sukkoth holiday, Avram praises him for the first time and refers to him as both a "man" and "a craftsman."[20] While Hirshkeh might not provide Avram with a heavenly reward, he betters his earthly existence.

One can read the story as a call for Jewish social transformation through adoption of a new masculine ideal type more in line with the physicality of Avram Leybush's non-Jewish neighbors and the call for productive labor advanced by Jewish socialists, Zionists, and non-Jewish reformers. Yet Avram's praise of Hirshkeh's sukkah yields a more sobering conclusion.[21] The sukkah, by law, constitutes a temporary shelter. Consequently, the text hints that the masculine ideal type tied to physicality and craftsmanship embodied by Hirshkhe cannot catalyze long-term Jewish improvement, even if such attributes allow Hirshkeh to display his virtue. Thus, we see Agnon rejecting facile imitation of non-Jewish masculine norms as no better than the rigid maintenance of traditional East European Jewish masculine norms or efforts to extract a new masculine norm from unrealistic models scattered throughout Jewish tradition.

Contemplating One's Craft: Writing and Masculine Transformation

Despite his reticence to advocate for Jewish men's physical transformation, Agnon did value Jewish men's assumption of secular crafts, as his sympathetic portrayal of Hirshkeh conveys, and he viewed writing as a craft whose practitioners could lead through communication. Consequently, he engaged with the prophetic ethos prominent in Hayyim Nahman Bialik's poetry to respond to pressing contemporary issues.[22] Disturbed by the Białystok pogrom of 1906 that left seventy dead and ninety wounded, Agnon composed the Yiddish poems "Azkores" (Memorial) and "Ir Zolt Nisht Meynen" (You shouldn't believe) in 1907.[23] In "You Shouldn't Believe," which evokes Bialik's "'Al ha-shehitah" (On the slaughter), the speaker communicates his people's anger at the wrongs perpetrated against them. Using his blood to write the poem whose words are like pieces torn from his heart, the speaker prosecutes the case against God, who overlooked the Jewish people's suffering. Furthermore, he expresses the Jewish people's unwillingness to accept the current state of affairs; he implicitly calls upon them to fight to change it. Meanwhile, in "Memorial," whose imagery recalls Bialik's "be-'Ir haharegah" (In the city of slaughter), the speaker explicitly stresses the Jewish people's readiness to struggle against atrocities perpetrated against them. The commemorative flame ceaselessly burning in Jewish hearts will be kept ablaze by unjustly spilled Jewish blood. Vengeful thoughts issue forth from these burning hearts together with the yizkor prayer; the speaker envisions that the vibrancy of these thoughts, hearts, and prayers will serve as a living monument to the disfigured corpses of victims of anti-Jewish violence.

The two poems express a communal Jewish will to live, with or without divine providence, and "Memorial" displays "moving rhetorical force." [24] Nonetheless, these poems do not instruct readers how to relate to the Jewish past or how to improve the Jewish people's condition. Consequently, Agnon abandoned the prophet's elevated vantage point. To better engage his male readers and foster social change, he concluded that he needed to interact with them on their level. To do this, he looked to make use of their connection to Jewish tradition, past, and community. Thus, despite the promise of his early Yiddish writing, Agnon wrote exclusively in Hebrew after his 1907 immigration to Palestine, implicitly linking his work to the vast Jewish textual tradition and imbuing it with the Hebrew language's long-standing authority.[25]

Agnon's Politically Engaged Art:
The Jaffa Period's Secular Tales

Judging by Agnon's most widely read stories from his first Palestinian period, claims about his fiction's political engagement seem strained. Yet this apolitical image is the product of the author's careful framing of his early literary career for public consumption and the selective reading this framing has engendered.[26] Published under the nom de plume Agnon, the short story "'Agunot" (Abandoned wives, 1908) eased Tshatshkes's movement in new literary directions by distancing him from his preimmigration life and work. Similarly, the novella *ve-Hayah he-'akov le-mishor* (And the crooked shall become straight, 1912) cast him as a writer whose work transcended his time and place.[27] Consequently, acceptance of this view shielded Agnon from criticism for disengaging from politics and allowed him to more effectively focus on his art's stylistic development. Furthermore, because the style of these *Kunstmärchen* proved "roughly continuous with the writer's mature style in their use of traditional Jewish symbols, folk motifs and the conventions of the Hasidic tale," most research on Agnon's initial Palestinian work focuses on them and helps spread the perception that he was an author dedicated to aesthetics with peripheral interest in broader political discourse.[28]

Nonetheless, many of Agnon's other period tales diverge intellectually, thematically, and stylistically from his mature work: "They are almost entirely secular; they have contemporary settings of Jaffa of the Second Aliya; and they are broadly autobiographical in spirit concerned as they are with young Hebrew writers recently arrived in Palestine." They also feature an "extravagantly expressive style (in contrast to the allusive classicism of the later works)" and prove thematically preoccupied "with erotic love."[29] One must turn to these secular tales, especially "Be'erah shel Miryam," "Ahot," and "Tishre," which constitute high points of Agnon's involvement with Self-Evaluative masculinity, to better understand how he exploits gendered representations to advance Zionism during this period.[30] While Agnon had previously put gendered images to use for programmatic purposes, their manipulation for advancement of Zionist aims assumed a clearer form when he engaged methods he shared with Self-Evaluative masculinity's other leading proponents. Consequently, attention to gender's function in these stories offers an effective point of entry for discussion of how these men's fiction worked to ideologically engage contemporary Palestinian male readers.

Who We Want to Be versus Who We Are: The *Talush* as Alternative Ideological Tool

Palestinian Hebrew writers looking to promote the idea that Jewish male immigrants could seamlessly transform themselves into healthy men through development of a connection to the Palestinian soil expressed this belief through the literary figure of the halutz (pioneer). The fiction of early twentieth-century writers such as Shlomo Tzemach (1886–1974) and Moshe Smilansky (1874–1953), as well as more obscure late nineteenth-century Palestinian Hebrew writers, provides examples of this.[31] Yet examination of the idyll "ba-Ya'ar be-Haderah" (In the Haderah forest, 1914) by David Shimoni (1886–1956), a leading early twentieth-century Palestinian Hebrew poet, more succinctly illuminates what underlay the Self-Evaluative writers' preference for a less overtly heroic model for their protagonists.

To create the perception that a new form of Jewish life had already taken root in Palestine, "In the Haderah Forest" presents a day in the life of a group of Jewish lumberjacks. The "broad dependable shoulders" of charismatic Naftali and the strong and equally broad shoulders of a young immigrant from Ukraine's Don region hint that the group is prepared to bear heavy burdens and will soon redeem the Jewish people, as alluded to by references to Passover deliverance and Joshua's conquest of Canaan. All these lumberjacks, who represent the Yishuv vanguard, need to do is just realize their potential through effective mimicry of the unseen pioneer Ben-Artzi (whose name means "son of the land"). Ben-Artzi enters the nearby malarial swamp daily to plant trees and "stay and disinherit its death / And hand it over to life."[32] Through a similar deferral of their personal needs, the lumberjacks will successfully bear the collective burden, and the nation will prosper.

While Naftali forecasts the Donny's successful mimicry of Ben-Artzi because he has "enough strength in [his] loins" and lacks "Torah in [his] skull' and "wisdom" to serve as a chair at meetings, Rav Pinchas, an older religious Jewish man who possesses a diasporic Jewish education and religious devotion, voices communal uncertainty about the future.[33] Exhausted, he is confronted by a sense of despair at the workday's conclusion. Malaria has killed his beloved wife, and he cannot provide for his dispersed children. Rav Pinchas questions the purposefulness of his actions. Yet when he looks over at his young compatriots, he sees the "iron in their blood," the laugh in their eyes, and their "confident stride."[34] Recognizing them as his true children, Rav Pinchas's doubts disappear and he feels confident that the group can realize its potential. Taking the lead, he pushes past his awareness that malaria, sword, and bullet have felled others looking to realize national liberation and calls upon his coworkers to commemorate the fallen by laboring alongside him in gladness and joy. Adopting this joyous approach portending national redemption, the group members burst into song and dance an impromptu hora.

Through effective exploitation of the idyll form and its characteristic features, "In the Haderah Forest" successfully promotes the idea that immigration to Palestine and physical labor on the land can seamlessly transform Jewish immigrants' individual and collective lives. The idyll form's limited temporal, spatial, and psychological focus and its generic reining in of perceptibly tragic elements, such as those characterizing Palestinian Jewish settlement, assist Shimoni in creating an invigorating "atmosphere of tranquility, certainty, peace, and harmony."[35] Doubt and despair confront only Rav Pinchas, the poem's elder, and he easily pushes them aside through effective recognition of the young Jewish immigrants' inspirational character. Successful resort to the idyll and the positive tone that characterizes it allow Shimoni to present an upbeat message about Palestinian Jewish settlement.

If, however, readers move beyond the idyll's arbitrary conventions, the discordance between the muscular anti-intellectual model of self-sacrifice that the poem promotes and the diasporic norms and cultural associations brought to Palestine by most contemporary Jewish male immigrants, including those in their late teens and early twenties, reemerges. In fact, immigrant readers capable of accessing the poem's Hebrew and Jewish cultural allusions would have found it easy to relate to Rav Pinchas's trepidation and difficult to disregard it to adopt Ben-Artzi's mentality and behavior that prove foreign to their experience.

Shimoni promotes his ideological message through coordinated use of the idyll form, the figure of the halutz, and the idea of epiphanic change. The Self-Evaluative writers opposed his efforts to downplay significant feelings of dislocation and alienation felt by Palestinian Jewish immigrants. Instead, they asserted that these feelings needed to be addressed to enable the progressive psychological change necessary for the early twentieth-century Palestinian Jewish community to develop. Consequently, Agnon and his cohort eschewed fictional use of the halutz and adopted the *talush* (uprooted) literary type for use in their Palestinian fiction. Thus, Agnon employs the talush in "Miryam's Well," "Ahot," and "Tishre," rather than modeling their protagonists on halutzim or traditional East European Jewish figures like those featured in most of his turn-of-the-century Hebrew tales.

A conflicted figure who loses touch with his religious and ethnic Jewish roots and finds himself incapable of acclimating to a non-Jewish environment, the talush (plural *tlushim*) achieved prominence in fin de siècle Eastern European Hebrew literature.[36] This figure's ability to voice feelings of uprootedness shared by most early twentieth-century Jewish men and women who turned to Zionism and Palestinian settlement out of frustration with European Jewish life led avant-garde Hebrew writers such as Agnon, Arieli, Brenner, and Reuveni to introduce it into Palestinian Hebrew literature. In addition to viewing the talush's importation as a way to more realistically portray Palestinian Jewish immigrants and better promote their belief that arrival in Palestine proved insufficient to actually transform immigrant Jewish men, they also recognized the political efficacy of its use.

The talush's exclusively male nature helps explain Self-Evaluative writers' literary adoption of it as well as the figure's relationship to broader national issues.[37] The predominantly male turn-of-the-century Hebrew literary community employed tlushim as allegorical figures simultaneously representing the incipient national community and its constituent male members. Allegorical use of tlushim helped Agnon and his cohort achieve the following: (1) It shed light on the perceived deficiencies of the Jewish male character that contributed to individual and communal Jewish decline and inhibited construction of a national community. The warm in-group environment created by the Jewish male writer's decision to address Jewish male imperfection before an overwhelmingly Jewish male audience created optimal conditions for this critique's consideration. (2) Once internalized, this critique delineated a narrative starting point for individual and collective Jewish improvement and an implicit end point when the individual Jewish male and his Palestinian community overcame their deficiencies and achieved "masculine" health. Such a narrative set a meaningful course for Palestinian Hebrew audiences confronted with a sense of purposelessness. (3) Resort to the talush also concretized the difficult struggles facing new immigrants attempting to build a successful new Palestinian community and highlighted the heroic nature of those men who, unlike tlushim, took steps to master their situation through introspection, confrontation with individual shame, and efforts to achieve individual and communal health. Talush narratives proved largely inclusive and, through their overlap with intersubjective reality, elucidated opportunities for heroic action available to Palestinian Jewish men regardless of their physique. (4) Finally, rather than portraying loyalty to one's past as an impediment to heroic action, as implied by praise of the Donny's ignorance of the Torah in "In the Haderah

Forest," Palestinian Hebrew tlushim tales promoted continued linkage to the Jewish past. It supplied useful tools for coping with the challenges to introspection posed by the individual psyche.

Masculine Critique and Homosocial Community in "Miryam's Well or Fragments from Human Life"

When forcibly placed into a cramped long boat and rowed from the ship that has brought him to the Palestinian shore, Hemdat, the protagonist of "Miryam's Well," is compared to a "fetus in his mother's womb . . . [who] emerged into the air of a new world."[38] Through this metaphor, Agnon ironically challenges the idea that mere presence in the Land of Israel enables personal transformation. If it did, this largely passive figure would prosper.

Instead, a strange passivity that inhibits Hemdat's ability to connect with others brings about his premature death. His isolation could be attributed to his arrival in a new land and his separation from his girlfriend, Miryam, whom he left behind in East Europe to pursue his literary calling, but when she arrives in Palestine, he does not work to renew their connection. Thus, when he travels north to meet her during Passover, their reunion voices neither the natural rebirth of spring nor the holiday's redemptive spirit. Hemdat hopes that his possession of an older and seemingly more mature man's travel documents will make others consider him worthy of her hand, but they fail to impress Miryam's father, who does not offer Hemdat her hand in marriage. Then Hemdat does not do anything more to draw Miryam near. He does not declare his love to her, propose marriage, or even initiate a sexual encounter that will bind Miryam to him through their shared sexual desire. He just stops pursuing her and takes a job working for her father. Ultimately, her proximity destabilizes Hemdat, and when he mistakenly imagines Miryam drowning in the Sea of Galilee, he drowns trying to save her.

Employing literary techniques that shed light on Hemdat's decision-making process, Agnon connects Hemdat's failed transformation to his psychological state.[39] Readers are exposed to Hemdat's "erotic yearnings, fantastic dreams of artistic beatitude, a relentless imagining of situations of heroism in which he . . . will save some damsel in distress and win her admiration and love," and "deep remorse about his tainted thoughts and life."[40] While not unusual, these thoughts prove striking, because they dominate Hemdat's psyche, paralyze him, and prevent his acclimation to life in Palestine.

Through analysis of these thoughts, the insecure gender and sexual identities that prevent Hemdat from acclimating to life in Palestine and thriving there reveal themselves. Hemdat's "insides filled with disgust at the sight of [his legs'] filthy appearance," and the sour "smell [of his body] wafting from his pillow and blanket" bothers him. Due to his inability to fully control his body, Hemdat finds his corporeality discomforting; it is his desire to punish his recalcitrant form that leads him to derive pleasure when mosquitoes prey on his naked body.[41] This masochism, however, proves a turning around on the self of its sadistic desire and points to a longing to "prey," or inflict pain, on others.

Hemdat identifies his sadism with heterosexual desire, and he does his best to repress this desire. Thus, when the "blood" he imagines issuing forth from his lips following perceived mastication of a spider seems to hint at a sexualized desire for flesh (*hemdat besarim*), Hemdat tries to bury sexual desire and issues of masculine identity deep within. Therefore, when he steps in a viscous blackish-red puddle upon getting out of bed, he interprets it as a sign of tuberculosis and sickness that distance him from the hint of carnal desire. However, neither renunciation of his body nor masochism reins in his heterosexual desire, and he feels impure. To assuage his sense of defilement and guilt, he partakes in increasingly intense and unsuccessful purification rituals that culminate with his death during imagined ritual immersion in the mythical well of Miryam.

More than aesthetic motivations led Agnon to describe Hemdat's psychological difficulties. Agnon intended for his readers to find his thought and behavior perplexing, just like Brenner who is confused by Hemdat coming "to Jaffa and [acting] as if the whole problem of the Jewish people's rebirth in the Land of Israel doesn't affect him in the least."[42] Agnon portrayed these difficulties to prod readers to examine Hemdat's lifestyle and literary approach more closely, reject them, and adopt a lifestyle, and potentially a literary approach, more attuned to national needs. In Agnon's paradigm, by avoiding introspection, Hemdat and his writing take on a feminine character. Thus, they contrast with Agnon and his writing that assume a masculine character through their embrace of introspection and homosocial community.

Like other Hebrew writers, Agnon incorporated tlushim into his fiction to catalyze discussion of normative Jewish values and steps necessary for individual and Jewish collective improvement. In "Miryam's Well," he utilizes Hemdat to address the interrelationship between individual Jewish behavior and collective Jewish existence and ways to improve the latter through modification of the former. Thus, even though Hemdat and Agnon share personal characteristics, Agnon chooses not to make him a vehicle for portraying his interior world. He dissociates himself from Hemdat and critiques his decision to live in isolation from broader Jewish national issues. The ironic comment that Hemdat "was a talented young man, at least that's what his naïve ancestors believed" emphasizes the distance separating the two writers.[43] Consequently, Agnon does not insert the saccharine and solipsistic excerpts from Hemdat's literary work into his story to highlight Hemdat's talent as a writer. Instead, these excerpts are intended to illustrate Hemdat's lack of emotional awareness and wisdom, and the work's "cultivation of tears and widespread sentimentalism" result from the author's desire to present Hemdat's limited and insular literary world.[44]

Hemdat's discomfort with introspection and self-exposure has long undermined his writing: "Hemdat's heart raged and divine fire ignited in his midst, but his ink was water, and, when it came time to employ it to release his choicest emotions, the flame was extinguished and the fire in his hands ceased."[45] Contemplating his literary failings, Hemdat perfunctorily casts blame on Miryam and his relationship with her. Feeling forced to choose between his personal feelings and a literary calling tied to his sense of collective belonging, Hemdat heads to the Land of Israel. He believes "his heart's freedom will be proclaimed" there.[46] Yet shame still prevents Hemdat from expressing his uncertainty about his gender and sexual identities.

Agnon manipulates descriptions of interior and exterior spaces to indirectly voice the fear of self-exposure that precipitates Hemdat's fatal descent into mental illness. Even though mosquitoes repeatedly prey on him in his stuffy, filthy, warm, and foul-smelling apartment associatively linked with his psyche, Hemdat will not leave it. The outdoors offers fresh clean air, cool breezes, and more pleasant smells symbolic of improved mental health, but Hemdat avoids them "in order not to be seen naked."[47]

Hemdat's discomfort with introspection and his reticence about self-exposure also underlie his seeming inability to acclimate to the Palestinian climate and the literary approach he develops:

> A burning sun came in through the door and pistol-whipped him in the face with its scepter. Alas, it jumps upon his head and there is no escaping it. In every corner of the room, it constitutes a danger. If only he had at least one window and didn't need to make use of the light entering through the door, he would put up a curtain. Then, in the morning, he would lie on his bed and read

a book, since reading while sitting had become difficult for him and when he began to read his head immediately began to sway.[48]

Like the curtain he imagines placing on his window, the literary approach Hemdat adopts is intended to cloak his shame and prevent self-exposure. By shielding him from uncomfortable reflection and providing him with a buoying and seemingly appreciative female audience, the approach, indeed, brings him short-term happiness. His female readers, who purportedly enjoy his entertaining fantasy tales and their ebullient style, do not critique his lifeless writing. Its insubstantial connection to his interior world and its failure to relate to personal and national issues animating it does not bother them.

By remaining at a distance from other men potentially ready to assist him in coping with his difficulties, however, Hemdat disregards his inner fire and hastens his demise by leaving gender and sexual issues unaddressed. Immersed in a world of emotion and fantasy, Hemdat produces "Luz," a maudlin text written in flowery derivative prose. It purportedly communicates the circumstances behind the death of Zoharah, the female embodiment of Hemdat's nonjudgmental audience. Yet it actually serves as a vehicle through which Hemdat bemoans his perceivably inalterable fate and writes off his failure to consummate sexual relations with Miryam and other interested women as inevitable. Left unaddressed in his life and work, Hemdat's pent-up desire ultimately finds expression in a phantasmagoric Miryam whom Hemdat dies trying to save.

Through his didactic presentation of Hemdat's manuscripts and story, the narrator of "Miryam's Well" employs a "masculine" literary approach; Agnon displays a greater affinity with him than he does with Hemdat: "This man was lost, as will subsequently be told, and he never voiced his song. He merely abandoned his heart's ruins [*bate nefesh*]. I, the youth who signed below, attempted to partially rebuild and plaster and paint them in accordance with my literary talents for when, if able to make his way amidst the ruins, the reader beholds [them]."[49] Editing cannot perfect Hemdat's bequeath, but it can help capture and maintain potential readers' attention. If and when readers take up this edited tale, it will offer more than its form would lead one to expect: "they are ruins, but he who has eyes will see; and, if he is a sensitive man, he will pay attention to the course of their owner's life."[50] By placing Hemdat's story before his intended readers, the narrator looks to address Hemdat's thought and behavior and work with these men to develop strategies and communities better able to foster personal and collective growth.

The narrator's desire to dispassionately explore Hemdat's thoughts and behavior differentiates the two men. While the narrator does not denigrate Hemdat for his weakness, he still interprets his fearful inability to address it as a distinctly feminine characteristic; he views those unwilling to work to overcome their weaknesses as unsuitable for membership in the masculine community he envisions. A self-critical attitude conducive to introspection would differentiate the imagined national community's normative male members from those who fail to dedicate their energies to achieving collective aims and choose to produce and consume escapist literature.

The intended Jewish male reader is left to consider whether he desires membership in such a community, and the narrator uses Hemdat's story to present the benefit of membership in a self-critical community dedicated to introspection. While identifying with him and implicitly struggling with similar shame-inducing gender and sexual issues, the narrator asserts that collective confrontation with such issues constitutes a way to limit their effects on individuals and the community by lessening the shame surrounding them and making it easier to address them. This belief underlies his decision to air Hemdat's dirty laundry. The narrator looks to bring together men who previously suffered from gender and sexual issues in isolation and create a self-critical reading community capable of initiating public discussion of gender and sexual issues previously shrouded in shame and advancing strategies to address them. Aware that most readers and writers would prefer not to expose themselves, the narrator points to Hemdat's mental collapse and death as a cautionary tale. Without self-exposure, the Palestinian Jewish community will lose contributors and fail to transform itself.

In "Miryam's Well," strategically placed elements of traditional Jewish life combine with meetings with older Jewish male figures to further delineate the purpose behind creation of the alternative masculine community the story promotes. While aboard ship, Hemdat struggles to understand what motivates him to travel to Palestine, a place, as one of his father's business colleagues reminds him, where observant Jews go to die. Yet he soon sees the issues he faces echoed in Abram's biblical journey to the promised land. Then, while contemplating his mission's rationale, he meets an old Sephardic man who points to self-improvement as one of immigration's primary objectives. If Hemdat pursues it, Palestine will offer him and his comrades an opportunity to achieve individual and collective goals denied them in the Diaspora.

Similarly, Palestine's Jewish environment pushes Hemdat to focus on his immigration's underlying purpose. On the Jewish New Year, known alternatively as the Day of Memory, Hemdat's memory disturbs his complacency. Neglected issues of familial responsibility and behavioral modification reassert themselves. Aware that he constitutes a financial burden to his family, Hemdat takes an important step to better their lives. He finds a job and achieves financial independence, something that demonstrates his ability to act to improve others' lives. Hemdat, however, fails to take further action. Nonetheless, his diasporic encounter with a Jew passionately praying "may our eyes witness Thy compassionate return to Zion" hints that he recognizes that a masculine achievement of collective spiritual return to a metaphorical Zion constitutes a daunting long-term group project, even if nothing prevents one from undertaking it.[51]

"Sister"—Confrontation and Renunciation of Inner Femininity

Neta Na'aman, the Jewish male protagonist of "Sister," who is promoted as a behavioral model for other Palestinian Jewish men, contrasts sharply with Hemdat. His two-year-long acclimation to Palestinian life initially seems to voice the basic difference between them. Yet his work as a business office copyist and his splitting of leisure time between creative writing and pursuit of romantic adventures merely mask his uprootedness and psychological difficulties. Nonetheless, Neta's ability to contemplate his situation and recognize his presence at a critical life juncture differentiates him from Hemdat. When forced to choose between continued avoidance of his problems and their repercussions and confrontation and tackling of difficulties underlying his unhappiness and frustration, Neta selects the latter option. His visit to his sister's apartment demonstrates this. There, confrontation with his sense of "feminine" weakness provides important insight. While women and children's weakness prevents them from bettering their lives, Neta's stereotypically feminine weakness aids both his development and the development of a healthier collective identity. By working to vanquish individual and collective Jewish weakness, Neta personifies Self-Evaluative masculinity and points the way to personal happiness.

"Sister" opens with Neta working on a hot summer day in the office. While the work bores him and he finds the heat uncomfortable, he projects poise, satisfaction, and a debonair masculinity that distinguish him from

European Hebrew fiction's neurotic tlushim. Palestine's self-proclaimed most eligible Jewish bachelor awaits feminine caresses and exudes confidence. Furthermore, he celebrates his freedom and independence: "In the prime of his life, he's free to do whatever his heart desires. He doesn't have a boss or a judge. Today Hannah and tomorrow Peninah, or perhaps both in one day. There's nobody to tell him what to do."[52]

Regardless of Neta's posturing, his raffish masculine persona quickly loses credibility. He walks past the homes of the two purported objects of his passions and arrives at his sister's apartment. After having ignored her since her arrival in Yafo two years earlier, Neta enters her apartment. Their meeting concludes with Neta kissing his sister's hand after "his suffering sliced open his eyes and the mysteries of eternal love sparkled amidst profuse tears."[53] This gesture marks an "ethical-existential-psychological change in the protagonist's consciousness" and communicates Agnon's promotion of Self-Evaluative masculinity in lieu of Neta's rakishness, because he pushes past fear and shame to aid somebody else.[54]

A retrospective reading of the story, prompted by its conclusion, reveals the dissatisfaction that Neta's previously tenuous gender and sexual identities fomented. When the text states that Neta stands on "hot broom-wood coals," communication of his subjective experience serves as its primary purpose.[55] Despite his praise of independence and his romantic pursuits, Neta perceives his life as hellish. His attraction to Tirtzah and his romantic involvement with her serve as tepid substitutes for the erotic appeal of her effeminate brother: "every time he looked at his beautiful profile a lovely and charming maiden's figure would rise up before his eyes. That's how he imagined Tirtzah's countenance."[56] Even before meeting her, Neta seemingly loves Tirtzah, a permissible sexual object. Yet he desires something she cannot offer and he finds pursuit of relations with her difficult. Similarly, Neta's attraction to Elnora, described in terms evocative of Medusa, reflect a desire to embrace his impotence and homosocial desire: "Those wild naked arms. Like snakes, love snakes opening the Garden of Eden's gates for Man, they encompass his neck."[57] Through her asphyxiating embrace, Elnora seems to offer castration and death. Alternatively, the phallic snakes' opening of Eden's gates can be interpreted as voicing a submissive desire for anal penetration. Neta's attraction to Tirtzah and Elnora points to urges that make it difficult for him to give expression to masculine heterosexual vigor.

Nonetheless, Neta's decision to bypass Elnora and Tirtzah's homes reveals a continuing desire for life, love, and happiness that neither relationships with these women nor pursuit of the desires that relations with them conceal can satisfy. Yet pursuit of an independent lifestyle divorced from his past prevents Neta from fulfilling his desire, because it fails to address his gender identity, his homoeroticism, his sadomasochistic tendencies, and his attraction to death and castration. Neta calls the individual freed of the yoke of family and one's paternal home happy, but true happiness, Agnon asserts, requires psychological advancement through ongoing encounter with individual, familial, and national pasts.

Through the story's timing and allusion to High Holiday liturgy, Agnon alludes to Neta's arrival at a critical life juncture. Twilight evokes the liminality of Palestinian Jewish life that hangs precipitously between death and renewed life. Neta and other seemingly independent Jewish men can either choose psychological confrontation with their past and potential happiness or the past's continued repression and lingering dissatisfaction. With the Palestinian Jewish future still open ended, a decision needs to be made before it is too late—something communicated in Neta's thoughts as he contemplates whether to head to Tirtzah's or Elnora's home: "Indeed, the day has declined, the night will come and will decline; therefore, young man, where to?" (*aval ha-yom panah, ha-laylah yavo ve-yifneh, uve-khen, bahur, le'an?*).[58] This sentence alludes to the neilah service when the congregation turns to God as the Day of Atonement concludes and begs for forgiveness and an opportunity to return to God before the gates of repentance close.[59] The allusion hints that before the opportunity is lost, Neta needs to choose once and for all between the powerful desires underlying his tangential relationships with Tirtzah and Elnora and important and emotionally wrought relationships directly tied to his past and the emergence of his problematic sense of masculinity.

Neta's eventide encounter with his sister constitutes a last-minute return. Yet Neta does not bask in God's mercy. Rather dark and uncomfortable truths that require examination, if he and Palestinian Jewry will experience a new day, confront him. Most significantly, his encounter with his sister raises the ennui, sense of impotence, and submissive tendencies he feels and connects to Jewish femininity. While this identification previously served as a source of discomfort and drove unsuccessful efforts to assume a masculine identity divorced from Jewish femininity, Neta's identification now produces a transformative empathy for his sister and those like her.

As Neta prepares to enter his sister's door, he recalls his last return home. When his sister tried to greet and kiss him, he forcibly pushed her away. This violent rebuff voices his discomfort with traditional Jewish society, whose feminized character he associates with his sister and his mother. Like his sister, who sought the comforting masculine embrace of a Polish Christian lover, Neta tried to abandon traditional Jewish society through assumption of Christian European masculine norms. Yet like his sister's Christian lover who leaves her heartbroken, Christian Europe rebuffs Neta, and he feels compelled to return to his family and feminized society. Thus, when his sister tries to greet him, she reinforces his perceived failure and incurs his wrath.

By traveling to Palestine, Neta looks to erase the memory of his humiliating rebuke through a dissolute lifestyle similar to that practiced by many Christian European men. Yet rather than constituting a masculine act, Neta's emigration and efforts at concealment echo his mother and sister's feminine behavior. Like his mother, who consoles herself with fictional happy endings, and his sister, who wears her overcoat during Palestinian summer to hold on to memories of her lover's wintertime embrace, Neta looks for a way to avoid self-exposure and confrontation with difficult truths.

Neta's face-to-face encounter with his sister and his recognition of their similarities, however, pushes him to cease his strategic avoidance. Previously, Neta's sister symbolized the best of life and its offerings. Her metamorphosis into a hopeless and despairing wreck pains Neta, who notes that he has undergone a similar change. Viewing his sister like a man viewing his wife's white wedding canopy after its transformation into an ark curtain following her death, Neta questions whether things are as hopeless and irreversible as his sister imagines, and by implication, whether his future is as hopeless as he has perceived it to be. While his sister might not be able to better her situation, Neta recognizes that he can improve it. By acting on the love glimmering amid his tears, Neta can better his sister's life. Simultaneously, he can improve his life through reconciliation with his people and his past. When he chivalrously kisses his sister's hand, he begins the reconciliation process and achieves a previously unattainable feeling of happiness.

Crisis of Authority, the Jewish Past, and Homosociality in "Tishre"

Agnon further develops his views of the desired relations between Hebrew literature, the imagined national community, and its male members in "Tishre."[60] While "Sister" points to the centrality of the individual male's confrontation with what he perceives to be characteristically feminine weakness and his efforts to address it for individual and communal betterment, it fails to expand on two issues raised in "Miryam's Well"—masculine community's important role in such confrontation and improvement efforts and ways that "masculine" writing can foster such behavior. In "Tishre," a story that again features a young single Palestinian male immigrant with literary pretensions as its protagonist, Agnon endeavors to integrate the concerns of both "Miryam's Well" and "Sister." In so doing, Agnon stresses how important mutual male support and literature offering Jewish men more effective ties to their collective past are to the Palestinian Jewish community's development.

Through use of a provocative framing device that introduces the protagonist's description of his failed relationship with a young immigrant woman named Ya'el Hayut, Agnon pushes readers to examine this relationship. Superficially, it proves unremarkable. Ya'el pursues a romantic connection with Na'aman. After repeated rebuffs, however, she moves on before he comes to terms with his attraction to her. Nonetheless, "two years after the tumult, at the end of his days," he still fixates on the perceived tempestuousness of their "breakup" and does not proceed with his life.[61] Because their relationship proves psychically significant to him, exploration of its painful demise may shed light on his life and his reasons for believing himself to be knocking on death's door despite his youth and health. Yet rather than investigating it and the homosocial ties his relationship with Ya'el helped him develop with other male suitors, Na'aman rejects this idea as purposeless and reverses course.

Agnon, however, marks Na'aman as an unreliable narrator whose actions and speech require careful examination. He communicates this through Na'aman's explanation of his decision not to investigate his earlier relationship. Na'aman simply states that "the mosquito in his brain flew off and everything resolved itself."[62] This capricious mosquito alludes to a mosquito in the Babylonian Talmud divinely directed to fly into Titus's brain through his nose as punishment for his role in the Second Temple's destruction (Gittin 56B), a reference widely known by contemporary readers. Titus's mosquito never flew off. Instead it inflicted immense pain and suffering before ultimately killing Titus seven years later. Consequently, Na'aman's mosquito evokes thoughts of rebelliousness and retribution, which despite their damaging and potentially deadly effects, Na'aman endeavors to deny. By languishing in a soporific state of melancholic depression, Na'aman quiets his mosquito. Yet his failure to address the thoughts the mosquito represents is precisely the reason that he cannot move beyond his failed relationship with Yaʻel. Thus, Agnon exhorts curious readers committed to the prospect of enlightenment and personal improvement to differentiate themselves from Naʻaman by carefully examining the protagonist's life. Male readers pursuing such examination will gain knowledge of Agnon's views about community, relations with the Jewish past, and masculinity that he looks for them to assume.

Naʻaman's uninspired fictive memoir points to his preimmigration past as the source of his unexamined feeling of rebelliousness and fear of retribution. By claiming that Naʻaman has been fated to unhappiness, the memoir does its best to remove causality and responsibility from discussion of his past. Following his circumcision, Naʻaman's mother showered him with kisses and did her best to keep him happy. Yet, the memoir explains, when the angel of life decreed that he was fated for eternal misery, his mother could not please him. This saddened her, but she never found a way to circumvent the angel's decree.

Close to the surface of Naʻaman's memoir is an unresolved oedipal rebellion that fuels Naʻaman's adult misery and emotional impotence. He clearly yearns for an intimate relationship with a woman, such as the one that he had with his mother when he was a young child, and the happiness and sexual pleasure that he imagines goes with it. Despite this desire's strength, the story of the angel of life's decree surfaces to neutralize any hint of incestuous attraction between Naʻaman and his mother. It simultaneously convinces Naʻaman that sexual pleasure is unattainable and it is purposeless to pursue it. Clearly, Naʻaman's sexual desire was not always repressed. It likely manifested itself in oedipal rebellion until fear of punishment and castration inhibited its direct expression.

When Yaʻel advances herself as an alternative sexual object to Naʻaman's mother, she offers Naʻaman a way to resolve his oedipal struggles, liberate himself from a burdensome past, and embrace life in Palestine. Naʻaman's discussion of his imagined past makes it seem that he would jump at such a chance. It would upend his belief in a tradition of Jewish impotence grounded in his interpretation of the story of his adopted ancestor Hemdat's failed quest to consummate his love for Salsibylla. Yet rather than pursuing Yaʻel and challenging the widespread racial antisemitic view of Jews as a mentally ill and degenerate people nearing extinction, Naʻaman accepts it: "His family's power has come to an end and Naʻaman was the final scion.

The time for his hoary family's departure had arrived" (*koah mishpahto le-kitzo higi'a ve-Na'aman ha-netzer ha-aharon. Zekenah mine yovlim mishpahto u-she'at selukah higi'ah*).[63] Consequently, one finds Na'aman vacillating between attraction to Ya'el and the vitality that his pursuit of her offers (her family name, *Hayut*, means *life force*) and dissociative efforts that offer him an ordered but unhappy existence.

A powerful and unarticulated desire to maintain continuity with his past through respect for paternal authority, voiced by adherence to the angel of life's decree that he will be eternally miserable, underlies Na'aman's surprising reticence to pursue Ya'el. As theorist Eve Sedgwick notes, erotic triangles featuring two men and a woman, normally seen as fostering competition between men, may instead help unite them: "In any erotic rivalry, the bond that links the two rivals is as intense and potent as the bond that links either of the rivals to the beloved: that the bonds of 'rivalry' and 'love,' differently as they are experienced, are equally powerful and in many senses equivalent. . . . In fact, . . . the bond between rivals in an erotic triangle [appear] even stronger, more heavily determinant of actions and choices, than anything in the bond between either of the lovers and the beloved."[64] Consequently, as Na'aman works to build a new life in Palestine, his unresolved oedipal struggle offers him a meaningful psychic connection to his father and an ongoing connection with his legacy in an unstable environment where such connections prove difficult to develop.

Despite Na'aman's initial reticence to pursue relations with Ya'el, things change when he imagines her marriage to a trusting spouse who fathers her children and welcomes Na'aman into their home. This scenario advances an erotic triangle that would allow Na'aman to replace his incestuous attraction to his mother with desire for a more socially acceptable erotic object and develop a significant homosocial tie with a contemporary Palestinian Zionist male capable of replacing his problematic paternal bond.[65] Prospects of attaining such a tie stimulate Na'aman's pursuit of Ya'el, and when Cohen begins pursuing Ya'el, Na'aman's hopes are realized.

Cohen invites Na'aman, his erotic rival, to visit him and his live-in girlfriend, Ya'el. Soon, Cohen appears in fantasies stimulated by a reproduction of Rembrandt's *The Jewish Bride* (1667) hanging in Na'aman's apartment. Just as before, when Na'aman perceived his image reflected between the couple in the reproduction, the role of erotic rival further invigorates him. Consequently, Na'aman escalates his pursuit of Ya'el and openly expresses his attraction. Muscular and virile, while also possessing a sense of humor, manners, and an appreciation of Naʻaman's poetry, Cohen is precisely the type of man with whom Naʻaman wishes to associate. Naʻaman does not see eye to eye with him on Zionist issues, but he proves worthy of engagement, and their continued relations hint at Naʻaman's potential integration as an active participant into the Palestinian Jewish community. When Yaʻel rejects both suitors, however, Naʻaman does not just lose touch with Yaʻel, but he also loses touch with Cohen and other like-minded men.

Unaware of homosocial ties' importance to his sense of self, his personal happiness, and his ability to develop, Naʻaman neither fully grasps what made his relationship with Yaʻel so significant to him nor how alternative means could be employed to develop similar homosocial ties. Nonetheless, the story's recurrent employment of the Hebrew month of Tishre, when the Jewish New Year is celebrated, points to the past's ability to aid Naʻaman in unraveling this relationship's dynamics. As Yom ha-zikaron (the Day of Memory), the Jewish New Year's alternative name, hints, Tishre and its approach rouse Naʻaman from the intellectual slumber brought on by his painful inability to choose between the vitality of pursuing a relationship with Yaʻel and dissociative efforts grounded in a desire to maintain a sense of connection with his paternal legacy. Flooding his mind with East European childhood memories, feelings of rebellion, fear of retribution, hopes for reconciliation, and carnal desire, memory pushes Naʻaman to reconcile with his past and proceed with his life—something that explains the clustering of significant narrative action around the High Holidays.[66] Thus, the beginning and ending of Naʻaman's relationship with Yaʻel as well as his renewed desire to investigate their relationship occur in Tishre.

Despite awareness of opportunities for psychic renewal created by periodic recollection of important elements of his past, Naʻaman characterizes himself as a "sleeping prince whose female love awakens him into a new slumber," and he fails to act on opportunities for individual or collective improvement.[67] Thus, Agnon censures him.[68] His oral and written tales, including the story of the angel of life's decree and Hemdat's failed relationship with Salsibylla, illustrate the aesthetic weakness of literature composed by individuals who fail to address their own psychic conflicts. Consequently, "Tishre" proves to be "a story of a progressive dispossession and dislodgement from a symbolic space (house = will)."[69] Having relinquished mastery of his home, his life, and his writing, Naʻaman cannot advance his or his people's lives. As a result, the story concludes with Naʻaman sitting forsaken on a sand dune, an image projecting his internal world's desolate state and the diminishing hope that he will build a future for himself or his people.

Nonetheless, Naʻaman's relationship with Ilanit demonstrates his discomfort with sexual ambiguity and his desire to act as a man within a national framework. In subsequent versions of the text, Agnon renames her Aylonit, a technical term for a genetically barren woman whose deep voice and coarse limbs make her largely indifferentiable from men; this hints at Ilanit's role as a sexually ambiguous figure that forces Naʻaman to consider his gender indeterminacy when he encounters her.[70] Thus, Ilanit appears at night on Hanukkah to disrupt Naʻaman's efforts to cleanse (*letaher*) his room. Not only does she prevent him from voicing the purity and spirit of rebirth symbolized by rededication of the Temple (*Bet ha-mikdash*) on the holiday, but she also arouses sexual thoughts that inhibit his ability to bring order to individual and national life. Then, when she leads Naʻaman in an impromptu dance, puts on his pants, expresses her desire to be a man, and states her envy of men's freedom, she proposes that they switch gender roles with Naʻaman assuming a more passive and "feminine" role. As this occurs, darkness envelops the room and alludes to this scenario's irrational and "dark" nature, but Naʻaman proves undeterred. Yet when two matches intended for candle lighting fail to ignite, Naʻaman senses that this darkness cannot coexist with the figurative rebirth of the Festival of Lights and its illuminating menorah candles. Viewing clear gender norms as necessary for national rebirth, Naʻaman distances himself from Ilanit and endeavors to maintain this distance.[71]

Dispossession and unhappiness are not Naʻaman's inevitable fate. Indeed, he does not successfully cultivate his masculinity through exploration of his past and creation of literature that points to ways Jewish men can maintain continuity with their collective past and more effectively act for individual and collective betterment. Nonetheless, ongoing attraction to Yaʻel and concerted resistance to Ilanit's appeal indicate that there is nothing deficient about his masculinity. In fact, his masculine potential attracts Yaʻel. While she pursues relationships with Shammai and Cohen, she only does so after Naʻaman spurns her. She goes for a walk with Shammai, whose hands are rough and masculine, rather than with Naʻaman, whose hands are soft like those of a young girl. Yet this occurs after Naʻaman leaves Yaʻel's party and denies her the opportunity to be with him. Similarly, she sleeps with Cohen, whose muscular arms Naʻaman notices, but only after Naʻaman repeatedly asserts his desire to be like a brother or father to her. Yaʻel does not commit to one of the martial watchman whose guard booths she visited in Rehovot either. Furthermore, her attraction to him is not diminished by his claim that time spent writing will render him a bald sunken-chested hunchback.

Yaʻel is attracted to Naʻaman because she believes that "there is something special about writers."[72] Their rich inner worlds that enable them to create literature offering an opportunity for greater self-understanding fascinate her. Consequently, by reading weighty literature by leading contemporary writers such as Yitzhak Leybush Peretz (1852–1915) and Bialik, Yaʻel hopes to better understand herself and her world. Therefore, even when Naʻaman pulls away from her sexually and intellectually and employs biblical passages to erect a fence between them, she still inquires about his past and tries to become close to him. Yet rather than believing that Yaʻel might be genuinely interested in him and capable of identifying with his inner struggles, Naʻaman supplies her with a fictive past lacking complexity and engagement. It finally drives her away by convincing her that he has nothing to offer.

Despite Naʻaman's fear of self-knowledge and expression, he does learn enough about himself to see that he is not a "feminine" figure incapable of acting to improve his and his people's fates. Contemplation of the possibility that he actually suffers from a hereditary illness compels him to accept that despite his similarities to a mentally ill female relative, an important difference separates them.[73] When Naʻaman last visited her on a Sabbath eve at twilight, it was two years since she last left her room. During this time, she decorated the room completely in white. She even covered a red rose bouquet in white powder. Dressed in white, she paced or lay on her white bed and never spoke. Even though it forced her to deny the vitality and sexuality evoked by red roses, the female relative, like Naʻaman, strove to attain a sense of virginal purity through the whiteness of her surroundings. However, this quest made her life a living death with her white clothing mimicking shrouds and her room resembling an enlarged coffin. All she could perceive in a large mirror was black, a possible allusion to her eventual death; she only recognized Naʻaman by running her long cold fingers across his forehead, temples, and eyes like a blind person.[74] Rather than exploring her internal darkness to achieve renewed vision and a return to life and sexuality, she passively waits for the impending arrival of death evoked by the setting sun and the approaching Sabbath.

The two years Naʻaman spends obsessed with his relationship with Yaʻel parallel the two years his relative spends enclosed in her room. Naʻaman, however, possesses skills that she lacks, and by making use of them, he can voice his masculinity and differentiate himself from her. Na'aman's mute relative lacked a voice, but his avocation points to his ability to express himself. To exploit his communicative abilities for his and his people's betterment, however, he must free his vision of the pessimism voiced when his relative's skeletal fingers passed across his eyes. This will enable him to bravely face his internal darkness, delineate its contours, and locate a way to convey the vigorous red of his and his people's passionate souls, hidden like the red of his relative's white-powder-covered roses, and their obscured vitality. Ultimately, this might not enable Na'aman and his male contemporaries to achieve a better long-term future in Palestine, but it elucidates a path forward that proves more compelling than the dead end Hemdat's story supplies. Rather than constituting a form of self-betrayal, such an approach offers Na'aman a way to finally start conveying authentic feeling in his writing.

Despite his ability to help other men adopt a worldview more in line with commitment to national rebirth and development of communal ties, Na'aman's problematic relationship with his past prevents him from assuming an authoritative authorial voice. In contrast, through presentation of their talush protagonists' reticence and unhappiness, Agnon and his contemporaries worked to develop connections between Palestinian Jewish men and get them working effectively toward national rebirth.

Conclusions

Rather than validating the treatment of early twentieth-century Hebrew literature and Palestinian Zionism as distinct phenomenon, Agnon's preimmigration Galician belles lettres and the three secular tales discussed above demonstrate how his literary work endeavored to address pressing Jewish national concerns. By 1905, with the publication of "The Pimp" and "The Letter," Agnon was employing gendered representations to communicate his belief that the Jewish people were in crisis. Portrayed as feminized, the Jewish people needed to undergo change to survive and thrive.

Requisite changes were the subject of fierce debate. Jewish masculinity constituted the lens through which Agnon and other contemporary Jews communicated what they viewed as necessary for Jewish prosperity. While many Zionists looked to Jewish tradition and history and contemporary non-Jewish culture for elements that could help promote their Jewish masculine ideal, Agnon advanced his ideal type through the figure of the talush in his secular Palestinian tales. Indeed, Agnon's tlushim suffered from a disabling lack of pride. Nonetheless, they pointed to Jewish men's possession of the spiritual resources necessary to transform their lives and the lives of their people.

In "Miryam's Well," "Sister," and "Tishre," Agnon rejects immigration to Palestine as a solution to Jewish national concerns. Instead, he argues that for the Jewish people's fate to improve, Jewish men needed to stop looking for external solutions and engage in a long-term process of psychological modification. While elaboration of an introspective and self-critical norm and assertion of the need for behavioral change constituted the distinct role of the Hebrew writer employing a "masculine" style, a broader community of Jewish men with shared ties needed to uphold this norm and undertake the behavioral modification it demanded. This required painful introspection involving confrontation with perceivably less flattering aspects of the individual psyche, such as weakness and associated feelings of shame, and efforts to combat these aspects through targeted action. This would not be easy, especially for those facing the harsh condition of early twentieth-century Palestine. They needed other Jewish men's love and support.

To foster such a supportive homosocial community, Self-Evaluative Hebrew writers needed to accomplish several tasks. First, they needed to naturalize individual and collective weakness and remove its stigma. Then they needed to locate a source of pride to unify members of the national community and steel them for long-term action. Agnon and the other Self-Evaluative writers saw a way to do this by addressing Palestinian Jewish men's relationship with their past. Rather than constructing community through a shared sense of rebellion, they saw a sense of continuity with the Jewish past as a way to endow the difficult and largely thankless tasks they placed before their male readers with meaning and significance. Striving for Zion, they would argue, had always linked collective improvement to self-improvement.

Agnon's secular Palestinian tales portray important instances of homosocial ties, with "Sister" highlighting Neta Na'aman's attraction to Tirtzah's brother and "Tishre" featuring the strong bond that develops between Na'aman and Cohen. Similarly, implicit ties exist between reader and editor in "Miryam's Well" and the implied author and intended reader in "Tishre." Nonetheless, male friendship assumes a secondary role in Agnon's work. This was not the case with other Self-Evaluative writers. As the next chapter demonstrates, Brenner placed male friendship at the heart of *mi-Kan umi-kan*, asserting the need to utilize homosocial ties for more effective communal construction. In doing so, Brenner addressed a subject that Agnon neatly sidestepped in "Tishre": Jewish male pathology. Were Jewish men degenerates nearing extinction incapable of changing their fate? Was their desire to associate with other Jewish men a manifestation of this degeneracy, or could such ties spark national renaissance by effectively promoting Jewish men's assumption of new masculine roles? Although *mi-Kan umi-kan* features a talush protagonist who seems to confirm the former, the next chapter reveals how the seminal novel points to the performative nature of gender identity and Jewish men's ability to improve Jewish life in the Yishuv through assumption of effective masculine roles.

Notes

1. *Kvutzah* is a term used to refer to a small largely agricultural communal settlement.

2. S. Y. Agnon, *Shira*, trans. Zeva Shapiro (New York: Schocken, 1989), 340; Shmu'el Yosef Agnon, *Shira* (Tel Aviv: Schocken, 1974), 337.

3. S. Y. Agnon, *Shira*, 352; Shmu'el Yosef Agnon, *Shira*, 348.

4. Robert Alter, afterword to S. Y. Agnon, *Shira* (New York: Schocken, 1989), 582.

5. Alter, afterword to *Shira*, 582.

6. For examples of Israeli historical studies that shift attention back to the early twentieth century, see Arieh Saposnik, *Becoming Hebrew: The Creation of a Jewish National Culture in Ottoman Palestine* (New York: Oxford University Press, 2008); Bo'az Neumann, *Land and Desire in Early Zionism* (Waltham, MA: Brandeis University Press, 2011); Gur Alroey, *An Unpromising Land: Jewish Migration to Palestine in the Early Twentieth Century* (Stanford, CA: Stanford University Press, 2014). Studies that examine Modern Hebrew literature outside the context of Zionism include Chana Kronfeld, *On the Margins of Modernism: Decentering Literary Dynamics* (Berkeley: University of California Press, 1996); Shachar Pinsker, *Literary Passports: The Making of Modernist Hebrew Fiction in Europe* (Stanford, CA: Stanford University Press, 2011); Allison Schachter, *Diasporic Modernisms: Hebrew and Yiddish Literature in the Twentieth Century* (New York: Oxford University Press, 2012). For an important critique of the failure to integrate Palestinian Hebrew culture into discussion of Israeli history, see Hannan Hever, review of *Becoming Hebrew: The Creation of Jewish National Culture in Ottoman Palestine*, by Arieh Saposnik, *Studies in Contemporary Jewry* 25 (2011): 222.

7. One need not view presentation of the socially engaged nature of Agnon's early Palestinian writing as a denial of his aesthetic aspirations. Instead, as was the case with other contemporary Hebrew writers, Agnon's aesthetic agenda and his self-perception as a communal leader existed in tension with each other. Unlike those who found this tension conducive to literary production, Agnon found it difficult to navigate. He worked hard to produce aesthetically accomplished belles lettres and social criticism promoting Jewish social

transformation, but the degree to which he obtained these objectives varied from work to work. Consequently, the stylistically and thematically diverse works he produced in Galicia and Palestine during his initial sojourn there parallel the "schizophrenic" writing produced by many of his contemporaries. Pinsker, *Literary Passports*, 14. Critic Ya'akov Rabinowitz first noted Agnon's early work's "schizophrenia." Ya'akov Rabinowitz, "Bentayim," *ha-Po'el ha-tza'ir*, November 29, 1912; Judith Halevi-Zwick, *Reshitah shel bikoret Agnon: 5669–5692* (Haifa: Haifa University Press, 1984), 33–35; Yitzhak Bakon, *Agnon ha-tza'ir* (Be'er Sheva: Singer Chair in Yiddish Studies, 1989), 80.

8. Oxford Dictionaries defines *Yishuv* as "the Jewish community or settlement in Palestine during the 19th century and until the formation of the state of Israel in 1948." See *Oxford Dictionaries*, s.v. "Yishuv," accessed November 12, 2018, https://en.oxforddictionaries .com/definition/yishuv.

9. Furthermore, Band notes "a clear logical progression" from this fiction's craftsmanship to that of his subsequent Jaffa work. Arnold Band, *Nostalgia and Nightmare: A Study in the Fiction of S. Y. Agnon* (Berkeley: University of California Press, 1968), 53.

10. Sh. Y. Tshatshkes, "ha-Sarsur la-'arayot," *ha-Mitzpeh* (Kraków), September 29, 1905; Sh. Y. Tshatshkes, "ha-Igeret," *ha-Mitzpeh* (Kraków), December 15, 1905.

11. Avraham Band, "Agnon lifne hayyoto Agnon: sippurav ha-'Ivriyim shel Shai Tshatshkes," *Molad* 175–76 (1963): 55.

12. Sholem Aleykhem, *Ale Verk Fun Sholem Aleykhem* (New York: Sholem Aleykhem Folksfond Oysgabe, 1923), 25:7–25.

13. Bakon, *Agnon ha-tza'ir*, 39–40.

14. Sh. Y. Tshatshkes, "Gibor katan," *ha-Mitzpeh* (Kraków), May 6, 1904.

15. Shmu'el Yosef Agnon, *Yiddishe Verk* (Jerusalem: Hebreisher Universitet in Yerusholaim, Yidish-Eptaylung, 1977), 3–7.

16. Sh. Y. Tshatshkes, "Yerushalayim," *ha-Mitzpeh* (Kraków), July 15, 1904. Yehuda Halevi (1075–1141) was one of the most prominent medieval Spanish Hebrew poets. For a bilingual version of "Tzion Halo Tish'ali," see Heinrich Brody, ed., *Selected Poems of Jehudah Halevi*, trans. Nina Salaman (Philadelphia: Jewish Publication Society, 1974), 3–7.

17. For two versions of the text and commentary, see Shlomo Tzuker, "Sipure Tshatshkes ve-tikune Agnon," in *Shai Agnon: mehkarim u-te'udot*, ed. Rafa'el Vayzer and Gershon Shaked (Jerusalem: Mosad Bialik, 1978), 12–20, 30–33.

18. Daniel Boyarin, *Unheroic Conduct: The Rise of Heterosexuality and the Invention of the Modern Jewish Man* (Berkeley: University of California Press, 1997), 271–312.

19. Shai Agnon, "Avram Leybush u-vanav," in *Shai Agnon: mehkarim u-te'udot*, ed. Rafa'el Vayzer and Gershon Shaked (Jerusalem: Mosad Bialik, 1978), 30.

20. Agnon, "Avram Leybush u-vanav," 30.

21. On productivization and Modern Jewish history, see Derek Penslar, *Shylock's Children: Economics and Jewish Identity in Modern Jewish Europe* (Berkeley: University of California Press, 2001), 107–23, 205–16.

22. On Bialik and the prophetic ethos, see Dan Miron, *The Prophetic Mode in Modern Hebrew Poetry* (Milford, CT: Toby, 2010), 127–76.

23. Agnon, *Yidishe Verk*, 11–12; Bakon, *Agnon ha-tza'ir*, 200–1.

24. Band, *Nostalgia and Nightmare*, 34–35.

25. On the aesthetic promise of Agnon's Yiddish writing, see Band, *Nostalgia and Nightmare*, 35; Dan Laor, *Haye Agnon* (Jerusalem: Schocken, 1998), 33; Dov Sadan, *'Al Shai Agnon: masah 'iyun ve-heker* (Tel Aviv: ha-Kibutz ha-Me'uhad, 1959), 139–54.

26. In addition to changing his name, Agnon altered his biography to allow it to more effectively serve his literary persona. See Yitzhak Bakon, "'Al shnat 'aliyato shel Agnon veha-mishtakef mimenah," *ha-Po'el ha-tza'ir*, April 29, 1968; Band, *Nostalgia and Nightmare*, ix.

27. Dan Laor, "'Ve-Haya he-Akov le-Mishor': A Century Later," (lecture, Association for Jewish Studies Conference, Chicago, December 18, 2012).

28. Alan Mintz, "Agnon in Jaffa: The Myth of the Artist as a Young Man," *Prooftexts* 1, no. 1 (1981): 63; Judith Halevi-Zwick, *Agnon be-ma'agalotav: iyunim be-omanut ha-sipur shel Agnon* (Tel Aviv: Papyrus, 1989), 45. In contrast with fairy tales that develop anonymously from one generation to the next within oral traditions, Kunstmärchen are fairy tales that have been artfully composed by specific authors.

29. Mintz, "Agnon in Jaffa," 64.

30. Agnon obscured the marked contrast between these secular tales and his subsequent fiction by never republishing "Miryam's Well" and intensively reworking "Sister" and "Tishre" before republishing them in the 1930s. Thus, critics who have investigated the initial versions of these works have done so for instrumental purposes, employing them to better understand their subsequent manifestations or how Agnon's style developed. Mintz, "Agnon in Jaffa," 62–83. Yet if one is interested in how the Palestinian Jewish context pushed even less overtly political Hebrew writers toward involvement with broader national concerns, one should examine the original versions of Agnon's secular tales and masculinity's role within them.

31. For more on representations connecting healthy new models of Jewish identity and Palestinian settlement, see Yaffa Berlovitz, *Lehamtzi' eretz lehamtzi' 'am: tashtiot sifrut ve-tarbut bi-yetzirah shel ha-'aliyah ha-rishonah* (Tel Aviv: ha-Kibutz ha-Me'uhad, 1996), 15–46.

32. David Shimoni, *Idylls* (Jerusalem: Youth and Hechaluz Department of the Zionist Organization, 1957), 6.

33. Shimoni, *Idylls*, 15.

34. Shimoni, *Idylls*, 19.

35. Barukh Kurtzveil, "Shorashav ha-nafshiyim veha-metafisiyim shel ha-yesod ha-idili," in *Sifrutenu ha-hadashah—hemshekh o mahpekhah?* (Tel Aviv: Schocken, 1960), 301.

36. This definition draws on Shimon Halkin's foundational discussion. See Shimon Halkin, *Mavo la-siporet ha-'Ivrit*, ed. Tsofiyah Hillel (Jerusalem: Akademon, 1958), 343–34. For English language treatments of the talush, see Nurit Govrin, *Alienation and Regeneration* (Tel Aviv: Mod Books, 1989), 11–30; David Roskies, *Against the Apocalypse* (Cambridge, MA: Harvard University Press, 1984), 143–49; Sheila E. Jelen, *Intimations of Difference: Dvora Baron in the Modern Hebrew Renaissance* (Syracuse, NY: Syracuse University Press, 2007), 1–25. For recent scholarship questioning this category's usefulness for understanding gender and sexuality's complex employment in turn-of-the century Hebrew literature, see Pinsker, *Literary Passports*, 169–84.

37. Jelen, *Intimations of Difference*, 13.

38. Shai Agnon, "Be'erah shel Miryam o kta'im me-haye enosh," in *Kovetz Agnon* 2, ed. Emunah Yaron, Rafa'el Vayzer, Dan Laor, and Reuven Mirkin (Jerusalem: Magnes, 2000), 19.

39. Band, *Nostalgia and Nightmare*, 63–67; Gershon Shaked, *Omanut ha-sipur shel Agnon* (Tel Aviv: Sifriyat ha-Po'alim, 1973), 30–42.

40. Band, *Nostalgia and Nightmare*, 65.

41. Agnon, "Be'erah shel Miryam," 20.

42. Yosef Hayyim Brenner, "Reshimato ha-genuzah shel Brenner al 'Be'erah shel Miryam' me-et Agnon," in *Gam ahavtem gam sene'tem*, ed. Hayyim Be'er (Tel Aviv: 'Am 'Oved, 2002), 364.

43. Agnon, "Be'erah shel Miryam," 11.

44. Yosef Hayyim Brenner, *Ketavim*, ed. Menahem Dorman and Yitzhak Kafkafi (Tel Aviv: ha-Kibutz ha-Me'uhad, 1978–85), 4:1027.

45. Agnon, "Be'erah shel Miryam," 12.

46. Agnon, "Be'erah shel Miryam," 13.

47. Agnon, "Be'erah shel Miryam," 20–21.

48. Agnon, "Be'erah shel Miryam," 21.

49. Agnon, "Be'erah shel Miryam," 12.

50. Agnon, "Be'erah shel Miryam," 12.

51. Agnon, "Be'erah shel Miryam," 14.

52. Shai Agnon, "Ahot," *ha-Po'el ha-tza'ir*, November 11, 1910.

53. Agnon, "Ahot."

54. Roman Katzman, "Mahvot be-sifrut: tihalukh kognitivi ve-semiozis tarbuti bi-shne mikre mivhan: 'Ahot' ve-'Ma'agale tzedek' me-et Shai Agnon," *Mehkere Yerushalayim be-sifrut 'Ivrit* 22 (2008): 426.

55. Agnon, "Ahot."

56. Agnon, "Ahot."

57. Agnon, "Ahot."

58. Agnon, "Ahot."

59. The liturgy reads as follows: "Open for us the gate of prayer, / Even at the closing of the gate, / Even now that the day has declined.// When the day declines into sunset, / O let us enter into thy gates.// O God, we implore thee, forgive us! / Pardon and spare us, grant us mercy; / Clear us and suppress iniquity." Philip Birnbaum, trans., *High Holiday Prayer Book* (New York: Hebrew Publishing Company, 1951), 988.

60. Agnon revised "Tishre" numerous times throughout his career. When he first republished it in 1920, he gave it a new name, "Giv'at ha-hol" (The hill of sand). Readers familiar with subsequent versions should be aware that notable differences exist between versions.

61. S. Y. Agnon, "Tishre," *Gazit* 33, nos. 9–12 (1977): 87.

62. Agnon, "Tishre," 87.

63. Agnon, "Tishre," 94.

64. Eve Sedgwick, *Between Men: English Literature and Male Homosocial Desire* (New York: Columbia University Press, 1985), 20.

65. For further discussion of erotic triangles in the story, see Michal Arbel, *Katuv 'al 'oro shel ha-kelev: 'al tefisat ha-yetzirah etzel Shai Agnon* (Jerusalem: Keter, 2006), 177–85, 194; Pinsker, *Literary Passports*, 233–35.

66. For Yom ha-zikaron's use, see Agnon, "Tishre," 97.

67. Agnon, "Tishre," 91.

68. Cf. Pinsker, *Literary Passports*, 228, 226, and 231; Arbel, *Katuv 'al 'oro she ha-kelev*, 196.

69. Mintz, "Agnon in Jaffa," 69.

70. Arbel, *Katuv 'al 'oro she ha-kelev*, 292; Pinsker, *Literary Passports*, 232–33. Pinsker incorrectly refers to this figure in the original as Aylonit.

71. Agnon, "Tishre," 97.

72. Agnon, "Tishre," 88.

73. Na'aman's intellectual confrontation with his female relative's approach to life parallels Neta Na'aman confrontation with his sister's worldview in "Ahot."

74. This version lacks any mention of the relative's artistic career attributed to it by Pinsker. Pinsker, *Literary Passports*, 228.

2

"HE NEEDS A STAGE"

Masculinity, Homosociality, and the Public Sphere

And what is the life of Man if not brotherhood and friendship.

—Yosef Hayyim Brenner to Uri Nisan Gnessin and
Gershon Ginsberg, April 20, 1897

Introduction

Regardless of homosocial relations' seemingly minor role in Agnon's early fiction, his development of a relationship with Brenner following the latter's arrival in Palestine points to their significance for him and for other early twentieth-century Palestinian Jewish men. A charismatic and established writer and editor, Brenner had numerous friends and acquaintances to catch up with in Jaffa. Yet when Agnon describes Brenner's first day there, he explains that Brenner brushed off friends, acquaintances, and assorted well-wishers to head off with him.[1] This might have proven unremarkable had the two men been renewing a close friendship, but as Agnon noted in retrospect, they had met only once before. As Agnon candidly explains, he was quite a fan: "I admired Brenner and loved him, and his words made an indelible impression on me."[2] Consequently, in pursuit of greater intimacy with his idol, Agnon did not leave things to chance. He carefully planned this and subsequent encounters with Brenner to best forge homosocial ties with him, just as he previously strove to fashion such ties with other older men who could mentor and advance him.[3] His pickup moves were not lost on contemporary Jaffa teenagers, such as artist Nahum Gutman (1898–1980).

Fig. 2.1 Yosef Hayyim Brenner, 1910. Central Zionist Archives: PHG\1011267/9038/2.

Gutman recalls watching Agnon orchestrate a seemingly chance encounter with Brenner during which he exploited his physical appearance to draw in the older man.[4] Agnon continued on this tack until he firmed up relations with Brenner.

In contrast with Agnon, whose bourgeois upbringing inhibited his ability to directly address his sexuality and how he exploited it to attract men, Brenner had little difficulty recognizing and expressing his attraction and love for other men. Their manifestation in his actions and correspondence proves easy to spot. It did not bother Brenner to pursue his relationship with Agnon to the point that one scholar refers to it as "wooing."[5] Brenner did not have a problem declaring his love for other men either, as the following excerpt from a letter to the bilingual Hebrew-Yiddish writer Zalman Yitzhok Anokhi (Aronsohn; 1878–1947) attests: "I only have two and a half more years left to lie alive in this grave, and then—we'll live together, we'll dwell together, and, perhaps, we'll wander together too. Find solace in your greatness, your deep and great understanding of the world and life, and, when you desire, my great and deep love for you."[6] Brenner's willingness to express his love for other men has led to unresolved scholarly consideration of his sexual orientation. Whatever the case, his tortured letters to his wife, Haya Broyde, demonstrate that he found it easier to express intimacy and love with men.[7]

Homosocial relations were paramount to Brenner, as the epigraph from his letter to Ginsberg and Gnessin attests. He spent considerable time contemplating them and their relationship to masculinity and Jewish nationalism. While aware of European antisemitic discourse concerning Jewish men's hereditary pathology and how it linked intimate relations between Jewish men to their castrated, feminine, and homosexual nature, Brenner rejected these assertions.[8] Furthermore, he rejected the implication that Jewish men's desire to spend time in each other's company proved incompatible with nationalism and advancement of communal needs. Rather than shying away from homosocial relations out of fear about how others might perceive them, he embraced them. They were something that could be harnessed for simultaneous transformation of Jewish masculine norms and construction of the Palestinian Jewish public sphere.

A New Critical Approach to Brenner's *mi-Kan umi-kan*

Arrival at Brenner's views on the interrelationship of masculinity, homosociality, and the public sphere voiced in his 1911 novel *mi-Kan umi-kan* (From here and from there) proves difficult. One must first navigate through the logjam caused by the century-old debate concerning the political and aesthetic character of his fiction. As the following anecdote illustrates, it was not initially viewed as aesthetic. One day, Brenner and Agnon stopped by to see the Hebrew writer and editor Simcha Alter Gutman (S. Ben-Tzion; 1870–1932). Told to wait for his impending return, Brenner took a literary journal off the bookshelf. Happening upon one of his own published stories, Brenner felt humiliated when he noticed that his host had made copious corrections to it. After showing the volume to a blushing Agnon, the two men promptly departed.[9] Gutman's emendations tangibly express a widespread view of Brenner's literary style as rough-hewn and sloppy and therefore unworthy of serious literary consideration. This view was counterbalanced, however, by a belief in Brenner's prophetic character and his literary work's seemingly divine origin that allowed it to speak directly to his readers' situation as individuals and Jews.[10]

Careful analyses that clarified the elements of Brenner's style and its aesthetic merit were published in the 1950s.[11] They transformed the perception and critical reception of his literary work so radically that scholars have emerged who frame it in exclusively aesthetic terms. They argue that Brenner purposefully distanced himself and his literary work from national considerations and needs. Thus, a recent scholarly analysis of Brenner's novel *Shekhol ve-khishalon* (Breakdown and bereavement) features the following assertion: "Brenner wrote his novel in the language of an emergent nationalism, but he refuted the territorial-linguistic claims of that nationalism. He did not allow his literary language to be conscripted into the service of nationalism."[12]

Rather than asserting Brenner's fiction's wholly aesthetic or wholly nationalist character, this chapter builds on earlier scholarship that employs a more nuanced approach.[13] Through exploration of "the connection between story and ideology in Brenner's work," its authors looked to better integrate analyses of his fiction into study of his ideological views.[14] Thus, through employment of new critical approaches to literature, this chapter looks to enhance scholarly understanding of how Brenner constructed fiction to advance his ideological message.

Employment of new critical approaches can allow for intersectional analysis capable of refining our understanding of the connections between Brenner's fiction and his ideological message previously addressed by Menachem Brinker and Bo'az 'Arpali.[15] Attention to representation of gender, sexuality, and the public sphere in *mi-Kan umi-kan* challenges Brinker's belief, shared with 'Arpali, that Brenner harbored a "deep suspicion about every national or cultural program."[16] Investigation of the role played by gender, sexuality, and the public sphere actually reveals how Brenner employs the novel to methodically construct "a narrative of . . . [a] 'nation' and . . . its relationship to . . . a potential state."[17] Framing the nation as "a community of sentiment which would adequately manifest itself in a state," Brenner works to foster belief in a collective commonality undergirding nationalist sentiment to push those adhering to it toward national improvement.[18]

Prior to Tamar Hess's pioneering 1995 article, gender theory had not been employed to analyze Brenner's fiction.[19] Subsequent literary scholars broke new ground by employing gender theory to study the feminine and masculine representations in his fiction.[20] Their research sheds light on masculinity's important role in early twentieth-century Hebrew culture, as well as how Brenner employs masculinity to assert his nationalist views.[21] As political scientist Cynthia Enloe astutely notes, "nationalism has typically sprung from masculinized memory, masculinized humiliation and masculinized hope."[22]

Dana Olmert illuminated sexuality's critical role in connecting masculinity and nationalism in Brenner's fiction. The attention she pays to homosociality in Brenner's novel *ba-Horef* (In winter, 1904) reveals protagonist Yirmiah Feuerman's sexual attraction to and repulsion from different male characters who represent divergent masculine models.[23] While paternal figures' appeal connects to a continuing attraction to extant social orders, such as traditional religious Jewish society, homoerotic attraction to contemporary males communicates readiness for change and willingness to assume new masculine norms.[24] Furthermore, the novel does not approve of every instance of homoerotic attraction to a contemporary male. Rather, it codes attraction to like-minded men with whom Feuerman could potentially share a "deep, horizontal comradeship" as "heterosexual" and positive and attraction to other men that will form connections lacking national import as "homosexual" and dangerous.[25] *In Winter* ends without fully clarifying Feuerman's homosocial feelings, but it points to how an author's perception of national needs can lead to sexuality's employment for valorization and admonishment of different forms of homosocial and masculine behavior.

Like representations of gender and sexuality, the public sphere's representation in *mi-Kan umi-kan* contributes to better understanding of the relationship between Brenner's thought and contemporary Palestinian Zionism. As "the sphere of private people come together as a public" and "a realm of . . . social life in which something approaching public opinion can be formed," the public sphere constitutes the domain where national publics coalesce to challenge alternative political and economic power centers.[26] While "a portion of the public sphere comes into being in every conversation in which private individuals assemble to form a public body," it comes together most effectively in the world of letters, where the written work alters the relationship between author and public.[27] In the world of letters, "intimate mutual relationships between privatized individuals . . . psychologically interested in what [is] 'human,' in self-knowledge, and in empathy" develop.[28] Subsequently, the public sphere expands to encompass institutions such as libraries, literary societies, drama circles, theaters, musical groupings, and learned societies.

Leading public sphere scholar Jürgen Habermas favors "the element of rational discourse in formation of the public sphere" and does not consider the degree to which its institutions were founded on "sectionalism, exclusiveness, and repression."[29] Historian Geoff Eley offers a less idealized model more applicable to early twentieth-century Palestinian Zionist developments. He views the public sphere as a site of contestation where "different and opposing publics maneuvered for space and from which certain 'publics' . . . may have been excluded."[30] Consequently, each public looks to achieve hegemony in the public sphere through demonstration of its "claims to 'intellectual and moral leadership,'" and this requires "a continuous labor of creative ideological interventions."[31]

Small early twentieth-century Palestinian Zionist groups made efforts after the fact to claim intellectual and moral leadership of the New Yishuv during the second wave of Zionist immigration (1904–14). Yet recent historical research has pointed to a distinct Palestinian Zionist public sphere's creation through a process of contestation that Brenner actively participated in through his journalistic and fictional writing.[32] Brenner's mythologization following his violent death at Palestinian Arab hands led to his repackaging as a martyr who laid down his life for the Zionist cause. Careful reading of literary texts such as *mi-Kan umi-kan,* however, clarifies the leadership role that early twentieth-century Palestinian Hebrew writers looked to assume and provides an opportunity to recover Brenner's distinct nationalist vision.[33]

With the image of an individual Jewish male serving as a metonymic representation of the nation, Brenner contests the prioritization of martyrial, aggressive, and agrarian images of Jewish manhood that he viewed as out of alignment with communal needs.[34] Instead, he promotes productive contribution to Palestinian Jewish society's provisioning, procreative, and protective needs as a paramount indicator of a healthy Jewish masculinity. In a properly functioning society, such a masculine model would achieve a place of prominence. Yet the Palestinian Jewish public sphere's incomplete development prevents its successful assertion. Even though productive contribution to societal needs places mental and physical demands on the individual that require the combating of inertia and fear, the commonplace character of most of these contributions inhibits people's ability to perceive the heroic nature of those making them.[35] Consequently, Brenner employs *mi-Kan umi-kan* to foreground his preferred masculine model in the public sphere. Simultaneously, he deploys sexual representations to promote the pleasure of Jewish male camaraderie achievable through widespread adoption of this norm and to marginalize and potentially even exclude those advancing divergent masculine forms supportive of alternative national visions. As a result, Brenner's advancement of Self-Evaluative masculinity in the novel proves more forceful than that found in Agnon's fiction.

Narrative Presentation and Homosociality's Advance in *mi-Kan umi-kan*

The fictional editor (*mevi' le-bet ha-defus*) who narrates *mi-Kan umi-kan*'s frame story fails to directly address what leads him to publish the subsequent embedded narrative. Nevertheless, his presentation of the embedded narrative as the "incomplete and disorganized writings" of an anonymous Jew divided into six "notebooks" and an additional three appendixes for which he must apologize proves disingenuous. He finds its portrayal of the narrator-protagonist's interior world—from just before he resolves to immigrate to Palestine until shortly before he decides to emigrate—both compelling and supportive of the message he looks to promote.[36]

Composed by the narrator-protagonist, who employs the pseudonym Oved 'Etzot (bewildered), during an extended hospitalization, the framed narrative constitutes a nonchronological retrospective narrative. It is composed through the seemingly haphazard combination of abstract reflections, sections from letters written to Oved 'Etzot or by him, and parts of articles by Oved 'Etzot published, archived, or in press; it displays the author and his good friend David Diasporin's unrealized potential to contribute to collective efforts.[37] These men's failure to realize their potential, due to the absence of a properly supportive homosocial environment, troubles the fictional editor, who looks to create a supportive homosocial environment and persuade intended male readers to take part in collective efforts. This is what motivates him to present Oved 'Etzot's narrative to the reading public. Discussion of the narrative's purported limitations proves a rhetorical strategy. The fictional editor employs it to delay reader perception of his clear identification with Oved 'Etzot and his yearning for a tie to like-minded men with whom he can form a community, something that could potentially undermine his efforts if misconstrued as homosexual desire at the novel's outset.[38]

The strength of Oved 'Etzot and Diasporin's homosocial tie and its potential to undergird the developing Palestinian Jewish community, as well as its potential to slide into potentially socially deleterious behavior, find voice in the following scene:

> And when I ascended to the moshava threshing floor at evening with Diasporin, and we concealed ourselves in the recesses of its sheaves, enveloped by a world of stalks and stars, and all around us, at a short distance, hushed voices, suggestive laughter, and wandering melodies,—and the "uncle" wasn't with us, because he was busy with his household chores—the two of us would lie down with our faces directed upwards and communicate things that this place hadn't heard for a thousand years, since prior to the arrival of youthful Israelites from the north . . .
>
> "Look!" . . . Diasporin would comment simply. "How good it is here . . ."
> "Yes, right now it is good . . ."[39]

Prior to his arrival in Palestine, Oved 'Etzot referred to himself as an Essene monk and a cloistered Torah scholar (*parush*), two types of Jewish men who refrain from sexual intercourse, and thereby communicated long-term sexual repression tied to feelings of self-loathing and stagnancy.[40] Yet Oved 'Etzot's recollection of the simple pleasure that he and Diasporin feel in each other's company points to his forging of an extremely powerful bond that brings about a positive change in his life. The setting, hushed voices, suggestive speech, wandering melodies, and mention of the failure of Diasporin's uncle to chaperone allude to the homoerotic nature of this unspoken bond.[41] While this bond could lead to sexual relations, an alternative interpretation would be that it serves as a benign way for Oved 'Etzot to start voicing his formerly repressed sexual desire and begin to work through the anxiety he feels about expressing his masculine potential.[42] Understood in this way, Diasporin and Oved 'Etzot's friendship can be seen as a prototypical connection capable of binding the Zionist project's male proponents one to another, getting them to advance collective efforts through shared assumption of normative masculine behavior, and allowing them to see that such efforts need not feel burdensome.

The Palestinian Jewish community's unwillingness to welcome Diasporin into its midst precludes further clarification of these men's relationship. Even so, their relationship catalyzes Oved 'Etzot's textual composition, and he endeavors to duplicate their prototypical connection through his writing. Feeling abandoned and adrift following Diasporin's departure for the United States, Oved 'Etzot becomes depressed. He ceases to perform everyday tasks and gets hospitalized for apparent psychological problems. Nonetheless, while hospitalized, he witnesses the slow painful death of his friend Aryeh Lapidot's hunchbacked son. It puts him in touch with simple pleasures that make life worth living: "A pleasing apartment. By the alcohol stove, a stinging fly buzzed. There was alcohol. There was bread. There was a blanket to cover oneself in too. Sleep at its proper time—a pleasure."[43] Therefore, when he receives a letter from Diasporin, who recently departed Palestine, Oved 'Etzot recognizes that their relationship constitutes his life's principal pleasure. In an expression of love, Oved 'Etzot takes up his pen and writes. Regardless of his letters' purported addressee and his desire to maintain his now attenuated relationship with Diasporin, Oved 'Etzot actually directs his writings to all Palestinian Jewish men. Writing in Hebrew, he knows that Diasporin, who knows only Russian and some Yiddish, cannot read his letters. Consequently, they constitute an effort to reach out to other Palestinian Jewish men in hopes of establishing strong ties with them that will either supplement or serve in lieu of his fraying connection with Diasporin.

The Modern Jewish Revolution and the Need to Redefine Brotherhood

Early twentieth-century efforts to create powerful homosocial ties grounded in a shared commitment to the Palestinian Jewish community might have seemed quixotic. Nonetheless, the novel points to them as preferable to the frequently antagonistic relations that developed between biological brothers following traditional Jewish society's breakdown. In contrast with Oved 'Etzot and Diasporin's largely idyllic interactions, exploitation and callousness typify Diasporin and his brother's relations, as well as the interactions of Aryeh Lapidot's two sons.

When Diasporin leaves Palestine and goes to Chicago to live with his brother, Hirsh treats him harshly. In America, Hirsh abandons his socialist ideals almost as quickly as he drops his given name to become Harris. He now looks to advance through appointment to factory supervisor, and when Diasporin arrives, Harris mocks him and tells him to stay out of his way. Furthermore, when Harris gets promoted, he tells David that he will need to work extra hard to show that Harris is not playing favorites. Rather than finding fraternal affection, David's interaction with his brother makes him feel like "one screw among the tens of thousands rotating within the machinery gears whose name is Chicago."[44]

The negative impact of Tzvi Lapidot's self-centered behavior dwarfs the effects of Harris's callousness. Tzvi's egoism precipitates his hunchbacked brother's death. Absent clear masculine norms, Tzvi exploits available freedom to fashion himself as a leading proponent of Palestinian Jewish self-defense modeled on members of Ha-Shomer (the Watchman) organization.[45] Consequently, he declares his readiness to take vengeance on those threatening the Jewish people's honor, even though he did nothing to protect his girlfriend, or her honor, when she was raped during a pogrom in Russia. Then, to broadcast his self-defense ethos's bona fides, he grows a huge forelock and starts carrying a Browning pistol. Yet when an Arab horseman happens upon him and his brother, Tzvi does not voice an assertive masculine identity. Instead, when asked two questions in Arabic that he cannot understand, he fearfully draws his pistol. Considering himself outnumbered, the horseman attacks and fatally wounds Tzvi's brother. Subsequently, Tzvi neglects to mention that he escalated things, and that when he did, he could not come to his or his brother's defense, because he did not know how to use his pistol. He lies to protect his reputation too. He claims that multiple horsemen attacked the two brothers and there was nothing he could do. With blood ties like those connecting the Diasporin and Lapidot brothers offering little succor, Oved 'Etzot's attempt to develop alternative homosocial ties capable of drawing Jewish men together for collective action proves admirable, regardless of its ultimate outcome.

Masculine Humiliation and Shame— Vehicles for Drawing Men Together

The novel portrays the five primary able-bodied men's failure to defend their people. It does so to exploit masculine humiliation for development of national sentiment and the strengthening of homosocial bonds.[46] Regardless of their differences, Oved 'Etzot and the Diasporin and Lapidot brothers do not nurture and protect those seemingly more vulnerable than them due to gender or age. Nonetheless, living their lives as private individuals, they do not recognize this collective failure. It is this regretful situation that Brenner highlights through portrayal of Hinde, 'Amram, and Aryeh Lapidot. Brenner views awareness of this failure as an important catalyst to development of an effectively functioning national public.

Oved 'Etzot portrays Hinde Lapidot as an almost saintly feminine figure who does not back down from challenges and does her best to care for her family until, at the novel's conclusion, she reaches her breaking point:

> Old aunt Hinde, Aryeh Lapidot's wife, had long been a small thin quiet modest woman, and her height [*shi'ur komatah*] hadn't increased any during the new period in her life. Therefore, when she carried the milk jugs to the market, they almost dragged on the ground. Yet she carried them. She'd carry the milk from the suburb where she resided to the market in the moshava. At the break of dawn, she'd walk to the Bedouins' tents, near the pool, negotiate with them in a language that nobody needed, with tongue wagging and finger waving, fill two tin milk canisters and carry them with the remainder of her strength. On the long path, the weight and fatigue made her hands like two metal bars, and, near the market, she would stand every five steps and take a break.[47]

Prior to immigrating, Hinde lived comfortably in Russia as a government-appointed rabbi's wife. Yet even after she arrives in Palestine and her family's dire financial straits force her to take up dehumanizing labor, she does not complain. Instead, she supports her husband's decision to live in Palestine. While her eldest son's murder leads her to question whether Palestine can offer a better life than Russia, Hinde does not blame anybody or anything for her situation. Rather, she holds herself accountable. She, rather than Tzvi, failed to protect her eldest son. Furthermore, she never lets her sense of pride interfere with her efforts to provide for her family. Not only does she soldier on performing animalizing labor, but she also humbly deigns to request charity. She does all that she can so that she will be able to bake bread for her husband and grandchild. Finally, even though she loses faith in her husband, who continues to preach physical labor's redemptive effects while failing to perform it, she never stops loving him.

Rather than portraying an actual Jewish woman, Hinde represents an idealized maternal figure symbolic of the Jewish nation, and Brenner introduces her to compel Palestinian Jewish male readers to action.[48] Hinde communicates the best elements of the women who have raised Oved 'Etzot and his contemporaries. Yet as age brings these devoted and nurturing women to the verge of physical and mental breakdown, these adult men do not lift a finger to help them. Their unwillingness to take up the burden that Jewish women have long carried on their behalf amounts to a betrayal of the Jewish nation and a failure to act like mature men. With this a matter of collective shame, the novel points to the need for a collective solution.

Brenner also employs ʿAmram Lapidot to goad his Jewish male readers toward collective action. As a Jewish child who struggles in the absence of adequate adult supervision, ʿAmram sheds light on the consequences of Jewish men's failure to develop a viable Jewish society capable of providing requisite security and protection to Jewish youth. Oved ʿEtzot and other adults happily delude themselves into believing that transplantation to Palestine's natural and healthy Hebrew environment transforms ten-year-old ʿAmram into a healthy New Hebrew (*ʿIvri hadash*). Nonetheless, examination of his behavior reveals him to be emotionally scarred and adrift following his father's murder. Traumatized, he acts out by refusing to say the kaddish prayer in his father's memory, impunibly breaking windows in the moshava, unprovokedly attacking local Arab shepherds, and dedicating himself to hunting and killing birds nesting in his grandfather's home.

Rather than helping ʿAmram work through his father's traumatic death, everybody interprets his acting out positively. Oved ʿEtzot praises ʿAmram's attacks on Arab shepherds, because they reveal his easy movement reminiscent of "an Arab in the desert"; he proudly refers to ʿAmram as a *baʿal guf*, a term for a physically developed Jew.[49] Similarly, Hinde praises ʿAmram's mischievous window breaking, and his grandfather praises him when he does not actually kill the birds he captures.

As in Hinde's case, the novel concludes with ʿAmram's future clouded. Oved ʿEtzot and his contemporaries do not communicate masculine norms to him effectively, and he is left unprepared to cope with his situation. Thus, when his teacher introduces the Arab practice of blood redemption during a discussion of its biblical antecedent, a dimwitted and preoccupied ʿAmram embraces the blood redeemer model to make sense of his life. His childish mind finds the system of justice it promotes compelling, and he aspires to become a moshava watchman meting out vigilante justice on Arab thieves. Yet adherence to the blood redeemer model does not address many of the psychological issues troubling ʿAmram. It neither brings him consolation nor explains why the Jewish community did not act in response to his father's death. Nonetheless, ʿAmram looks likely to act violently against the surrounding Arab population and meet an untimely end without advancing broader communal concerns. The tableaux vivants presented toward the novel's conclusion, with 'Amram lying in his grandfather's lap with thorns in his hair, supports this likelihood. It does this by evoking Michelangelo's *Pietà*, with 'Amram paralleling a dead Jesus sacrificed for others' sins. While the boy subsequently rises, others' betrayal of him and the unlikelihood that they will assist him in the future does not bode well.

Due to Aryeh Lapidot's similarity to the venerated Labor Zionist leader A. D. Gordon, critics have failed to appreciate that he also functions as a vulnerable figure intended to prod able-bodied Jewish men to participate in collective action.[50] Like Hinde, he looks ready to collapse under a self-assumed burden at novel's end. Since arriving in Palestine, he has ignored his limitations. He refuses to acknowledge that he is a middle-aged man ill-suited to the physical demands of nonmechanized agricultural labor and moves to a moshava to work the land. His primary motivation for doing this, however, is his desire to assume the role of a wise guru on the moshava's main stage and gain the fame that goes with it.

Drawing an audience of young natives and immigrants together to listen to his monologues on the best way to advance the Zionist project, Lapidot achieves his goal, but he never considers whether the ideas he spouts are any good. Never sounding preachy, Lapidot publicly asserts his assumption of the best possible path and calls on others to follow his lead: "The conditions aren't so bad; they're just difficult, and there's a real possibility that everything will turn out alright. If they just wanted to do this and that— it'd be great. . . . They'd live the good, moral, rational life."[51] While thoroughly vague, this statement, when asserted by a charismatic figure like Lapidot, convinces others of his model's feasibility. Consequently, Aryeh even persuades skeptics. Thus, we see Oved 'Etzot parroting his views in one of his articles: "village construction everywhere is of principle importance," and committed Zionists "should be like old Lapidot! They should sacrifice their souls!"[52] Through his efforts, Lapidot initiates development of a cultural sphere uniting Palestinian Jews and preparing them to assume collective action. "An atmosphere of speeches, discussions, careful investigation, demands, complaint, questions, and problems" arises around his home.[53] Hence, he elevates his monologues above cultural alternatives like soirees and Land of Israel folk songs (*Shire Eretz Yisra'el*) that do not get people thinking beyond themselves. Yet Aryeh fails to consider what will be required to sustain long-term support for his program and whether it promotes the Yishuv's best interests.[54]

Aryeh initially contributes as a convincing advocate of an agrarian Zionist masculinity and as a public sphere developer. Nonetheless, his grandstanding and his model's unsuitability for widespread imitation hint that he needs to step aside and cede the Zionist project's foreground to a broader male public prepared to assume more sustainable roles better attuned to Palestinian realities. Aryeh's advanced age (fifty-three years old), his inability to get hired to perform agricultural labor and to provide for his family, and his principled refusal to accept charity to support his family place the aptness of the agrarian Zionist masculinity his performance promotes into question. Even an ardent supporter like Oved 'Etzot begins to see beyond Aryeh's facade. Aryeh avoids looking him or Hinde in the eye when he deceitfully proclaims himself "like a fish in water" in Palestine.[55] Eventually, Aryeh's actions appear as little more than acting to Oved 'Etzot: "The whole matter of this suburb that Aryeh Lapidot lived in was a type of game, and the game was not amusing: a game in farming, a game in social reformation."[56]

Beyond what his acting proffered others in Palestine, it initially provided Aryeh with a sense of pride his earlier life lacked. This pride, however, eventually dissipates. Oved 'Etzot naively captures what drew Aryeh to his role: "This quiet man by his nature is a hero . . . a hero every hour of the day. The whole battalion fled and he remains alone to face the enemy, and the flag is in his hand. That is grandiose! Lest you think that at such an hour he expects some type of reward? No, one who is a hero by his character—it is impossible for him otherwise."[57]

By assuming the tragic hero's role, Aryeh feels pride in transcendence of his discernable petit bourgeois origins. Yet this role proves onerous and restrictive, because it inhibits fellowship and does not offer reward. Tragedy only guarantees its heroes' defeat and death. Consequently, the tragic hero's role becomes increasingly difficult for an isolated individual to maintain, especially as conditions impede effective performance.

Despite Aryeh's best efforts, his audience perceives him assuming an altogether different role, the role of a beggar happy with his lot. Viewed as one resigned to his fate, rather than a heroic figure challenging it, Aryeh's sense of pride dissolves. At novel's end, he momentarily assumes the feminine role of Mary, a woman helpless to save her beloved son, in the tableaux vivants. The able-bodied male reader is left to ponder whether this role and the self-perception that goes with it should be Aryeh's reward for his critical role in the public sphere's development.

Acting, Composing, Producing—Public Sphere Development as Unrealized Solution

The Lapidot trio faces serious difficulties at the end of *mi-Kan umi-kan*, and no able-bodied Jewish male protagonists appear ready to aid them, but the novel's concluding sentence offers a surprising affirmation of life: "The whole account was not yet closed."[58] This hints at potential improvement and pushes readers to reexamine the novel to discover the source of its optimism. Such reexamination reveals that Palestinian Jewish men could potentially coalesce to proclaim viable masculine norms that would remove feelings of shame and humiliation, employ homosocial ties to draw together those maintaining these norms and distancing those unwilling to adopt them, and model the pleasing roles available to those acting in accordance with these new masculine norms. This possibility's advancement can be gleaned through perusal of key scenes set in proximity or in relationship to the theater, the library, and the newspaper, three key public sphere institutions that do not contribute to the Jewish public sphere's development in the novel.

The Theater

The presence of a viewing "public" both in theater and popular politics has long made theater a central metaphor for popular politics; this fact helps explain the central role that theater plays in the lives of Oved 'Etzot and Diasporin.[59] First and foremost, the overlapping realms of theater and politics help Diasporin and Oved 'Etzot express their sense of exclusion in the Diaspora and their implicit desire to overcome it in Palestine: "In Diasporin's party . . . there was an accepted custom to organize fictitious marriages between male and female members from time to time for purposes of assembly and propaganda. Brides and grooms would sit at the head of the table at their forbidden gatherings—to trick the police, initially, if they were to come. And he, David Diasporin, son of Bunem the middleman, the eternal best man, would call on his comic theatrical talent for assistance."[60] Diasporin's desire to act both politically and theatrically propels him to active party membership. Yet his loyalty and his commitment to advancing his party's agenda do not prevent his marginalization. His fellow party members view his national and gendered character suspiciously. Rather than being given the opportunity to put his prodigious talents to use in the role of groom, he is perpetually assigned a subordinate comedic role.

Nonetheless, Diasporin struggles for inclusion as an equal. Consequently, in accordance with the party line, he valorizes Bogdan Khmelnitsky, leader of a popular revolt against the Polish-Lithuanian Commonwealth and its magnates, who perpetrated some of the worst anti-Jewish violence in history. Unfortunately, however, Diasporin only ends up alienating his father. Eventually, he tires of the inferior position the party offers him. His immigration to Palestine voices his desire to participate as an equal within a community and vie for more compelling theatrical and political roles.

Similarly, theater proves integral to Oved 'Etzot's expression of his sense of diasporic exclusion and his desire for equal membership in a national community. Three years before immigrating to Palestine, he sits on a park bench in the Galician city L., not far from the ornate local theater where a play by the prominent Young Poland movement member Stanisław Wyspiański (1869–1907) is premiering.[61] Observation of a beautiful Jewish woman entering the premiere together with Polish Jewish and Christian men arouses Oved 'Etzot's sexual desire and his desire for inclusion in a national public. Simultaneously, however, it sparks a sense of masculine and national impotence. Communion with Poles, who flock to the theater to view a Wyspiański drama exploring past Polish national failures in hopes of unifying the Polish national public and bringing about its collective rebirth, proves impossible for Oved 'Etzot. To commune with them, Oved 'Etzot would need to accept the drama's antisemitic message and its portrayal of Jews as nationally and sexually inferior. Yet even if he accepted this message, he would still be forced to recognize his unsuitability for communal inclusion as a non-Polish speaker.

The double bind Oved 'Etzot faces leads to his alienation, and as he reads through Goethe's *Faust* for the third time, he feels a sense of connection to Goethe's alienated hero. Like Faust, Oved 'Etzot wants liberation from ennui, and like Faust, he hesitates to embrace Mephistopheles's suggestion to take up agricultural labor to attain a sense of purpose and to regain his lost youth. Nonetheless, he puts aside his doubts and commits himself to agrarian Zionism.[62]

Although agrarian Zionism fails to address the fundamental issues underlying Oved 'Etzot's alienation, it gets him to Palestine, where his earlier thoughts on theater present a better way for him to employ his time. More than a site for potential Jewish conquest of the land, Palestine offers a location where Jews can develop a theater capable of drawing them together for national improvement, just as L.'s theater brings Poles together and strengthens their commitment to national revival. As Oved 'Etzot asserts, "there we will also build our own new stage."[63]

The Library

Through employment of his literary ability, Oved 'Etzot can create compelling and more historically appropriate roles for himself, as well as other Palestinian Jews, that can model the actions necessary for an altered fate. Unbeknownst to him, his personal experience offers sufficient material to create such roles, as he demonstrates through dramatization of a Sabbath morning spent waiting outside Jerusalem's National Library.

Like so many of his Palestinian Jewish brethren, Oved 'Etzot looks to satisfy his heterosexual desire and his desire for collective redemption. Yet unexplored feelings of impotence and their relationship to his national status lead him to believe that these desires prove unrealizable: "Family life—it is probably best for somebody like me, especially when I am in good spirits. Yet it is only an attic in this life, an attic without a home, without a lower floor, to be a father and a brother for those who need it."[64] Construction of the lower floor in Oved 'Etzot's spatial description requires that Jewish men clarify and properly direct their erotic urges. In this way, they can create the conditions for construction of positive fraternal and paternal bonds conducive to national success. As the library scene implies, such a solution will require that Jewish men confront their individual and collective problems. Yet because they would prefer to cast blame on others, introspection needs to become one of Zionist masculinity's key features.

When he describes "the fierce heat of the ever-turning lock set on the inside [of the National Library] door," Oved 'Etzot playfully alludes to Genesis 3:24. Through this allusion, he points to the need for Jewish men to abandon personal narratives to construct a collective one more attuned to contemporary Jewish life.[65] In Genesis, "the fiery ever-turning sword" guards the Garden of Eden's eastern entrance following Adam and Eve's expulsion. Consequently, unto death the first couple will be unable to re-enter Eden and will be forced to work to survive. Yet the diverse group of Jewish men assembled outside the library's doors refuses to accept this foundational story's pronouncement of the unavoidable need to face life's challenges. Instead, they impatiently wait for the library to open, because it can supply them with diverse narratives to distract them from their responsibilities to the Palestinian Jewish community. Scanning through the library's linguistically diverse Jewish newspapers and its traditional and modern Jewish scholarly books, each man looks for a choice narrative with which to sequester himself.

The gathered Jewish men only act as a public addressing its shared problems when the library's delayed opening places them in a conscious state of exile. Nonetheless, this impromptu assembly's deliberation about the propriety of Jewish participation in military service demonstrates Jewish men's ability to grapple with erotic and national issues inhibiting expressions of Jewish fraternity and paternity. It does so when it touches on homosexuality's prevalence in the Ottoman military and Jewish recruits' inability to resist their Ottoman counterparts' advances.

While several men find it difficult to address Jewish homosexual behavior, the topic does not get tabled and debate arises. Instead, Jewish soldiers unable to resist their Arab counterparts' advances are explicitly compared to Jewish women in Buenos Aires forced into prostitution by familial abandonment and the Jewish Colonization Organization's stringent rules. Thus, we hear that "several heads were lowered. A heavy lead weight was cast down from above."[66] Confronted by Jewish prostitution's existence in Argentina, the waiting men see their manhood placed in question and unite in their shared shame and humiliation. Again, efforts to foreclose discussion fail, and two questions remain in the air. How can Jewish men allow such a fate to befall their sisters, and are Jewish men no different than Jewish women? Oved 'Etzot sees "the *audience* listening," and it seems to him that "their interest in the matter was great and even if they opened up ten doors at that moment, the discussants wouldn't leave their places and wouldn't cease their conversation touching upon the most important thing."[67] As the newly formed audience's attentiveness grows, the exchange shifts to Zionism—the national movement potentially able to provide an effective response to the two lingering questions. When the library doors open, however, discussion breaks off and neither masculine nor heterosexual norms are advanced for the national community.

The Newspaper

Oved 'Etzot's continued contemplation of Palestinian Zionist settlement's theatrical potential finds voice in his dramatized portrayal of a typical day in the editorial office of the newspaper *ha-Mahreshah* (The plow). In this scene, he struggles to find the mode best suited to promotion of a Self-Evaluative male heterosexual norm conducive to communal improvement. Questioning the fatalism and sustainability of the tragic mode favored by Aryeh Lapidot, he toys with a more sustainable and open-ended hybrid: "In the heart there are divergent prophecies, and, in any case, it is the heart, our heart, in which various prophecies about the nation's life and death run about—won't it die?! Nevertheless? It will certainly die; nevertheless, as long as it has its soul within it, we don't cease living, worrying about our lives, thinking about our lives."[68] Jewish life's open-ended nature precludes its deterministic conversion into tragedy, but it also will not permit its carefree transformation into comedy.

Oved 'Etzot searches for an intermediary mode capable of integrating settlement's humorous moments with its more compelling and riveting ones: "'Comedy? Tragedy?'—repeated Oved 'Etzot and recalled Mrs. Tumarkin's question only an hour earlier, and immediately a response formed in his head: Vaudeville, a publicistic vaudeville . . . it should be this evening . . . ah, yes, he'll write this vaudeville . . . and he'll give it the name 'The Banquet' . . . 'The Banquet' . . . 'The Celebration' . . . alas in Palestine they so frequently celebrate . . . especially before guests . . . they think that it's natural for a living nation in its land."[69]

The envisioned vaudeville performance will mix high and low to produce a variation on Wyspiański's *The Wedding*. It will employ occasional humor to address serious topics such as the Jewish people's fate in a less anxiety-inducing manner. For example, in one sketch, Oved 'Etzot will have Zionist activists of different stripes ingratiating themselves to a big donor in hopes of convincing him of their approach's validity, gaining his support, and having him use his wealth to resolve the Jewish people's problems. This messianic figure, however, will not give anything to anybody, and the activists, who fail to actively initiate change, will fall silent. Indeed, this envisioned sketch offers Oved 'Etzot a humorous way to playfully critique contemporary politicians' ineffective verbiage and inaction. More significantly, however, it would shine light on what he sees as Jewish society's pathological desire for external salvation.

If employed in isolation, the slapstick of this scene will prove too constricting, because it will deny Oved 'Etzot and his contemporary audience viable masculine alternatives capable of bringing about change through emulation. This difficulty, however, can be resolved through Oved 'Etzot's assumption of the Faustian role he looked to assume with immigration to

Palestine. By employing *The Plow* to better voice Palestinian Zionist settlement's variegated drama and viable dramatic roles for Jewish male adoption, Oved 'Etzot can enact Mephistopheles's advice to Faust: "dig and plow" to find personal meaning and regain lost youth.[70]

The Undeveloped Public Sphere and Negative Denouement

Unaware of the pressing need for appealing Jewish male roles, Oved 'Etzot ceases to look for the most effective theatrical mode for their promotion. Yet he subsequently learns the cost of their absence and the absence of dramas transmitting them—the loss of capable immigrants like Diasporin who can contribute to the New Yishuv's development. Indeed, this oversight factors into Oved 'Etzot's loss of a sustaining homosocial relationship that makes his life pleasurable and pushes him toward positive social engagement.

Unlike Aryeh Lapidot, whose energies are sapped, and Oved 'Etzot, whose literary talents constitute his primary strength, Diasporin has various talents employable for the New Yishuv's development. Aryeh Lapidot enviously recognizes this: "Indeed, what would I lack if I was young like you, . . . a youth who has strength in his loins and power in his stomach muscles."[71] Encouraged to take up agricultural labor, Diasporin's physical abilities allow him to quickly and easily succeed at it. Furthermore, his presence of mind permits him to find enjoyment in the largely barren land even when unable to secure work. Diasporin embraces his unusual new surroundings and the freedom of action they offer. He revels in the informal dress and the opportunity to walk barefoot. Letting past traumas roll off him, Diasporin finds Palestine's sights and smells captivating, and he feels like a son returned to his mother.[72] Even malarial fever does not make a negative impression. Yet as Oved 'Etzot understands from personal experience, Diasporin's honeymoon period will ultimately end; he requires a role capable of fully engaging him. Assumption of such a role will keep him in Palestine alongside close friends; it will allow him to support them and assist them in overcoming hardships.

When a bored Diasporin looks beyond agricultural labor for a more captivating role, he encounters a paucity of options and barriers inhibiting his adoption of the available ones. Just as his Jewishness previously prevented his assumption of the groom's role in party weddings, his limited Hebrew language knowledge is used against him by the leader of Jaffa's

Hebrew Theater Lovers' Union. He is denied a meaningful place in the union's ranks. Once again, Diasporin's capabilities gets overlooked. Yet rather than letting his rejection affect him negatively, he works to develop the skills necessary to succeed as "the first Hebrew actor."[73] Denied assistance by his friend Oved 'Etzot and dismissed by his uncle Aryeh for engaging in a trivial pursuit, Diasporin, who lacks familiarity with modern Jewish culture, joins a traveling Yiddish theater troupe as a first step toward full Palestinian public sphere participation. As he explains, "he needs a stage, a stage, a stage," and he looks to build one for himself and others.[74]

Ideological rigidity and limited theatrical vision ultimately shatter Diasporin's hopes of building a Hebrew theater capable of guiding Palestinian Zionists to national rebirth. Consequently, he leaves Palestine to search for a more captivating role in America. Oved 'Etzot's fellow Palestinian Jewish intellectuals refuse to accept Yiddish as the most viable medium for communicating with both Ashkenazic and Sephardic Jews in Palestine, as well as modern Yiddish theater's popularity and budding sophistication. Thus, they attack Diasporin and his troupe for purportedly undermining Hebrew's hard-fought ascendance as the language of the New Yishuv.[75] The attack's bitterness surprises Aryeh Lapidot: "He brings Jewish dramatic art to the Jewish street in their spoken language, and behold the papers rebuke him and the whole intellectual community reprimands him—what a shock!"[76]

Deeply hurt by his contributory efforts' summary dismissal, Diasporin perseveres in the belief that performing the role of Hershele Dubrovner, whom he refers to as "the Jewish Faust," will constitute an engaging and didactically significant challenge. Like Oved 'Etzot, who is captivated by Goethe's *Faust*, Diasporin finds *Got, Mentsh, un Tayvel* (God, man, and devil, 1900) by leading Yiddish dramatist Jacob Gordin (1853–1909) irresistible due to the way it portrays temptation. Hershele, a poor shtetl resident lacking the means to help himself and others, appears righteous. Yet when God accedes to the devil's request, his righteousness is tested. The devil grants him the financial means to alter his and others' lives. Inexperienced in making important moral choices, Hershele errs. When the negative repercussions of his identity's unflattering aspects manifest themselves, he commits suicide. Hershele fails to learn from his mistakes.

Regardless of its unhappy ending and its East European setting, *God, Man, and Devil* treats issues pertinent to Palestinian Jewish life. Like Hershele following his lottery win, Palestinian Jewish immigrants can transform their and their fellow Jews' lives. Balancing individual and collective needs will prove difficult, because Palestinian Jewish immigrants will need to confront their faults and weaknesses to find a moral path forward—something that Hershele fails to do in isolation. Yet a properly functioning Palestinian Jewish public sphere coalescing around discussion of dramas such as *God, Man, and Devil* will enable Jewish men to chart such a path and advance together.[77] This important melodrama offers all Palestinian Jewish men, not just Diasporin, a fundamentally compelling role. It is easy to see why it attracts Diasporin.

Ultimately, Diasporin does not spark debate about the proper moral path for Palestinian Jewish men to assume, because the Yiddish theater producer chooses not to put on *God, Man, and Devil*. Preferring more lighthearted fare and accompanying profits, he selects *Di Kaprizne Kale Moyd: Oder Kavtzanzon un Hungerman* (The capricious bride, or Beggarson and Hungryman, 1877) by Yiddish theater pioneer Avrom Goldfadn (1840–1908) for performance. He then offers Diasporin the choice between the roles of Kavtzanzon and Hungerman. Neither option satisfies him. They are both Jewish con artists who never display empathy or remorse for their actions as they team up to swindle a naive young woman. Rather than serving as compelling figures capable of catalyzing Palestinian Jewish men's self-transformations, they resemble antisemitic caricatures of Jewish men as dubious figures incapable of change. Diasporin has no interest in portraying such morally reprehensible figures. As staged in Palestine, Yiddish theater does not provide Diasporin and other contemporary Palestinian Jewish men with dramatic roles pertinent to their lives. Therefore, Diasporin's feeling that an abyss has opened beneath him proves understandable.[78] Having lost his sense of purpose and his desire to perform on a Palestinian stage, Diasporin becomes "incredibly angry" and "madness dwells within him."[79] No longer capable of appreciating Palestinian Jewish life, he departs never to return.

Conclusion: Masculinity, Sexuality, and Brenner's Efforts to Construct a Palestinian Jewish Public Sphere

Brenner's dramaturgy influenced Palestinian Hebrew drama's development.[80] His contribution to it, however, increased exponentially following his arrival in Palestine.[81] Viewing Hebrew theater as an important tool for the Palestinian Jewish public sphere's development, he strove to catalyze its expansion and exploit it to draw together and unify Jews possessing diverse cultural backgrounds for pursuit of a broader nationalist program.[82] Consequently, in contradistinction to his fictional alter ego Oved 'Etzot, he set aside time, despite a busy schedule, to cultivate it.[83]

Although Brenner never composed a drama that portrayed the settlement project, he integrated facets of drama into *mi-Kan umi-kan* and voiced his dedication to it in other ways.[84] First and foremost, he translated dramas into Hebrew. Carefully selected translations supplemented the limited number of dramas available to Hebrew directors and the limited roles available to performers. Furthermore, they introduced other Palestinian Hebrew writers to useful models for dramatic composition. Brenner turned to the well-developed field of Yiddish drama for relevant Jewish content, translating David Pinski's *Yankele der Shmid* (Yankele the blacksmith) in 1910 (staged soon thereafter by the Amateur Dramatic Arts Company).[85] Brenner drew from European languages too, selecting plays by Nobel laureate Gerhart Hauptmann (1862–1946) for translation. Brenner also served as a drama critic, reviewing performances of Pinski's drama and other plays.[86]

Brenner's implicit approach to Palestinian drama was tied to his views about masculinity and can be extrapolated from his critical writings, translated plays, and *mi-Kan umi-kan*. He saw masculinity as an internal characteristic continually tested by circumstances. It was not something visible to the naked eye. Consequently, emergent models of Zionist masculinity tied to visible markers, specific professions, aspects of upbringing, or the way one died were anathema to him. Indeed, Tzvi Lapidot dresses like a watchman and carries a gun, Aryeh Lapidot proudly brags of his tangible connection to the soil created through agricultural labor, 'Amram Lapidot's erratic and combative "native Palestinian" behavior is praised by characters in the novel, and 'Amram's father is killed by Arabs. Yet Brenner opposed those who would view the watchman, the agricultural laborer, the native or near-native Palestinian Jew, and the martyr as models for emulation. He sought out a dramatic style capable of generating discussion about appropriate gender and sexual norms and moral action, sparking introspection and gaining new adherents to Self-Evaluative standards.

The ability to externalize internal everyday struggles and offer audiences a way to collectively confront pressing social psychological concerns drew Brenner to the melodramatic mode, a prominent alternative to tragedy and comedy. Thus, one finds Brenner employing a key melodramatic technique in *mi-Kan umi-kan*—exploitation of the distinction between surface and depth for externalization of psychic struggles.[87] Consequently, the contrast between a superficial portrayal of Oved 'Etzot as a bent fatigued figure with a mammoth head and short legs, seemingly unworthy of further consideration, and description of his bright virtuous pupils and his facial "expression of great strength going to waste" pushes the reader, like the fictional editor before him, to examine Oved 'Etzot's psychological world.[88] Brenner's presentation of Oved 'Etzot's pupils as a gateway to his virtuous soul, and the great strength present in his facial expression hint that his physical appearance belies his ongoing and observable inner struggle to act virtuously.

Indeed, serious consideration of Oved 'Etzot's narrative reveals hidden strength and virtue, with Oved 'Etzot striving to convert his personal experience into a plan for communal action. As the fictional editor recognizes, Oved 'Etzot's narrative has him assuming implicit blame for Diasporin's departure from Palestine. He failed to actively develop the Palestinian Jewish public sphere through drama. Ceasing to stew in the painful loss of Diasporin's companionship, he takes up pen and paper to alert other Palestinian Jewish men to the importance of homosocial ties and the ability of (in Nagel's words) "a community of sentiment" to foster such ties and promote virtuous masculine behavior.[89]

Oved 'Etzot also exposes the existence of shared Jewish male humiliation that leaves Jewish men uncomfortable with their gender and sexual identities and inhibits the development of the type of sustaining ties to like-minded men he unabashedly yearns for. Oved 'Etzot's narrative points to the cost of overlooking this discomfort. Oral deliberation in the library scene, discussion of relevant dramas such as *God, Man, and Devil*, examination of literature such as Oved 'Etzot's manuscript, and the viewing of theater all serve as ways to address Jewish male failure to protect and serve Jewish women, youths, and elders. These acts can stimulate introspection and help convert shameful ties into positive bonds grounded in shared gender and sexual norms compelling Jewish men to address communal needs together. In this way, a viable Palestinian Jewish public sphere and a better Palestinian Jewish future could be created. Diasporin and Oved 'Etzot's ultimate failure to strike root in Palestine implies that absent a mature Palestinian Jewish public sphere, a strong culture of introspection, stout homosocial bonds, and effective valorization of critical male efforts to contribute to Palestinian Jewish society's needs, little hope existed for the Palestinian Jewish community.

Both Brenner's mythologization and *mi-Kan umi-kan*'s stylistic complexity have inhibited readers' recognition of the connection between story and ideology in his fiction. Through attention to representation of gender, sexuality, and the public sphere in *mi-Kan umi-kan*, this chapter illuminates how Brenner strove to develop the Palestinian Jewish public sphere and realize Zionist aims through promotion of a masculine ideal grounded in introspection, moral action, and supportive homosocial ties. Awareness of these promotional acts aids in clarification of Brenner's ideological stance and illuminates his dissent from other masculine forms popular in the New Yishuv, including the labor movement ideal, with which he has been identified.[90]

A Look Ahead

Brenner's composition of literature to help Self-Evaluative masculinity's proponents assume intellectual and moral leadership in the coalescing Palestine Jewish public sphere was not the only way he went about this task. He played a critical role in getting other Palestinian Hebrew writers to contribute to local theater's development by creating the perception among them that it was necessary for development of the public sphere. This helps explain David Shimoni's and Arieli's decisions to forgo their preferred forms of literary expression to compose the pioneering Palestinian Jewish settlement dramas *Laylah ba-kerem* (A night in the vineyard, 1910) and *Allah Karim!* (1912).

The following chapter will turn its attention to Arieli's drama to explore how it works to promote Self-Evaluative masculinity. While it has much in common with other works by proponents of Self-Evaluative masculinity, Arieli introduces new elements and develops others that make it unique. In it, Arieli, like Brenner, rejects emergent models of Zionist masculinity tied to visible markers, specific professions, aspects of upbringing, or the way one died. The drama incorporates characters who embody these models to highlight their limitations. Simultaneously, Arieli takes up the tension between surface and depth found in Brenner's portrayal of Oved 'Etzot and Agnon's depiction of Na'aman to powerfully assert Self-Evaluative masculinity's superiority. This is particularly noteworthy in the presentation of Noah Yonter. At the outset, he appears an unredeemable schlemiel, but his inner virtue is gradually revealed. Furthermore, if he upholds the tenets of Self-Evaluative masculinity, the drama argues, even he can give tangible expression to this virtue through heroic action. As in Agnon's "Sister," life lived in accordance with Self-Evaluative masculinity's tenets requires confrontation with "feminine" weakness. Yet Arieli lays greater stress on this lifestyle's painful nature and the need for it to be taken up together with others. Thus, homosociality proves pivotal for Arieli, and he advances a usable Jewish past to provide community members with a positive shared foundation offering continuity with the past and a feeling of pride—something noticeably absent in Brenner's and Agnon's works.

Notes

1. Shmu'el Yosef Agnon, "Yosef Hayyim Brenner be-hayyav uve-moto," in *Y. H. Brenner: mivhar divre-zikhronot*, ed. Mordehai Kushnir (Tel Aviv: ha-Kibutz ha-Me'uhad, 1971), 121.

2. Galyah Yardeni, *Tet-zayin sihot 'im sofrim* (Tel Aviv: ha-Kibutz ha-Me'uhad, 1962), 59.

3. Yitzhak Bakon, *Agnon ha-tza'ir* (Be'er Sheva: Singer Chair in Yiddish Studies, 1989), 15.

4. Nahum Gutman, *Ben holot u-khehol shamayim* (Tel Aviv: Yavneh, 2001), 87–96.

5. Hayyim Be'er, *Gam ahavtem gam sene'tem* (Tel Aviv: 'Am 'Oved, 2002), 107.

6. Yosef Hayyim Brenner, *Kol Kitve Y. H. Brenner*, ed. Menahem Poznanski (Tel Aviv: ha-Kibutz ha-Me'uhad, 1955–67), 3:227.

7. Mishpahat Brenner, "Halifat mikhtavim ben Y. H. Brenner, ra'yato Hayah Broyda u-vnam Uri," in *Mahbarot Brenner 3–4*, ed. Menahem Dorman and Uzi Shavit (Tel Aviv: ha-Kibutz ha-Me'uhad and Tel Aviv University, 1984), 9–91.

8. Yosef Hayyim Brenner, *Ketavim*, ed. Menahem Dorman and Yitzhak Kafkafi (Tel Aviv: ha-Kibutz ha-Me'uhad, 1978–85), 4:1293. For more on European antisemitic, homophobic, and misogynistic discourses' confluence, see Lewis Aron and Karen Starr, "Freud and Ferenczi: Wandering Jews in Palermo," in *The Legacy of Sandor Ferenczi: From Ghost to Ancestor*, ed. Adrienne Harris and Steven Kuchuck (New York: Routledge, 2015), 150–68.

9. Shmu'el Yosef Agnon, "Yosef Hayyim Brenner," in *Y. H. Brenner: mivhar divre-zikhronot*, ed. Mordehai Kushnir (Tel Aviv: ha-Kibutz ha-Me'uhad, 1971), 129; Gutman, *Ben Holot*, 90–91; Be'er, *Gam ahavtem gam sene'tem*, 110–11.

10. Anita Shapira, *Brenner: Sipur hayyim* (Tel Aviv: 'Am 'Oved, 2008), 362–65; Yitzhak Bakon, "Brenner ha-mesaper be-'eyne ha-bikkoret," in *Yosef Hayyim Brenner: mivhar ma'amare bikoret 'al yetzirato ha-sipurit*, ed. Yitzhak Bakon (Tel Aviv: 'Am 'Oved, 1972), 25–27.

11. Bakon, "Brenner ha-mesaper be-'eyne ha-bikoret," 31; Dan Miron, "Giluye nof be-sipure Eretz-Yisra'elim shel Y. H. Brenner," *Zemanim*, October 28, 1955 and November 4, 1955; Dan Miron, "Al ba'ayot signono ha-omnuti shel Y. H. Brenner be-sipurav," in *Yosef Hayyim Brenner: mivhar ma'amare bikoret 'al yetzirato ha-sipurit*, ed. Yitzhak Bakon (Tel Aviv: 'Am 'Oved, 1972), 174–86.

12. Allison Schachter, *Diaspora Modernisms: Hebrew and Yiddish Literature in the Twentieth Century* (New York: Oxford University Press, 2012), 76.

13. Menachem Brinker, *'Ad ha-simtah ha-tveryanit* (Tel Aviv: 'Am 'Oved, 1990); Bo'az 'Arpali, *ha-'Ikar ha-shlilit* (Tel Aviv: ha-Kibutz ha-Me'uhad, 1992).

14. Avner Holtzman, "Poetics, Ideology, Biography, Myth: The Scholarship on J. H. Brenner, 1971–1996," *Prooftexts* 18, no. 1 (1998): 87; see also 82–83, 87–90. See also Bakon, "Brenner ha-mesaper be-'eyne ha-bikoret," 30–36.

15. Brinker, *'Ad ha-simtah ha-tveryanit*; 'Arpali, *ha-'Ikar ha-shlilit*.

16. Holtzman, "Poetics, Ideology, Biography, Myth," 89.

17. Joane Nagel, "Masculinity and Nationalism: Gender and Sexuality in the Making of Nations," *Ethnic and Racial Studies* 21, no. 2 (1998): 247.

18. Nagel, "Masculinity and Nationalism," 247.

19. Holtzman, "Poetics, Ideology, Biography, Myth," 90; Tamar Hess, "'Tzarikh lenashek lah'—dimui feministi bi-'Shekhol ve-khishalon' le-Y. H. Brenner," *Mehkere Yerushalayim be-sifrut 'Ivrit* 15 (1995): 197–221.

20. Dana Olmert, "Shama halo lo po: kri'ah bi-shne sipurim mukdamim shel Yosef Hayyim Brenner," *Mehkere Yerushalayim be-sifrut 'Ivrit* 19 (2003): 123–41; Dana Olmert, "Miniut ve-merhav be-'ba-Horef' le-Y. H. Brenner—he'arot ahadot," in *Rega' shel huledet: mehkarim be-sifrut 'Ivrit uve-sifrut Yidish li-khvod Dan Miron*, ed. Hannan Hever (Jerusalem: Mosad Bialik, 2007), 387–401; Mikha'el Gluzman, *ha-Guf ha-Tzioni: le'umiut, migdar u-miniut ba-sifrut ha-'Ivrit ha-hadashah* (Tel Aviv: ha-Kibutz ha-Me'uhad, 2007), 136–81; Mikhal Dekel, *The Universal Jew* (Evanston, IL: Northwestern University Press, 2011), 190–203.

21. On the relationship between masculinity and nationalism, see George Mosse, *The Image of Man* (New York: Oxford University Press, 1996).

22. Cited in Nagel, "Masculinity and Nationalism," 244.

23. Olmert, "Miniut ve-merhav be-'ba-Horef' le-Y. H. Brenner."

24. As previously discussed, homoerotic attraction functions in the same way in Agnon's short story "Tishre."

25. See Benedict Anderson, *Imagined Communities: Reflections on the Origins and Spread of Nationalism* (New York: Verso, 2006), 7, for this felicitous phrasing.

26. Jeffrey Veidlinger, *Jewish Public Culture in the Late Russian Empire* (Bloomington: Indiana University Press, 2009), 8.

27. Jürgen Habermas, "The Public Sphere: An Encyclopedia Article (1964)," *New German Critique* 3 (Autumn 1974): 49; Craig Calhoun, "Introduction: Habermas and the Public Sphere," in *Habermas and the Public Sphere*, ed. Craig Calhoun (Cambridge, MA: MIT Press, 1992), 10.

28. Calhoun, "Introduction," 12.

29. Geoff Eley, "Nations, Publics, and Political Cultures: Placing Habermas in the Nineteenth Century," in *Habermas and the Public Sphere*, ed. Craig Calhoun (Cambridge, MA: MIT Press, 1992), 321.

30. Eley, "Nations, Publics, and Political Cultures," 325–26.

31. Eley, "Nations, Publics, and Political Cultures," 323.

32. Examples of such retrospective leadership claims include Brakhah Habas, ed., *Sefer ha-'aliyah ha-shniyah* (Tel Aviv: 'Am 'Oved, 1947); Shomer Organization, *Kovetz ha-Shomer: te'udot zikhronot ve-divre ha'arakhah ketuvim bi-yede vatike "ha-Shomer"* (Tel Aviv: Arkhiyon ha-'Avodah, 1937). For a more sophisticated discussion of the Zionist public sphere's development in late Ottoman Palestine, see Arieh Saposnik, *Becoming Hebrew: The Creation of a Jewish National Culture in Ottoman Palestine* (New York: Oxford University Press, 2008). For a discussion of the importance of political newspapers for early public sphere development, see Habermas, "The Public Sphere," 53.

33. On Brenner's mythologization, see Shapira, *Brenner*, 355–78.

34. For a discussion of masculinity's use as a metonym for the nation, see Todd Reeser, *Masculinities in Theory: An Introduction* (Malden, MA: Wiley-Blackwell, 2010), 174–80.

35. For a brief discussion of masculinity's role in getting men to make social contributions, see David Gilmore, *Manhood in the Making: Cultural Concepts of Masculinity* (New Haven, CT: Yale University Press, 1990), 220–31.

36. The role played here by the fictional editor parallels the one played by the editor of Hemdat's story in Agnon's "Miryam's Well" discussed in the previous chapter.

37. On the straightforward construction of the framed narrative, see Brinker, *'Ad ha-simtah ha-tveryanit*, 72–81.

38. Iris Milner notes homosociality's centrality to the novel. She, however, views it as a key element in presentation of the traumatic feelings of loss felt by Oved 'Etzot following Diasporin's departure from Palestine, feelings parallel to those felt by Brenner following dissolution of his friendship with Uri Nisan Gnessin. See Iris Milner, "Yosef Hayyim Brenner's *Mikan umikan*: The Telling of Trauma," *Prooftexts* 32 (2012): 33–62.

39. Brenner, *Ketavim*, 2:1366; ellipses in the original.

40. For a description of Oved 'Etzot as an Essene, see Brenner, *Ketavim*, 2:1281; for his description as a parush, see Brenner, *Ketavim*, 2:1391.

41. On this scene's homoeroticsm, cf. Milner, "Yosef Hayyim Brenner's *Mikan umikan*," 40–41; for a discussion of heterosexual relations' tertiary position in the novel and how it contrasts with Brenner's other fictional work, see Brinker, *'Ad ha-simtah ha-tveryanit*, 56–59.

42. Despite his comic portrayal of himself as a clumsy schlemiel-like Diaspora Jew incapable of land redemption, Oved 'Etzot has bright virtuous eyes and "a countenance of power going to waste." See Brenner, *Ketavim*, 2:1391.

43. Brenner, *Ketavim*, 2:1271–72.

44. Brenner, *Ketavim*, 2:1298.

45. On stable gender norms' absence in early twentieth-century Palestine, see Bili Melman, "Min ha-shulayim el ha-historiyah shel migdar ve-Eretz Yisra'eliyut (1890–1920)," *Tzion* 62, no. 3 (1997): 243–78; on Ha-Shomer, see Yaakov Goldstein, *From Fighters to Soldiers: How the Israeli Defense Forces Began* (Portland, OR: Sussex Academic Press, 1998), 27–105.

46. For more on Hebrew literature's employment of masculine humiliation to create nationalist sentiment, see Dekel, *The Universal Jew*, 139–67.

47. Brenner, *Ketavim*, 2:1306.

48. For more on idealized maternal figures and their relationship to the nation, see Reeser, *Masculinities in Theory*, 188; Mosse, *The Image of Man*, 8–9.

49. Brenner, *Ketavim*, 2:1416. For more on the ba'al guf figure, see David Roskies, *Against the Apocalypse* (Cambridge, MA: Harvard University Press, 1984), 141–44.

50. For an important warning about the interpretive dangers of viewing Aryeh Lapidot as a mere personification of A. D. Gordon, see Brinker, *'Ad ha-simtah ha-tveryanit*, 29–64; for recent scholarship on Gordon's thought and his place in early twentieth-century Palestinian culture, see the essays by Gid'on Katz, Motti Ze'ira, and Shalom Ratzabi in Avner Holtzman, Gid'on Katz, and Shalom Ratzabi, eds., *mi-Saviv la-nekudah: mehkarim hadashim 'al M. Y. Berdich'evski, Y. H. Brenner, ve-A. D. Gordon* (Kiryat Sede-Boker: Mekhon Ben-Guryon le-heker Yisra'el veha-Tzionut, Universitat Ben Guryon ba-Negev, 2008); Bo'az Neumann, *Teshukat ha-halutzim* (Tel Aviv: 'Am 'Oved, 2009).

51. Brenner, *Ketavim*, 2:1361.

52. Brenner, *Ketavim*, 2:1397–98.

53. Brenner, *Ketavim*, 2:1371–72.

54. For presentation of moshava parties and Land of Israel folk songs as ineffective means for advancing the New Yishuv's political and cultural life, see Brenner, *Ketavim*, 2:1370–71.

55. Brenner, *Ketavim*, 2:1360.

56. Brenner, *Ketavim*, 2:1368.

57. Brenner, *Ketavim*, 2:1362.

58. Brenner, *Ketavim*, 2:1440.

59. David Blackbourn, "Politics as Theatre: Metaphors of the Stage in German History, 1848–1933," *Transactions of the Royal Historical Society*, 5th Series, 37 (1987): 149–67.

60. Brenner, *Ketavim*, 2:1284–85.

61. The performed play appears to be Wyspiański's symbolist drama *Wesele* (The wedding, 1901).

62. Oved 'Etzot conveys his doubts about agrarian Zionism when he compares it to the spark that ignites the Torah scroll enveloping Rabbi Hananiah ben Teradion and kills him.

63. Brenner, *Ketavim*, 2:1282.

64. Brenner, *Ketavim*, 2:1278–79.

65. Brenner, *Ketavim*, 2:1327.

66. Brenner, *Ketavim*, 2:1341.

67. Brenner, *Ketavim*, 2:1343.

68. Brenner, *Ketavim*, 2:1394.

69. Brenner, *Ketavim*, 2:1406.

70. Brenner, *Ketavim*, 2:1276.

71. Brenner, *Ketavim*, 2:1360–61.

72. Brenner, *Ketavim*, 2:1364.

73. Brenner, *Ketavim*, 2:1365.

74. Brenner, *Ketavim*, 2:1365.

75. Many scholars speak of Hebrew's achievement of linguistic dominance in the New Yishuv starting in the 1920s. This, they assert, was due in large part to efforts, like the one featured in the novel, to block linguistic diversity. Recent scholarship, however, points to a more complex multilingual environment where Yiddish as well as non-Jewish languages played a much greater role than previously acknowledged up until the State of Israel's establishment. Yael Haver, *What Must Be Forgotten: The Survival of Yiddish in Zionist Palestine* (Syracuse, NY: Syracuse University Press, 2004), 1–44; Liora Halperin, *Babel in Zion: Jews, Nationalism, and Language Diversity in Palestine, 1920–1948* (New Haven, CT: Yale University Press, 2015).

76. Brenner, *Ketavim*, 2:1418.

77. Such a discussion would parallel the communal deliberation outside the national library.

78. Brenner, *Ketavim*, 2:1421.

79. Brenner, *Ketavim*, 2:1417.

80. Gid'on 'Ofrat identifies his play *Me'ever la-gevulin* (Out of bounds, 1907) as an important Diaspora precursor. Gid'on 'Ofrat, *Adamah, adam, dam: mitos he-halutz ve-fulhan ha-adamah be-mahazot ha-hityashvut* (Tel Aviv: Ts'erikover, 1980), 19–42.

81. For a firsthand account of Brenner's growing involvement with drama in Palestine, see Menahem Gnessin, "Tehilato shel ha-te'atron ha-'Ivri," in *'Al Y. H. Brenner: od zikhronot*, ed. Yitzhak Kafkafi and Uri Brenner (Tel Aviv: ha-Kibutz ha-Me'uhad, 1991), 65–68.

82. For a more expansive discussion of Palestinian Hebrew drama's early development, see Shimon Lev-Ari, "Hitpathut ha-te'atronim," in *Toldot ha-yishuv ha-Yehudi be-Eretz-Yisrael me-az ha-'aliyah ha-rishonah: beniyatah shel tarbut 'Ivrit be-Eretz-Yisrael*, ed. Zohar Shavit (Jerusalem: Mosad Bialik, 2002), 343–66.

83. For more on Brenner's dominant role in the development of the New Yishuv's world of letters from the time of his immigration until his death, see Zohar Shavit, *ha-Hayyim ha-sifrutiyim be-Eretz Yisrael, 1910–1933* (Tel Aviv: ha-Kibutz ha-Me'uhad, 1982), 28–72.

84. For more on Brenner and Hebrew theater, see Shapira, *Brenner*, 188–90.

85. Palestine's most important contemporary Hebrew theater company.

86. Brenner, *Ketavim*, 3:458–65, 4:1029–30.

87. This component can be found in Hauptmann's *The Weavers, Fuhrmann Henschel*, and *Michael Kramer*, Pinski's *Yankele the Blacksmith*, and Gordin's *God, Man, and Devil*, works Brenner either wrote on, translated, or referenced. For his discussion of the surface/depth dichotomy in Hauptmann's work, see Brenner, *Ketavim*, 4:1068.

88. Brenner, *Ketavim*, 2:1391; Peter Brooks, *The Melodramatic Imagination: Balzac, Henry James, Melodrama, and the Mode of Excess* (New Haven, CT: Yale University Press, 1995), 9.

89. Nagel, "Masculinity and Nationalism," 247.

90. For a discussion of the labor movement ideal as one of four masculine forms competing for dominance in the contemporary New Yishuv, see Anita Shapira, "ha-Mitos shel ha-Yehudi ha-hadash," in *Yehudim hadashim Yehudim yeshanim* (Tel Aviv: 'Am 'Oved, 1997), 155–74.

3

CONTESTED MASCULINITY AND THE REDEMPTION OF THE SCHLEMIEL

Bemokem she-eyn ish iz a hering oykh a fish
(Where there is no man, a herring is a fish too).
—Yiddish Proverb

A Friend and Colleague: Levi Aryeh Arieli as a Self-Evaluative Hebrew Writer

Earlier scholarship on Arieli and his oeuvre does not support the claim that Arieli and other prominent Palestinian Hebrew writers employed literature to promote a Zionist message. In fact, seminal articles by Gershon Shaked and ʿAdi Tzemah portray Arieli as a writer whose literary career and aesthetic achievements can only be understood once one recognizes his opposition to Zionism.[1] Thus, Shaked overlooks the personal issues underlying Arieli's decision to immigrate to the United States, asserts that he lacked Zionist commitment, and alleges that he wrote nothing significant after abandoning Palestine's supportive literary environment. Similarly, Tzemah, who draws on Shaked's conclusions, contends that Arieli's opposition to Zionism predated his departure from Palestine and that awareness of this opposition proves necessary to understand his narrative art.[2]

Tzemah's insightful discussion of aesthetic issues has led subsequent scholars to unquestioningly accept his assertions about Arieli's politics. Thus, the unverified connection between Arieli and Otto Weininger (1880–1903), an apostate Jew and a highly prominent early twentieth-century proponent of racial antisemitism, first voiced in Tzemah's work, recurs in subsequent scholarship.[3] In fact, this connection is used to support the

claim that Arieli, like Agnon and Brenner, was "equally suspicious of ostentatious Zionist ideology and rhetoric and the attempts to harness literature
and politics."[4] Consequently, this scholarship implies that one should avoid
making any connection between Arieli's immigration to Palestine and the
fifteen years he spent there and Zionist commitment. On the contrary, he
should be understood as a vagabond whose primary affiliation was to other
Hebrew writers fully committed to aesthetic achievement.[5]

Shaked and Tzemah's characterizations of Arieli's politics do not take
published and archival materials into account. Furthermore, they stand in
marked contrast with the author's own self-perception and how his contemporaries perceived him. Therefore, this and the subsequent chapter
employ Arieli's own writings to present a more accurate depiction of his
political views and the relationship between them and the literature that
he produced.[6] Careful examination of his drama and prose reveals him to
be working alongside other Palestinian Hebrew writers to promote Self-
Evaluative masculinity in the Palestinian Jewish public sphere. Thus, one
finds him to be an individual actively engaged in the life of the New Yishuv
working to harness literature to politics.

Arieli's nonliterary writings prove a useful source for those looking to
understand his connection to Brenner and the Self-Evaluative camp, as well
as what he perceived his role to be as a writer. His elegiac and emotionally
laden response to Brenner's premature death in May 1921, published in the
pages of the newspaper *ha-Aretz* (The land), exemplifies this. Addressing
"our beloved brother," Arieli turns to Brenner and asks him from whose
mouth the Jewish people would now hear the bitter sad truth about life,
their personal affairs, and the Jewish condition in Palestine and the world,
"the same truth that so many didn't love to hear, but that would fertilize
[the Jewish people's] thought and push [them] to the pure, elevated and
concrete path of national service."[7] Arieli leaves this question unanswered
for rhetorical reasons. Nonetheless, he and Brenner had long shared the
task of composing fiction and drama intended to confront male Palestinian Hebrew readers (the implied collective readership referenced through
use of first-person plural) with the sad bitter truth of their contemporary
existence and push them to work collectively for achievement of communal
goals. In fact, even after his close friend's death, Arieli proved committed
to such activity.

Described soon after his arrival in Palestine as an attractive young man
with smiling blue eyes, one who displayed experience in physical labor and

Fig. 3.1 Tiberias Grammar School staff photo, 1920. From right to left: author Ya'akov Horgin, Aryeh Kutler, Mikhal Kutler, Asher Erlikh (principal), Yehuda Beker, Levi Aryeh Arieli, Tzvi Milin (Avital). Central Zionist Archives: PHG\1019513/ 16892/13.

skillfully performed fieldwork, Arieli does not initially seem like somebody who would go on to promote Self-Evaluative masculinity with Brenner.[8] Yet agricultural and subsequent security work failed to intellectually or emotionally engage him. Work in these professions did not supply him with the type of homosocial community he desired either. Appreciative of the Hebrew literary community's esprit de corps, impressed by its contribution to Zionist aims' realization and intrigued by the aesthetic challenges it posed to its members, Arieli turned to literature for the first time. Publication of his short story "Shavrire kolot me'ever la-gey: Haynrikh ha-hiver" (Voice shards from across the valley: Pale Heinrich) in July and August 1909 bestowed the status of a leading Palestinian Hebrew author on him and earned him full communal membership.

Both Arieli's literary status and communal membership prove inextricably tied to Brenner. Brenner viewed Arieli as a potential contributor to the incipient Hebrew literary community, who, with proper cultivation, could emerge as an important ally in Self-Evaluative masculinity's advancement. Therefore, Brenner discussed literature and corresponded with him throughout his career. Like Agnon, Arieli felt honored by Brenner's commitment to his development and embraced his mentorship. This fealty was not lost on Brenner, who in the weeks following the publication of "Pale Heinrich" referred to Arieli and Agnon as "two talented emerging writers devoted to me with their whole souls [*be-khol nafsham*]."[9] The two men would publicly display their fidelity to Brenner in the coming years, such as when Brenner came under attack in Hebrew Zionist circles for perceived pro-Christian views.[10]

Brenner's fiction constituted one of the primary vehicles through which he communicated his ideas about literature and life to his fellow Palestinian Hebrew writers; Agnon recalls the anticipatory excitement with which the literary community greeted *mi-Kan umi-kan*.[11] Arieli, who mentions the novel in two commemorative articles dedicated to Brenner, undoubtedly read it. Due either to reading it or conversing with the author about it, Arieli took up Brenner's call for the Palestinian Jewish public sphere's development and devoted himself to composition of the first full-length drama dedicated to Zionist settlement in Palestine.[12]

Allah Karim!—Brenner's Influence and Beyond

The content, style, and message of Arieli's 1912 drama *Allah Karim!* bear the mark of Brenner's influence. Like other elements in Brenner's fiction, an Arab rider's attack on Aryeh Lapidot's two sons during a journey between settlements and the hunchbacked son's death after a long hospitalization in *mi-Kan umi-kan* draw on actual events. In spring 1909, Arabs from the village of Lubia attacked Berl Shveiger and a companion when they were traveling from Sejera to Mitzpeh, and Shveiger, who suffered only minor gunshot wounds, died of blood poisoning after a long hospitalization.[13] Thus, Arieli's selection of the increasingly tense relationship between Palestinian Arabs and Zionist settlers as an important component in his drama suggests Brenner's influence.

Arieli's effective employment of drama to persuasively advance Self-Evaluative masculinity, in contradistinction to other forms of Zionist masculinity, points to his skill as a dramatist. His successful wielding of dramatic form, however, did not occur in a vacuum. His employment of the melodramatic mode to interweave pathos and humor points to how he shared Brenner's belief that it constituted the optimal means for Palestinian Jewish life's dramatic portrayal.[14] Furthermore, his utilization of the melodramatic mode to undercut the pathos of the watchman Shmaryahu

Fogel's death at Arab hands and support the drama's rejection of martyrdom indicates his shared understanding of the political implications of his aesthetic choice.[15]

Despite significant overlap in their views, Arieli displayed a more developed approach for promotion of productive homosocial ties than Brenner did. While concurring with Brenner's belief in identity's performative nature, Arieli nonetheless saw the internalized discourse of racial antisemitism as a factor inhibiting creation of productive homosocial ties and adoption of Self-Evaluative masculinity. Therefore, rather than fostering such ties through promotion of a shared sense of rebellion against the Jewish past, Arieli looked to advance them through creation of a usable past. Through a reenvisioning of Jewish history and tradition, Arieli strove to offer Jewish men a way to move beyond burdensome elements of their past and self-perception, arrive at a positive feeling of continuity and pride, and attain confidence in their ability to sustain their community through work alongside other Jewish men, just as their forefathers did before them. Like Agnon, he argued that striving for Zion had always linked collective improvement to self-improvement efforts. Through provision of a usable past, Arieli looked to endow the difficult and thankless tasks of communal construction performed by his Palestinian Jewish male readers with meaning and significance and thereby steel them for long-term action alongside their compatriots. This chapter will explore the means Arieli employed to accomplish this task in *Allah Karim!*

After introducing the drama's historical context, anthropologist David Gilmore's conceptual approach to masculinity, and the relationship between masculinity and the act of reading, the chapter will explore the drama's showcasing of four well-known models of Zionist masculinity. The chapter argues that Arieli presents these models competing for supremacy in late Ottoman Palestine to clarify their limitations and promote productive homosocial ties capable of producing widespread adoption of Self-Evaluative masculinity and effective communal development.

Contextualizing *Allah Karim!*

Transformed political conditions in Ottoman Palestine following the Young Turk Revolution of 1908 pushed Zionist settlers to better clarify their views concerning the New Yishuv's character. With imperial control weakened, land disputes broke out between indigenous Galilean Arabs and wealthy Arab landowners and Jewish settlers considered responsible for displacing farmers from their land.[16] In April 1909, three prominent Jewish settlers died in these disputes. As previously noted, Arab villagers from Lubia attacked Berl Shveiger during a journey between Sejera and Mitzpeh; he died of his wounds. When the guard Israel Korngold went to question suspicious Arabs near Sejera, they shot and killed him. Immediately thereafter, farmer Shimon Melamed died in a confrontation between Jewish settlers and residents of Sejera.[17] Acquainted with Shveiger, Brenner's close friend Yehoshua Radler-Feldman (1880–1957) initiated commemorative efforts that soon encompassed the three dead men and provoked intense debate concerning Zionist masculinity and the Jewish people's past, present, and future.

Brenner and Alexander Ziskind Rabinovich (1854–1945) soon assumed editorship of a planned volume to memorialize the previously mentioned victims and other "workers and guards who [had] been killed guarding the Jewish colonies in our country."[18] As the predominant cultural figure, Brenner initially dominated affairs. He prompted leading contemporary stylists including Berdichevsky, Agnon, and Reuveni to contribute. In contrast, Rabinovich, a practitioner of the passé social realist new wave prose style, contributed his administrative abilities.[19] Despite their unequal status, Rabinovich did not defer. He, Radler-Feldman, who would anonymously pen the volume's introduction, and the volume's editorial board advanced positions on Jewish-Arab relations, the proper relationship to the Jewish people's religious traditions and history, and the memorialization of fallen Zionist pioneers that Brenner found objectionable.[20] Viewing collaboration as morally compromising, Brenner resigned editorship and published his intended contribution elsewhere.

A controversy centered on masculinity soon raged around the volume, *Yizkor: matzevet zikaron le-halele ha-po'alim ha-'Ivriyim be-Eretz Yisrael* (Yizkor: Memorial stone for the dead Hebrew workers in Palestine, 1911). It promoted a masculinity of national self-sacrifice to its male audience through blood and death's mythologization, and many Palestinian Zionists found this unpalatable.[21] The following excerpt from the contribution of Galician Zionist leader Yehoshua (Osias) Thon (1870–1936) succinctly voices what the volume promoted: "Unless people lay down their lives for their sake, national aspirations . . . cannot be realized. Without the sign of blood, . . . no national hope . . . was ever fulfilled. Our hopes have already recognized the stamp of blood, warm blood, young blood. Now we can rest assured that their time will come. The nation will live forever and the memory of the young men who shed their blood guarantees that our hope, eternal [life], will never be erased from our history."[22] The dissonance between this elevated rhetoric and the banal circumstances of the memorialized pioneers' deaths certainly irked Brenner.[23] Rather than emphasizing the importance of how one died, Brenner's withdrawn contribution stressed the need to make the most of one's life.[24] Consequently, his view of Zionist masculinity diverged significantly from that of Thon and Rabinovich.

A 1911 letter Arieli wrote to Brenner attests to similar disillusionment with the volume's direction. As he explains, "several things lead me to believe that the Yizkor volume won't be the best thing."[25] It appears, however, that he committed to participation during Brenner's editorship and planned to contribute *Allah Karim!*[26] The drama's portrayal of a Palestinian Arab youth murdering a Jewish watchman against the backdrop of increasing Jewish-Arab tensions clearly evokes Shveiger and Korngold's deaths. Yet Arieli had only begun writing it when Brenner resigned editorship. Nonetheless, he felt obligated to submit something and considered offering the editors his nearly completed story "Hagadat ha-mavet" (The death tale).[27] Through its proffering to Brenner for publication elsewhere, however, Arieli looks to be asking Brenner's permission to forgo his earlier commitment. Brenner's publication of "Hagadat ha-mavet" as a separate book in 1912, after its publication in the newspaper *ha-Ahdut* (The unity), where he served as literary editor, communicates his consent.

Viewing *Allah Karim!* as representative of shared ideological and aesthetic values, Arieli considered dedicating it to Brenner.[28] Arieli abandoned this idea, but Brenner remained committed to the project and submitted it to Editor Yosef Klauzner (1874–1958) for publication in *ha-Shiloah*.[29] From its 1896 founding by cultural Zionist leader Ahad Ha-Am (Asher Ginsberg; 1856–1927), *ha-Shiloah* constituted Hebrew literature's premier contemporary journal.[30] Despite its diasporic publication sites, *ha-Shiloah* offered Arieli's drama Palestinian and diasporic readerships on par with those enjoyed by the original Yizkor volume. Consequently, his drama's publication in *ha-Shiloah* allowed Arieli to assert his belief that how one lived one's life was more important than how one died. This belief undergirded Self-Evaluative masculinity and contrasted sharply with Thon's model.

Manhood Is in the Making

While genetic factors underlie production of male and female offspring, scholars agree that masculinity and femininity constitute cultural constructions with diverse manifestations. Thus, before exploring masculinity's place in *Allah Karim!* and its relationship to Palestinian Jewish culture's development, it proves useful to backtrack and briefly consider the connection between masculinity and culture previously touched on in this book. Although lacking a deep structure, anthropologist David Gilmore argues that masculinity assists societies in confronting "the existential 'problem of order' that all societies must solve by encouraging people to act in certain ways, ways that facilitate both individual development and group adaptation."[31] Manhood ideals contribute to social systems' continuity. In the case of developing national communities facing major obstacles with limited resources, masculinity can be used to psychologically integrate men into a community as well as encourage their selfless contribution to it.

In contradistinction to femininity, which most societies confer on females largely through their arrival at sexual maturity, Gilmore notes the precarious nature of masculinity that males struggle to attain. Requiring provisioning, procreation, and protection for their maintenance, societies continually turn to males to assume these burdens. Yet such demands frequently pain, endanger, or even cause the death of those assuming them. As a result, "manhood ideals force men to overcome their inherent inertia and fearfulness and to 'work,' both in the sense of expending energy and in the sense of being efficient or 'serviceable' in doing so."[32]

Masculinity pushes males to continually renounce bonds to their mothers, with whom they maintained a sense of unity during their childhoods, as well as escapist wishes tied to efforts at regressing to this primal state, to achieve and maintain a psychologically integrated identity meeting societal expectations. Consequently, masculinity's successful deployment, especially in a developing community, requires elucidation of communal boundaries, communication of masculine norms, justification for societal expectations, and clarification of noncompliance's costs. While much has been made of how tests, rituals, and shared narratives help various societies satisfy these preconditions, the act of reading prose fiction can accomplish the same goals.

Manhood and Reading in Late Ottoman Palestine

In Palestine, as in East Europe, the Hebrew reading public "looked up to literature (including fiction and poetry), expecting it to tell it what to do and where to go."[33] Yet these expectations were not met through direct acquisition of knowledge or truth. Involving itself in the existential issues facing writers and readers alike, the best Palestinian Hebrew literature addressed readers' moods and concerns by temporarily severing them from extratextual reality and creating an imaginary space where they could rationally contemplate their situation.[34] Readers, however, were not free of outside influence in this imaginary space, because "when the subject is separated from himself, the resultant spontaneity is guided and shaped by the text in such a way that it is transformed into a new and real consciousness."[35] Thus, reading reshaped individual consciousness and influenced behavior. Consequently, with Hebrew literature the most authoritative, best developed, and most widely consumed turn-of-the-century Palestinian Jewish cultural form, the act of reading became a central process by which Jewish men internalized masculine norms that cemented their identification with the New Yishuv, pushed them to withstand difficult conditions, and kept them dedicated to a collective effort whose fruits they were unlikely to savor.[36]

Late Ottoman Palestine constituted an almost ideal location for Hebrew literature advocating adherence to new masculine norms to impact its audience. By the 1910s, a significant portion of its writers, editors, and critics resided in Palestine, where they constituted an important component of a developing national community that used Hebrew as its primary means of communication.[37] Furthermore, young males who had severed themselves from earlier familial, social, religious, and geographic ties constituted a disproportionate portion of the literary community, as well as of the thirty thousand to thirty-five thousand immigrants who arrived in Palestine between 1900 and 1914. [38] Consequently, facing disorienting Palestinian conditions, evocative of the befuddling conditions previously experienced in European urban centers such as Warsaw, uprooted young men, both writers and readers, turned to literature treating issues of communal affiliation.

Like the turn-of-the-century Warsaw Jewish journalists discussed in the introduction, Self-Evaluative Hebrew writers portrayed early twentieth-century Palestine's modern Jewish community as emasculated and feminine. They did this to impart the feelings of disorientation felt by Jewish male immigrants encountering a new land, their impaired senses of self, and their experience of Jewish communal suffering. In addition, they employed such portrayals to advance ordered gender and sexual norms as a way for Jewish men to remasculinize themselves and their symbolically male nation. To ease feelings of confusion and inability to cope and to offer male readers a potential source of pride, Self-Evaluative Hebrew writers implored them to act in accordance with Self-Evaluative masculine norms and steel themselves for attainment of a "deep, horizontal comradeship," with like-minded individuals.[39] Moreover, these writers' literary works pushed readers to view failure to assume Self-Evaluative masculine norms as a violation of proper relations between Zionist men, or Zionist homosociality, meriting exclusion from the national community.[40] While other contemporary Palestinian Jewish intellectuals followed the same strategy to advance divergent Zionist masculine forms, Self-Evaluative Palestinian Hebrew writers set themselves apart by asserting the primacy of a form appropriating and transforming, rather than negating, diasporic Jewish masculine elements.

Negation, New Jews, and the Schlemiel

Benjamin Harshav has convincingly asserted that a sense of crisis spread among large portions of East European Jewry following the 1881–82 pogroms and catalyzed a secular Jewish revolution. Dissatisfied with their lives, overwhelming numbers of East European Jews felt compelled to act to change them, either in East Europe or elsewhere, and to attain a different public image for themselves and, sometimes, their people. Consequently, divergent individual and group identities rejecting extant or imagined elements of East European Jewish life arose.[41] The individual Jew's ability to successfully immigrate, to participate in Bolshevik or socialist activities, Zionism or European nationalism, scholarship or visual art, sport or music, demanded that something be left behind for something to be gained.

With a negative antisemitic-inspired portrait of Jewish men as nerdy, weak, and bookish an important element in Western discourse, Zionism and other variations of the Modern Jewish Revolution prioritized Jewish masculinity's transformation.[42] Yet these efforts were propelled by more than just Jewish men's desire for self-respect and respect of their non-Jewish peers. Contemporaries viewed masculinity as a key indicator of a national community's vibrancy and health and believed that only through achievement of masculine health would the Jewish people prove capable of caring for their members and achieving acceptance as a peer nation.[43]

Arriving in Palestine with a greater sense of urgency than their predecessors, the late Ottoman period's predominantly East European immigrant settlers worked to shape its modern Jews into a national community

capable of withstanding contemporary existence's vagaries. General agree-
ment existed among them that this would require negation of prominent
aspects of diasporic Jewish masculinity. Yet no consensus existed concerning which aspects required negation, and what, if any, of its aspects could
be appropriated or transformed for incorporation into Palestinian Jewish
culture.

Overlooking the less-than-heroic circumstances of Shveiger, Melamed,
and Korngold's deaths, writers such as Thon used them to promote a Zionist
masculinity grounded in mortal sacrifice in service of the nation. Members
of the clandestine organization Bar-Giora,[44] who established Ha-Shomer
(the Watchman), a legal organization dedicated to Jewish self-defense, in
1909 promoted a similar Zionist masculinity. Through Ha-Shomer's attainment of mythological status as a forbearer of the Israeli Defense Force, many
people now view this model as synonymous with Zionist masculinity.[45] Yet
the idea of sacrificing oneself for the nation broke with the Jewish martyrological tradition, superficially mimicked an element popular in other
contemporary national traditions, and lacked broad consensus within the
contemporary Yishuv.[46]

The farmer Sami Tolkovsky, who in 1913 wrote to the Rehovot town
council calling for dismissal of a local Jewish watchman whose misbehavior
disturbed him, represents an alternative Zionist masculine form rooted in
the prophets' moral vision. Tolkovsky spoke candidly about Eli'ezer Fin-
kelstein's brutal, inhumane, and frequently capricious use of force against
Arab workers, which he saw as damaging to the New Yishuv's moral and
spiritual development.[47] Such a stance, which required individual distance
from the community, proved popular among contemporary Hebrew writers, such as Bialik, who were influenced by both the prophetic tradition and
Russian literature, whose writers widely embraced the prophetic persona.[48]

As previously noted, Aharon David Gordon propounded still another popular masculine form that found its greatest appeal among early
twentieth-century affiliates of *ha-Po'el ha-tza'ir* (The young worker). Believing each Diaspora Jew to have "an unnatural, defective, splintered person within him," Gordon looked to manual labor on Palestinian soil as a
method for overcoming self-alienation and achieving a healthy connection to the world.[49] Such an approach to masculinity jibed effectively with
European critiques of the Jews as unproductive, due to underrepresenta-
tion in farming and crafts, but lacked earlier Jewish precedent. Gordon's
preference for soil tilling, construction of buildings and homes, and road

paving over cultural work betrays the distinctly anti-intellectual and quasi-mystical character of his propounded masculinity.

Another decidedly anti-intellectual masculine form frequently overlapping with that of the watchman was grounded in an Orientalist idealization of native Palestinian Arabs, especially Bedouins. For example, Radler-Feldman expressed the fallen watchman Shveiger's attraction to such masculinity: "[Shveiger] was becoming—or, at least, wished to become—Arabized; to be like the best among the Arabs. In seeking to be totally Hebrew, he wanted to be like them. He wanted the Hebrew in him to be like the Arab in them."[50] Rather than censoring Shveiger's effort, Radler-Feldman viewed it as legitimate and even admirable. Proponents of idealized oriental masculinity viewed Palestinian Arab men as embodiments of the Rousseauian noble savage free of civilization's chains. Thus, they looked to mimic them by similarly freeing themselves of diasporic Jewish culture's perceived disabling effects. The dissonance between this idealized image and Palestinian Arab men encountered by immigrants limited this form's spread. Yet Canaanite ideology, which subsequently looked to sever Israeli culture and society from its diasporic roots and reconnect it with its Middle Eastern environment, demonstrates this form's enduring attraction.[51]

Although lacking vocal advocates, the final masculine form hovering over the Yishuv was that of the schlemiel, who at first glance resembles anti-semitic caricature.[52] As literary scholar Ruth Wisse explains, the schlemiel was "vulnerable, ineffectual in his efforts at self-advancement and self-preservation" and "emerged as the archetypal Jew, especially in his capacity of potential victim."[53] Consequently, many Jews attempting to transform Jewish society viewed the schlemiel as a negative unmanly figure whose memory needed to be erased from Jewish history. Yet challenging historic conditions and the prominence of antisemitically tinged racial science led many Jewish men, including would-be reformers, to internalize the schlemiel's negative characteristics and question their transformative efforts.

Zionist reformers looking to re-create Jewish men as martial figures prepared for national sacrifice, prophetic figures, agricultural laborers psychically integrated through reconnection to Palestinian soil, and noble savages free of cultural baggage hesitated to directly address the problematic association of Jewish men with the feminized schlemiel. They feared what they might discover. Yet nationalists might "make their own history, but not entirely as they please; not with cultures of their own choosing, but with cultures directly encountered, given, and transmitted from the past."[54] Unlike the schlemiel, all the masculine models advanced by Palestinian Zionists, except the prophetic model, had little Jewish precedent, especially in the last two millennia. In contrast, the figure of the schlemiel resonated among Jews. Furthermore, closer examination showed its possession of positive characteristics such as fortitude, incorruptibility, and unshakable awareness of individual weakness that prevented seduction by might's brutalizing potential.[55] These attributes could serve as an effective basis for a model of masculinity for the New Jewish Man promoting provisioning, procreation, and protection necessary for the New Yishuv's ongoing development. Promotion of these positive attributes as core aspects of Self-Evaluative masculinity, attainable by all Jewish immigrant males and capable of unifying them for successful pursuit of personal and national goals, constitutes Arieli's objective in *Allah Karim!* Utilizing drama's ability to transform individual consciousness, Arieli promoted a nuanced form of Zionist masculinity employing elements from the diasporic Jewish past.

A Cast of Masculine (Stock) Characters

Fictional characters based on common literary or social stereotypes constituted an important feature of East European Jewish and non-Jewish literatures brought by Hebrew writers to Palestine.[56] Review of the major male dramatic personae in *Allah Karim!* reveals that each one corresponds to one of the masculine models detailed above. Twenty-two-year-old Shmaryahu Fogel, an orchard guard who wears a wide brimmed hat, a black Russian peasant shirt, and a bullet-laden belt typical of period watchman, represents watchman masculinity. Despite his provincial dress, twenty-five-year-old writer Shimshon Bronskul self-importantly asserts authority over his fellows and portrays himself as a righteous upholder of prophetic masculinity. A gray-bearded fifty-five-year-old agricultural laborer, Kalman Vaynsheynker evokes Gordon and his nature and manual labor–centric masculinity. Despite laboring as a pastry salesman, Ali, a tan, attractive twenty-year-old Palestinian Arab youth, wears a blinding white kaffiyeh, an ornamental dagger, blue pants and shirt, and red shoes to suggest the noble savage's untainted masculinity. Finally, dressed in a tropical pith helmet, cloak, and high-water pants, twenty-four-year-old Noah Yonter, who chews on his goatee, stutters, and speaks in a nasal voice, suggests the schlemiel's problematic and sometimes comical masculinity.

Femininity—Masculinity's True Test

Arab herders illegally graze animals in the orchards Fogel protects, and growing tensions between them lead to his murder. Yet the drama intentionally avoids using his murder to promote a martial masculinity and the centrality of bloodshed to Jewish national aspirations. It does this to encourage rereading and meaningful consideration of Zionist masculinity. Thus, after Fogel receives an uncontested sword blow to his nape, he mumbles a few words and expires. The aspiring martyr takes momentary pride in his approaching death, but it accomplishes little and the drama questions its social utility. Fogel's death robs his comrades and the woman who loves him of something precious. Furthermore, it undermines the New Yishuv's ability to complete important tasks, including tedious everyday ones, by robbing it of necessary manpower.

Once the martial form is placed in question, readers are pushed to consider what the alternative Zionist masculine forms embodied by the drama's other male characters can offer individual Jewish men and Yishuv society. These men's interaction with eighteen-year-old Naomi Shatz serves as a yardstick by which readers can evaluate the Zionist masculinities they personify.

Naomi's structural role sets her apart from the other dramatis personae and explains Arieli's decision not to portray her in a psychologically realistic manner.[57] He intends for her to be larger than life like Sanin, the eponymous protagonist of the best-selling novel *Sanin* (1907) by Mikhail Artsybashev (1878–1927), whom she references in the drama.[58] A character modeled on the Nietzschean Übermensch, Sanin returns to his hometown for a visit, tests the identities of its inhabitants, and challenges their sense of order. Similarly, Naomi, an embodiment of anarchic feminine modernity, arrives in Palestine, puts the extant identities of Ali and the drama's Jewish men on trial, and challenges the sense of order their distinctive identities provide them. The texts' conclusions also run parallel. *Sanin* concludes with Sanin's departure after he lifts the deceptive veils of decency and order erected by the townspeople and exposes the anarchic nature of contemporary existence. Similarly, *Allah Karim!* concludes following Naomi's revelation of the previously unrecognized limitations of the various masculine forms assumed by the drama's men, as well as the illusory nature of the sense of order the New Yishuv's members possess.

While Bronskul, Fogel, Vaynsheynker, and Ali proudly maintain what they perceive as viable masculinities when the drama opens, they harbor an unrestrained and amoral egoism that prevents them from nurturing children and limits their ability to provision and protect their societies. Unaddressed, this egoism isolates and inhibits them. Naomi embodies this egoism, and when she declares that she will accede to "a man who will command [her] and demand compromises from [her]," she challenges the drama's men to prove themselves by vanquishing "feminine" egoism.[59] Achievement of individual and collective aims requires that each male confront his identity's "feminine" egotistical side, prioritize paternity and women's integration into society through motherhood, and sublimate unbridled desire and fear.

Test Preparation

Exasperating Diaspora experiences inhibit Fogel's, Vaynsheynker's, and Yonter's assumption of the challenge Naomi symbolically poses. Lacking a viable norm for judging their behavior, doubts about the appropriateness and morality of their actions paralyze them; they travel to Palestine hoping to overcome their paralysis. An early Russian Jewish proponent of Enlightenment, Kalman breaks with traditional Jewish society to embrace modernizing trends, but his wife's premature death and his children's wayward behavior make him question his embrace of Modern Hebrew culture. He looks to agricultural labor in Palestine for salvation. Yonter, who abandons traditional society to immerse himself in European culture and achieve his non-Jewish neighbors' loving acceptance, does not consummate his plan. Uncertainties about it, its morality, and its realizability prevent him from sleeping with his non-Jewish girlfriend. After an acquaintance beds her, Yonter's doubts multiply. He decides to pursue a teaching degree in Palestine to change things. Finally, despite education in Kropotkin's Yeshiva, Fogel cannot bypass his heritage.[60] Viewing Jews as egotistical and ideologically questionable, Fogel's Russian anarchist colleagues doubt his commitment and set him up for arrest. Disillusioned, he travels to America to prove his ideological commitment, but its temptations prove too strong. Fogel then travels to Palestine believing that its barren character will check his antisocial desire.

Rather than displaying ideological commitment or pursuing self-transformative efforts in Palestine, these men regress to a fetal state and ignore Jewish communal challenges. Pooling their resources and forming a commune with Bronskul, they retreat to a one-room apartment, where they eat, sleep, and conduct their lives. There, the "tender grace" spilling onto the "delicate thought-drenched face" of the German Jewish teacher Tzipporah Engelbrand, Naomi's virtuous feminine antipode, nurtures them and renews their sense of self-worth.[61]

Tzipporah cannot sustain the men indefinitely and her strength wavers. Yet Fogel works as a watchman, Kalman labors in agriculture, and Yonter prepares to enter a teacher's seminary; the commune members appear ready to forgo her nurturing support and confront previously side-stepped masculine challenges. Unfortunately, their increased confidence and demonstrated abilities fail to eliminate lingering doubts about their facility for tackling the challenges facing them outside their apartment's womb-like environment. Tzipporah believes that the men, who constitute a microcosmic New Yishuv, can meet the challenges in front of them, and she even looks to Fogel to lessen her load through marriage. The men do not reward her belief in them. Nonetheless, with Naomi's arrival, their masculinities will be tested.

The Commune's Dissonant Song and Its "Missing String"

Having enjoyed the praise of Odessa's aged literary establishment, symbolized by Naomi's father, who refers to him as "our literature's Samson," Bronskul confidently assumes prophetic masculinity's mantle.[62] He considers his Hebrew poetry to be capable of providing his fellow commune members with moral guidance, and he fervently believes that it will enable them to move beyond experiences that forced them to accept their limitations and generated self-doubt.[63] Bronskul's limited self-perception, however, inhibits his ability to offer moral direction and belies his superior air. While he confidently assumes that Naomi will accede to his will and marry him upon arrival in Palestine, the challenge she poses quickly exposes his literary and masculine limitations. Failure to deal with these shortcomings does not just inhibit Bronskul's personal growth—it also prevents him from composing literature capable of guiding his fellow commune members and uniting them to address Palestine's challenges.

Even when Naomi emphasizes his failings, as in the following passage, Bronskul refuses to change his attitude and approach to earn her devotion and more effectively realize his literary aspirations:

> And this . . . look . . . [She immediately jumps up on a crate standing in the middle of the room and reaches out her hand. She plucks the three strings

of a dusty violin with one of her fingers, and, afterwards, she runs her finger across them all. The violin gives off a quiet dissonant moan.] Ha-ha-ha! What a strange song! That is your commune's symbol that you wrote me about? . . . Four strings representing four members, ha-ha-ha! Yet there are only three strings here. The missing string hints that the song of one of the four members has been fully sung. Bronskul, isn't it your song?[64]

The violin's symbolism communicates that successful communal construction requires that members transcend their differences to work harmoniously like violin strings mellifluously performing a musical score. Yet Bronskul does not consider how to harmonize the commune's members. Although he unconsciously senses the validity of Naomi's critique, his immaturity prevents him from facing the masculine limitations and doubts that unite him with the others. Consequently, he does not employ them as a starting point for change. This failure raises the possibility that Hebrew literature, a prominent feature of Diaspora Jewish culture, cannot contribute to the commune and the New Yishuv's success.

Rejecting Primitivism's Allure

When the "spectacular wide landscape of an Eastern city with its mosques, towers, and flat roofed homes" becomes visible through the commune's apartment windows, the possibility of a new Jewish beginning in the Orient seductively asserts itself.[65] The windows do not muffle the sound of jingling camel bells, reciting muezzins, and Ali's mercantile cry, "Allah Ka-rim!" His handsome appearance, elegant attire, and self-confident behavior, visible when Naomi calls him to the apartment, mark Ali as a seemingly viable masculine alternative to the drama's Jewish men weighed down by a diasporic legacy reflected in the apartment's filth and disorder. Consequently, when Naomi remarks on Ali's power and demands liberation from the apartment's dismal atmosphere, it appears that the drama advocates a break with previous Jewish forms as the only way for Jews to meet individual and societal challenges.

Despite superficial differences, however, Ali and other Palestinian Arab characters face modern trials like those faced by the commune members. The primary difference being that the Palestinians have not fully engaged the modern challenges that the Jews have failed to meet. [66] A burdensome and threatening past weighs Ali down, just as similar pasts weigh down commune members. When Ali was ten, one of his mother's former suitors killed his father. Arab custom obligates him to avenge his father's death, and a ten-year stay of vengeance concludes as the drama opens. Until then, Ali successfully responds to changing Palestinian conditions to satisfy both his wants and broader societal needs by working in his uncle's bakery and learning Hebrew to better market its goods. His earnings permit him to purchase a Martin rifle and a curved sword and assist his aged uncle. When the need to avenge the death of his father reemerges, it prevents Ali from simultaneously pursuing self-interest and meeting societal demands and his incipient modern Palestinian masculinity faces its first serious test. Ali is pushed to choose between meeting the demands of his past through vengeance or ostracism.

Distracted by Naomi and the aggressive egoism that she symbolizes, Ali fails to address how to meet the challenge before him. Even though vengeance will likely cause his death, Ali long assumes that when of age, he will act. Yet when Naomi arrives and offers her affection, he unconsciously grasps what he will lose if he pursues vengeance blindly. With his self-interest aroused, a previously concealed fear of death and a reticence to pursue vengeance assert themselves. Nonetheless, Ali maintains communal commitment and hesitates to pursue Naomi. Sensing his indecisiveness, she plays with him and chastises him both for betraying his past and lacking commitment to a shared romantic future with her.

Rather than investigating his feelings of impotence and working to overcome them by either clarifying his relationship to his community or redefining it by asserting an alternative form of fealty to his past, Ali refuses to address the issues troubling him. Instead, he lashes out at others. Initially, he blames Naomi and looks to violently subdue her. Yet he fails to neutralize her and, in despair, charges her hoping she will kill him. When Fogel blocks his path, Ali kills him instead. Rather than a triumphant masculine voicing of Palestinian Arab nationalism, Ali's shocked expression betrays frustration with his inability to control his desire or find liberation from it. Ali's failure to subjugate Naomi and the anarchic feminine modernity she embodies points to the native Palestinian Arab male's inadequacy as an object of emulation for Jewish men.

The Last Man Standing

Through the failure of Ali, Bronskul, Kalman, and Fogel to meet the challenge Naomi poses, the drama critiques and rejects the masculine models they represent, but their failures do not reflect fundamental pessimism on the part of their creator.[67] Before the Balfour Declaration, Palestinian realities greatly restricted what Zionist settlers could accomplish; expectation management constituted one of Palestinian Hebrew literature's most serious challenges. Rather than "beating on the expanding revival drum," Arieli, like Brenner, developed a literary strategy that allowed him to deliver hope in measured quantities.[68] The centrality of negation or rejection to a literary work does not necessarily translate to a nihilistic message. Rather, through the process of negation, one can gradually reveal a more hopeful outlook.[69]

While indeterminate ending allows readers to interpret Arieli's drama as viewing the Jewish future pessimistically or optimistically, careful reading exposes Yonter's keen self-awareness, fortitude, and incorruptibility and its promotion as a model for emulation. Despite his seeming schlemiel-like character, he best meets Naomi's challenge. While Naomi escapes subjugation, Yonter's transformed attitude hints that one's Diaspora Jewish upbringing need not impede one's successful meeting of Palestine's challenges.

As he works to express his manhood for individual and collective betterment, Yonter does not conceal his feelings of impotence. Instead, he struggles with them. Thus, with Naomi's arrival and his erotic desire's arousal, Yonter ceases looking outward for guidance and directs his search for meaning inward. Painful self-examination reveals a debilitating fear of immoral action and a childish desire to avoid decisive action. Even though Bronskul sadistically belittles him to elevate himself and Naomi works to obscure his actions' virtuousness, Yonter does not let shame crush his hope or derail attempts to overcome past failures.

When Naomi selects Yonter to stroll with her, she pushes him toward successful heterosexual expression. He initially rejects her overture, but his accession to her wish betrays his continuing desire for betterment and openness to behavioral change. Prepared to sacrifice to prove his manhood, Yonter does not flinch when Naomi jokingly threatens to sell him. Yet when she calls a policeman to inform him that Yonter is stalking her, Naomi arouses Yonter's fears concerning his actions' propriety. Harboring seduction and rape fantasies, Yonter feels shamefully exposed. Furthermore, fearful of his erotic feelings' consequences, he flees and contemplates suicide as a form of liberation from a mature relationship's challenges. Nonetheless, when he backs away from a poison container that he has just ordered and tips over an oil bottle, the oil dripping on his head symbolically anoints him and expresses his readiness to act. Yonter puts his previous Diaspora failure behind him and returns to pursue Naomi.

Despite Yonter's attitudinal change, the psychological issues motivating his planned suicide remain and pose an ongoing threat to collective betterment efforts. Consequently, Naomi exploits them when he confesses his love. She denies the possibility of self-transformation arguing that individuals cannot transcend their past. Noting elements of Yonter's yeshiva education littering his speech, Naomi argues that the life he pursues does not differentiate him from embalmed pharaohs. Furthermore, she denies the bravery of his actions and labels them a cowardly betrayal of Jewish martyrs who unhesitatingly killed themselves to sanctify God's name. When faced with these sophistic claims, Yonter looks out with the eyes of "an accused righteous man." Unable to point to traditional Jewish elements employed as building blocks of an improved Jewish future or to verbally refute Naomi's accusations, he faces renewed doubt about individual and communal betterment efforts.[70] Recognizing that weakness does not preclude success, however, Yonter will not be cowed. Consequently, he seizes hold of Naomi's locket engraved with the aphorism, "Life is steadfast, and only he who a steadfast spirit moves will catch it and obtain it."[71]

Yonter exhibits an increasingly crystallized worldview grounded in introspection by the third act. For him, manhood requires confrontation with one's fears and assumption of full responsibility for one's actions. Only in this way can excuses be avoided and aims achieved. While he previously deferred to Bronskul, Yonter now rejects his misogyny and struggles to explain his incipient outlook:

BRONSKUL: Noah, have you read about the female spider that eats the male after they mate?

YONTER: What about it?

BRONSKUL: Naomi's that kind of spider.

YONTER: [A painful grimace distorting his facial muscles] Oh, stop it, stop it, Shimshon . . . you do not n-n-need to speak like that . . . you don't need . . . everything around lacks consolation . . . so . . . a-a-ah . . . so . . . and you add more . . . of these emasculated sentences . . .

BRONSKUL: Where are these emasculated sentences?

YONTER: Geldings . . . [Silence] The spiders are us . . . all of us and not her . . . yet we are defeated spiders; we don't eat, rather they eat us . . . and these are seventy times more abominable . . .

BRONSKUL: [derisively] Excuse me, philosopher.

YONTER: [continuing bitterly without paying attention to Bronskul] And every one of us crawls and carries with him his bundle of tiny abominations, the seed of his shameful weakness . . . this one here and this one there . . .[72]

With Naomi embodying both procreative and destructive potential in Bronskul's metaphor, Yonter's substitution of the commune members for her as the metaphoric tenor communicates his recognition of their concurrent possession of similar procreative and destructive powers. Hiding their immoral thoughts and actions like a "bundle of abominations," the commune members rein in their destructiveness, but they simultaneously deaden desire and its ability to propel individual and social betterment. To effectively tap this desire, they must overcome feelings of regret and shame by confronting the thoughts and actions that produce them and by acting morally to prevent their manifestation. Such confrontation requires painful self-exposure, but its avoidance will have negative consequences. Blame for these consequences will land squarely on the passive commune members' shoulders.

Yonter's limited persuasiveness and Bronskul's unwillingness to listen prevent Yonter from gaining devotees to his emergent outlook or successfully employing it. Prior to pledging love to Naomi, proposing marriage, and demanding that she rein herself in to contribute to the New Yishuv, Yonter tries confessing regrettable past actions he now seeks to avoid. Yet Naomi aggressively silences him. Taking advantage of an initial admission, she asserts that it proves that mentally ill and incurable Jews cannot better their lives. Thereafter, she spuriously lauds alternative masculine models, including Ali's, as preferable to one Yonter looks to voice. Then she exits the stage and avoids subjugation.

Ultimately, Yonter's failure to control Naomi and what she represents results from a lack of allies. Thus, rather than calling for the Jewish cultural past's wholesale rejection, the drama asserts the need for its more effective employment in a secular Hebrew tradition capable of cultivating productive homosocial ties and successfully unifying Jewish men for realization of group aims.

Cultural Continuity and Adaptation of Tradition

While Naomi belittles Yonter's tie to Jewish religious culture, Arieli rejected efforts to sever Jewish men's ties to it. Instead of viewing such ties as a disability, he and other Self-Evaluative writers saw Jewish religious culture as a readily exploitable resource capable of drawing Jewish men together in support of social continuity. While Jewish men might abandon their faith, the individual and collective issues they confront resemble those their predecessors previously faced. Consequently, by reestablishing connection to their cultural past, Jewish men could draw strength from their male predecessor's successes and the traditions that enabled them. Therefore, Arieli drew upon earlier Jewish traditions and texts to create a secular collective redemption narrative he subsequently embedded in the fabric of *Allah Karim!* This narrative provides male readers with a viable way to interpret the commune's failure to meet the challenge Naomi posed, and advances Self-Evaluative masculinity's collective adoption as the most effective path to communal success.

An off-handed remark about the Fast of the Firstborn made by Kalman, the commune's most culturally literate member, clarifies the Jewish temporal setting of the three-act drama's action and points to tradition's potential significance for the New Yishuv.[73] The first act transpires on the twelfth of the Hebrew month of Nisan, two days before the fast; the second act starts three days later on the fifteenth of Nisan, Passover's first day; the third act occurs five days later on Passover's sixth day.

Despite the drama's timing, the commune members do not observe the religious traditions of the Passover holiday. Instead, Bronskul reads his poem "la-Shemesh" (To the sun) for the first time as night descends in the second act. His reading constitutes an alternative to the traditional Haggadah reading done in the Diaspora on Passover's second night, thereby raising the possibility that Modern Hebrew literature could assume social functions previously fulfilled by the Jewish religious tradition. Yet beyond bringing the play's Jews together, Bronskul's reading does not perform any meaningful social function. His failure to consider the experiences of the other commune members alongside his own and offer a communal response to them leaves him expressing repressed and seemingly insurmountable feelings of impotence instead. His speaker's description of a loss of sustenance and protection with the setting of a maternal sun recalls a yearning infant's wailing desire to return to the mother's breast. Consequently, Bronskul's reading does not impel masculine transformation and unified communal action. Instead, Arieli's juxtaposition of Bronskul's reading with Naomi's decision to turn her attention to Ali emphasizes the limitations of the Hebrew cultural form Bronskul advances. Thus, it engages the possibility that Jews might benefit from sloughing off their culture.

Arieli does not expose the limitations of Bronskul's work to reject Hebrew culture outright. Instead, he employs Kalman to model a more viable and socially engaged alternative grounded in the Haggadah. Composed in the tumultuous period following the Second Temple's destruction, the Haggadah narrates the Exodus in support of the belief that God will redeem the Jewish people, just as he did when he liberated them from Egypt. By ritualizing the Exodus narrative's retelling and combining it with the seder's other ritualized acts, the Haggadah provides a compelling justification for communal participation and unifies Jewish society. While God's redemptive role inhibited nonbeliever's use of the traditional Haggadah narrative, Hebrew writers still envied the commitment and sense of cohesion that it produced. Thus, rather than starting anew, Hebrew writers looked for ways to advance the New Yishuv through selective appropriation of its elements and elements of religious Jewish culture still resonant with the New Yishuv's formerly religious members.

To create a secular alternative to the Haggadah capable of achieving the commitment and cohesion the religious text formerly produced, Arieli drew on the seder traditions of consuming four cups of wine and the *afikoman*. While tea is proffered during Bronskul's seder night reading, the bottle of brandy Kalman brings births a new narrative. Brandy, referred to in Hebrew as *yayin saruf*, evokes the wine, or *yayin*, drunk at the seder. Therefore, when Kalman raises the bottle, his intended consumption is endowed with meaning that his toast further expands: "For the last time . . . we'll drink our master Daihis's poison cup until we drain its dregs and then we'll never drink again!"[74] The Hebrew term for poison cup, *kos ha-tar'elah*, constitutes a biblical dis legomenon used only in Isaiah 51. There, the prophet offers the people consolation, informing them that the period of suffering that serves as their punishment for blasphemy, compared to a cup of poison that they must drink to completion, nears its end. When over, the people will assume honored status in a new age dominated by virtuous rule.

Informed by the prophetic message, Kalman's statement offers a way to modify both Isaiah and the Haggadah's religious vision to suit contemporary reality. Lacking divine compulsion, the New Yishuv's Jewish men do not reflect on their misdeeds, an action parallel to drinking poison. Consequently, they wallow in suffering and do not produce the virtuous society that confrontation with their improprieties would help create. For example, Kalman receives brandy for betraying his principles and becoming an agricultural overseer. Yet rather than looking to understand his actions, he consumes the brandy to forget. Consequently, if things do not change, he and the other commune members will never arrive at the desired "afikoman of their drinking," because their unexamined lives will multiply their misdeeds.[75]

Promoting self-examination and subsequent moral action through both reconstructed ritual and dramatic composition, Arieli advances the type of introspection and constructive action Yonter displays as a masculine behavioral norm for all New Yishuv men. Collective redemption will not be achieved through one individual's sacrifice akin to a Christologically tinged paschal offering. Instead, as Kalman's reference to seder participants' collective consumption of the afikoman hints, introspection constitutes a less draconian form of sacrifice. Nonetheless, it can achieve its aim through its adoption by a broad spectrum of Jewish men working in tandem. Lacking the sense of safety provided by strong homosocial ties, the commune members prove unwilling to sacrifice their pride and risk self-exposure to undertake this endeavor. Thus, they fail to assume the collective narrative laid out through Arieli's creative reworking of traditional Jewish ritual and text. Instead, Kalman seals the brandy bottle with a cork given to him by Naomi. The poison cup of personal shame remains full. A Self-Evaluative male brotherhood pursuing introspection and moral action and unwilling to admit unreflective men needs to emerge before a better future can be realized.

Conclusion

A product of the "Yizkor" Book of 1911 controversy, *Allah Karim!* reflects both Zionist masculinity's use as a proxy in increasingly intense late Ottoman period debates about the Yishuv's future character and Arieli's employment of drama to actively participate in these debates. Thus, rather than revealing Arieli's opposition to Zionism or his failure to engage politics, one sees him engaging drama to advance Self-Evaluative masculine norms for the Palestinian Jewish community's widespread adoption. Protagonist Shmaryahu Fogel takes on the Jewish watchman's role, assumes appropriate guise, and finds his death in struggle with the Palestinians, but Arieli intentionally subverts his death's tragic possibilities. By undermining its potential use to promote a Zionist masculinity grounded in mortal sacrifice, Arieli pushes readers to consider Self-Evaluative masculinity and its widespread adoption's ability to transform the New Yishuv.

True heroism, Arieli believed, involved confrontation with a more abstract opponent—modernity—gendered feminine and personified in the drama by Naomi Shatz. Powerful and emasculating, yet simultaneously willing to yield to and reward those who subdue her, Naomi voices the challenges posed by the complex reality Palestinian Jewish men face and the potential reward for those capable of working together to meet them. Clear moral vision and coordinated effort, rather than brute force, prove necessary to accomplish this; these prerequisites demand that Palestinian Jewish men not jettison their diasporic Jewish past. Fogel, né Barukh Shnaydbroyt, adopts a surname voicing his desire to take birdlike flight and fly free of his past, but this proves unattainable. In contrast, Noah Yonter, whose comical appearance and stutter lead readers and the other commune members to disregard him, addresses the possible. He takes up the challenge posed by his individual and collective Jewish pasts and the commune's shameful failure to chart a moral path forward. Arieli employs melodrama, a mode of excess, to effectively externalize Yonter's inner struggle with his deleterious "feminine" side and his efforts to combat it—a key act that points to his masculine exemplarity.

Yonter's inability to transform Palestinian conditions singlehandedly by forcing Naomi and the modern condition she personifies to yield to his will precludes a happy ending. Nonetheless, Arieli does not lay exclusive blame on him for this failure. Instead, as discussion of the invented Passover tradition advanced by Kalman clarifies, he asserted that for Palestinian Jewish men to impact their surroundings, they needed to unite to assume the burden previously shouldered by Yonter alone. Embrace of such invented traditions and the Jewish texts and traditions capable of generating them offered Palestinian Jewish men an enriching sense of continuity with the past, a positive foundation for homosocial ties, and a stimulus to collective efforts.

Arieli envisions the development of invented cultural traditions as an effective noncoercive method for cultivation of homosocial ties and achievement of social aims. Yet as he saw it, contemporary conditions were producing highly stable homosocial ties less conducive to the Palestinian Jewish community's development. Arieli placed such unproductive ties at the heart of his first short story, "Voice Shards from across the Valley: Pale Heinrich."[76] Narrating the lead-up to and early twentieth-century marriage of Naftali Shvartzbeyn to Dinah 'Ori, the story presents the challenge posed by the homosocial ties between Naftali and his best friend, Yitzhak

Blum. These ties threaten the idyllic Palestinian Jewish future the marriage portends. While Naftali marries, his ties of love to his friend, voiced largely through infliction and reception of pain, prove more powerful than his tie to his new wife; the story concludes with him leaving his wedding reception to be with Yitzhak. Through its ability to provide them with a way to simultaneously express their ongoing rebellion against their Jewish pasts and their feelings of loyalty to them, the two men's sadomasochistic relationship proves highly durable. Neither immigration to Palestine nor marriage to Dinah 'Ori, a woman Naftali has known for only a short time, function as effective alternatives to it.

Sadomasochistic relations that result from ineffective efforts to come to terms with the Jewish past and inhibit advancement of Zionist aims can also be found in *Allah Karim!* Prior to Naomi Shatz's arrival, the four male commune members do little to effect positive change. Instead, they pair up. Shimon Bronskul and Noah Yonter form one pair and Kalman Vaynsheynker and Shmaryahu Fogel form the other. Sadomasochism characterizes both pairings. Bronskul bitterly ridicules a prematurely balding Yonter; Kalman and Fogel trade bitter barbs aimed at each other's hypocrisies. Encounters with Naomi disrupt these pairings. Yonter is pushed to psychological development and breaks with Bronskul, and Fogel commits assisted suicide, liberates himself from the need to change, and isolates Kalman. Nonetheless, these developments do not inhibit the creation of new sadomasochistic pairings or make the stability of these pairings any less attractive to Jewish male immigrants.

Arieli wanted Palestinian Jewish men to forgo such homosocial ties in favor of more socially productive ties created through invented traditions. Such ties could offer an enriching sense of continuity with the past and spur collective efforts through widespread assumption of Self-Evaluative masculinity. Yet Arieli recognized that invented traditions alone would not prove sufficient to induce many Jewish men to embrace socially productive homosocial ties and Self-Evaluative masculinity. Many men felt that the sadomasochistic ties binding them to other Jewish men enriched their lives and saw no convincing reason to forgo them. As Yitzhak Blum explains to Naftali Shvartzbeyn, "If it is only possible to experience life and live it to the fullest in a state of sickness or disease, then it is better to be sick."[77] Consequently, Arieli saw the need for a way to compel reticent Palestinian Jewish men to sever socially deleterious homosocial ties and join more socially engaged men working to meet the developing Palestinian Jewish community's provisioning, procreative, and protective needs. As discussion of the novella *Yeshimon* in the next chapter will demonstrate, Arieli made use of the increasing early twentieth-century importance of sexuality, or one's sexual interests and attraction for others, as well as one's capacity to have erotic experiences and responses, to oblige Palestinian Jewish men to adopt Self-Evaluative masculine norms or face ostracism.

Notes

1. Gershon Shaked, "ha-Te'om she-yarad—'al yetzirato shel L. A. Arieli-Orlof," *Siman Kri'ah* 5 (February 1976): 481–91; 'Adi Tzemah, "Min ve-ofi le'umi: tzemed nos'im be-'Yeshimon' shel L. A. Arieli," *Moznayim* 53, nos. 5–6 (1982): 371–83.

2. Tzemah, "Min ve-ofi le'umi," 380–81. Tzemah does not mince words when asserting his view of Arieli's opposition to Zionism: "And Jewish nationalism? This, as we will see in Arieli's eyes, is not possible for us, because we are whores in our souls, we need the gentiles of the world to be our masters, to swear fealty to them, to be intercessors and notables amongst them, and to betray them. We Jews are women (and also, as we will subsequently discuss, mosquitoes): bloodsuckers, traitors, and abominations. That is, in my opinion, the central theme of 'Wasteland.'"

3. Shachar Pinsker, *Literary Passports: The Making of Modernist Hebrew Fiction in Europe* (Stanford, CA: Stanford University Press, 2011), 166. The first part of the title of Tzemah's article *Min ve-ofi le'umi* [Sex and national character] constitutes a clear evocation of Weininger's famed volume *Geschlecht und Charakter*; see *Sex and Character: An Investigation of Fundamental Principles*, ed. Daniel Steuer and Laura Marcus, trans. Ladislaus Löb (Bloomington: Indiana University Press, 2005).

4. Pinsker, *Literary Passports*, 394.

5. Pinsker, *Literary Passports*, 179.

6. For a statement of the similarity between Arieli's attitude to Jewish life and those of his contemporaries, see Yeshurun Keshet, *Omadot* (Jerusalem: Hotza'at Shalem, 1970), 139.

7. Levi Aryeh Arieli, *Kitve L. A. Arieli: sipurim, mahazot, hagadot, ma'amarim, igrot*, ed. Mikha'el Arfa (Tel Aviv: Dvir, 1999), 2:129.

8. For Shimon Kushnir's description of Arieli, see Gila Ramraz-Ra'ukh, *L. A. Arieli (Orlof): hayyav ve-yetzirato* (Tel Aviv: Papirus, 1992), 11.

9. Yosef Hayyim Brenner, *Kol Kitve Y. H. Brenner*, ed. Menahem Poznanski (Tel Aviv: ha-Kibutz ha-Me'uhad, 1955–67), 3:347. The Hebrew phrase *be-khol nafsham* evokes the phrase *be-khol nafshekha*, used to describe the ideal cleaving of the Jewish soul to God in the Shema prayer.

10. On the controversy over Brenner's perceivedly pro-Christian views that engulfed the Hebrew and Zionist literary worlds, see Nurit Govrin, *'Me'ora' Brenner': ha-ma'avak 'al hofesh ha-bitui (1911–1913)* (Jerusalem: Yad Ben Tzvi, 1985). On Agnon and Arieli's participation in a gathering held in support of Brenner on a stormy winter evening in 1911, see R' Benyamin, "me-Asefat ha-sofrim," *ha-Po'el ha-tza'ir*, February 20, 1911.

11. Shmu'el Yosef Agnon, "Yosef Hayyim Brenner be-hayyav uve-moto," in *Y. H. Brenner: mivhar divre-zikhronot*, ed. Mordehai Kushnir (Tel Aviv: ha-Kibutz ha-Me'uhad, 1971), 142.

12. L. A. Arieli, "'Alav. shuv 'alav. . . ,'" *ha-Po'el ha-tza'ir* April 12, 1923; Levi Aryeh Arieli, "Y. H. Brenner," *ha-Do'ar*, April 12, 1941. On the place of Arieli's drama in the development of Palestinian Jewish settlement drama, see Gid'on 'Ofrat, *Adamah, adam, dam: mitos he-halutz u-fulhan ha-adamah be-mahazot ha-hityashvut* (Tel Aviv: Ts'erikover, 1980), 41–49.

13. Sha'ul Avigur et al., eds., *Me-hitgonenut le-haganah*, vol 1., *Sefer toldot ha-Haganah* (Jerusalem: ha-Sifriyah ha-Tzionit, 1956), bk. 1, 213.

14. Employment of melodrama in *Allah Karim!* challenges Mikhal Dekel's assertion of tragedy's centrality to emergent Palestinian Hebrew culture. Mikhal Dekel, *The Universal Jew: Masculinity, Modernity, and the Zionist Movement* (Evanston, IL: Northwestern University Press, 2011), 133–224.

15. For a fuller discussion of melodrama in *Allah Karim!*, see Philip Hollander, "Between Decadence and Rebirth: The Fiction of Levi Aryeh Arieli" (PhD diss., Columbia University, 2004), 172–94.

16. Neville Mandel, *The Arabs and Zionism before World War I* (Berkeley: University of California Press, 1976), 66–67.

17. Avigur et al., eds., *Me-hitgonenut le-haganah*, bk. 1, 212–14.

18. Jonathan Frankel, "The 'Yizkor' Book of 1911: A Note on National Myths in the Second Aliya," in *Crisis, Revolution, and Russian Jews* (New York: Cambridge University Press, 2009), 187.

19. Shaked, *ha-Siporet ha-'Ivrit, 1880–1980* (Tel Aviv: ha-Kibutz ha-Me'uhad, 1977–98), 1:219–50; Getzel Kressel, *Leksikon ha-sifrut ha-'Ivrit ba-dorot ha-ahronim* (Merhavyah: Sifriyat ha-Po'alim, 1967), 2:814–16.

20. Frankel, "The 'Yizkor' Book of 1911," 189.

21. For the pioneering study of this controversy, see Frankel, "The 'Yizkor' Book of 1911," 183–215; Yael Feldman, *Glory and Agony: Isaac's Sacrifice and National Narrative* (Stanford, CA: Stanford University Press, 2010), 84.

22. Frankel, "The 'Yizkor' Book of 1911," 192.

23. See Feldman, *Glory and Agony*, 41–128.

24. Yosef Hayyim Brenner, *Ketavim*, ed. Menaham Dorman and Yitzhak Kafkafi (Tel Aviv: ha-Kibutz ha-Me'uhad, 1978–85), 3:565.

25. Arieli, *Kitve L. A. Arieli*, 2:15. The volume errs in dating this letter to 1912. A discussion concerning contribution to a volume must predate its publication.

26. In a March 1910 letter, Arieli asks Brenner about a collection he plans to put out and hints at a possible request to participate in the Yizkor volume. Furthermore, Arieli asks Brenner for the Hebrew equivalent for the word *fez*. In Arieli's corpus tarbush, the Hebrew term for *fez*, appears exclusively in *Allah Karim!* See Arieli, *Kitve L. A. Arieli*, 2:9–10.

27. For the shift in attention from *Allah Karim!* to "Hagadat ha-mavet," see Arieli, *Kitve L. A. Arieli*, 2:13.

28. On potential dedication of *Allah Karim!* to Brenner, see Arieli, *Kitve L. A. Arieli*, 2:17.

29. Arieli, *Kitve L. A. Arieli*, 2:18.

30. See Steven Zipperstein, *Elusive Prophet: Ahad Ha'am and the Origins of Zionism* (Berkeley: University of California Press, 1993), 96–169; Ali Attia, *The Hebrew Periodical ha-Shiloah (1896–1919): Its Role in the Development of Modern Hebrew Literature* (Jerusalem: Magnes, 1991).

31. David Gilmore, *Manhood in the Making: Cultural Concepts of Masculinity* (New Haven, CT: Yale University Press, 1990), 3.

32. Gilmore, *Manhood in the Making*, 227.

33. Dan Miron, *From Continuity to Contiguity: Towards a New Jewish Literary Thinking* (Stanford, CA: Stanford University Press, 2010), 52.

34. Miron, *From Continuity to Contiguity*, 115–17.

35. Wolfgang Iser, *The Act of Reading* (Baltimore: Johns Hopkins University Press, 1980), 157–59.

36. For more on literature's central place in Palestinian Hebrew culture, see Zohar Shavit, "Mavo," in *Toldot ha-yishuv ha-Yehudi be-Eretz-Yisrael me-az ha-'aliyah ha-rishonah: beniyatah shel tarbut 'Ivrit be-Eretz-Yisrael*, ed. Zohar Shavit (Jerusalem: Mosad Bialik, 2002), 4–5. No mention is made of a contemporary Palestinian performance of *Allah Karim!* This chapter treats it as a closet drama read by individuals or small performance groups who experienced it exclusively through the act of reading.

37. On the turn-of-the-century Hebrew literary community, see Dan Miron, *Bodedim be-mo'adam: li-deyoknah shel ha-republikah ha-sifrutit ha-'Ivrit bi-thilat ha-me'ah ha-'esrim* (Tel Aviv: 'Am 'Oved, 1987), 9–111. On the Palestinian Hebrew literary community through the World War I, see Shavit, *ha-Hayyim ha-sifrutiyim be-Eretz Yisrael, 1910–1933* (Tel Aviv: ha-Kibutz ha-Me'uhad, 1982), 28–72.

38. On the turn-of-the-century Hebrew literary community's male character, see Sheila Jelen, *Intimations of Difference: Dvora Baron in the Modern Hebrew Renaissance* (Syracuse, NY: Syracuse University Press, 2007), 1–25; Naomi Seidman, *A Marriage Made in Heaven: The Sexual Politics of Hebrew and Yiddish* (Berkeley: University of California Press, 1993), 11–39; Iris Parush, *Reading Jewish Women*, trans. Saadyah Sternberg (Waltham, MA: Brandeis University Press, 2004), 57–133, 207–41. Statistical data confirm young males' predominance among Jewish immigrants to Palestine. For more on this, as well as contemporary Palestinian Jewish immigration, see Gur Alro'ey, *Imigrantim: ha-hagirah ha-Yehudit le-Eretz-Yisrael be-reshit ha-me'ah ha-'esrim* (Jerusalem: Yad Yitzhak Ben-Tzvi, 2004).

39. Benedict Anderson, *Imagined Communities: Reflections on the Origins and Spread of Nationalism* (New York: Verso, 2006), 7.

40. For fuller discussion of homosociality, see Eve Sedgwick, *Between Men: English Literature and Male Homosocial Desire* (New York: Columbia University Press, 1985); Eve Sedgwick, *Epistemology of the Closet* (Berkeley: University of California Press, 1990). On ties between homosociality and nationalism, see Eve Sedgwick, "Nationalism and Sexualities: As Opposed to What?" in *Tendencies* (Durham, NC: Duke University Press, 1993), 143–53.

41. Benjamin Harshav, *Language in the Time of Revolution* (Berkeley: University of California Press, 1993), 17.

42. For more on the European manifestation of antisemitic rhetoric and racial antisemitism, see Sander Gilman, *Jewish Self-Hatred: Anti-Semitism and the Hidden Language of the Jews* (Baltimore: Johns Hopkins University Press, 1992); Sander Gilman, *Franz Kafka, the Jewish Patient* (New York: Routledge, 1995), 101–68; John Efron, *Defenders of the Race: Jewish Doctors and Race Science in Fin-de-Siècle Europe* (New Haven, CT: Yale University Press, 1994); Mitchell Hart, *Social Science and the Politics of Modern Jewish Identity* (Stanford, CA: Stanford University Press, 2000). On the Modern Jewish Revolution, see Harshav, *Language in the Time of Revolution*, 3–80.

43. See George Mosse, *The Image of Man* (New York: Oxford University Press, 1996); Daniel Boyarin, *Unheroic Conduct: The Rise of Heterosexuality and the Invention of the Modern Jewish Man* (Berkeley: University of California Press, 1997).

44. The Bar-Giora organization was named in honor of Shimon Bar Giora, a military leader in the first-century Jewish revolt against Roman rule.

45. For a representative work supporting Ha-Shomer members' mythological portrayal, see Yaakov Goldstein, *From Fighters to Soldiers: How the Israeli Defense Forces Began* (Portland, OR: Sussex Academic Press, 1998).

46. See Anderson, *Imagined Communities*, 9–10; George Mosse, *Fallen Soldiers: Reshaping the Memory of the World Wars* (New York: Oxford University Press, 1990). Feldman, *Glory and Agony*, 70–84; Gur Alro'ey, "Mesharte ha-moshavah o rodanim gase ruah?—me'ah shanah le-agudat 'ha-Shomer'—perspektivah historit," *Katedra* 133 (2009): 77–104.

47. Alro'ey, "Mesharte ha-moshavah," 88.

48. Khone Shmeruk, *ha-Kri'ah le-navi: mehkere historiyah ve-sifrut*, ed. Yisra'el Bartal (Jerusalem: Merkaz Zalman Shazar, 1999), 278–85; Dan Miron, *The Prophetic Mode in Modern Hebrew Poetry* (Milford, CT: Toby, 2010), 127–90.

49. Arthur Hertzberg, *The Zionist Idea: A Historical Analysis and Reader* (Philadelphia: Jewish Publication Society, 1997), 377; for recent scholarship discussing Gordon's thought and his place in turn-of-the-century Palestinian culture, see Meir Chazan, Eli'ezer Shvid, and Motti Ze'ira's essays in Avner Holtzman, Gid'on Katz, and Shalom Ratzabi, eds., *mi-Saviv la-nekudah: mehkarim hadashim 'al M. Y. Berdich'evski, Y. H. Brenner, ve-A. D. Gordon* (Kiryat Sede-Boker: Mekhon Ben-Guryon le-heker Yisra'el yeha-Tzionut, Universitat Ben Guryon ba-Negev, 2008); Bo'az Neumann, *Teshukat ha-halutzim* (Tel Aviv: 'Am 'Oved, 2009).

50. Frankel, "The 'Yizkor' Book of 1911," 190; similarly, Brenner's brother Binyamin lived among the Bedouin and contemplated joining a tribe. Binyamin Brenner, *Gedolah haytah ha-bedidut* (Tel Aviv: 'Am 'Oved, 1978); Yael Zerubavel, "Memory, the Rebirth of the Native, and the 'Hebrew Bedouin' Identity," *Social Research* 75, no. 1 (2008): 315–52.

51. On Orientalism and Hebrew literature's relationship between 1900 and 1930, see Yaron Peleg, *Orientalism and the Hebrew Imagination* (Ithaca, NY: Cornell University Press, 2005). For an overview of the Canaanite movement, see James Diamond, *Homeland or Holy Land? The "Canaanite" Critique of Israel* (Bloomington: Indiana University Press, 1986).

52. For more on this cultural type, see Ruth Wisse, *The Schlemiel as Modern Hero* (Chicago: University of Chicago Press, 1971), 3–24.

53. Wisse, *The Schlemiel as Modern Hero*, 4–5.

54. Geoff Eley and Ronald Suny, "Introduction: From the Moment of Social History to the work of Cultural Representation," in *Becoming National: A Reader*, ed. Geoff Eley and Ronald Suny (New York: Oxford University Press, 1996), 23.

55. Wisse, *Schlemiel as Modern Hero*, 5.

56. For discussion of one of Russian literature's most prominent character types, see Ellen Chances, "The Superfluous Man in Russian Literature," in *The Routledge Companion to Russian Literature*, ed. Neil Cornwell (London: Routledge, 2002), 111–22; on the *ba'al guf* and *talush*, two prominent character types in East European Jewish literature, see David Roskies, *Against the Apocalypse* (Cambridge, MA: Harvard University Press, 1984), 141–55.

57. Scholarly consensus concerning Naomi Shatz's character and dramatic role does not exist. Nonetheless, her centrality has been widely noted. Yehoshu'a Bar-Yosef, "Akh eleh hem hayyim: al 'Allah Karim' me-et L.A. Arieli," *ba-Mahaneh*, October 15, 1980, 53; Ramraz-Ra'ukh, *L. A. Arieli (Orlof)*, 133; Yaron Peleg, "Reinterpreting the East: Orientalism in Hebrew Literature, 1890–1930" (PhD diss., Brandeis University, 2000), 154; Hollander, "Between Decadence and Rebirth," 182–87. On the lack of psychological realism in Naomi's portrayal, see Brenner, *Ketavim*, 4:1029–30.

58. For more on *Sanin* in its Russian context, see Otto Boele, *Erotic Nihilism in Late Imperial Russia: The Case of Mikhail Artsybashev's Sanin* (Madison: University of Wisconsin Press, 2009).

59. Arieli, *Kitve L. A. Arieli*, 1:405; for the drama's initial publication, see L. A. Orlof (L. A. Arieli), "Allah Karim!" *ha-Shiloah* 27 (1912): 51–65, 107–19, 204–21, 323–36, 401–11, 501–8.

60. Arieli, *Kitve L. A. Arieli*, 1:343. Pyotr Kropotkin (1842–1921) was a prominent anarchist who advocated for a communist society governed by voluntary workers' associations rather than a centralized government.

61. Arieli, *Kitve L. A. Arieli*, 1:334.

62. Arieli, *Kitve L. A. Arieli*, 1:352.

63. Arieli, *Kitve L. A. Arieli*, 1:352.

64. Arieli, *Kitve L. A. Arieli*, 1:347.

65. Arieli, *Kitve L. A. Arieli*, 1:335.

66. Cf. 'Ofrat, *Adamah, Adam, Dam*, 44–46.

67. Cf. Tzemah, "Min ve-ofi le'umi," 371–83.

68. Brenner, *Ketavim*, 3:572.

69. For a full discussion of this point in reference to Brenner's fiction, see Bo'az 'Arpali, *ha-'Ikar ha-shlili* (Tel Aviv: ha-Kibutz ha-Me'uhad, 1992).

70. Arieli, *Kitve L. A. Arieli*, 1:374.

71. Arieli, *Kitve L. A. Arieli*, 1:394.

72. Arieli, *Kitve L. A. Arieli*, 1:413.

73. The Fast of the Firstborn commemorates the Israelite firstborns' salvation when the Plague of the Firstborn beset Egypt just prior to the Exodus.

74. Arieli, *Kitve L. A. Arieli*, 1:389.

75. Arieli, *Kitve L. A. Arieli*, 1:390. The afikoman is a half piece of matzah, symbolic of the paschal offering, set aside early in a seder for consumption after the meal. The seder cannot be completed until it is consumed by all present.

76. For a fuller discussion of this story, see Hollander, "Between Decadence and Rebirth," 28–83.

77. Arieli, *Kitve L. A. Arieli*, 1:151.

4

HOMOSEXUAL PANIC AND MASCULINITY'S ADVANCEMENT

Not similar is the love of men, not at all similar;
The hearts of true men will not be filled with women's love;
As hard as iron is their heart, the hammer alone will subdue it.
Without fuss or capering, one's heart stamps the other;
And when a man's love conquers another's and sinks to the bottom of his soul,
It will burn there sure and modest, without explosion or rainbow colors
And nourish feelings in its nurturing warmth, and youthful hidden powers.

—Zalman Shneour, "The Gift"

Homoeroticism and Early Twentieth-Century Hebrew Literature

In a famous scene from Brenner's *In Winter*, its narrator recounts an encounter in a paramour's darkened room. Following his arrival, the two greet each other and sit together in the darkness. Experiencing an "unnatural pleasure" in each other's company, they share their innermost thoughts and feelings. Then they hear footsteps. Yirmiyah Feuerman compares their surprise to that of "two lovers hidden in forest brush when passersby discover them."[1] When their friends enter the room and turn on the lights, the first to enter playfully comments, "a silent meeting in the dark . . . Song of Songs."[2] The "pleasure," albeit "unnatural," the two feel in each other's company, the association that pops into Feuerman's mind, and the friend's reference to the erotic love poem Song of Songs push readers to view this encounter as a secluded romantic rendezvous. It starts with intimate conversation and, prior to interruption, seems to be moving in an erotic direction.

Indeed, my reference to Feuerman's male friend Dawidovsky as a paramour might disturb some readers. Reticent to acknowledge the homoerotic nature of the two men's rendezvous, they would likely point to the passage's use of irony and Feuerman's unrequited heterosexual attraction to Rahil Moiseyevna to shift attention away from it.[3] Yet neither fictional characters nor real people need limit their sexual desire to women or men; it proves more productive for readers to engage with Freud's view of sexuality as polymorphously perverse, with every individual capable of assuming different sexual objects and aims.[4] Greater understanding of this tryst and other represented homoerotic encounters and the role they play in fin de siècle Hebrew literature and contemporary Palestinian Hebrew literature can be achieved by analyzing them rather than sweeping them under the carpet.

Literary scholar Yaron Peleg's pioneering research constitutes an important first step in addressing the role played by homoerotic representations in early twentieth-century Hebrew fiction.[5] Yet his assertion that five works, including Arieli's *Yeshimon*, constitute "almost all of the instances in which the subject [of homosexuality and homoeroticism] appeared in [Hebrew fiction] from the beginning of the Haskalah until the 1960s" proves surprising.[6] In fact, the widespread portrayals of intimate male relations in additional early twentieth-century works of Hebrew fiction have led scholars to discuss homoeroticism's role in them as well as their authors' sexual orientation. For example, because powerful portrayals of homosociality proliferate in Brenner's oeuvre, earlier critics have written about his sexual orientation, his potential homosexuality, and his characters' homosexuality.[7] Other critics have investigated the nature of the relations between Yitzhak Kummer and his male friends Sweet Foot and Rabinovitch in Agnon's famed Second Aliyah period novel *Tmol shilshom* (Only yesteryear, 1945); chapter 1 pointed to the homoerotic nature of male relations in "Sister" and "Tishre."[8] Similarly, several critics have noted Brenchuk's attraction to Me'ir Funk in Reuveni's *Till Jerusalem*, which will be treated in depth in chapter 5.[9] These examples, I would argue, constitute the tip of the iceberg. Thus, contrary to Peleg's claim, it seems that this fiction was indeed concerned with homosexuality and homoeroticism.[10]

To account for homosexuality and homoeroticism's place and role in early twentieth-century Hebrew literature, one must acknowledge the contemporaneous link between Zionist culture and Hebrew literature and Hebrew literature's role in the advancement of Zionist values.[11]

Turn-of-the-century Zionists feared for the future of the Jewish people and its constituent members, and they strove to regenerate the Jewish body politic. Familiar with contemporary European imagery of individual and communal death and degeneration, they incorporated depictions of weakness, passivity, effeminacy, and homosexuality into their portrayal of personal characteristics they believed needed to be overcome for Jews to work toward individual and communal health.[12] Consequently, early twentieth-century Hebrew writers, especially those participating in Palestinian Zionist settlement, created literature that also drew on representations of male weakness, passivity, effeminacy, and homosexuality to demonize elements of Jewish identity that its authors believed needed to be overcome for a better Jewish future to be achieved.[13]

As analysis of Agnon's early work has demonstrated, Jewish effeminacy constituted the central element in Hebrew writers' depiction of the crisis facing fin de siècle Jewish society; weakness, passivity, and homosexuality served as secondary elements in this portrayal. Consequently, in its effort to resolve the depicted crisis, mainstream turn-of-the-century Hebrew literature worked to reshape Jewish masculinity.[14] Indeed, individuals influenced by German culture, such as political Zionist leaders Theodor Herzl (1860–1904) and Max Nordau (1849–1923), considered efforts to bring the Jewish male body into conformity with Western European physical standards as central to Zionist efforts to "cure" national and individual cases of Jewish "femininity." Yet the body-centered Zionist masculinity they promoted did not resonate any more effectively with predominantly East European–born turn-of-the-century Hebrew writers than those tied to the use of force, agriculture, indigeneity, or the way one died discussed in previous chapters.[15] Thus, even after Nahum Sokolow (1859–1936) translated Herzl's *Altneuland* into Hebrew in 1902, masculine models grounded in bodily transformation attracted little attention from a Hebrew literary community closely affiliated with cultural Zionism's proponents.[16] Furthermore, one can find little support for the assertion that *Altneuland* introduced a body-centric masculine "cure" into Hebrew literary discourse.[17]

As discussion of *mi-Kan umi-kan* and *Allah Karim!* elucidated, Self-Evaluative masculinity's proponents viewed homosociality, rather than the male body, as the primary means through which to advance a "curative" form of Jewish masculinity. This fact contributes significantly to explaining homosociality, homoeroticism, and homosexuality's ubiquitous presence in turn-of-the-century Hebrew literature. In contrast with the invented traditions deployed in *Allah Karim!* to foster positive homosocial ties and advance Self-Evaluative masculinity, *Yeshimon* portrays homosocial relations that it sees working in opposition to the spread of Self-Evaluative masculinity as sadomasochistic, counterproductive, negative, and homosexual. Like in *mi-Kan umi-kan*'s library scene, where "homosexual" Jewish behavior is also stigmatized, *Yeshimon* pillories "homosexual" relations to prod Palestinian Jewish men to abandon them and adopt homosocial ties with other men advancing the national interest through adherence to Self-Evaluative masculine norms.[18] Thus, rather than constituting an effective harbinger of a homosexual tradition in Hebrew literature as Peleg claims, *Yeshimon* is a product of its time. Like similar works found in other national literatures, *Yeshimon* exploited the relatively new concept of "homosexuality" to restrict homosociality and thereby advance national aims.

After introducing queer theorist Eve Sedgwick's theoretical model of sexuality and gender's interrelationship, exploring how this model can be used to better understand Palestinian Hebrew literature's use for advancement of Zionist views, and supplying historical contextualization pertaining to World War I and its aftermath, this chapter will turn its attention to Arieli's *Yeshimon*. Analysis of *Yeshimon* will demonstrate how the novella exploits homosociality to advance Self-Evaluative masculinity.

Nationalism and Manipulation of the Homosocial Continuum

Eve Sedgwick, like David Gilmore, whose work was discussed in the previous chapter, rejects the assertions of masculinity theorists, like George Mosse, who posit national movements mobilized around stable masculinities.[19] Instead, she argues that national communities effectively function as patriarchies through manipulation of the relations between men, who inevitably interpret their masculinity and the sexual and gender roles available within their society in diverse ways. Rejecting a fixed heterosexuality/homosexuality binary, Sedgwick offers a different way to understand these terms. These two terms, in her view, merely refer to different places along a continuum of "male homosocial desire" that voices different types of male interaction. At one end lie things such as mentorship relationships and shared participation in sports leagues, and at the other end lie things such as fellatio and anal sex. Every manifestation along this continuum involves similar emotional ties. Therefore, assignment of the terms *heterosexual* and *homosexual* to this continuum's different ranges proves a random act motivated more by efforts at social organization than essential character.

Rather than dismissing homophobia as a marginal modern social phenomenon, Sedgwick provides a political rationale for the repression and persecution of individuals occupying the homosocial continuum's "homosexual" range. Failure to clearly articulate the point at which "acceptable" homosocial bonds and homosexuality diverge creates an underlying uncertainty among a nation's male population about whether their ties to other men in their national community as well as men outside it implicate them in "homosexual" action. Thus, if "homosexuals" exist as a stigmatized and/or persecuted group, "homosexual panic," the internalized fear of being categorized as a "homosexual," opens men to manipulation. Once most men look to avoid categorization as "homosexual," "a relatively small exertion of physical or legal compulsion potentially rules great reaches of behavior and filiation."[20] Put differently, by influencing men's perception of their sexuality through physical or textual means, one can push them to abandon their extant masculine identity and adopt new masculine norms. Hence, the national group member's uncertainty about his sexuality and gender and his desire to fit in can lead him to modify his behavior to better meet promoted standards of sexuality and gender.

Palestinian Zionism and Homosociality's Intersection

Application of Sedgwick's model to the Jewish national context contributes to our understanding of what made Zionism's male proponents susceptible to sexual and gender norms promoted within Hebrew literature.[21] In the early twentieth century, an entire generation of young East European Jewish men transitioning from smaller Jewish communities and familiar environments to developing European cities experienced feelings of bewilderment and paralysis.[22] Close male friendships helped these men cope with them and fostered creation of "alternative frameworks that could somehow replace traditional family and communal structures in changing times."[23] Thus, homosocial ties were "of central importance to" the sense of culture and community shared by an "entire generation of young Jewish men," who "resisted continuous, real relationships with women, [and] postponed the creation of their families," and they eventually became an integral component of Jewish nationalism.[24]

Therefore, with Palestinian Zionism a subset of Jewish nationalism, homosocial ties can be understood to have played a similarly important role in early twentieth-century Zionist settlement. Historians long lauded the ideological certitude of this period's Jewish immigrants and viewed it as pivotal to their contribution to the State of Israel's establishment. Yet these immigrants' steadfastly ideological image has recently been challenged, and other explanations for their behavior need to be considered.[25] Furthermore, ideologically committed Zionists, who arrived in Palestine in the early twentieth century, were only a small percentage of immigrants.[26] A sense of connection to the New Yishuv and its emergent Palestinocentric ideology was ultimately what kept immigrants in Palestine; this link was formed in Palestine.[27] Palestinian Hebrew literature written by Self-Evaluative masculinity's proponents proved an important and cost-efficient tool for strengthening Jewish male immigrants' connection to the Yishuv community and shaping their participation in it. At its most effective, it exploited homosocial ties to push Palestinian Jewish men toward adoption of Self-Evaluative masculine norms. Despite the questionable way that these writers manipulated homosocial bonds, this manipulation provided immigrant Jewish men with a way to overcome a paralyzing sense of confusion and despair brought on by the difficult conditions they faced as Jews and immigrants and advance toward individual and collective goals' accomplishment.

Tlishut, Homosexuality, and the Push for Self-Evaluative Masculinity

With the exception of atypical works such as "Khawadja Nazar" by Moshe Smilansky, "Yehudah noter-ha-pardes" (Yehuda the orchard-watchman, 1912), and "Yo'ash" (1912) by Joseph Luidor (1856–1921), and "In the Haderah Forest" by David Shimoni, one is hard-pressed to find strong-bodied, healthy, and vigorous masculine figures in early twentieth-century Palestinian Hebrew literature capable of serving as emulative models for a national community.[28] Instead, with the early twentieth-century arrival of Self-Evaluative masculinity's leading proponents, who doubled as Palestine's most prominent Hebrew prose writers, the figure of the *talush* transitioned from the Diaspora to Palestine, and assumed a prominent role in the literary landscape.[29]

As chapter 1 explains, *tlushim* evoked many early twentieth-century Jewish men. Consequently, leading members of the predominantly male turn-of-the-century Palestinian Hebrew literary community employed them as allegorical figures representing the developing national community and its constituent male members. Thus, representation of the talush's imperfect maleness offered the Jewish male writer a way to present his overwhelmingly Jewish male audience with the individual and collective deficiencies he saw besetting the Jewish male character in a nonthreatening manner. Furthermore, this variety of talush narrative advanced a flawed and unimposing protagonist with whom Jewish male readers could identify and an implicit narrative that they could assume in their own lives. This narrative started with efforts to improve individual and collective Jewish conditions and would conclude with arrival at individual Jewish male and national communal health. A talush's demonstration of the inner strength necessary to take up this narrative came to alert Jewish male readers to their possession of similar internal resources that would allow them to effectively participate in the difficult struggle to build a successful new Jewish community in Palestine.

Because improvement of the lives of individual Jews as well as the Jewish collective motivated Self-Evaluative Hebrew writers, they introduced uprooted fictional characters to help their readers clarify their priorities and arrive at a more effective way to realize their goals. Thus, the inward turn of their fiction and the innovative techniques it employed to make the interior worlds of uprooted figures visible was not an exclusively aesthetic enterprise. Presentation of the interior worlds of tlushim, who allow their preoccupation with their erotic passions, their inevitable mortality, their guilt-ridden relationship to their Jewish past, and their fear of failure sidetrack them from their goals' accomplishment, has a clear purpose. It enabled Self-Evaluative masculinity's proponents to clarify the dangers of limited consciousness, something that led individuals to act in opposition to their conscious goals, and push their male readers to adopt introspective strategies intended to assist them in avoiding this quagmire. Carefully planned action could assist Palestinian Jewish readers in achieving both individual and collective long-range goals. Furthermore, it would provide them with an immediate sense that they were doing their manly best, despite their limited abilities, by taking control of their lives and helping their community better itself.

While Self-Evaluative Hebrew writers could employ the talush in their fiction to present a blueprint for male change and assumption of an alternative masculinity, it proved difficult to get male readers to follow this scheme. Confrontation with the least flattering elements of one's past, including failures and manifestations of personal weakness, was what the

Self-Evaluative writers argued was necessary for satisfaction of Palestinian Jewish needs. Yet many Jewish men hesitated to take up this challenge. The Self-Evaluative writers took pains to explain that this critical confrontation would prove less onerous when undertaken alongside like-minded Jewish men with little success. They promoted it through use of invented traditions offering a sense of continuity with the Jewish past to little avail. Palestinian Jewish men still wavered.

Proponents of Self-Evaluative masculinity found such reticence suspect. Hence, they looked to counter it by stigmatizing those failing to engage in self-transformative efforts as individuals engaged in homosexual behavior with whom other Jewish men should avoid contact. Thus, Kalman, Bronskul, and Fogel from *Allah Karim!* and Yitzhak Blum and Naftali Shvartzbeyn from Arieli's "Voice Shards from across the Valley: Pale Heinrich," who hesitate to direct their gaze inward, are depicted embracing sadomasochistic relations with other men that offer pleasure without burdening them with additional obligations.

Self-Evaluative masculinity's proponents, however, did not look to permanently brand Palestinian Jewish men who did not engage in introspection and subsequent moral action as homosexuals. They implicitly understood homosexuality as a range on the homosocial spectrum. Consequently, they looked to activate the internalized fear of being placed in the stigmatized category of "homosexual" to compel those deviating from Self-Evaluative masculine standards to change their place on the continuum of male homosocial desire to the heterosexual range occupied by those bonded by their shared adherence to Self-Evaluative masculine norms. Effective use of homosexual panic required successful communication of designated homosexual behaviors' dangers, the pain suffered by those engaging in them, and their marginalizing effects. Once their dangers, pain, and marginalization were recognized, male readers would more readily adopt promulgated masculine standards together with other heterosexual men.

In Self-Evaluative Hebrew writers' works open ending combines with Palestinian Jewish life's mimetic portrayal to push male readers to adopt proper masculine and heterosexual norms. With these literary works concluding without clear resolution, they leave readers with a confused textual reality evocative of their everyday lives. While readers could passively accept this indeterminacy and despair of the future, textual reality provided them with an opportunity for mastery and knowledge difficult to attain in their regular lives. Through retroactive reading of texts, contemporary readers could analyze uprooted protagonists' actions and note how homosexually tinged behavior inhibited achievement of their goals and left them dissatisfied and endangered. With the protagonists and their fictional world bearing a marked resemblance to the Palestinian male reader and his reality, mastery of the literary text and proper understanding of how to cope with the psychological situations its characters face constituted a form of knowledge that readers could take with them. This knowledge pushed those readers who attained it to adopt Self-Evaluative masculine norms that pushed them to clarify their individual and collective goals and desires and enabled them to act more confidently and effectively. Pursuit of these goals, alongside other heterosexual Jewish men pursuing similar ones, offered personal satisfaction, even if these men's goals were not ultimately realized.

Yeshimon—Background

Ottoman imperial participation in World War I and Palestine's subsequent transition to British mandatory rule profoundly affected the Palestinian Jewish community. *Yeshimon*'s composition, publication, and content reflect both these influences and Self-Evaluative Hebrew writers' response to changing circumstances. Hebrew literary works such as *Allah Karim!* reflect the New Yishuv's inward-looking gaze and its internecine strife. Yet the difficult conditions and social change brought on by World War I forced the Self-Evaluative Hebrew writers to adopt a more complex worldview that accounted for Palestinian Jewish life's geopolitical context and European-born Zionists' minority position within it.

European-born Palestinian Zionists perceived the effects of the 1908 Young Turk Revolution largely through the increasingly frequent clashes between Arab villagers and Zionist settlers mentioned in chapter 3. In contrast, native-born Sephardim, who were Palestinian Jewry's predominant and most powerful ethnic group, took part in the general euphoria that engulfed the empire and raised hopes of an Ottoman future based in liberty, equality, fraternity, and justice.[30] Like the Ottoman Empire's other Jewish citizens, Palestinian-born Sephardim, especially members of the community's young intelligentsia, saw the progressive imperial framework envisioned by the revolutionary elite as the best way to neutralize Arab opposition and advance Jewish national interests in Palestine. Through their Hebrew newspaper *ha-Herut* (Freedom), they looked to gain adherents among the general Palestinian Jewish population. To advance this "inclusivist Zionist" approach, *Freedom*'s authors called on Palestinian Jews to adopt Ottoman citizenship, enlist in the Ottoman military that now admitted non-Muslims into its ranks, and cooperate with Palestinian Arabs in local development.[31]

Having seen similar hopes to those held by the Palestinian Sephardic intelligentsia crushed by pogroms and the return of czarist tyranny following the 1905 Russian Revolution, European-born Palestinian Zionists like Arieli placed little stock in the 1908 Young Turk Revolution's promise. The Jewish national project constituted their sole priority. While prepared to display loyalty to the Ottoman Empire and to maintain transnational and cross-ethnic ties, they viewed such loyalty and ties as instrumental rather than principled.

Despite European-born Palestinian Zionists' certitude concerning the validity of their approach, wartime circumstances challenged it. Ottoman Jews, by and large, received better treatment than non-Ottoman Palestinian Zionists, who were deported and expelled from their homes. Thus, while leading Palestinian Hebrew newspapers such as *The Young Worker* and *The Unity*, expressing "exclusivist Zionist" views, were forced to cease publication, *Freedom* continued to publish up until 1917. Nonetheless, wartime conditions were not good for either Ottomans or non-Ottomans. A naval blockade on Palestinian shores combined with locust swarms to limit grain supplies. Hunger and starvation spread throughout the land, and the hardships of war forced many women to take up prostitution to survive. Zionists effectively mobilized international support to provide relief aid to the suffering Jewish population, but the Ottoman authorities and emergent Muslim-Jewish organizations also implemented plans to alleviate suffering and meet civilian needs. Thus, the Jerusalem municipality organized efforts to stem the locus plague and import grain for its inhabitants from east of the Jordan, and the Red Crescent Society, a Jewish-Arab relief organization, treated the sick and wounded and strove to relieve wartime suffering.

With war affecting social structure and social cohesion, World War I pushed Palestinian Jews to consider what social formation could best advance their needs and aspirations and what types of social ties could contribute to such a social formation's stability or exist alongside it. While the British conquest of Palestine subsequently obviated the need to consider Palestinian Jews' relationship to the Ottoman Empire, Palestinian Jews still needed to consider their attitude toward their British overlords as well as the nature of their interaction with the Palestinian Arab population.

Yeshimon, a work begun in 1916, while Arieli served in the Ottoman army, actively engages homosexual panic to oppose fraternal ties with imperial rulers, mandatory rulers, or Arab neighbors. Furthermore, it asserts the exclusive legitimacy of homosocial bonds with other Jewish men prioritizing the Palestinian Jewish collective's needs, a position strengthened by contemporary circumstances. The 1920 Nabi Musa riots challenged Palestinian Jewish faith in British mandatory rule prior to its establishment and undercut the Palestinian Sephardic intelligentsia's efforts to advance Jewish national aims through cultivation of expanded ties between Palestine Jews and Arabs.[32]

Yeshimon—Composition, Publication, Overview

Cursory perusal of *Yeshimon*, with its fictional portrayal of a short period in its naturalized Ottoman protagonist's life, shows its evident basis in Arieli's wartime experience. Following his assumption of Ottoman citizenship and military conscription, Arieli served in the Djemal Pasha Orchestra, and *Yeshimon* starts with David Ostrovsky's arrival at a desert military base to begin service in an Ottoman band unit.[33] Similarly, both men initially find their military experience exhilarating. In fact, while stationed in Damascus in 1916, an inspired Arieli began work on *Yeshimon*. Ultimately, just prior to the British conquest of Palestine, dissatisfaction led both protagonist and author to desert and return to Jerusalem. Yet Arieli's journey back would last years. Unlike bachelor David, who solipsistically wallows in his fiancée's presumed unfaithfulness at the end of the novella, Arieli took his family's needs into consideration when he decided to desert. Thus, before reestablishing himself in Jerusalem, as British civilian rule over Palestine took effect, he spent years in wartime and postwar Tiberias combating the hunger and material want he, his wife, and his children faced. Having continued work on *Yeshimon* following his desertion, Arieli completed work on it in 1922. Two years after its previous installments' postwar publication, its third serial installment finally appeared.[34]

As just noted, David initially feels euphoric about his mobilization. He finds the desert environment and the variegated group of soldiers he serves with, drawn from throughout the Ottoman Empire, fascinating. Consequently, he downplays tension in his relationship with his Damascene Arab superior, overlooks the poor treatment received by the unit's other Jewish member, and fails to consider his seemingly arbitrary elevation by the

Fig. 4.1 Members of the Tiberias Grammar School Marching Band with band director Levi Aryeh Arieli. Central Zionist Archives: PHG\1019515/16892/15.

band's conductor that saves him from the general indignities suffered by new military enlistees. While under the conductor's protective wing, David has time to think about what type of husband and father he'd like to be following his upcoming wedding. Yet rather than exploiting this opportunity, he gravitates to a misogynistic middle-aged Arab drummer and storyteller, who gladly abandons his wife and children to serve alongside the unit's other men, and fails to contemplate various masculine models presented to him.

Only during participation in a general's funeral does David look beyond his unit's seemingly warm homosocial environment to reveal its dysfunction and the potentially disastrous consequences of his service. Confronted with unprocessed feelings of grief that arose following his best friend's death, David sees that they have pushed him to unconsciously mimic his friend to draw closer to him. Consequently, David, who is not an Ottoman patriot, enlisted. When hospitalized and placed in bed with an infected fellow soldier, his best friend contracted typhus and quickly died. "Sharing a bed" with a fellow Ottoman soldier (a possible euphemism for homosexual relations) and death during military service constitute ways for David to follow in his friend's footsteps. Nonetheless, they need not preclude other ways of honoring his friend's legacy. Recognizing this, David chooses life. Masculine oversight over his community's Jewish women, who prove vulnerable, constitutes an alternative way to voice his homosocial solidarity with his friend. Furthermore, endogamous heterosexuality and efforts to give succor to his feminized nation, embodied by his mother and fiancée, offer David ways to overcome his grief and endow his life with meaning. Having detected this new path, David deserts and heads out in search of his fiancée.

Despite David's identification of a new way to voice his ongoing connection to his dead friend, individual transformation proves difficult and his homosocial desire threatens to derail his efforts. David's efforts to locate his fiancée, Rachel, at a nearby hospital prove arduous and wearying. Thus, when he meets an attractive German military train conductor, David's commitment to his feminized nation wavers, and he allows his homoerotic attraction to distract him. David accepts the conductor's suggestion that he board a Jerusalem-bound train and then engages the conductor's supposition that Rachel has betrayed him. Thus, when David does not find Rachel in Jerusalem (where he did not earlier believe her to be), he concludes that she betrayed him. Rather than questioning his new male friend's assertion and what led him to believe it, David labels Rachel a whore, asserts his impotence and inability to improve conditions for himself and the Jewish people, and withdraws inward.

At Homosociality's Cusp:
Spectral Homosexuality in the Opening Scene

To push readers to adopt gender and sexual norms to which David has difficulty adhering, Arieli structures the novella's opening to create immediate male reader identification with him.[35] Arieli plays on the rabbinic literary trope of a Jewish youth enslaved by gentiles to achieve this effect.[36] Thus, when David assumes a subservient position in a non-Jewish hierarchy, contemporary readers lower their guard and sympathize with him. Then David's physical beauty combines with a fancy new suit, accessorized with a gold watch chain, a clean white handkerchief, and a pair of freshly shined shoes, as well as his fluent unaccented Turkish, his musical talents, and his engagement to a young Jewish woman, to further draw in contemporary male readers.

This homosocial attraction initially appears quite different from the homoerotic attraction felt by David's fellow soldiers:

> All the eyes rose from the cards and turned toward the tent opening. From there, even before the flap burning with the Tammuz sun was raised by the hand of one of the shadows that appeared outside, a mature man's rich healthy voice was heard:
>
> "There's a recruit for you Hamdi . . . a student . . . just arrived. Fate has given you another stand and score carrier to replace that deserting Armenian pig Georgie, may Allah curse him."
>
> The tent flap was opened. In the opening there appeared, as they bent their heads to enter, the first sergeant's face saturated with a wide smile and cheap wine, and, behind his shoulder, a beautiful and delicate youth around twenty-two years of age dressed in elegant urban attire.
>
> This outfit and this beauty struck all those present in the tent with a sudden astonishment. Only once, when, in this desolate and remote location, a kitten with a pink ribbon and a bell upon its neck appeared, were the musicians so astonished. The card game was forgotten and everyone sunk their hungry eyes into the young visitor.[37]

David's striking physical beauty and attractive attire led the Ottoman soldiers to sink their sex-starved eyes into his flesh; they view him like a red-ribbon-and-bell-accessorized "sex kitten" ready for initiation. While these soldiers' predatory sexuality would have scandalized Arieli's contemporary male readers, these male readers' hunger for a healthy and politically attuned "New Jew" led them to derive similar homoerotic pleasure from David's appearance. Their longing for somebody capable of resolving the Jewish people's problems pushed them to read on curious as to whether David could avoid harm at his fellow soldiers' hands and help realize Palestinian Zionist efforts. Yet such passive reading caused them to forgo important clues foreshadowing David's subsequent failures. Consequently, contemporary readers were just as frustrated as David at the work's conclusion. Their unquestioning acceptance of his attitudes and activities, as well as similar attitudes and activities they maintained, performed, or witnessed in their everyday lives, proved embarrassing.

Analysis of the opening scene shows that attention to detail and what attracts one to others offers a way to pursue effective action and avoid David's fate. Although David's attire finely compliments his physical beauty, it proves inappropriate for military service. Furthermore, it hints at David's obliviousness to his actual goals, his motivations, and his actions' implications. Thus, even though he transmits a coquettish readiness for sexual engagement, David tries to convey his repulsion from the tent's inhabitants and their "dark ways" by hesitating to cross from light to darkness at the tent threshold. Similarly, when he raises his "handkerchief, white like a sea gull's wing," to wipe the sweat off his brow and chase away buzzing flies, he seeks to communicate a pure character in stark contrast with that of his libidinous superior Hamdi whose fellows label him a black "crow."[38] Yet as previously discussed, David's primary drives prove pivotal to his decision to put off his marriage and its consummation to serve in the Ottoman army. In fact, his fellow soldiers immediately recognize his "dark" and passionate side, embodied by the shadow that constitutes his comrades' first glimpse of him. Therefore, they laugh off the air of cultured superiority and purity of character he looks to transmit. Instead, his "primitive" comrades interpret his evasiveness as flirtatiousness and look forward to the chance to mold him to their will, just as they have broken and shaped the unit's other Jewish soldier.[39] Unless David changes, he and his lifestyle prove unworthy of emulation.

Homoerotic Feelings—Readers and Characters

David proves perceptive and capable of anticipating others' actions, but his smug self-satisfaction prevents introspection and inhibits his effective response to his circumstances. Feeling "a light imperceptible push in his depths" soon after meeting Hamdi, David anticipates a clash and senses the need to prepare for it.[40] Yet he disregards his intuition. Preferring immediate pleasure, David does not prepare to meet the challenges his fellow soldiers and his primary drives pose to his perceived goals. This carefree attitude manifests itself in the strong homoerotic attraction that David and his Jewish comrade Shmil feel toward their fellow soldiers; the novella's captivating style pushes unrestrained male readers toward similar feelings:

> The evening had already begun to spread its dominion. From the midst of the fading western glow and the light of the new moon's rays, the whistling of the clarinet was so enticing, and, for David, the *debitzah* dance accompanying it was so new. The faces of the shadows circle dancing and rubbing up against each other, shoulder to shoulder, with a desirous yearning, were already a bit difficult to discern. Yet in the movement of their loins and the spasms of their bellies, there was no small measure of licentiousness—this was sensed and felt by all even in the descending darkness. Yet the rhythm was wonderful, intoxicating, a rhythm measured in the ears of the children of the silent and still mountains and balanced in the muscles of the fellaheen, for generations the children of the wide invigorating Aravah.[41]

David gladly imbibes the intoxicating music and undulating male bodies that distract him from contemplation of soon-to-be-assumed marital responsibilities and the Jewish people's future fate. More than mere curiosity, a subsequent dream voicing David's unconscious homoerotic desire hints that he has long fantasized about inhabiting such a world.[42]

Even when his "Hebrew" masculine facade gets challenged, David proves reticent to consider the national implications of homosocial relations with his fellow soldiers. Hamdi looks to gauge David's gender and sexual identity and clarify their future relations, so he invites David to stroll with him. Seduced by Hamdi's attractive countenance, his smooth tanned skin, his beautiful eyes, and his vivacious character, David, oblivious to the sexual attraction that motivates him, accepts without considering Hamdi's motivations. If beneath his "Hebrew" facade David resembles the Jewish men with whom he is familiar, Hamdi intends to exploit David. Therefore, when Hamdi expresses interest in David's sisters, he tests David's masculine vigor, and he interprets David's reticence to repel his rhetorical advance as a sign of Jewish weakness. Furthermore, David's declared virginity and his squeamishness about issues of gender and sexuality lead Hamdi, who perceives David's sexual attraction to him, to conclude that David unconsciously desires sexual relations and just finds it difficult to verbalize this desire. Therefore, Hamdi hints that if David submits to him, he would be open to a relationship. Only at this point, when Hamdi pushes David to come to terms with his sexual proclivities, does David walk away. Declaring his readiness to protect his Jewish military comrade from harm, David employs a gesture of national pride to mask his sexual attraction. Through this assertion of national and sexual boundaries, David regains reader sympathy, but in the absence of any serious attempt at introspection, it rings hollow. If not for David's elevated status gained through a problematic willingness to serve as a go-between for his Ottoman unit commander and his Jewish mistress, it seems that Hamdi would manipulate David's sexual desire and gradually mold him to his will.

Masculine Options and the Absence of a Path Forward

Two deficient diasporic masculine models dominate David's thoughts and impede his arrival at a clear moral framework capable of aiding his pursuit of his sexual desire and his emergence as an effective Zionist settler. Arieli introduces David's seemingly random and purposeless encounters with Reb Ber Tuneyadiver and the Bedouin leader Abu Salim to indirectly voice his psychological relationship to the masculine models that the two men embody.[43] Consequently, through analysis of David's relations with the men, one is alerted to the two masculine models that impede David's personal progress.

Reb Ber represents a connection to what David perceives as an outdated masculinity rooted in religious Judaism. Due to a lack of faith, David proves incapable of upholding it; following his immigration to Palestine and his concerted effort to start life anew, he believes that he transcended it. Therefore, he finds Reb Ber Tuneyadiver's "packed sack worn out from use" and his "handled staff" disturbing.[44] They serve as metonymic reminders of a diasporic Jewish existence he believed he had risen above. The sack and staff evoke the cursed figure of the Wandering Jew doomed to roam the earth until the Second Coming. Simultaneously, Reb Ber's last name evokes the fictional East European shtetl of Tuneyadevke featured in Abramovitsh's aforementioned *Kitser masoes Binyomin hashlishi*, in which male characters have been characterized as "mentally castrated."[45]

Regardless of David's initially negative attitude to Reb Ber, additional meetings propel him to greater sympathy for Reb Ber and the outlook he represents. Consequently, David and the text's male readers are pushed to abandon a wholly negative view of the Jewish past and to appreciate and preserve the Jewish past's positive aspects. Motivated by love and devotion to God's law, the physically imposing Reb Ber raises his son Leibushel in the Lord's ways. Fatherly nurturing helps Leibushel emerge as one of Jerusalem's leading yeshiva students. Reb Ber, however, cannot protect Leibushel from being drafted into an Ottoman labor detail, where he is reported to have died. Yet when a conflicting report emerges, Reb Ber puts aside concern for his physical health and journeys to save his son. His paternal love and his desire for a viable legacy lead him to commit an act of understated heroism. Indeed, Reb Ber's eventual return to Jerusalem with his dead son's body places the viability of a masculinity grounded in Torah Judaism into question. Nonetheless, events leave David and the novella's intended readers to consider whether the masculine model Reb Ber represents must be completely abandoned or elements of this model can be appropriated for subsequent use. Should Reb Ber's love and devotion be discounted, or can his failure to leave a paternal legacy be tied to inadequate means?

In contrast with Reb Ber, the Bedouin leader Abu Salim personifies a masculine model defined by pleasure's amoral pursuit. Abu Salim's physical and mental abilities propel him to tribal leadership that he exploits to advance his personal agenda. He accepts money for services rendered to both sides in the war, and he proves ready to kill other tribal members whose interests do not align with his own. Envying Abu Salim's ability to decisively pursue and attain what he wants, David is drawn to the masculine model he represents.

Regardless of David's attraction to him, however, Abu Salim and his Bedouin tribe, whom many Zionist thinkers would have viewed as an ideal toward which Palestinian Jewish immigrants should aspire, warn the novella's readers about what elements of the Diaspora past need to be forgone for a better Jewish future's realization.[46] Through evocation of Numbers 14:24 at the end of the novella's first part, Arieli creates a parallel between the Israelites in the desert and Abu Salim and his tribe. Unlike the biblical Hebrews, who wander through the desert, spiritually advancing toward their goal, the Bedouins wander it aimlessly. Consequently, they symbolize a degenerate modern Jewry lacking a collective narrative capable of moving them forward: "Every man would dream his dream alone."[47] Even fulfillment of primal desires only temporarily satisfies the Bedouins. Consequently, "from above one of the pillows oscillating like a ship at sea, a solitary song, a continuous indecipherable wail of the wretched son of the wasteland, will suddenly rise up and cut through the bitterness of the day."[48] Such unhappiness and isolation underlie Abu Salim's distrust of other tribal members and his unwillingness to accept a match for his daughter. Consequently, Abu Salim's legacy proves no more certain than that of Reb Ber.

Fraternal Homosociality and a New Hebrew Masculinity's Development

David perceives the limitations and strengths of Reb Ber and Abu Salim's masculine models. Nonetheless, just as he did when he postponed his marriage to enlist, he defers further thought concerning paternity and individual legacy. Only during forced participation in General Hussein's funeral march, when thoughts of his mortality push him to introspection, does David contemplate life's meaning and proper moral action. The cacophony produced by the orchestral performers contrasts sharply with the rhythmic music that earlier accompanied the lithe dancers and drew David to the unit's homosocial environment. David senses his life's purposelessness and considers what he truly values.

Like the hospitalized Oved 'Etzot in *mi-Kan umi-kan*, who at his lowest point recollects Diasporin and the homosocial bond that they share, David recalls his friend Yerahmiel and their homosocial tie. This recollection prompts his recognition that Ottoman military service cannot provide him with what he actually desires: "Ach, Yerahmiel! Ach, Krankin! How many nights Yerahmiel slept together with him in the same room under a single blanket. They would move about and act mischievously like young kittens. And now where were that white flesh and that sunburned neck which he used to caress? How beautifully he would declaim Italian poems in the evenings by the light of a green shaded lamp . . . by that light all of Italy was green."[49]

Finding Yerahmiel's death painful, David represses it. Yet this inhibits his working through of his grief and leads him to indiscriminately try to replicate the powerful homosocial bond he shared with Yerahmiel.[50] While David can re-create the physical sensation of "kitten-like" homoerotic behavior with other soldiers and forge homosocial ties in the Ottoman military, these bonds cannot match the intellectual bond he shared with Yerahmiel—something voiced by their mutual love of Italian poetry. Yerahmiel's readiness to admit Jewish society and tradition's limitations and to search outside these boundaries for enhanced experience and solutions to Jewish problems proved an important part of what attracted David to him. Similar openness underlies David's musical training, his immigration to Palestine, his acquisition of Turkish language and Ottoman citizenship, and his enlistment in the Ottoman military. Consequently, the homosocial environment of the Ottoman military cannot actually provide David with what he desires.

Once General Hussein's funeral raises repressed thoughts and feelings, David can start working through his grief. He can analyze his relationship with Yerahmiel, locate aspects of it that he can carry into the future, develop a more viable masculinity than the ones Reb Ber and Abu Salim represent, and employ this new masculine form to forge healthy homosocial bonds with other Palestinian Jewish men—a process that evokes the behavior of Oved 'Etzot and the fictional editor who narrates the frame story in *mi-Kan umi-kan*. When Reb Ber explains, "[Jewish] daughters, God please forgive me for my words, despite all their good work are a type of merchandise . . . that demands superior protection. . . . They're really like one of the tenderest of the most tender oranges sent to Liverpool," he cast aspersions on Jewish men for their inability to protect Jewish women's virtue.[51] Yet, as David's behavior demonstrates, Jewish men also require the imposition of behavioral boundaries for Jewish society to return to health. Jewish religious law, however, no longer aids in production of viable boundaries. Through incorporation of elements drawn from non-Jewish society, however, David and like-minded contemporaries can establish masculine and homosocial norms that will reconfigure Jewish social boundaries for Jewish society's preservation and satisfaction of its members' needs. This would constitute a way to honor the noblest elements of Yerahmiel's legacy. In such a scenario, homosocial ties lacking shared Jewish social commitment would become stigmatized as transgressive homosexuality.

Improved understanding of his relationship with Yerahmiel pushes David to sever ties with his fellow Ottoman soldiers, whom he previously viewed as brothers linked together by shared communal ties, and work toward Jewish social boundaries' reestablishment. Thus, as the novella's third section opens, one finds David struggling to disentangle himself from his Ottoman superior's malevolent grasp. David had previously looked upon the conductor as a benefactor looking to better his and his fellow soldiers' lives. Yet when the conductor's Jewish mistress transfers her affection to another Turkish officer, David finally recognizes his capriciousness and his indifference to the imperial community's broader concerns. The conductor angrily calls on David to refer to his mistress as "the daughter of a filthy race" in a letter to be sent to her that he dictates to David for translation into Hebrew.[52] Not only does the conductor's request serve as a way for him to reassert his beleaguered masculine pride at David and his former mistress's expense, but it also foregrounds the religious, ethnic, and national tensions that ultimately make an Ottoman imperial community unfeasible. David's refusal, under the threat of severe punishment, to degrade himself and his people to please his malicious commander proves significant. It marks his readiness to abandon an unsteady imperial framework and work toward establishment of a stabler national one.

When David confronts the implications of his assertion of Jewish masculine standards, however, thoughts of the cost of their assertion and what he will need to do to maintain them overwhelm him. First and foremost, his personal security will be threatened. His insubordinate behavior angers his commander, who will soon deny him the elevated status that kept him safe from his fellow soldiers. Newly cognizant of the flimsy fraternal bonds he shares with them, David forecasts that he will soon be mercilessly abused like Shmil. Consequently, he weighs his commitment to the developing

Palestinian Jewish community against death and liberation from the burden imposed by assertion and maintenance of Jewish communal standards and fear.

When captured by a British patrol while on assignment, David drifts off into a reverie. He seems resigned to death. Then renewed vigor pushes him to consciously commit to serving his national community:

> Behold they're leading him, David, to execution, but it appears, there's another with him. . . . Suddenly the one divides into three and they stand like chess pawns. . . . All around them there are only knights, knights, and exposed knees. . . . Who's walking to his right? It's either Yerahmiel or Leibushel . . . reciting Dante. . . . How terrible that the head's voice changed so . . . two columns. . . . They remind David of something and he exclaims: "Ah! That is a death suitable for a Jew!" . . . Inside of him, in that that's hidden within, something sublime and awesome grows and flourishes . . . the son of a proud ancient people digs a grave for himself! . . . Tens of thousands of eyes, the eyes of thousands of persecuted and martyred from generation to generation, look to him to see his work . . . binding him with Rachel's braided hair to a sycamore with Hebrew charm . . . a dark red charm. . . . To his right they are doing the same thing to Yerahmiel. . . . Already? "I still haven't played the dark red . . . Air Varie of Beriot! I still haven't read Tennyson in the original! . . . I still haven't kissed one with Hebrew charm! . . . Mommy! Mommy! Why did you give birth to me and nurse me with your milk? The miserable woman! When they tell her! . . . Rachel! Rachel! You are so close to me here. . . . Come, come, my dove, my poor babe. . . . You'll remain 'in mid-sea,' 'in mid-sea.'"[53]

Following his capture, David fears that the British will turn him over to their Russian allies, and as a Russian subject, he will be executed for treason. Consequently, one can construe the image of David bound to a tree by Rachel's hair as a prelude to an imagined execution. David pathetically interprets such an execution as an instance of the Jewish martyrological tradition's sublime manifestation with his binding paralleling the binding of the patriarch Isaac, the prototypical Jewish martyr, to the altar. On the other hand, David's binding to the tree by Rachel's hair communicates his fear that commitment to heterosexuality, marriage, and family will lock him into a demanding, joyless, and static masculine existence. Believing that Yerahmiel preferred death when faced with this life choice, David considers following suit. Yet this would betray the martyred, who bind David, and their commitment to the Jewish people. David concludes that life and pursuit of a Jewish future achievable through commitment to the beleaguered feminine nation that his mother and his fiancée personify prove preferable to death.[54] When he was a defenseless infant, his mother nurtured him, even though the breast milk he consumed leached calcium from her bones. Now, when circumstances leave her vulnerable, he can protect her. Similarly, he can reward Rachel's devotion to him by supporting her. By not prematurely embracing death, David can better these women's lives and the lives of other Jews. Participation in the New Yishuv need not be onerous either. Opportunities for pleasures experienceable within the confines of a heteronormative Yishuv, including music, poetry, and erotic relations with Rachel, exist.

Through his homosexual desire's sublimation, David can access the energy necessary to act on his commitment to the nation's feminine representatives. Furthermore, this newly accessed power can aid him in balancing social responsibility with individual pleasure. Options besides those embodied by Reb Ber and Abu Salim exist. Through consideration of the lives of Leibushel and Yerahmiel, whom he imagines marching beside him, David can produce such an alternative. Neither Leibushel's overly strict commitment to Jewish tradition nor Yerahmiel's excessive reliance on external influences improves conditions for Jews. Yet David can forge a more constructive approach through Jewish and non-Jewish elements' synthesis within a Jewish national framework. Even if David died prior to Jewish communal needs' full realization, such a synthesis would offer him and other Jewish men a greater sense of communal cohesion and more meaningful and qualitatively better lives. David, Yerahmiel, and Leibushel might be like pawns when compared with knight-like British mounted soldiers, but the Jewish people's fate remains unsealed. Just as strategically played pawns can defeat more powerful chess pieces, relative weakness need not inhibit effective action and national success.

David's conscious embrace of this new approach indeed unleashes heretofore untapped internal resources. Thus, he successfully escapes captivity and makes his way to Rachel: "Filled with both fear and hope, David began to run forward. The blood didn't stop beating in his temples. Yet some stream of new powers, which he had never imagined, flew into his legs. . . . Several times he fell and again he rose and ran."[55] The knowledge that he is headed to Rachel to honor his commitment to her "breath[es] the spirit of courage and renewed hope into his heart."[56]

Reading Ending in "Wasteland"

Despite the important conclusions that David draws, life lived in accordance with them proves difficult without the support of other Jewish men who share similar goals. Consequently, when he encounters "the beautiful and mischievous eyes" of the German train conductor, his commitment to Rachel and the nation she represents fall victim to his homoerotic desire.[57] Rather than searching for her at the nearby Red Crescent hospital where she works, David travels back to Jerusalem at the conductor's suggestion. Arriving at dawn, he imagines a new chapter opening in his life. Yet Rachel's absence from Jerusalem shatters his hopeful sense of renewal. Unlike during the general's funeral or after his capture, David avoids looking inward to discover personal shortcomings. He fails to note that his homoerotic desire has distracted him from his long-range goals. Instead, he blames the Jewish people, whom he portrays as whorish, immoral, and incapable of changing its destiny. Subsequently, he expresses his self-pitying sense of his existence's hellish and inalterable nature through evocation of the lines appearing on hell's gates in Dante's *Divine Comedy*: "Through me you will pass into the valley of tears / Through me you will pass into the sorrows of eternity, / through me you will pass into a lost nation. . . ."[58]

While David fatalistically views his life as inalterable at novella's end, his personal and his people's narratives remain open. In fact, the above-mentioned quotation offers an alternative to utter despair that parallels the narrative advanced through reworking of Jewish ritual and sacred text in *Allah Karim!* In the *Divine Comedy*, Dante, like David, faces a personal crisis that prevents him from proceeding directly to his desired destination. Yet he does not despair. Instead, he enters hell, descends deeper and deeper into its depths, and ultimately achieves a heavenly reunion with his beloved Beatrice. If David desires a union with Rachel, a reborn nation, and a perceptibly different Jerusalem, he must continue the type of painful introspection synonymous with his desert experience and parallel to Dante's descent into the depths of hell. It will empower him to change his fate, bring meaning to his life, and improve his nation's status. Without it, David's life in Jerusalem will mimic his desert life.

While Arieli stigmatizes David's reticence to engage in introspection and to act on the insights he draws as homosexual behavior, he fails to place exclusive blame on him. Instead, he pushes his Jewish male readers to recognize their possession of a similar reservedness that produces equally deleterious results. Furthermore, they have permissively accepted reticent Palestinian Jewish men into their midst and enabled them to injure other community members.

David's case emphasizes that adoption of the Dantean narrative will prove difficult in isolation. Yet Arieli stresses what Jewish male readers have the power to do. They can work together to embrace Self-Evaluative masculine norms, offer support to those struggling to maintain these norms, and censure those unwilling to adhere to such standards. Ultimately, Jewish male readers are left to choose their own paths, and they need not act like homosexuals. If they desire to achieve social rootedness in Palestine, they need to embrace, internalize, and uphold the gender and sexual norms promoted in the novella.

Conclusions

Prompted to bolster support for Self-Evaluative masculinity following the outbreak of World War I and the challenge to it mounted by inclusivist Zionists, Arieli engaged sexuality more extensively in his fiction. Consequently, he incorporated homoerotic elements into *Yeshimon*. Their analysis reveals how he employed homosexual panic and its distinguishing of proper and improper homosocial ties to communicate masculine behavior he considered best able to advance national aims. Thus, *Yeshimon* exposes how Hebrew writers exploited the widespread contemporary linkage of homosexuality and Jewishness to promote new forms of Jewish masculinity and homosocial connection considered more attuned to collective needs. Therefore, awareness of how Arieli employs homoeroticism and homosexual panic in *Yeshimon* offers a way to better understand a panoply of turn-of-the-century Hebrew literary works written in the Diaspora and Palestine, especially those written by Self-Evaluative masculinity's other literary advocates.

As next chapter's discussion of Reuveni's novelistic trilogy *Till Jerusalem* demonstrates, Reuveni makes use of homoeroticism and homosexual panic for advancement of Self-Evaluative masculinity in *Till Jerusalem* in a similar manner to that engaged by Arieli in *Yeshimon*. The primary difference involves his decision to shift his portrayal of World War I–era Palestine to the home front. Hence, when Arieli, Reuveni, and other leading early twentieth-century Hebrew modernists produced Hebrew literary representations of gender and sexuality, they almost always had political and aesthetics motivations that influenced how they portrayed gender and sexuality.

The distaste for homosexuality that underlies the way that proponents of Self-Evaluative masculinity such as Arieli and Reuveni employed homoeroticism and homosexual panic in their work links fin de siècle Zionist culture with other contemporaneous national cultures. Consequently, *Yeshimon* fails to live up to the sexually progressive label that Yaron Peleg assigns it in an effort to find literary precursors who laid the foundation for a blossoming of gay Hebrew fiction in the 1960s. Social structures and cultural institutions necessary for the development of a vibrant homosexual subculture did not exist in the early twentieth century. Thus, neither early twentieth-century homoerotic literary representation nor publication of a gay Hebrew poet's homoerotic poetry in the 1920s and 1940s proved capable of stimulating a continuous and self-aware gay Hebrew culture in Palestine or abroad.[59] Only in the state period, when requisite social structures and cultural institutions developed, would gay Hebrew fiction effectively blossom.

Yeshimon and *Till Jerusalem* stigmatize homosexuals and homosexual behavior, so they and their authors' reception of decadent labels that linked them with homosexuals and marginalized them prove surprising. Yet in the interwar period, their ideas were increasingly out of step with the broader zeitgeist of the Yishuv. Euphoric Zionists interpreted historic events such as the Balfour Declaration as signs that a new era in Jewish history was taking shape in Palestine; they did their best to project the sense that Palestinian Jews had left diasporic degradation behind them and were in the midst of a renaissance. The unblemished figure of the native-born Palestinian Jewish male, or sabra, was vigorously advanced as the embodiment of this new era community.

Self-Evaluative masculinity's proponents came to advance it due to their possession of a radically different worldview. They failed to privilege the present over the past and the Land of Israel over the Diaspora. Instead, they saw forces working to psychologically fragment individuals and disorganize societies in both locations. Consequently, they strove to portray Palestinian Jewish men as flawed and in need of reliable allies if they were to better Jewish lives in Palestine. Representations of gender and sexuality that were not always flattering to Jewish men were a pivotal part of this portrayal.

Instead of tackling the positions held by Self-Evaluative masculinity's proponents head-on, its opponents took advantage of representations of psychic fragmentation, effeminacy, and homoerotic attraction found in their literary depictions of Palestinian Jewish life to delegitimize their views. These opponents pointed to these depictions as evidence of the decadent character of the literary works and their authors. It would be these efforts that brought about Self-Evaluative masculinity's eclipse during the mandate period and lessened its impact on the social norms and culture of the inchoate national community. Through explication of the role representations of psychic fragmentation, effeminacy, and homoerotic attraction play in advancement of Jewish national interests in *Till Jerusalem*, the next chapter looks to remove the decadent label from literary works promoting Self-Evaluative masculinity once and for all.

Notes

1. Yosef Hayyim Brenner, *Ketavim*, ed. Menahem Dorman and Yitzhak Kafkafi (Tel Aviv: ha-Kibutz ha-Me'uhad, 1978–85), 1:199.

2. Brenner, *Ketavim*, 1:199.

3. For a fuller discussion of this "homosexual" moment, see Alan Mintz, *Banished from Their Father's Table: Loss of Faith and Hebrew Autobiography* (Bloomington: Indiana University Press, 1989), 172–74.

4. Sigmund Freud, *Three Essays on the Theory of Sexuality*, trans. James Strachey (New York: Basic Books, 1975).

5. Yaron Peleg, *Derekh gever: siporet homoerotit ba-sifrut ha-'Ivrit ha-hadashah, 1880–2000* (Tel Aviv: Shufra le-sifrut yafah, 2003), 5–86; Yaron Peleg, "Heroic Conduct: Homoeroticism and the Creation of Modern, Jewish Masculinities," *Jewish Social Studies: History, Culture, Society* 13, no. 1 (Fall 2006): 31–58.

6. Peleg, "Heroic Conduct," 44.

7. See Hayyim Be'er, *Gam ahavtem gam sene'tem* (Tel Aviv: 'Am 'Oved, 2002), 107; Avner Holtzman, *Temunah le-neged 'eynay* (Tel Aviv: 'Am 'Oved, 2002); Ariel Hirshfeld, "Deyokan 'atzmi o ha-deyokan ba-derekh el 'atzmi,'" *Helikon* 5 (Winter 1992): 30–54.

8. On *Only Yesteryear*, see Michal Arbel, *Katuv al 'oro shel ha-kelev: 'al tefisat ha-yetzirah etzel Shai Agnon* (Jerusalem: Keter, 2006), 207–54; Amos Oz, *Shtikat ha-shamayim: Agnon mishtomem 'al elohim* (Jerusalem: Keter, 1993), 110–79.

9. On *Till Jerusalem*'s homosexual and homoerotic aspects, see Dan Miron, *Kivun orot: tahanot ba-siporet ha-'Ivrit ha-modernit* (Jerusalem: Keter, 1979), 395–430; Yig'al Shvartz, *Le-heyot ke-de li-heyot: Aharon Re'uveni—monografiyah* (Jerusalem: Hotza'at Magnes, 1993), 175–221; Peleg, "Heroic Conduct," 56.

10. Cf. Peleg, "Heroic Conduct," 44. For a discussion of homoeroticism in Hebrew literature after World War I, see Ehud Ben 'Ezer, "'Eynayim lahem velo yir'u oznayim," *Moznayim* 68, no. 1 (1993): 24–25.

11. For more on this topic, see Dan Miron, *Im lo tihyeh Yerushalayim* (Tel Aviv: ha-Kibutz ha-Me'uhad, 1987), 9–92.

12. Arieh Saposnik, "Exorcising the 'Angel of National Death'—Nation and Individual Death (and Rebirth) in Zionist Palestine," *Jewish Quarterly Review* 95, no. 3 (2005): 559; Peleg, "Heroic Conduct," 33; Daniel Boyarin, *Unheroic Conduct: The Rise of Heterosexuality and the Invention of the Modern Jewish Man* (Berkeley: University of California Press, 1997), 271–312.

13. Others disagree with my position; cf. Shachar Pinsker, "Imagining the Beloved: Gender and Nation Building in Early Twentieth-Century Hebrew Literature," *Gender and History* 20, no. 1 (April 2008): 105–27.

14. See Mikh'ael Gluzman, *ha-Guf ha-Tzioni: le'umiut, migdar u-miniut ba-sifrut ha-'Ivrit ha-hadashah* (Tel Aviv: ha-Kibutz ha-Me'uhad, 2007), 11.

15. East European Zionists lacking Hebrew literary connections displayed greater affinity to their West European brethren. For more on such Zionists, see Yisra'el Bartal, *Kozak u-bedvi: "am" ve-"eretz" ba-le'umiut ha-Yehudit* (Tel Aviv: 'Am 'Oved, 2007), 68–79.

16. Ahad Ha'am bitterly criticized this work from a cultural Zionist perspective, and the Hebrew literary elite almost certainly shared his sentiments. See Ahad ha-'Am, *Kol kitve Ahad ha-'Am* (Tel Aviv: Dvir, 1956), 313–20.

17. Cf. Gluzman, *ha-Guf ha-Tzioni*, 34–66; Pinsker, "Imagining the Beloved," 106–7. Gluzman asserts that male bodily transformation proved central to Hebrew literary discourse, and Pinsker accepts this claim. Nonetheless, he proceeds, like Gluzman before him, to show how prominent early twentieth-century Hebrew writers stood in opposition to the bodily norms promoted by figures such as Herzl and Nordau. This muddies the actual nature of the relationship between male bodily transformation and Hebrew literary discourse and weakens both men's claims concerning the centrality of male bodily transformation. Proponents of Self-Evaluative masculinity failed to take the assertion that male bodily transformation would alter the Jewish people's fate seriously. Thus, Arieli employs the bodily ideal for comic effect in *Allah Karim!* This occurs when Naomi Shatz views the physical beauty of an Aryan-looking German turnverein member she deems worthy of being her boy toy and comments approvingly to another female character, "Wow, what a stud that one is! . . . Look how strong his muscles are! And ankles . . . beautiful ankles!" Levi Aryeh Arieli, *Kitve L. A. Arieli: sipurim, mahazot, hagadot, ma'amarim, igrot*, ed. Mikha'el Arfa (Tel Aviv: Dvir, 1999), 1:366. For a fascinating but equally problematic assertion of *Altneuland*'s promotion of a Hebrew literary prototype, see Yigal Schwartz, *The Zionist Paradox: Hebrew Literature and Israeli Identity* (Waltham, MA: Brandeis University Press, 2014), 49–96.

18. Others disagree with my position; cf. 'Adi Tzemah, "Min ve-ofi le'umi: tzemed nos'im be-'Yeshimon' shel L. A. Arieli," *Moznayim* 53, nos. 5–6 (1982): 371–83; cf. Peleg, "Heroic Conduct," 40–42.

19. Eve Sedgwick, "Nationalism and Sexualities: As Opposed to What?" in *Tendencies* (Durham, NC: Duke University Press, 1993), 143–53. For a fuller exposition of Sedgwick's views, see Eve Sedgwick, *Between Men: English Literature and Male Homosocial Desire* (New York: Columbia University Press, 1985); Eve Sedgwick, *Epistemology of the Closet* (Berkeley: University of California Press, 1990). For Mosse's position, see George Mosse, *The Image of Man* (New York: Oxford University Press, 1996); George Mosse, *Nationalism and Sexuality: Middle-Class Morality and Sexual Norms in Modern Europe* (Madison: University of Wisconsin Press, 1985).

20. Sedgwick, *Between Men*, 89.

21. Scott Ury, "The Generation of 1905 and the Politics of Despair: Alienation, Friendship, Community," in *The Revolution of 1905 and Russia's Jews*, ed. Stefani Hoffman and Ezra Mendelsohn (Philadelphia: University of Pennsylvania Press, 2008), 96–110.

22. Ury, "The Generation of 1905 and the Politics of Despair," 99.

23. Ury, "The Generation of 1905 and the Politics of Despair," 101.

24. Dan Miron, *Bodedim be-mo'adam: li-deyoknah shel ha-republikah ha-sifrutit ha-'Ivrit bi-thilat ha-me'ah ha-'esrim* (Tel Aviv: 'Am 'Oved, 1987), 420–22, quoted in Ury, "The

Generation of 1905 and the Politics of Despair," 103; Ury, "The Generation of 1905 and the Politics of Despair," 104.

25. See Gur Alro'ey, *Imigrantim: ha-hagirah ha-Yehudit le-Eretz-Yisrael be-reshit ha-me'ah ha-'esrim* (Jerusalem: Yad Yitzhak Ben-Tzvi, 2004).

26. Alro'ey, *Imigrantim*, 208–28.

27. Alroey notes that many workers' connection to the New Yishuv was created and gradually strengthened when membership in national organizations proved useful and necessary to attain a job and keep it. Early twentieth-century Palestinian Zionist organizations, however, had few patronage opportunities to offer, and one must consider other methods that developed immigrants' connections to the New Yishuv. Gur Alroey, "'Olim' or Immigrants: The Jewish Migration to Palestine in the Early Twentieth Century" (Lecture, Arizona State University, Tempe, February 5, 2006).

28. On Smilansky and Luidor and their works, see Peleg, "Heroic Conduct," 38–40; Gershon Shaked, *ha-Siporet ha-'Ivrit, 1880–1980* (Tel Aviv: ha-Kibutz ha-Me'uhad, 1977–98), 2:44–55, 2:59–61; others view Smilansky and Luidor's work as exemplary; cf. Gluzman, *ha-Guf ha-Tzioni*, 26, 149, 185; Schwartz, *Zionist Paradox*, 97–141.

29. For more on Agnon, Arieli, Brenner, Reuveni, and early twentieth-century Hebrew literature, see Shaked, *ha-Siporet ha-'Ivrit*, 2:17–33.

30. Michelle Campos, *Ottoman Brothers: Muslims, Christians, and Jews in Early Twentieth Century Palestine* (Stanford, CA: Stanford University Press, 2011).

31. On the Palestinian Sephardic proponents of "inclusivist Zionism," see Abigail Jacobson, *From Empire to Empire: Jerusalem between Ottoman and British Rule* (Syracuse, NY: Syracuse University Press, 2011), 82–116; Campos, *Ottoman Brothers*, 197–223.

32. On the Nabi Musa riots, see Jacobson, *From Empire to Empire*, 172–77.

33. For background on Palestinian Jews' conscription into the Ottoman military during World War I and their difficult wartime experiences, see Glenda Abramson, "'Perhaps We'll Meet Again'—Moshe Sharett's Military Service," *Israel Studies* 20, no. 3 (Fall 2015): 18–38; Glenda Abramson," Haim Nahmias and the Labour Battalions: A Diary of Two Years in the First World War," *Jewish History and Culture* 14, no. 1 (2013): 18–32.

34. Gila Ramraz-Ra'ukh, *L. A. Arieli (Orlof): hayyav ve-yetzirato* (Tel Aviv: Papirus, 1992), 160; Levi Aryeh Arieli, "Yeshimon," *ha-Adamah* 1, no. 3 (Tishrei-Adar 1920): 253–73; Levi Aryeh Arieli, "Yeshimon," *ha-Adamah* 1, no. 7 (Iyar 1920): 2–17; Levi Aryeh Arieli, "Yeshimon," in *Dapim [kovetz rishon]*, ed. Dov Kimhi (Jerusalem: Defus Y. Helperin, 1922), 4–18; Arieli, *Kitve L. A. Arieli*, 1:221–73.

35. This strategy, which is frequently employed in talush literature, has been more fully explored in relationship to the Victorian novel. See D. A. Miller, *The Novel and the Police* (Berkeley: University of California Press, 1988).

36. Tzemah, "Min ve-ofi le'umi," 371; for additional readings of *Yeshimon*, see Shaked, *ha-Siporet ha-'Ivrit*, 2:124–25; Yehoshu'a Bar-Yosef, "bi-Mekom hemdat libi . . . al 'Yeshimon' me-et L. A. Arieli," *ba-Mahaneh*, November 23, 1979, 35–36; Ramraz-Ra'ukh, *L. A. Arieli*, 145–60; Philip Hollander, "Between Decadence and Rebirth: The Fiction of Levi Aryeh Arieli" (PhD diss., Columbia University, 2004), 281–378; Glenda Abramson, *Hebrew Writing of the First World War* (London: Valentine-Mitchell, 2008), 298–328.

37. Arieli, *Kitve L. A. Arieli*, 1:221.

38. Arieli, *Kitve L. A. Arieli*, 1:222.

39. As is common throughout Western literature, this text sees a correspondence between sexual dominance and political dominance with one penetrated considered to have abdicated

power. For more on this frequent connection and its Greek origins, see Leo Bersani, "Is the Rectum a Grave?" in *Is the Rectum a Grave? and Other Essays* (Chicago: University of Chicago Press, 2010), 3–30.

40. Arieli, *Kitve L. A. Arieli*, 1:224.

41. Arieli, *Kitve L. A. Arieli*, 1:230.

42. Arieli, *Kitve L. A. Arieli*, 1:238. For analysis of dreams in *Yeshimon*, see Hollander, "Between Decadence and Rebirth," 302–8.

43. This literary strategy is known as the technique of meetings. For more on it, see Shaked, *Omanut ha-sipur shel Agnon* (Tel Aviv: Sifriyat ha-Poʻalim, 1973), 57.

44. Arieli, *Kitve L. A. Arieli*, 1:247.

45. Dan Miron, *The Image of the Shtetl and Other Studies of Modern Jewish Literary Imagination* (Syracuse, NY: Syracuse University Press, 2000), 116.

46. For more on Arabs' idealization in early twentieth-century Hebrew thought and literature, see Frankel, "The 'Yizkor' Book of 1911: A Note on National Myths in the Second Aliya," in *Crisis, Revolution, and Russian Jews* (New York: Cambridge University Press, 2009), 189–90; Yaron Peleg, *Orientalism and the Hebrew Imagination* (Ithaca, NY: Cornell University Press, 2005).

47. Arieli, *Kitve L. A. Arieli*, 1:243.

48. Arieli, *Kitve L. A. Arieli*, 1:243.

49. Arieli, *Kitve L. A. Arieli*, 1:263.

50. Tzemah, "Min ve-ofi leʼumi," 375.

51. Arieli, *Kitve L. A. Arieli*, 1:249.

52. Arieli, *Kitve L. A. Arieli*, 1:260.

53. Arieli, *Kitve L. A. Arieli*, 1:265–66.

54. For more on the frequent feminization of the nation as a woman, especially a wife, mother, or maiden, within various national discourses, see Mosse, *Nationalism and Sexualities*, 90–97; Pinsker, "Imagining the Beloved," 110–13.

55. Arieli, *Kitve L. A. Arieli*, 1:266–67.

56. Arieli, *Kitve L. A. Arieli*, 1:267.

57. Arieli, *Kitve L. A. Arieli*, 1:268.

58. Arieli, *Kitve L. A. Arieli*, 1:273.

59. On this gay Hebrew poet, Mordechai Langer, and his poetry, see Shaun Halper, "Mordechai Langer (1894–1943) and the Birth of the Modern Jewish Homosexual" (PhD diss., University of California, Berkeley, 2013), 112–89.

5

SELF-EVALUATIVE MASCULINITY'S INTERWAR APEX AND ECLIPSE

Our people is formed by Exile and is sick. As it walks, it stumbles.
Seven times it falls and gets back on its feet. It is for us to raise it up.
Its willpower is weakening—it must be strengthened. Let us become stronger.
Israel has no Messiah—let us develop the strength to live without the Messiah.

—Yosef Hayyim Brenner, "Ba-ʿitonut uva-sifrut"
(In the newspapers and literature)

Reuveni and ʿAd-Yerushalayim's Reception

When Aharon Reuveni arrived in Palestine in 1910, he knew little Hebrew and had limited literary experience. Nonetheless, the merit of his Yiddish prose and its ability to encapsulate Palestinian Jewish life impressed readers who sought out ways to cultivate his talents and incorporate his work into the developing Palestinian Hebrew literary canon.[1] Looking to reward the confidence Palestinian Hebrew writers had in him and make good on the claim that he was "a powerful new talent who promises a great deal," Reuveni worked hard developing his literary style.[2] His efforts culminated with the publication of ʿAd-Yerushalayim (Till Jerusalem). He and the novelistic trilogy soon won a rave review: "He is one of the important prose writers in Hebrew literature. He powerfully and realistically portrays Palestinian life during wartime. His novel Shamot [Devastation] constitutes one of Hebrew literature's best works."[3] Reuveni seemed to have met the Palestinian Hebrew literary community's expectations and rewarded its support.

More than eighty years later, Hebrew literary critics widely concur with this earlier evaluation. By the late 1960s, the influential literary scholar Dan

Miron and the seminal poet Natan Zakh were penning criticism delving into the trilogy's merits; Zakh boldly proclaimed that it had "no second in its panoramic character . . . in the whole of Hebrew literature."[4] Yigal Schwartz's masterful 1993 study *Li-heyot ke-de li-heyot* (To live to live) further cemented Reuveni's literary status.

This triumphant recounting of Reuveni's embrace by the Hebrew literary community belies a more complex reality. From the mid-1920s until the mid-1950s, Hebrew readers, by and large, ignored him.[5] Meanwhile, the individuals who actually read *Till Jerusalem* found its distant and aloof narration at odds with the zeitgeist and its provocative portrayal of figures, based on early twentieth-century Palestinian Zionist settlers, brutal and unsympathetic.[6]

Gradualism, Depiction of Gender and Sexuality, and Reuveni's Marginalization

Reuveni's literary reception alerts one to how, even as the literary works of Self-Evaluative masculinity's proponents were reaching new aesthetic heights, a wedge was developing between them and wider circles within the Palestinian Jewish community. By the late 1910s, a new horizon of expectations, at odds with Self-Evaluative masculinity's tenets, had started entrenching itself. While death, deprivation, and hardship characterized wartime Palestinian Jewish life, a series of events had nonetheless transformed how many Palestinian Jews viewed the Zionist project. The Jewish Legion's establishment by the British in August 1917 kicked off this perceptual shift, with prominent Zionists excitedly proclaiming it a critical step toward statehood and the cessation of Jewish exilic suffering.[7] The Balfour Declaration, the Bolshevik Revolution, World War I's conclusion, repatriation of exiled Palestinian Jews, reopening of Jewish immigration to Palestine, postwar reconstruction, and the planned British Mandate for Palestine led growing numbers of Zionists to believe that a new era in Jewish history was unfolding.

In contrast with giddily exuberant potential readers, Reuveni stayed true to the sober gradualist worldview he shared with Self-Evaluative masculinity's other proponents.[8] Indeed, Reuveni avoided wartime deportation and brutal army service by adopting Ottoman citizenship and paying a costly twenty-five gold Napoleon military substitution tax.[9] Nonetheless, he endured existential uncertainty, hunger, and privation during the war.

This experience influenced his mind-set during composition of his trilogy, as an article published in June 1918 effectively conveys. The article does make begrudging reference to the Balfour Declaration's groundbreaking character.[10] Yet Reuveni's juxtaposition of comic description of the ceremonial laying of the Hebrew University's cornerstone with somber reference to thousands of Jewish deaths in Ukrainian pogroms and the Ottoman authorities' ongoing wartime execution of Palestinian Jews for spying and desertion points to his belief that things remained much as they were before. He desired to temper the exhilaration so many Zionists were displaying: "What has been accomplished constitutes only one aspect of the coin; it is possible to say the external, the external political aspect. The truth is that the work is difficult, and it will extend for years and years. The work of returning an exiled nation and reestablishing it in the land stands before us in full force."[11] For Zionism to truly accomplish its mission, Palestinian Jews needed to transform themselves from within. Outside powers' actions could not promote internal psychological change and the Palestinian Jewish community needed to take up this task.

While Reuveni composed his trilogy, he saw his warning about the need for psychological change going unheeded: "During 1919 and 1920, Zionist hopes soared. It appeared as though all the dreams of Jewish independence in Palestine were on the verge of immediate realization."[12] Then, as he neared completion of the trilogy's third novel, external events took him from his desk to Jerusalem's streets and reinforced his earlier message's importance.[13] Muslim celebrants from throughout Palestine traditionally commemorated the Prophet Moses with a weeklong festival. In April 1920, the festival took on a distinctly political character. Palestinian nationalist leaders employed it to galvanize participants in opposition to Zionism and British support for it. After these leaders spoke in Jerusalem, the festival descended into violent riots and four days of bloodshed in the Old City and its environs. Six Jews died, hundreds were wounded, and extensive material damage resulted.[14]

A British army battalion thwarted Reuveni's attempt to join other Jews defending their vulnerable brethren trapped within the Old City walls. They, thereby, prevented him from beholding the worst perpetrated atrocities. Nonetheless, he witnessed an important historic event that revealed the limited nature of British support and the Palestinian nationalist movement's increasingly organized opposition to Zionism.[15] Rather than heralding a messianic age, the British Occupied Enemy Territory Administration's leaders sympathized with Palestinian national interests, and willingly promoted them by allowing Palestinian leaders to instigate violence against Jerusalem's Jewish community. Consequently, the Palestinian Jewish community began to reevaluate its situation vis-à-vis the British and the indigenous Palestinian population. Reuveni's article "Anu Ma'ashimim" (We accuse) voiced the evolving consensus among gradualists—mistrust of British authority, belief in the need for political advocacy to ensure British advancement of Zionist aims, and a clear preference for independent Jewish action for promotion of the Palestinian Zionist agenda.[16] Reuveni would subsequently travel to London as part of a three-man delegation sent by the Jerusalem City Council to report to the British government on the Nabi Musa riots, demand an end to the Occupied Enemy Territory Administration, and seek compensation for the riots' victims.

As Reuveni retrospectively observed, the Nabi Musa riots proved pivotal to his trilogy's ultimate form. Not only did they lead him to abandon his initial plan to compose a hexalogy, but they also pushed him to more carefully formulate his literary response to events he saw paralleling the Palestinian Jewish community's wartime experience. Reuveni rejected the widespread use of the term *riots* to describe them. He considered the word *pogrom* better able to capture the situation the Palestinian Jewish community faced.[17] First and foremost, the term evoked Jewish life in the Diaspora and its use in the Palestinian context stressed the shared nature of Palestinian and diasporic Jewish experience. Rather than liberating Jewish men from psychic fragmentation and social institutions' fragile and temporary nature, Palestinian Jewish life presented them to Jewish men as fundamental and unavoidable characteristics of Jewish modernity.

Reuveni did not embrace the common pogrom discourse portrayal of Jewish men as innocent victims hectored by forces beyond their control.[18] Instead, he turned to pogrom allusions and wartime events' depiction to direct attention to the psychological issues he saw preventing the Palestinian Jewish community and its male members from realizing their goals. He looked to arouse feelings of masculine shame and humiliation among Palestinian male readers and compel them to address internal impediments preventing them from achieving personal and communal goals. To evoke these feelings, voice the psychological problems that he saw birthing them, and promote Self-Evaluative masculine norms' collective adoption as the best way to combat them and promote a nationalist agenda, Reuveni, like other Self-Evaluative writers, turned to representations of gender and sexuality. Adoption of these norms, Reuveni believed, constituted a way for Jewish men to make Palestine Jewish life fundamentally different and arguably better than its diasporic alternative.

Through exploration of seemingly decadent depictions of Jewish gender and sexuality in *Till Jerusalem* that likely contributed to its failure to achieve a significant initial readership, this chapter will advance three principle assertions. First, it claims that Self-Evaluative masculinity's proponents were engaged with the political here and now. As analysis of Reuveni's trilogy demonstrates, this led them to vigorously incorporate arguably decadent gender and sexual representations into their writing. Their presence in their works reflects their intimate familiarity with similar depictions found in European literature but should not be interpreted as evidence of exclusively aesthetic motivations. Second, this chapter avers that Reuveni, like Self-Evaluative masculinity's other proponents, utilized questionably decadent gender and sexual representations to promote widespread adoption of gender and sexual norms he considered best able to assist Palestinian Jewish men in overcoming individual weakness and participating in the national community's gradual development. As part of this process, Reuveni promoted the Self-Evaluative Hebrew writer, who explores his psyche, chooses to combat the weaknesses he reveals, and acts to achieve individual and collective betterment. He presented him as an alternative to an increasingly prominent Zionist masculine ideal type that sidestepped the existence of personal deficiencies and promoted an invincible air. Following the Self-Evaluative Hebrew writer's lead, Reuveni believed, offered a better way for potential male readers to meet their needs and work toward realization of their long-term desires. Consequently, the trilogy's portrayal of gender and sexuality do not promote an openness to gender and sexual diversity. Finally, this chapter contends that the Self-Evaluative masculine ideal type and the seemingly decadent depictions of Jewish gender and sexuality its proponents employed for its advancement put them up against those who believed that East European Jewish male immigrants and their progeny could radically transform themselves and rapidly realize Zionist aims. Palestinian Jewish men, who looked to generate the perception that Palestinian and diasporic Jewish life were fundamentally different and thereby create such a reality, reimagined or rejected the literary work produced by Self-Evaluative masculinity's proponents. They did this, because they saw this literature and its assertion that communal development was a difficult and gradual process running counter to the self-perception they looked to propagate.

Decadence, European Hebrew Literature, and Jewish Nationalism

Widespread challenges to normative behavior characterized turn-of-the-century Europe, and decadent was a term frequently employed by contemporaries to describe this period of sexual anarchy when "men became women. Women became men. Gender and country were put in doubt."[19] While decadence can be defined as "the process of falling away or declining (from a prior state of excellence, vitality, prosperity, etc.); decay; impaired or deteriorated condition," the scholar Charles Bernheimer, drawing on Nietzsche's discussion of it, views it more as a constellation of different ideas and phenomena. These include decadence as something pathological that "disorganizes and fragments individuals and societies"; as a defining characteristic of modernity and most of humankind; as a repulsive femininity best kept at a distance; and as "an aesthetics of superficiality and artifice . . . [deploying] fetishistic strategies and emergent homosexual tropes."[20]

In an atmosphere of "changing historical and cultural paradigms," where innovative aesthetic and literary trends were spreading, European-based Hebrew writers engaged with decadence in its various permutations; this engagement drew them to decadent writers such as Oscar Wilde whose aesthetic approach to gender and sexuality's representation contributed to Hebrew modernism's emergence.[21] Thus, the appearance of the "effeminate 'dandy' male, the homosexual, the androgyne, the femme fatale and the masculinized women" in Hebrew literature owes a debt to Wilde and Russian Silver Age authors such as Fyodor Sologub (1863–1927) and Mikhail Kuzmin (1872–1936).[22]

Indeed, literary decadence's study can contribute to understanding of Hebrew modernism's emergence in Europe. Yet one needs to study it alongside decadence's other facets to effectively understand its influence on Hebrew modernism. Decadent thought forecast the fragmentation and dissolution of Jewish society and the demise of the pathological men who belonged to it. This assertion made early twentieth-century Hebrew writers deeply uncomfortable. Accordingly, even as they drew on elements of literary decadence, they distanced themselves from decadent thought.[23] Thus, despite acute interest in the stylistics of European decadence and Silver Age Russian symbolist writing, prominent Hebrew writers such as Brenner saw the need for literature "to directly involve itself in the existential issues the writer and his readers were facing."[24] This led them to advance "a masculine

ideal for the emerging Jewish (or 'Hebrew') national identity" capable of re-
futing the "imbrication of Jewishness, effeminacy, and sexual decadence."[25]

Decadence, Zionism, and the Palestinian Context

The issues and phenomena of decadence stimulate efforts to attain "a position outside of decadence that [will] enable one to judge it as such" with
"some mode of knowledge, some standard of ethics, [or] some conception
of health" necessary for its attainment.[26] Consequently, many Zionists
pointed to national affiliation and immigration to Palestine as ways to escape from decadence to health. The 1920 battle of Tel Hai was used to mark
out a new beginning indicating the transition from an exilic Jewish period
of abjection to a period of national revival; the idealized figure of the native-
born Palestinian Jewish male, or sabra, with his attractive appearance, his
physical rootedness in the land, and his moral character served as an exem-
plar of the emerging Palestinian Zionist community, wholly distinguishable from its purportedly outmoded and decadent diasporic predecessors.[27]

As previously noted, early twentieth-century Palestinian Hebrew literature offers few strong-bodied, healthy, and vigorous masculine figures for
emulation. On the contrary, even after 1920, one finds Self-Evaluative masculine works, such as *Yeshimon* and *Till Jerusalem*, featuring representations of Jewish gender and sexuality similar to those found in European fin
de siècle works of literary decadence.[28] Those promoting the figure of the
sabra and looking to immunize both individual Jews and the whole Jewish people against decadence viewed such works as a threat to their efforts
to create a new beginning for Jews in Palestine. Not only did these works
infer contemporary Palestinian Jewish life's similarity to earlier Jewish life,
both in Palestine and abroad, they presented psychic fragmentation and
social institutions' limitations as key aspects of Jewish modernity. Furthermore, they inhibited creation of a new reality through radical transformation of how Palestinian Jews, especially the young, perceived themselves.
Not only did such purportedly decadent depictions disturb mature Palestinian Hebrew readers involved in Jewish self-perception's transformation,
but they also proved especially difficult for youth socialized to sabra norms
to process. Thus, Palestinian Hebrew literary works written by important
proponents of Self-Evaluative masculinity such as Arieli and Reuveni were
misread, underappreciated, or ignored by critics in the 1920s through the
early 1950s.

Hebrew critics' discomfort with decadent motifs' presence in Palestinian Hebrew literature first found expression in the late Ottoman period with prominent critic Ya'akov Rabinowitz (1875–1948) chastising Arieli for their use in his story "ha-Na'ar Bunyah" (The youth Bunyah, 1912).[29] Yet Sh. Levitan's early review of Reuveni's trilogy points to increased discomfort with decadent motifs and imagery during the interwar period. Levitan felt that the trilogy's principle characters should voice "the spirit of their generation"; he chastised Reuveni for his decadent representations of sexuality and gender.[30] Reuveni overpopulated his trilogy with prostitutes and defamed the Old Yishuv's women when he portrayed one of them engaging in premarital sex. Furthermore, Levitan disapproved of Reuveni's representation of "unnatural" heterosexual relations, Turkish officers' homosexual proclivities, and the rape of Jewish soldiers in the Ottoman military—things that "make a bad impression."[31]

Despite current appreciation of Reuveni and Arieli's prose, these writers still retain a decadent label. Just as 'Adi Tzemah praises "Wasteland" in spite of his belief that Arieli was a Hebrew Otto Weininger, literary scholar Nili Sadan-Loebenstein extols Reuveni's fiction even though she sees it undergirded by a belief in the Zionist revolution's ultimate failure.[32]

Indeed, Reuveni viewed Jewish modernity as characterized by psychic fragmentation and unstable social institutions, an idea that Bernheimer links to decadence. Nonetheless, this chapter stresses that his classification and classification of other proponents of Self-Evaluative masculinity as decadent inhibits understanding of them and their work. They did not view themselves as decadent writers. On the contrary, this label was thrust on them by their political opponents to delegitimize them and their Zionist views. Acceptance of it severs them from their immediate cultural context and overlooks their enduring dedication to the Palestinian Zionist project. Self-Evaluative masculinity's proponents turned to fiction to offer a more sophisticated modern justification for Zionist action—one that acknowledged that Zionist aims could only be realized over the long term and that pinning one's hopes for improving Jewish lives on the emergence of a masculine ideal type wholly divorced from decadence proved illusory.

Jewish Masculinity and Decadent Hebrew Representation

Awareness of Hebrew literature's participation in broader efforts to create a new Jewish society proves integral to understanding purportedly decadent

Hebrew literary representations of gender and sexuality created in Pre-State Palestine. Like all incipient societies, the New Yishuv struggled with "the existential 'problem of order.'"[33] Solving this problem, as previously noted, required that the New Yishuv "encourag[e] people to act in certain ways, ways that facilitate[d] both individual development and group adaptation."[34] The advancement of masculine norms constituted one of the best ways to do this. Because the Palestinian Hebrew reading public, like its East European counterpart, looked to belles lettres for guidance, Palestinian Hebrew literature proved a valuable vehicle for masculine norms' promotion.[35]

The Jewish male's outsider status in the European modernization process led to his portrayal as a gentle and weak countertype associated with femininity and homosexuality. This characterization and its relationship to the difficult social, political, and economic conditions facing fin de siècle European Jewry seriously impacted Jewish men. Many of them, at least in their fantasy lives, looked to assume a more heroic male image and participate in individual and/or Jewish collective improvement. Consequently, Jewish male fantasies prove central to the fin de siècle creation of a Jewish national or Zionist imaginary working to unite Jewish men for the Jewish people's transformation into a sovereign Palestinian majority.[36]

While scholars of Jewish masculinity agree that efforts to transform masculinity played an important role in the State of Israel's ultimate creation, disagreement exists concerning the essence of the Zionist masculinity that took hold in Palestine and catalyzed individual and communal advance, as detailed above. Nonetheless, many scholars agree that "to create a heroic Jewish male image one must abandon the Jewish component and rely on the dominant culture's version of the heroic male. Jewish male heroes must be non-Jewish Jews."[37] Thus, some cultural critics posit that the Zionist masculinity central to the state-building enterprise centered on the Jewish male body's transformation to accord with European physical ideals; some assert the primacy of a Zionist masculinity grounded in mimicry of a "vengeful, violent . . . ideal Aryan male"; still others contend that the Zionist movement focused on valorizing an ideal male willing to sacrifice his life for the nation, similar to ideal male figures championed by various European nationalisms.[38]

As was the case with previously discussed Self-Evaluative masculine works, proper understanding of *Till Jerusalem* and decadent representation's role within it requires that one move beyond the binary approach to Jewish masculinity reflected in the various models mentioned above.[39] Debates concerning a variety of Zionist masculine forms, including many blending Jewish and non-Jewish elements, and which of them deserved primacy animated the Palestinian Jewish public sphere. Despite Zionist pioneers' efforts to restart Jewish history, many Palestinian Jewish men, especially immigrants, viewed it as impossible to realize the total masculine transformation implied by abovementioned Zionist masculine models and the sabra ideal. They recognized that the individual and collective vulnerability gendered feminine in Zionist discourse could be fought through "masculine" action, but it could never be fully transcended. Thus, they proved open to a soberer Zionist masculinity. Reuveni and his cohort looked to persuade these men to embrace Self-Evaluative masculinity, and they championed it in ongoing struggles among Palestinian Zionists concerning Zionist masculinity's proper form and the relationship between such a form and the Jewish nation's future character.

Reuveni, like Self-Evaluative masculinity's other promoters, opposed utopian masculine ideals that viewed radical individual transformation as feasible. Devotion to ideals grounded in bodily development, aggressive behavior, or readiness for self-sacrifice might boost individual self-confidence and produce a short-lived sense of self-transformation. Yet they proved less effective at mobilizing men to achieve the procreative, provisioning, and protective goals societies look to realize through masculine norms' imposition. Therefore, when Self-Evaluative Zionist masculinity's promoters turned to literature, they advanced it as more realizable and better suited to group aims than the masculine ideals they opposed.

Homosociality, introspection, and ongoing commitment to achievement of communally shared goals constitute key aspects of the Self-Evaluative masculine agenda Reuveni advances in *Till Jerusalem*. *Till Jerusalem* does not call on Zionist-affiliated Palestinian Jewish men to negate their earlier lives. Instead, it compels them to confront their sense of psychic fragmentation and their polymorphously perverse sexuality, recognize the need for collective action to achieve their goals, create or commit themselves to a viable plan of action, and embrace the pleasure inherent in working alongside Jewish men making similar efforts.[40] This masculinity involved taking responsibility for one's actions, ceasing to blame others for one's problems, and working to avoid antisocial behavior. Nothing about it necessitated an alteration of one's character. Rather than denying Jewishness, Self-Evaluative masculinity's collective embrace would transform it.

Till Jerusalem—Plot Summary and Associative Structure

be-Reshit ha-mevukhah (When confusion began), *ha-'Oniyot ha-ahronot* (The last ships), and *Shamot* (Devastation), *Till Jerusalem*'s three component novels, employ different novelistic forms, proceed at divergent paces, and focus on different protagonists. Nonetheless, through complex portrayal of Palestinian Jewish life during World War I, they together produce an important statement about Palestinian Jewish society.[41]

Although *When Confusion Began* focuses on the accountant Aharon Tzifrovitz and depicts the collapse of his life in Palestine, it revolves around the Jerusalem political journal *ha-Derekh* (The way), whose contributing writers and staff, including Tzifrovitz, constitute its primary characters. Tzifrovitz prepares to marry his fiancée and firmly root himself in the Jerusalem landscape on the eve of the war, but he cannot cope with war-provoked feelings of insecurity. Consequently, as he prepares to abandon Palestine, attention shifts to other staff members.

Like the fictional newspaper *The Plow* featured in Brenner's *mi-Kan umi-kan*, which is loosely based on the important labor newspaper *The Young Worker*, *The Way* resembles *The Unity*, the newspaper of Po'alei Tzion (Zion Workers) party. Therefore, one can view the paper and characters Hayyim Ram, Giv'oni, and Ben-Mattiyahu, who prove similar to Yitzhak Ben-Zvi, the State of Israel's second president, David Ben-Gurion, the State of Israel's first prime minister, and Labor Zionist leader Ya'akov Zerubavel (Vitkin) (1886–1967), as part of a veiled portrayal of actual events. Nonetheless, it proves more fruitful to view the paper and its staff as fictional elements employed to indirectly comment on the New Yishuv's social organization.

In *The Last Ships*, which opens following Tzifrovitz's departure from Palestine, the trilogy shifts its focus to Gedalyah Brenchuk, a staff writer at *The Way*. A misanthrope, he welcomes the Ottoman Empire's declaration of war and Jewish flight en masse from Jerusalem, because he believes, once disencumbered from social relations, he will become a more productive writer. Yet writer's block plagues him. He only overcomes it following participation in large-scale efforts to stem massive locust swarms that plagued Palestine in March 1915 and threatened the food supply. With his novel's completion, Brenchuk travels to Jaffa to board the last ship scheduled to depart Palestine. The Ottoman authorities, however, prevent his escape from Palestine and the harsh existential conditions it represents. After being

Fig. 5.1 Group picture of *ha-Ahdut* editorial board members, Jerusalem 1911. From right to left: sitting—Yitzhak Ben-Zvi, David Ben-Gurion, Yosef Hayyim Brenner; standing—Aharon Reuveni, Ya'akov Zerubavel. National Library of Israel. Photographs Collection.

beaten for draft evasion together with other escapist Jewish men, Brenchuk is released. He flees inland, and the novel concludes with his reacquisition of his lost manuscript.

Brenchuk appears in *Devastation*, the trilogy's concluding novel. Yet Me'ir Funk, a young worker, who fought the locusts with him, assumes center stage. *Devastation* pits him against his non-Zionist Jewish surroundings represented by Jerusalem's Nahalat Ya'akov neighborhood and Doberman House, where he resides. Employing members of the Doberman House–based Wetstein family to offer a panoramic portrait of these environs, the novel engages the possibility of Jewish social transformation. *Devastation* begins optimistically, but following Funk's unexpected arrest by Ottoman authorities, a series of events gradually undermines his self-confidence. After Funk marries Esther Wetstein and fathers a child, his surroundings slowly overwhelm him and prevent him from meeting Palestinian Jewish needs. Despite possession of the money necessary to pay the military substitution tax, Funk mobilizes and soon commits suicide.

Associative links connect the trilogy's three novels.[42] Therefore, identification of the trilogy's preferred form of masculinity requires analysis of all three novels and consideration of their interrelationship. While the trilogy can be viewed as a "thicket composed of the characters' psychology and the randomness of the circumstances that bring these characters to action," comparison of the seemingly separate plot lines taking place against a shared societal background offers a path through this covert.[43]

The following comparative analysis concentrates on four portrayed men—Funk, Tzifrovitz, Brenchuk, and Leyzer Wetstein—to demonstrate how Reuveni employs their failures to elucidate how Palestinian Jewish men could best meet their developing society's needs. First, through Funk's story, Reuveni rejects Zionist efforts to base their settlement project on a yet-to-emerge masculine ideal, parallel to the Nietzschean Übermensch, untroubled by psychic fragmentation. Next, through Tzifrovitz's portrayal, Reuveni voices the sense of psychic fragmentation and accompanying weakness that he saw troubling, either consciously or unconsciously, all Jewish male immigrants to Palestine. While other immigrant men marginalize Tzifrovitz to distance themselves from these feelings, Reuveni emphasizes the need for communal leaders, including writers, to avoid scapegoating. Instead, they need to address these feelings and develop strategies for working them through. In this way, Jewish men can better achieve their collective aims.[44] Leyzer Wetstein's narrative shifts attention to Palestinian Jewish men who do not find feelings of psychic fragmentation troubling enough that they will adhere to collective-oriented strategies for overcoming them. Reuveni marks such men as possessors of non-normative gender and sexuality who need to be placed outside communal boundaries until they change their behavior. Finally, through Brenchuk's narrative, Reuveni demonstrates how Palestinian Hebrew writers can become leaders and role models. They can use literature to express feelings of psychic fragmentation and weakness revealed through introspection and then point to how Palestinian Jewish men can advance their personal and collective agendas by addressing them and working with other Jewish men to overcome them. If Hebrew writers perform this critical social function, they can give meaning to their writing and their lives.

Skin-Deep Masculinity

Hebrew readers awaited the appearance of an idealized Palestinian Jewish male, whose attractive appearance, physical rootedness in the land, and moral character would herald Zionism's successful distancing of the Jewish people from diasporic decline.[45] Thus, Me'ir Funk, who embodies the body-centered Jewish masculine ideal type, captured their imagination. Long muscular arms, broad shoulders, and a calm, strong facial expression communicate his potential energy. His carpentry, "productive labor" distancing him from "parasitic" Jews critiqued in antisemitic discourse, does too.[46] Both his physique and productivity attract men and women. Consequently, his future wife, Esther, decides to sleep with him out of wedlock, and Tzipporah Blumenthal readily consents to an adulterous affair with him. Then, when he avenges the rape and murder of a vulnerable Jewish girl, he voices his power. Finally, when called to military service, Funk unhesitatingly enlists and appears to display his bravery.

Despite Funk's seeming exemplarity, Reuveni challenges those who would elevate him above other Jewish men and employ his life to illustrate a Jewish superman's emergence on Palestinian soil. Lacking self-control, Funk commits suicide and bequeaths state-building efforts to other Jewish men.[47] Rather than standing apart, his psychology unites him with other Palestinian Jewish men.[48] Exploration of this shared psychology elucidates what Reuveni sees as a key impediment to the New Yishuv's development.

The description of the Nahalat Ya'akov neighborhood and Doberman House that opens *Devastation* proves significant. In contrast with newly founded kibbutzim, the recently created city of Tel Aviv, and other Jerusalem neighborhoods, where members of the Hebrew literary and Zionist political circles reside, Nahalat Ya'akov does not embody the future. Instead, as in Brenner's contemporaneous novel *Breakdown and Bereavement* and Agnon's subsequent novel *Only Yesteryear*, this Old Yishuv neighborhood stands in for diasporic Jewish existence and the Jewish past. Thus, Funk's placement within this setting symbolically communicates Jewish men's ongoing confrontation with the diasporic past; description of the urinal and fecal stench enveloping Doberman House's courtyard voices Reuveni's belief in the perceivably flawed nature of this past. Consequently, by having Funk rent a room in Doberman House, Reuveni asserts that Palestinian Jewish immigrants cannot transcend their problematic past and the anarchic psychological elements tied to it. Immigrants like Funk maintain an insuperable psychic connection and even an attraction to this past, including its decadent elements. Confrontation with this past, rather than its repression, constitutes the best way of moving beyond its deleterious manifestations.

Indeed, Funk wants to move beyond his diasporic past's negative elements. Yet his decision to act in isolation and his lack of an appropriate plan cause him to fail. His physique and physical strength teach less about him than his social views. Inspired by the Russian Narodniks, whose late nineteenth-century commitment to the Russian peasantry he idealizes, Funk strives to cultivate the Jewish folk's pure spirit for social betterment.[49] Consequently, while living in the Wetstein family's home, he assumes responsibility for their development. Yet he never considers the feasibility of his approach. The sacrifices prove tremendous, he finds little satisfaction, and his dedication does not change the Wetsteins. Rather, his fiancée and her mother strive to mold him to meet traditional Jewish masculine standards. They push him to assume a religious lifestyle and study sacred texts. Aware that his social reform plan has failed, Funk does not know how to pivot.[50]

Funk's temporary imprisonment for suspected draft evasion further challenges his sense of self-worth and provokes the reemergence of deleterious and previously repressed psychic forces. Identifying with Jewish men who hid in cellars and under beds during Russian pogroms, Funk views himself as "an object denied individual will, given into the hands of the willful to do with as they please."[51] His state-building efforts and his ongoing struggle against objectification seem quixotic. While an early fantasy of death by hanging highlighted his fear of death and objectification, subsequent fantasies of being whipped, shot, and stabbed voice a masochistic desire for humiliation, suffering, and death.[52]

Rather than addressing his masochism's inhibiting effect, Funk perseveres in a life he finds increasingly restrictive. After Esther pays to temporarily defer his military service, he marries her out of a sense of obligation. Yet she does not attract him, and "her adherence to him was somewhat like a burden."[53] Even premarital sex does not draw them together. As Funk tersely puts it, "the awakening of the flesh and the flood of new life did not envelop him to the degree that it enveloped her."[54]

Despite their relationship's deadening nature, Funk possesses tremendous vitality harnessable for collective goals' realization. Adulterous sex reveals it: "His ego, the everyday one, that thinks and thinks, the one that maintains permissive and prohibitive standards, suddenly was cast down from the heights of its throne, it was canceled and it was as if it never was, and its place was taken by a savage force, that burst forth from the unknown depths, and this force was also him, Me'ir Funk, yet it was a completely different him."[55] The shattering of an ego grounded in outdated social values reveals a potentially new identity capable of making Me'ir feel alive. Indeed, his adultery arouses feelings of guilt and shame that make Funk uncomfortable. Nevertheless, a vital new identity grounded in transvalued Jewish values could dispel these feelings and counterbalance his passive masochistic tendencies and his feared repetition of past Diaspora events. Yet outside a social framework capable of reassuring Funk of his emergent identity's propriety, he fails to maintain its associated masculine standards.

Funk's confrontation with the Arab watchman Hadj Youssef reveals both temporary embrace of a new transvalued Jewish identity and the psychological issues preventing its ultimate adoption. Youssef's broad muscular body, dark skin, "primitive" Arab identity and emergent vitality mark him as a potential model of emulation for Funk.[56] Like Funk, his obedience to external authority leaves him feeling impotent and dissatisfied. He views the world as a desert, whose rewards others deny him. Yet he throws off his perception of himself as a harem eunuch and resolves to possess the naked Jewish female bodies he secretly observes.[57] Unhesitatingly embracing his submerged sense of masculine vitality, Youssef rapes and murders a Jewish girl. Furthermore, he proves ready to do it again. Elevated above the herd by his disregard for external authority, Youssef presents Funk, who is aware of his crime, with a manifestation of the vital superman that he yearns to become. Consequently, through confrontation with this consummate Arab Other, Funk achieves greater clarity about his character.[58]

Funk tries to avoid confrontation with Youssef, but he cannot conscience his amoral behavior. The vitalistic Nietzschean model Youssef personifies disgusts him. Consequently, when a suspicious Youssef attacks and beats him, Funk fights back and emerges victorious. In doing so, Funk embraces a new transvalued Jewish identity that combines a vitality previously engaged for perceivably unconscionable acts with assertion of basic moral standards.

Unable to comprehend the significance of his momentary integration of vital experience into a new moral framework, an isolated Funk steps back from establishment of new Jewish standards. He judges himself a murderer, in accordance with extant Jewish moral standards, and punishes himself by disengaging his vital core. Accordingly, his dissatisfaction with his banal existence festers. Even military mobilization does not liberate him from it. Fearful that he will prostitute himself to Ottoman officers, like other young Jewish men, Me'ir commits suicide. Rather than bettering the Wetsteins' lives and constructing a new Zionist society, Funk's unaddressed sadomasochism leads him to abandon his wife and newborn child, whose ability to fend for themselves proves doubtful. Consequently, Funk fails to embody an elevated form of Jewish masculinity. On the contrary, he betrays a troubled Jewish masculinity similar to the troubled masculinity voiced by the Jewish watchman Shmaryahu Fogel in *Allah Karim!* Just as Arieli relies on Fogel's assisted suicide to shift his readers' attention to other forms of Jewish masculinity, Reuveni makes use of Funk's suicide to push his readers towards consideration of the trilogy's other male characters and Self-Evaluative masculinity as the most productive form of Zionist masculinity.

Blaming the Victim: Aharon Tzifrovitz and Stillborn Zionist Community

Besides unduly elevating Funk, literary critics have unnecessarily denigrated Aharon Tzifrovitz.[59] By concentrating on these characters' differences and overlooking their fundamental similarity, critics have come to view Tzifrovitz as a degenerate figure incapable of effective Zionist involvement. Consequently, they fail to note that Reuveni introduces this character to critique Zionist leaders for their failure to develop a national consciousness capable of bringing together diverse elements for pursuit of shared aims.[60]

Zionists had little tangible political power in late Ottoman Palestine. Nonetheless, the persuasive power wielded by Palestinian Hebrew literature and journalism endowed these institutions with the ability to shape an effective response to the crises the New Yishuv faced following World War I's outbreak. Yet the trilogy's allusion to a female Jerusalem's rape by the Ottoman Empire personified as a man points to their failure to provide such a response. Furthermore, it assigns blame to the political leadership, embodied by those united around the Jerusalem political journal *The Way*, for this failure.

As the New Yishuv coalesced in the interstices between European and Ottoman power, its self-appointed leaders, blind to potential dangers and extant possibilities, failed to elaborate and effectively promote viable norms for a unifying national consciousness.[61] As Tzifrovitz notes, *The Way*'s leading figures "did everything like they did it in Vilna or Kiev ten years earlier. Nothing in them changed, except that their skin got thicker."[62] Palestinian conditions did not mimic those faced by Russian Jewish politicians during the 1905 Russian Revolution, when mass followings could be easily mustered. Nonetheless, *The Way*'s leading figures prove increasingly insensitive to others' feelings and needs. They stubbornly forgo opportunities for greater self-knowledge and development of more effective group mobilization strategies.

Tzifrovitz's emigration from Palestine has been marshaled to demonstrate his flawed character. Yet, less judgmentally, one can view him as a critical but realistic reflection of the type of individual that the trilogy looked to mobilize for early twentieth-century Palestinian Zionist aims' realization.[63] Tzifrovitz's immigration to Palestine and his affiliation with *The Way* indicate an incipient connection to the Palestinian Zionist project, akin to the one Funk maintains, as well as a readiness to work with other men for its realization. Indeed, Tzifrovitz's advanced age (thirty-five years old), balding head, limited physical strength, hypochondria, and erotic timidity differentiate him from Funk and evoke the *talush* and the schlemiel, but these differences prove superficial.

Tzifrovitz and other Palestinian Zionist figures, including Funk, could be viewed as *tlushim* searching for rootedness in Palestine. Yet uprooted figures emerge from the Jewish intelligentsia's ranks, and Tzifrovitz and Funk lack the intellectual and social independence that typify them.[64] Instead of producing ideas or art that would encourage intricate portrayal of his unique and expansive interiority, Tzifrovitz searches for ideas and art to consume. Thus, he devoutly reads the leading contemporary Hebrew intellectual journal *ha-Shiloah*, and looks to develop social ties with the writers of *The Way*, whom he idolizes. Furthermore, Tzifrovitz lacks grandiose aspirations. His primary goals are a stable livelihood, a home, and a wife with whom to share them. His accounting job and his engagement show him working to achieve these goals. Rather than undermining his Zionist commitment, these banal goals push him to more active political involvement in hopes of strengthening his economic position and his erotic ties.[65]

A follower, Tzifrovitz, like Funk, represents the Jewish masses that the Zionist avant-garde needs to mobilize for its aims' realization. This avant-garde's failure to effectively mobilize Jewish men to its cause constitutes its primary shortcoming, and it underlies the Yishuv's failed wartime response detailed in *Till Jerusalem*. Tzifrovitz allies himself with *The Way*'s intellectuals, because he is literally searching for "the way" to realize his personal aims. Yet these intellectuals completely dismiss him, preferring to obscure their similarities to him. Consequently, rather than asserting normative masculine standards intended to advance communal objectives, they traffic in standards that belittle Tzifrovitz and others like him and push them away from community-building efforts.

Megalomaniacally viewing themselves as the inchoate New Yishuv's principle policy makers, Ram and Giv'oni unilaterally center the Yishuv's response to war on full adoption of Ottoman citizenship. Worried about their and their families' well-being, however, immigrant Jews see it as prudent to maintain loyalty to their original countries, which provide them with extraterritorial protection, and hesitate to fully renounce previous affiliations. Nonetheless, Ram and Giv'oni fail to address their concerns. The perceived strategic value of Ottoman citizenship blinds them. They never consider the perspective of their policy's potential victims. Such consideration requires introspection and confrontation with long-suppressed feelings of weakness and doubt like those felt by ordinary Yishuv men. Yet it can help Ram and Giv'oni explain why no other option exists—something that can assist their position in achieving a privileged place in the Yishuv's discussion of the general interest.

Ram and other purported Zionist leaders' failure to effectively communicate their ideas and persuade their audience explains their mobilization failure: "Ram's words didn't disperse his doubts' clouds. That Ram and other members of *The Way* were prepared to cast down their lives for their ideals wasn't a surprise to him. They'd surely done that their whole lives. They took it upon themselves. And yet it wasn't very consoling. He couldn't and didn't want to take part in public matters. He didn't desire to sacrifice himself and he didn't demand that others sacrifice themselves for him. His only desire was that they'd allow him to live in peace. He didn't demand anything more. And as it concerned Manyah . . . "[66] Seeing no connection between the self-sacrificial masculine norm Ram asserts and a healthy sexual relationship with his fiancée, Manyah, that he sees as a lynchpin of a better life, Tzifrovitz dismisses Ram and the position he asserts. Thus, Ram fails to advance new masculine norms, even those demanding less draconian forms of sacrifice, among uncertain and sexually reticent men, like Tzifrovitz, who find action difficult. As Reuveni recognizes, clarification of the type of future such norms could make possible and the reasonable nature of the demands they would place on Yishuv men could have altered the future.

Gender, Sexuality, and Novelistic Assertion
of Communal Boundaries

Although Reuveni believed that individual human weakness was an insurmountable aspect of modern life, he considered the Yishuv capable of realizing its goals through imposition of new normative standards that addressed this weakness and could pave the way toward their achievement. Through presentation of Tzifrovitz and Funk's failure to achieve their individual and collective aims due to personal weakness, Reuveni looked to make readers who were ashamed by their own repeated failures aware of just how ubiquitous personal weakness made such failure. In contrast with Tzifrovitz and Funk, who conceal their feelings of weakness and shame and allow themselves to be paralyzed and defeated by them, Yishuv men could confront and transcend such feelings. This would prepare them to undertake collective action that could better their lives and the lives of others.

Interested in promoting coordinated efforts that would aid individuals in succeeding at things they had failed at in isolation, Reuveni worked to redefine what constituted shameful behavior. One's inability to achieve one's long-term goals was not something to be ashamed about. Rather, failure to struggle against individual and collective Jewish weakness and pursue long-term goals was shameful. This redefinition, he believed, could best advance collective aims. Furthermore, independent of long-term goals, this redefinition offered those struggling against Jewish weakness an esprit de corps through association with others also struggling against it and separation from those embracing it—something that endowed their lives with greater meaning and pleasure.

To convey a new standard of virtue grounded in shameful behavior's redefinition and promote its adoption by readers, Reuveni links reticence to struggle against individual and collective Jewish weakness with negative representations of homosexuality and effeminacy. He does this through the way he crafts the figure of Leyzer Wetstein. To understand how this works, one must remember that Reuveni did not believe that a "healthy" masculine New Hebrew wholly free of perceived decadent attitudes and behaviors existed. Therefore, as in *Yeshimon*, homosexuality and heterosexuality function as points on a continuum charting the ways that men relate one to another, and in the absence of an agreed-upon definition of homosexuality, every Jewish male, whether fictional or real, becomes a potential addition to the stigmatized homosexual category. With contemporary Jewish men, by and large, maintaining an internalized fear of such categorization, the association of the term *homosexual* with certain behaviors and the stigmatization of their fictional practitioners had the power to compel real men to cease partaking in these behaviors. Thus, Reuveni's interest in promoting individual and collective struggles against Jewish weakness leads him to mark avoidance of introspection and the unwillingness to struggle against Jewish weakness as key features of "homosexuality" and engagement in these behaviors as "heterosexual." If Jewish men do not engage in these behaviors, they are placed at the stigmatized margins far from healthy male Zionists, and if they do, they are accepted as heterosexual equals. Consequently, social pressure ostracizes those like Leyzer who shirk such behavior and pressures men like Funk and Tzifrovitz to adopt these behaviors and advance individual and collective aims.

Despite their differences, Funk, Tzifrovitz, and Brenchuk sense feelings of weakness like those felt by Leyzer. Nonetheless, their struggles against them, as well as accompanying feelings of guilt and shame, differentiate them from Leyzer, who guiltlessly and shamelessly embraces his weakness. Leyzer's lack of empathy and identification with others underlies his behavior. As his scornful attitude to his aged grandfather Zalman, who symbolizes the Old Yishuv's former moral and social vigor, communicates, Leyzer senses little connection to this community. Similarly, he does not exhibit loyalty to the New Yishuv or the Ottoman Empire either. Therefore, when looking to lighten the burden of Ottoman military service, he entertains his superiors by sadistically caricaturing his weak and oppressed fellow soldiers.[67]

Because Leyzer's social disconnection and disregard for others' opinions and needs typify his character and prevent him from feeling shame, guilt, or weakness, the trilogy stigmatizes these characteristics through graphic portrayal of his homosexuality and effeminacy. Leyzer's flirtatious speech and his hand and facial gestures, which resemble those of a female Arab prostitute, speak to his effeminacy and communicate that his engagement in anal sex with his male superiors is consensual and a reflection of his powerful homosexual desire. Only when frequent intercourse produces syphilitic sores requiring medical intervention does Leyzer desert. While his wounds heal, Leyzer retains his earlier mannerisms and turns to women to satisfy his sexual needs. He, nonetheless, retains a desire for sexual domination and his girlfriend Rosa soon finds his effeminacy abhorrent. Yet this does not faze him, and Leyzer merely turns to another woman to engage his fantasies of anal sex with Ottoman officers.[68]

Leyzer's combination of effeminacy and homosexuality with cravenness and disloyalty promotes a negative Jewish male image similar to the one racial antisemites advanced as a countertype to "healthy" national manhood. Yet *Till Jerusalem* does not portray Leyzer's identity as a manifestation of his Jewish essence.[69] Self-Evaluative masculinity's promoters, who were aware of the antisemitic image of the Jew, challenged such essentialism. They argued that integration into a social framework promoting healthy norms could even transform somebody as loathsome as Leyzer. No Jew was doomed to degeneracy and suffering.

Toward Engaged Literature—Introspection, Performative Identity, Homosociality

Reuveni asserts the need for Hebrew writers to accomplish an important task that politicians such as those who work for *The Way* did not undertake. They need to develop intimate mutual relations between Palestinian Zionists that will promote the type of collective action absent from the New Yishuv's wartime response. Yet Hebrew writers needed to abandon autonomous conceptions of art to achieve this. Rather than employing art for escape, Hebrew writers needed to use it to promote self-knowledge, the creation of pleasurable and productive homosocial relations, and collective action.[70]

While critics assert that Reuveni based Brenchuk on himself, Brenchuk's biographical similarity to Reuveni, as well as Brenner, should not distract readers from the critical distance employed in Brenchuk's depiction.[71] Through portrayal of Brenchuk, a skilled writer whose social limitations prevent him from successfully moving beyond autonomous art and instead lead him toward homosexuality, Reuveni elucidates his own engaged aesthetics. Only through production of literature advancing gender and sexual norms, he argued, would the Yishuv succeed.

Brenchuk, in contrast with Tzifrovitz and Funk, possesses a keen intellect and sharp observational and analytical skills. Thus, he perceptively notes "that the line that separated him and Tzifrovitz was a very thin line— so thin that it frequently was completely erased and proved invisible to the eye."[72] Yet he neither addresses this similarity's social significance nor makes use of his intellect or his observational and analytical skills to better himself or the collective. Instead, judging himself against history's Nietzschean great men, Brenchuk finds his and Tzifrovitz's weakness shameful.

To avoid such painful awareness, he creates a seemingly autonomous art that produces reassuring feelings of vitality. Eventually, this art becomes a hard and insulating shell employed to protect him from seemingly threatening relationships and external stimuli.[73]

Unexpectedly, following the Ottoman declaration of war, Brenchuk's isolation and resultant writer's block force him to confront the bankruptcy of his escapist aesthetics. His stalled writing becomes like a Sisyphean boulder "used to pave a wide smooth path that neither departed nor led to a settlement. An indistinct path—flat, wide, dead, in the middle of the wasteland."[74] Brenchuk's writing does not provide a starting point, a destination, or a compelling reason to travel the path it helps readers perceive. Hence, it serves nobody. Nonetheless, the metaphor hints that Hebrew literature could serve its readers. Production of a wide path through the wilderness could provide everyday Palestinian Jews with a way to meaningfully respond to their travails and move together toward their goals' fulfillment. Embrace of such a literary approach, however, requires that Brenchuk remove his protective shell and experience life.

When Brenchuk exposes himself, he attains increased self-knowledge that pushes him toward a new life and new aesthetics: "Inside the peel sat a different man, simple and small, and seemingly composed of mercury. Truthfully it was not a man at all; it was scattered drops of mercury that rolled around without any resting place, separating and scattering in all directions before again meeting and joining into one body of living trembling silver."[75] Here, Brenchuk painfully confronts his fractured sense of self. Yet this confrontation reveals a vital and infinitely malleable interior world that can be harnessed for individual and communal betterment. Acting like a "body of living trembling silver," Brenchuk can overcome feelings of stagnancy. To do so, however, he needs to first accept his and fellow Yishuv members' limitations.

When massive locust swarms hit Palestine, the resulting crisis advances Brenchuk's thinking about Yishuv members' limitations. Instead of utilizing the eighth plague wrought by God on the pharaoh or the plague of locusts used to voice God's wrath in Joel 2 to comprehend the situation, Brenchuk employs rational thought to critically examine it. He investigates the locust's physiognomy. Its vitality and determinedness strike him and get him thinking about the Yishuv. Brenchuk previously scorned run-of-the-mill people incapable of elevating themselves above the crowd, but he now reconsiders this view. Despite their tiny intellects and individual vulnerability, locusts' coordinated efforts make them nearly unstoppable. Similarly, if a national community's affiliates disregarded personal limitations and worked toward a common goal's realization, they could accomplish even daunting tasks.

Building on his insight, Brenchuk departs Jerusalem to join coordinated efforts to combat the locusts' spread. Through this work, he meets Funk. The men's shared commitment to the crisis-stricken Yishuv sparks mutual admiration and feelings of physical attraction that draw them together. Rather than devolving into Leyzer-like asocial behavior, however, Brenchuk and Funk's mutual attraction enhances their relationship, strengthens their resolve, and pushes them to improve communal conditions together. They spend weeks digging pits, where the locust larvae are pushed and buried alive, but the physically taxing labor does not faze them. Instead, their time together proves to be one of their lives' most pleasurable periods: "Nothing happened, nothing out of the ordinary. Nevertheless, that day shined in their memory like a bright ray of light amid the remaining gray days of the year."[76] Brenchuk's experience reveals that even when confronting difficult conditions, a shared path and a common destination offer men a way of transcending feelings of stagnancy. Furthermore, in such a situation, anxieties about the future flee the mind.

Brenchuk fails to realize his literary potential when he gravitates from healthy heterosexuality toward deviant homosexuality. Absent promulgated masculine heterosexual norms or like-minded Jewish men's presence, he befriends the Viennese Jewish bank clerk Anselmus Mayer. As a result, he squanders the "feeling of great wealth [that] beat in his heart" following participation in collective survival efforts and does not voice important insights he derived from them.[77] Instead, he reverts to his earlier aesthetics, and the trilogy ends with the two men's homosexually tinged relationship intact—something that hints at an ominous future.

Mayer fails to push Brenchuk toward self-improvement or participation in collective efforts. On the contrary, he pushes him to inaction and embrace of masochistic pleasure.[78] Suffering from writer's block, Brenchuk's self-esteem plummets. He views himself as a physically repulsive figure lacking cultured charm and sexual magnetism. At this moment, he encounters Mayer. His superficial human warmth, masculine charisma, and simple intellectual curiosity attract Brenchuk and he looks to Mayer to buoy him. Yet rather than looking inward and informing his friend that they share similar deficiencies best addressed through collective improvement efforts, Mayer basks in Brenchuk's adulation and projects his feelings of weakness onto him. Furthermore, he takes sadistic pleasure in critiquing Brenchuk's deficiencies. Aware of Brenchuk's concealment of sexual insecurities behind Victorian sexual mores, Mayer sets him up with women to watch him squirm. Similarly, rather than helping Brenchuk cope with his sense of physical repulsiveness, Mayer enjoys repeating hurtful comments made about his appearance. Yet just as a "frozen wanderer" enjoys "being showered by warm water," Brenchuk derives masochistic pleasure from Mayer's company and cannot stay away from him.[79]

Nonetheless, Brenchuk remains uncomfortable with the sadomasochistic nature of their relationship. Mayer demands that Brenchuk uphold his misogynistic and hedonistic standards to gain his approval and love, but Brenchuk proves reticent to accept these standards and continues to challenge Mayer's worldview. Even before heading off to combat the locust, he considers alternative moral standards and looks for ways to extricate himself from their relationship. In spite of this, when Manyah Appelbaum invites Brenchuk back to her apartment, his displeasure at her rejection of his sexual advances leads him to act like his mentor and use his narrative skills to seduce her. Brenchuk tells her salacious stories, sexually arouses her, and gains her assent for intimacy. But on the verge of sexual conquest, Brenchuk steps back. Finding greater pleasure in controlling his desire than hedonistically expressing it, he leaves her room. Indeed, Brenchuk remains in Mayer's shadow at the end of the trilogy and fails to produce a novel capable of promoting Self-Evaluative masculinity and productive homosocial ties. Even so, his self-restraint and concern for Manyah points to his ability to maintain Self-Evaluative masculine standards and hew to associated heterosexual norms.

Like Brenchuk, the New Yishuv's other men can maintain these standards and uphold these norms for the betterment of their community. To be sure, such standards and norms were not in place during the war. Nonetheless, Reuveni makes use of *Till Jerusalem* to disseminate and promote them to better conditions in the postwar New Yishuv. Their further promulgation and promotion, however, required other introspective authors capable of publicly addressing personal deficiencies in support of normative change and public discussion of strategies for achievement of a unified Palestinian Zionist community's collective aims. As portrayal of Brenchuk comes to show, authors unwilling to adopt such a socially engaged aesthetic would merely reveal their questionable character and the irrelevance of their work. Reuveni looked to his Hebrew literary counterparts to help him take up an important social project neglected by their political contemporaries.

Conclusions

Israeli society and culture's Pre-State development has been portrayed as a seamless process advanced through development of new prototypes of Jewish manhood such as the sabra model. Because literary works written by Reuveni, Arieli, Brenner, and Agnon did not support these paradigms, scholars have not considered their role in Israel's social and cultural development. Rather than confirming these writers' dedication to autonomous conceptions of art, this oversight proves inextricably bound to political struggles that took place in the 1910s and 1920s.

Proponents of Self-Evaluative masculinity maintained positions that put them at odds with many of their contemporaries, and they turned to literature to disseminate and promote their views. To argue the validity of their positions, including their view that community and state building constituted difficult long-term processes, they made use of literary representations of gender and sexuality. Their use allowed them to shine light on Jewish weakness, the insurmountable nature of psychic fragmentation, and continuity with the diasporic Jewish past, and advance changes in male behavior they deemed necessary for Jewish men to maximize their potential and advance communal interests.

Those maintaining alternative plans for the Zionist project's advancement and advocating adoption of divergent masculine models found Self-Evaluative masculinity and its associated tenets a challenge to their success and looked for a way to shunt them aside. Representations of psychic fragmentation, homoerotic attraction, and effeminacy in literary works by proponents of Self-Evaluative masculinity helped them accomplish this. Rather than examining the role these representations played in advancement of Jewish national interests, Self-Evaluative masculinity's opponents pointed to them as decadent elements that delegitimized the literary works that featured them and the writers that employed them. While the decadent label has stuck more persistently to Arieli and Reuveni and their literary work, it was used widely to undermine literary works promoting Self-Evaluative masculinity that could not be reinterpreted in support of alterative views.

By removing the decadent label from Hebrew literary works such as *Till Jerusalem* and reading them in accordance with authorial intention, one sees that Israeli norms were not seamlessly produced through facile imitation of non-Jewish ideals with little precedent in diasporic Jewish life. Hebrew literature written by Self-Evaluative masculinity's advocates alerts scholars to widespread early twentieth-century debate concerning what constituted Zionist masculinity and what would best advance Jewish collective interests.

More interested in social mobilization than individual pride, Reuveni, like Agnon, Brenner, and Arieli before him, challenged those who advanced the Nietzschean superman or the individual ready to sacrifice his life for the collective as viable exemplars for Palestinian Jewish men. Therefore, rather than focusing on unachievable or potentially undesirable masculine ideals, Reuveni promoted a masculine form that strove to address, rather than resolve, existential conundrums inhibiting immigrant Jewish men and preventing them from bettering their lives and communal life. Modern Jewish life might be characterized by psychic fragmentation and individual and collective weakness. Nonetheless, individual and collective Jewish life could be improved. Consequently, Reuveni employed the trilogy to push Palestinian Jewish men to act regardless of their doubts. Diasporic failures and humiliations might have scarred immigrant Jewish men and made them feel ashamed of their limited abilities, but participation in a joint struggle against psychic fragmentation and its deleterious effects could combat feelings of shame. Furthermore, it could provide Jewish men with a sense of pride as they strove to meet the community's provisioning, procreative, and protective needs. For Self-Evaluative Hebrew writers, such participation defined masculine health and would reward Jewish men with enriching homosocial bonds.

A community of like-minded Jewish men virtuously working to meet the New Yishuv's collective needs constituted an ideal scenario for Self-Evaluative Hebrew writers. Nonetheless, they recognized that a combination of fear, inertia, self-interest, and shame inhibited Palestinian Jewish men's advancement of communal interests. Hence, as discussion of Arieli's and Reuveni's work has demonstrated, these writers increasingly drew on sexuality, in addition to gender, to mark out communal boundaries. Consequently, they categorized introspection and communal improvement efforts, undertaken as part of the struggle against psychic fragmentation and its deleterious effects, as healthy heterosexual behavior—and the shirking of these behaviors as deviant homosexual conduct indicative of unsuitability for membership in the New Yishuv. Thus, *Till Jerusalem*'s extensive portrayal of aberrant sexuality enabled it to demarcate proper social behavior and place pressure to conform on Palestinian Jewish men interested in other Jewish men's company. Not only did proper deportment provide entrée into New Yishuv society, but it also conferred membership in a select group to which Jewish men could take pride in belonging.

As with previously discussed literary works written by Self-Evaluative masculinity's advocates, *Till Jerusalem* does not end happily. Palestinian Jewish society has not embraced the values and associated gender and sexual norms advanced by Self-Evaluative masculinity's proponents. The Jewish future remains indeterminate in literature, just as it remained indeterminate in life. Consequently, if contemporary male readers truly desired change, they were going to have to help realize it. This could be done by assuming the masculine and heterosexual norms that the trilogy promotes and installing them as the basis for New Yishuv membership.

If *Till Jerusalem* pushed Palestinian male readers to act in this manner, it certainly made an important contribution to Palestinian Zionist culture and contemporary discussions of most effective forms for collective action. Such a direct link between Self-Evaluative Hebrew works and their readers will likely never be located. Nonetheless, showing how *Till Jerusalem* transcends purely aesthetics concerns and employs gender and sexuality in an effort to define incipient Israeli society and culture proves historically and culturally significant. The impatience of the postwar period, Palestinian Hebrew literature's increasing focus on young readers, and delegitimation efforts made by those holding alternative views caused most works written by Self-Evaluative Hebrew writers to be classified as decadent, marginalized Self-Evaluative Hebrew writing and obscured the existence of a Zionist masculine form offering great continuity with the past and fewer utopian demands. Not only will further study of this literature offer a way toward a more complex understanding of Israeli culture and society, but it will also provide further evidence of a historic Zionist masculine form in better accord with the way many contemporary Israeli Jewish men desire to see themselves today.

Notes

1. For a positive review of Reuveni's work, see Yosef Hayyim Brenner, *Ketavim*, ed. Menahem Dorman and Yitzhak Kafkafi (Tel Aviv: ha-Kibutz ha-Me'uhad, 1978–85), 4:1339–43.

2. Aharon Kabak, *Masot ve-divre bikoret* (Jerusalem: Shalem, 1978), 228.

3. Yod Beyt [Natan Bistritzky], "Vegn der Hebraisher literature un teater in Palestine," *Literarishe Bleter* 10 (October 11, 1927): 3, quoted in Yig'al Shvartz, *Mah she-ro'im mi-kan* (Or Yehudah: Dvir, 2005), 156–57.

4. Natan Zakh, "Omanut ha-sipur shel A. Re'uveni," in *Aharon Re'uveni: mivhar ma'amare bikoret 'al yetzirato*, ed. Yig'al Shvartz (Tel Aviv: ha-Kibutz ha-Me'uhad, 1992), 110; Dan Miron, *Kivun orot: tahanot ba-siporet ha-'Ivrit ha-modernit* (Jerusalem: Keter, 1979), 395–430.

5. On Reuveni's work's literary reception, see Shvartz, *Mah she-ro'im mi-kan*, 149–200. Hebrew readers' lack of appreciation for Reuveni's work contributed significantly to his almost complete literary silence from the early 1930s until the late 1950s.

6. On the trilogy as a roman à clef, see Yeshurun Keshet, "'Al A. Re'uveni," in Shvartz, *Aharon Re'uveni*, 86–104.

7. Sh. Yavni'eli, "Divre ha-mehayvim," in *'Al ha-saf: kovetz le-'inyane ha-hayyim vela-sifrut* (Jerusalem: Mifleget Po'ale Tziyon be-'Eretz Yisra'el, 1918), 14. For a more sober assessment of the Jewish Legion, see Derek Penslar, *Jews and the Military: A History* (Princeton, NJ: Princeton University Press, 2013), 195–200.

8. On the debates between gradualists and those harboring messianic hopes tied to the Jewish Legion's establishment, see Anita Shapira, *Land and Power: The Zionist Resort to Force, 1881–1948*, trans. William Templer (Stanford, CA: Stanford University Press, 1992), 89–98.

9. On his payment of the military substitution tax, see Nili Sadan-Loebenstein, *Aharon Re'uveni: Monografiyah* (Tel Aviv: Sifriyat Po'alim, 1994), 22.

10. Aharon Re'uveni, "The London Zionist Committee in Palestine," *Di Varhayt*, June 16, 1918, quoted in Sadan-Loebenstein, *Aharon Re'uveni*, 34 and 38. He started the trilogy in winter 1917 and completed it in spring 1920.

11. Re'uveni, "The London Zionist Committee in Palestine."

12. Shapira, *Land and Power*, 117.

13. Aharon Re'uveni, "le-Toldot ha-trilogiyah sheli," *Davar*, December 26, 1969.

14. Sha'ul Avigur et al., eds., *Me-hitgonenut le-haganah*, vol 1., *Sefer toldot ha-Haganah* (Jerusalem: ha-Sifriyah ha-Tzionit, 1956), bk. 2, 614.

15. On the Nabi Musa riots as a turning point, see Abigail Jacobson, *From Empire to Empire: Jerusalem between Ottoman and British Rule* (Syracuse, NY: Syracuse University Press, 2011), 175.

16. Reuveni's article's title clearly evokes Emile Zola's "J'accuse" (I accuse) that reproached the French government for antisemitism and unlawful jailing of the Jewish officer Alfred Dreyfus on trumped-up charges. On the article, see Avigur et al., eds., *Me-hitgonenut le-haganah*, bk. 2, 620.

17. Re'uveni, "le-Toldot ha-trilogiyah sheli." The term *pogrom* was an important element in the discourse surrounding anti-Jewish violence in Palestine in 1920–21. Shapira, *Land and Power*, 111–14.

18. On the discourse of pogrom literature, see Shmu'el Verses, "Ben tokhehah le-apologetikah: 'be-'ir ha-haregah' shel Bialik umi-saviv lah," in *bi-Mevo'e 'ir ha-haregah: mivhar ma'amrim 'al shiro shel Bialik*, ed. Uzi Shavit and Ziva Shamir (Tel Aviv: ha-Kibutz ha-Me'uhad, 1994), 23–54.

19. Karl Miller, *Doubles: Studies in Literary History* (London: Oxford University Press, 1985), 209.

20. Charles Bernheimer, *Decadent Subjects* (Baltimore: Johns Hopkins University Press, 2002), 26–27.

21. Shachar Pinsker, *Literary Passports: The Making of Modernist Hebrew Fiction in Europe* (Stanford, CA: Stanford University Press, 2011), 159, 147–64.

22. Pinsker, *Literary Passports*, 163.

23. Hamutal Bar-Yosef, *Maga'im shel dekadens: Bialik, Berdichevski, Brenner* (Be'er Sheva: Hotza'at ha-sefarim shel Universitat Ben-Guryon ba-Negev, 1997), 13–41. On contemporary Jewish anxieties about individual and collective Jewish demise, see Arieh Saposnik, "Exorcising the 'Angel of National Death'—Nation and Individual Death (and Rebirth) in Zionist Palestine," *Jewish Quarterly Review* 95, no. 3 (2005): 557–78.

24. Dan Miron, *From Continuity to Contiguity: Towards a New Jewish Literary Thinking* (Stanford, CA: Stanford University Press, 2010), 117.

25. Cf. Pinsker, *Literary Passports*, 158, 168, 162.

26. Bernheimer, *Decadent Subjects*, 26–27.

27. Yael Zerubavel, *Recovered Roots: Collective Memory and the Making of Israeli National Tradition* (Chicago: University of Chicago Press, 1995), 33–34; Oz Almog, *The Sabra: The Creation of the New Jew*, trans. Haim Watzman (Berkeley: University of California Press, 2000), 76–96.

28. For a contextual discussion of literary decadence's presence in Palestinian Hebrew literature, see David Biale, *Eros and the Jews: From Biblical Israel to Contemporary America* (Berkeley: University of California Press, 1997), 176–203. Reuveni composed *Till Jerusalem* between 1917 and 1920, but its publication extended well into the 1920s. The first novel was published in serial form, while the two subsequent novels were published as independent books. Aharon Re'uveni, "be-Reshit ha-mevukhah," *ha-Adamah* 1 (1919–20): 11–30, 141–59, 338–43, 392–415, 501–23; Aharon Re'uveni, *ha-'Oniyot ha-ahronot* (Warsaw: Shtibel, 1923); Aharon Re'uveni, *Shamot* (Warsaw: Shtibel, 1925).

29. Ya'akov Rabinovitz, "Bentayim," *ha-Po'el ha- tza'ir*, November 29, 1912.

30. Sh. Levitan, "Shamot," *Do'ar ha-yom*, May 15, 1925.

31. Sh. Levitan, "Shamot," *Do'ar ha-yom*, May 15, 1925.

32. 'Adi Tzemah, "Min ve-ofi le'umi: tzemed nos'im be-'Yeshimon' shel L. A. Arieli," *Moznayim* 53, nos. 5–6 (1982): 371–83; for a similar argument, see Gershon Shaked, "Ha-te'om she-yarad—'al yetzirato shel L. A. Arieli-Orlof," *Siman Kri'ah* 5 (February 1976): 481–91; Nili Sadan-Loebenstein, "Magemot dekadentiot be-siporet ha-mehagrim bi-shnot ha-'esrim be-Eretz-Yisrael" (PhD diss., Bar Ilan University, 1976); for more on Sadan's dissertation, see Avidov Lipsker, introduction to *Aharon Re'uveni: Monografiyah*, by Nili Sadan-Loebenstein (Tel Aviv: Sifriyat Po'alim, 1994), 7–10.

33. David Gilmore, *Manhood in the Making: Cultural Concepts of Masculinity* (New Haven, CT: Yale University Press, 1990), 3.

34. Gilmore, *Manhood in the Making*, 3. Similarly, George Mosse points to manhood ideals' centrality to the European nation-state's development. See George Mosse, *The Image of Man* (New York: Oxford University Press, 1996), 77.

35. Miron, *From Continuity to Contiguity*, 52.

36. Mikhal Dekel, *The Universal Jew: Masculinity, Modernity, and the Zionist Movement* (Evanston, IL: Northwestern University Press, 2011), 5–6.

37. Harry Brod, "Of Mice and Supermen," in *Gender and Judaism*, ed. Tamar Rudavsky (New York: New York University Press, 1994), 283.

38. For placement of emphasis on bodily transformation, see Mikha'el Gluzman, *ha-Guf ha-Tzioni: le'umiut, migdar u-miniut ba-sifrut ha-'Ivrit ha-hadashah* (Tel Aviv: ha-Kibutz

ha-Me'uhad, 2007); Todd Presner, *Muscular Judaism: The Jewish Body and the Politics of Regeneration* (New York: Routledge, 2007), 1–23. Dekel, *The Universal Jew*, 108. On the importance of mimicry of an Aryan model, see Daniel Boyarin, *Unheroic Conduct: The Rise of Heterosexuality and the Invention of the Modern Jewish Man* (Berkeley: University of California Press, 1997), 271–312. For stress on the importance of readiness to sacrifice one's life, see Dekel, *The Universal Jew*, 34; Yael Feldman, *Glory and Agony: Isaac's Sacrifice and National Narrative* (Stanford, CA: Stanford University Press, 2010), 51–105.

39. Leading masculinity scholars recommend such an analytical shift. Raewyn C. Connell and James Messerschmidt, "Hegemonic Masculinity: Rethinking the Concept," *Gender and Society* 19, no. 6 (2005): 829–59.

40. Freud, *Three Essays on the Theory of Sexuality*, trans. James Strachey (New York: Basic Books, 1975), 57, 97–109.

41. For recent scholarly discussions of *'Ad-Yerushalayim*, see Glenda Abramson, *Hebrew Writing of the First World War* (London: Valentine-Mitchell, 2008), 261–97; Andrea Siegel, "Rape and the 'Arab Question' in L. A. Arieli's Allah Karim! and Aharon Reuveni's Devastation," *Nashim* 23, no. 1 (2012): 110–28. For earlier readings, see Yig'al Shvartz, *Li-heyot ke-de li-heyot: Aharon Re'uveni—monografiyah* (Jerusalem: Hotza'at Magnes, 1993), 155–255; Nili Sadan-Loebenstein, *Aharon Re'uveni: Monografiyah* (Tel Aviv: Sifriyat Po'alim, 1994), 143–243; Gershon Shaked, *ha-Siporet ha-'Ivrit* (Tel Aviv: ha-Kibutz ha-Me'uhad, 1977–98), 2:143–50; Yig'al Shvartz, ed., *Aharon Re'uveni: mivhar ma'amare bikoret* (Tel Aviv: ha-Kibutz ha-Me'uhad, 1992).

42. Miron, *Kivun orot*, 419; Shvartz, *Li-heyot ke-de li-heyot*, 164–66; cf. Shaked, *ha-Siporet ha-'Ivrit*, 2:144; cf. Abramson, *Hebrew Writing*, 276–95.

43. Gershon Shaked, *Omanut ha-sipur shel 'Agnon* (Tel Aviv: Sifriyat ha-Po'alim, 1973), 47.

44. Like Freud, Reuveni posited the need to confront traumatic psychological material to avoid repeating it. Sigmund Freud, "Remembering, Repeating, and Working-Through," in *The Standard Edition of the Complete Psychological Works of Sigmund Freud*, trans. and ed. James Strachey (London: Hogarth, 1956–74), 12:147–56.

45. Almog, *The Sabra*, 73–137; Avner Holtzman, *Ahavat Tziyon* (Jerusalem: Carmel, 2006), 320. For examples of Funk's attractiveness to Hebrew readers, see Miron, *Kivun orot*, 414–17; Shvartz, *Li-heyot ke-de li-heyot*, 185–90. For more on a new body-centered Jewish masculine form's turn-of-the-century assertion, see Boyarin, *Unheroic Conduct*; Gluzman, *ha-Guf ha-Tzioni*; Presner, *Muscular Judaism*.

46. For further discussion of productivization and modern Jewish history, see Derek Penslar, *Shylock's Children: Economics and Jewish Identity in Modern Jewish Europe* (Berkeley: University of California Press, 2001), 107–23, 205–16.

47. Arieli employs the figure of Shmaryahu Fogel for similar ends in *Allah Karim!*

48. Alexander Karmon, "'Shamot' le-A. Re'uveni," *Do'ar ha-yom*, July 26, 1925.

49. Miron, *Kivun orot*, 407.

50. For a fuller description of Funk's mental limitations, see Re'uveni, *Shamot*, 22.

51. Re'uveni, *Shamot*, 98.

52. See Re'uveni, *Shamot*, 27–28, 108, and 113–14, for prominent examples of these fantasies. These masochistic fantasies connect Funk with the Jewish men in Arieli's *Allah Karim!* discussed in chap. 3.

53. Re'uveni, *Shamot*, 128; Re'uveni, *Shamot*, 105, 128.

54. Re'uveni, *Shamot*, 136.

55. Re'uveni, *Shamot*, 205.

56. On Youssef's role in this scene, see Andrea Siegel, "Rape and the 'Arab' Question," 120–24; on Arabs' idealization in contemporary Hebrew fiction and their role in the reimaging of Jewish identity, see Yaron Peleg, *Orientalism and the Hebrew Imagination* (Ithaca, NY: Cornell University Press, 2005), 75–99.

57. Re'uveni, *Shamot*, 186.

58. Reuveni and his contemporaries parodied Hebrew literature's idealized Arab and worked to construct an Israeli identity in stark contrast to Arab primitivism. See Yohai Openhaimer, *Me'ever la-gader: yitzug ha-'Aravim ba-siporet ha-'Ivrit veha-Yisra'elit (1906–2005)* (Tel Aviv: 'Am 'Oved, 2008), 52–81.

59. For this view's most sophisticated assertion, see Shvartz, *Li-heyot ke-de li-heyot*, 185–90.

60. Reuveni's representation of Zionist leaders' inability to effectively exploit the Palestinian Jewish public sphere for nationalist sentiment's development parallels Brenner's portrayal of similar leadership failures in *mi-Kan umi-kan*.

61. On the New Yishuv in the late Ottoman period, see Saposnik, *Becoming Hebrew*.

62. Re'uveni, "be-Reshit ha-mevukhah," 24–25.

63. For a dispassionate study of early twentieth-century Palestinian Jewish immigrants, see Gur Alro'ey, *Imigrantim: ha-hagirah ha-Yehudit le-Eretz-Yisrael be-reshit ha-me'ah ha-'esrim* (Jerusalem: Yad Yitzhak Ben-Tzvi, 2004).

64. See Miron, *Kivun orot*, 407.

65. See Re'uveni, "be-Reshit ha-mevukhah," 25.

66. Re'uveni, "be-Reshit ha-mevukhah," 151.

67. For discussion of his survival in the army at others' expense, see Re'uveni, *Shamot*, 59.

68. See Re'uveni, *Shamot*, 155, 160; for Leyzer's comparison to a female Arab prostitute, see Re'uveni, *Shamot*, 29; for reference to Leyzer as a male prostitute, see Re'uveni, *Shamot*, 42.

69. On racial antisemitism and its rhetoric, see Sander Gilman, *Jewish Self-Hatred: Anti-Semitism and the Hidden Language of the Jews* (Baltimore: Johns Hopkins University Press, 1992); Gilman, *The Jew's Body* (New York: Routledge, 1991); John Efron, *Defenders of the Race: Jewish Doctors and Race Science in Fin-de-Siècle Europe* (New Haven, CT: Yale University Press, 1994); Mitchell Hart, *Social Science and the Politics of Modern Jewish Identity* (Stanford, CA: Stanford University Press, 2000). On "healthy" masculinity's connection to nationalism and the European Jewish countertype, see Mosse, *The Image of Man*; Mosse, *Nationalism and Sexuality*.

70. For an important call for Hebrew literature to assist its readers in achievement of self-knowledge, see Yosef Hayyim Brenner, "Ha'arakhat 'atzmenu bi-shloshat ha-kerakhim," in *Ketavim*, 4:1223–96.

71. Shaked, *ha-Siporet ha-'Ivrit*, 2:144; Abramson, *Hebrew Writing*, 263.

72. Re'uveni, "be-Reshit ha-mevukhah," 152.

73. For reference to Brenchuk's art as a hard peel, see Re'uveni, *ha-'Oniyot ha-ahronot*, 19; for impotent feelings caused by interpersonal relations, see Re'uveni, *ha-'Oniyot ha-ahronot*, 5.

74. Re'uveni, *ha-'Oniyot ha-ahronot*, 31.

75. Re'uveni, *ha-'Oniyot ha-ahronot*, 20. This perception parallels the way that Funk feels after committing adultery and the concomitant revelation of internal vigor recalls David Ostrovsky as he makes his escape from his British captors.

76. Re'uveni, *ha-'Oniyot ha-ahronot*, 99.

77. Re'uveni, *ha-'Oniyot ha-ahronot*, 105. These "feelings of great wealth" parallel the "stream of new powers" felt by David in *Yeshimon* after he momentarily embraces the tenets of Self-Evaluative masculinity.

78. For more on the two men's relationship, see Shvartz, *Li-heyot ke-de li-heyot*, 211. This loss of direction at the end of the trilogy parallels David's loss of direction in *Yeshimon* after his encounter with the German train conductor.

79. Re'uveni, *ha-'Oniyot ha-ahronot*, 22.

AFTERWORD

The Lesson, Legacy, and Implications of Self-Evaluative Masculinity

How much better to get wisdom than gold, to
gain insight rather than silver.

—Proverbs 16:16

Parting Thoughts

Many East European Jewish men understood modernity in gendered terms and considered themselves "feminized" by the changes it effected. The nationalists among them, who stressed the connection between individual and collective Jewish impotence, responded to these feelings by promoting nationalist values and norms as a way to "remasculinize" the Jewish people. Hebrew writers, who had been socialized to the idea of engaged literature since their youth, felt compelled to take part in these efforts.

My study has focused on four prominent early twentieth-century Hebrew writers who immigrated to Palestine prior to World War I and took part in these remasculinization efforts. Through their literary works, they advanced a new form of Jewish masculinity intended to promote a shared future vision for the Palestinian Jewish community. Alluding to Brenner's famed essay "Self-Evaluation in Three Volumes," I referred to this masculinity as Self-Evaluative masculinity.[1] Its key features are self-examination, clarification of individual priorities, and moral pursuit of these objectives alongside like-minded Jewish men.

Self-Evaluative masculinity does not equate with Zionist masculinity. Masculinity was a highly contested topic in the emerging Palestinian Jewish public sphere with different groups promoting different models of the New Jewish Man that reflected different views about what the New Yishuv's most pressing needs were and how best to meet them. The Palestinian Hebrew literary works analyzed here are rhetorical tools constructed to convince Palestinian Jewish men to adopt Self-Evaluative masculinity rather than a myriad of alternatives.

Homosociality is central to these literary works' rhetoric. As David Gilmore argues, manhood is something thrust on men to get them to meet societal needs. Consequently, men frequently prove reticent to adopt externally imposed masculine standards. Proponents of Self-Evaluative masculinity turned to homosociality as an important way to draw men toward its adoption. Independent of what those maintaining Self-Evaluative masculine norms could potentially achieve, promoters of these norms asserted that those adopting them would be rewarded with strong erotic ties with like-minded Jewish men that could endow even difficult lives with pleasure and a reason to endure. Furthermore, these backers invented traditions that drew on religious Jewish texts and customs to argue that continuity with the Jewish past could be achieved through adherence to Self-Evaluative norms and maintenance of homosocial ties with others upholding them too. Finally, promoters of Self-Evaluative masculinity employed homosexual panic to advance it. By categorizing those who failed to act in accordance with Self-Evaluative norms as homosexuals and promoting their stigmatization, they put pressure on those desirous of homosocial ties with men adhering to Self-Evaluative standards to alter their behavior and conform.

Nonetheless, Self-Evaluative masculinity never achieved hegemonic status within Israeli culture, and I have drawn on the misattribution of the term *decadent* to Self-Evaluative Hebrew writers to explain this. The representations of sexuality and gender employed by these writers were ultimately used to delegitimize them and their works as sick and incapable of contributing to the development of Israeli society and culture. Their belief in continuity between the Diaspora and the Land of Israel, psychic fragmentation as an inalterable part of the modern condition, and the necessarily gradual nature of community and state building in Palestine set adherents of Self-Evaluative masculinity apart from their contemporaries in the interwar period. Due to increasing support for the use of idealized sabra masculinity to voice desired national character, Self-Evaluative masculinity and the alternate national image that it presented were shunted aside.

In the remainder of this afterword, I will touch on what I see as the lesson, the legacy, and the scholarly implications of this study of Self-Evaluative masculinity. First, the use of sexuality for the advancement of masculine standards voicing a broader social vision is not unique to the literary work of those advocating Self-Evaluative masculinity. Other Hebrew writers used representations of gender and sexuality to promote their values too. Second, while the sabra masculine norm attained hegemonic status with the establishment of the State of Israel, both prominent native-born Palestinian Jewish men and immigrant youth who arrived during the interwar period, who are considered to have most effectively brought this norm to life, never fully identified with it. While this incomplete identification long simmered close to the surface, prominent Hebrew writers including Yehuda Amichai (1924–2000) and Amos Oz (1939–2018) employed gender to express feelings of psychic fragmentation and gradually brought new masculine forms, evocative of Self-Evaluative masculinity and displaying greater openness of Diaspora life, to mainstream Israeli cultural discourse. As a result, social pressure to conform to sabra masculine norms has progressively diminished in Israel. Finally, the implications of this exploration of Self-Evaluative masculinity merit new research in Modern Hebrew literature and Israel studies.

Cultural Norms' Advancement through Divergent Representations of Gender and Sexuality

Many prominent mid-twentieth-century Israeli writers advanced cultural norms through representation of gender and sexuality, just as Self-Evaluative masculinity's supporters did before them. Consequently, as brief discussion of Moshe Shamir's *be-Mo yadav: pirke Elik* (With his own hands: The Elik chapters, 1951) demonstrates, analysis of gender and sexual representation enables one to discern divergent cultural and political positions various Hebrew and Israeli writers advocated. In contrast with previously discussed fiction and drama, *With His Own Hands* promotes a body-centered self-sacrificial form of Israeli masculinity. Analysis of three scenes, two drawn from Shamir's portrayal of the events of November 29, 1947, when the New Yishuv celebrated the United Nations' approval of Palestine's partition, and a third coming at the work's conclusion, points to how scattered gender and sexual representations help accomplish this task.

The second November 29 scene pursues this goal through presentation of the protagonist Elik's thoughts as he observes his celebrating Palmach comrades:[2] "There's no finer sight tonight than all these lads together. All he saw was the solidity of their broad backs as enthusiastic song rose from them. . . . Pressed closely together the others danced with their girls.

He observed the full length of their backs, from boot to crown. Good-natured, pliant lads, they were always ready to forgive a slight, and they loved the girls they held in their arms."[3] Elik's homoerotic attraction to the young men is conveyed through his attentiveness to their broad backs and fit bodies. Nonetheless, foregrounding of the loving care the Palmachniks provide their girls, paralleling Elik's bond to his unnamed girl, defuses the hint of homosexuality. Thus, the text successfully conveys the "healthy" homosocial bonds linking the Palmachniks. Simultaneously, it pushes Palestinian Jewish men to befriend similar men, whose physical attributes combine with less visible characteristics, such as their unity, enthusiasm, good nature, flexibility, forgiveness, and normative heterosexuality, to make them objects of emulation. Hence, the text exploits Elik's homoerotic tie to his comrades to draw male readers to the ideal community they embody.

Shortly before Elik enters the café where this celebration takes place, a group of artists blocks his and his comrades' path to ideal masculine community's expression: "Approaching their destination, which lay at an intersection, they came to a halt before a strange slow group that passed going in another direction . . . among them were a few young girls with an affected ladylike air about them and young men whose expressions testified to something, though one couldn't tell exactly what this was. A bunch of artists always aroused an impulse to laugh, as well as a desire to tease. . . ."[4] The passing male artists embody an alternative homoerotically tinged masculinity, but the text distances them from the idealized Palmachniks and from readers. These self-important men have little substantive to say. Nonetheless, they forgo communal activities and dedicate their time to self-reflection and self-expression. Yet in their self-absorption, these effete men do not pair off with their group's women. Instead, they mirror their haughty female companions. Thus, the text implies, individual males must forgo their solipsism and their company to number alongside the young Palmachnik men.

Aware of the differences between the groups, Elik, who spots his brother among the artists, ultimately feels obliged to distance himself from him. Elik, however, initially attempts to bridge the divide separating him and his brother. He invents and performs a theatrical scenario that has him physically grabbing his brother "like a kid from a flock" and shepherding him into his group.[5] Meanwhile, Elik's brother, who views his artistic endeavors as legitimate, does not understand his brother's reticence to unconditionally embrace him. Gazing into his brother's eyes, he sees "the love of a lout who was ready to embrace everything and everybody that night, even a telegraph pole, but was too shy to embrace his own brother, and had sought an outlet for his pent-up affection by pulling this wild stunt."[6] Despite Elik's desire to connect with his brother, his Palmach community values action. Absent his brother's sincere desire to renounce the contemplative life and join them, Elik feels remiss maintaining a connection with him. Thus, the two biological brothers part never to meet again; Elik goes to serve alongside his imagined brothers.

Just prior to Israeli independence, Elik participates in the armed struggle between Jews and Arabs for territorial control of Palestine. He thereby promotes the masculine heterosexual norm he shares with his Palmach brethren, and they reward him with their friendship. Then, when he dies at Palestinian Arab hands, the comrades' masculine norm finds consummate expression. If his fellows want to maintain their homosocial tie with him and remain worthy of service alongside their comrades, they too must prove ready to sacrifice their lives.

Roots in the Palestinian Soil

As European-born men, Self-Evaluative Hebrew writers naturally addressed Palestinian Jewish settlement from an immigrant perspective; they structured their fiction and drama to promote their preferred gender model among other immigrant Jewish men. Furthermore, as discussion of their literary work has shown, they convincingly advanced a viable gender model for the developing national community. Yet beginning in the 1920s, this model's inherent conservatism, especially its demurral of Zionism's ability to rapidly and irrevocably transform Palestine's Jewish inhabitants, diminished its prominence. Advocates of more revolutionary forms of Zionism, who proselytized the unlimited possibilities open to Palestinian Jewry, developed and promoted Hebrew cultural alternatives that more effectively spoke to natives and immigrants alike.

Sabra masculinity, as voiced in Shamir's *With His Own Hands*, constitutes the most successful alternative to Self-Evaluative masculinity to arise. Its success rested on two central pillars. First and foremost, its immigrant proponents created a hybrid form that derived from disparate forms of Palestinian Zionist masculinity and benefited from a wide preexistent base of support. It drew on Nordauian body-centered Zionist masculinity, the Trumpeldorian martyrological model, the Gordonian agricultural model, and the idealized native model tied to Palestinian Arabs that Ali voices in *Allah Karim!* Then its supporters allowed native-born youth to embellish it at the margins. The native generation added ornamental elements such as straightforward or *dugri* speech, in-group slang and humor, and fashion.

Connection to the Diaspora and associated feelings of individual and collective fragmentation proved integral to Self-Evaluative masculinity, but the sabra model refused this connection and attendant feelings. Instead, its supporters promoted immigrant and native ties to the physical Land of Israel. As part of this process, they amplified the significance of largely forgotten historical events, such as Masada's fall and the Bar Kochba revolt, and seemingly marginal contemporary events, such as the Battle of Tel Hai, to synthesize ideologically sound ties to the Land of Israel for young Palestinian Jews.[7] This, they believed, would supply Palestinian Jewry with a sense of rooted confidence.

The second pillar undergirding sabra masculinity's success was its promoters' dedication and perseverance during the interwar and early state periods. They enabled effective inculcation of sabra masculinity to the native-born generation and youth immigrants in Palestine's Hebrew-Zionist educational system. Teachers in the "schools and boarding schools affiliated with the labor movement" and "schools belonging to the general educational system sponsored by the Jewish agency," counselors directing children and teenagers participating in youth movement activities, and moshav and kibbutz members directing urban youth sent to assist in agriculture participated in this indoctrination process.[8] While the character of socialized youths never really aligned with sabra archetype, those hewing closely to sabra norms constituted a generational nucleus that "served as a behavioral model" for both the first native-born generation and their immigrant contemporaries.[9]

Postindependence memorial culture played up the sabra character of those among the first native-born Hebrew generation who died defending the incipient nation; it "contributed to the impression that the Sabra elite . . . had brought about the victory in the War of Independence and had paid the heaviest price."[10] Thus, it did more than push surviving native-born Hebrew males to cleave closely to sabra masculinity as a way of honoring their fallen brethren. It pushed Jewish men possessing looser ties to sabra masculinity to prove their masculinity by partaking in activities closely tied to sabra identity. Participation in combat roles in the newly formed Israel Defense Forces constituted one way to do this. Yet joining a kibbutz and working the land constituted an even more popular and significant way to voice sabra masculinity. Thus, years of service in kibbutz agriculture constituted an important biographical stage in the lives of many native-born men.

Indeed, sabra masculinity was successfully transmitted to a core group of native-born Palestinian Jewish youth, as well as to youth immigrants socialized alongside them, during the interwar period; through its subsequent promotion to even broader swaths of Israeli society, it achieved unquestioned ascendancy in the 1950s and 1960s. Nonetheless, native-born Hebrew men, both members of the generational nucleus and closely affiliated fellow travelers, as well as associated youth immigrants, had already begun to question it and the intentions of pioneering generation members who had actively inculcated it to them. The connections to the Land of Israel developed to provide native-born youth with rooted confidence proved too superficial. They failed to address serious existential issues that emerged in the mid-1940s, like the Holocaust, Palestinian Jewry's relationship to Diaspora Jewry and the diasporic past, the best way to honor those who fell in the State of Israel's defense, mass immigrations, and the ingathering of exiles. Taken together, these issues made more thoughtful native-born and immigrant men aware of sabra masculinity's limitations.

The sabra masculine form outlined above remained central to Israeli culture into the twenty-first century. Yet it brought on a conceptual crisis by making it increasingly difficult for those who embraced it to comprehend their world and their place within it. Consequently, Amos Oz's autobiographical novel *Sipur al ahavah ve-hoshekh* (A tale of love and darkness, 2002) proved pivotal, because it helped tens of thousands of secular Jewish Israeli male readers work through this crisis.[11] By supplying them with a composite lens synthesizing elements drawn from both sabra and diasporic Jewish masculinities, the novel offered them a new way to view the surrounding world and themselves. As a result, they successfully incorporated long-suppressed aspects of their experience into more nuanced senses of self that better reflected contemporary Israeli society's complex and frequently contradictory nature. Moreover, it enabled them to move forward with their lives with confidence that they were proceeding down paths previously trod by their fathers and forefathers.

Awareness of Zionist masculinity's intense Pre-State contestation and Self-Evaluative masculinity's role in these struggles helps illuminate the gradual movement from sabra masculinity to new Israeli masculine forms. Key literary works by five prominent Israeli writers who contributed to sabra masculinity's dislodgement from its exclusive cultural position and the ongoing challenge it currently faces from alternative masculine forms more open to Diaspora experience, and the psychological mind-set identified with it, will now be briefly discussed.

Recovered Diasporic Roots

Excepting Amos Oz, the four Israeli authors whose literary works will now be discussed had their work appear in *Dor ba-aretz* (A generation in the land, 1958), a literary anthology seen to have canonized Palmach-generation literature. Initially, this might prove surprising, because the literature featured in the anthology, written by young native-born and youth immigrant Israelis in the state's first decade, is widely considered to have advanced sabra masculinity and provided readers a gateway to indigenous Israeli culture grounded in local experience.[12] Yet literary scholar Avner Holtzman recently called for Palmach-generation literature's reevaluation due to its frequent discomfort with and opposition to sabra masculinity and its associated values previously overlooked by scholars.[13] Writers such as Moshe Shamir, S. Yizhar (Yizhar Smilansky, 1916–2006), Hanoch Bartov (1926–2016), and Yehuda Amichai expressed this discomfort and their sense of alienation from contemporaries who unselfconsciously promoted it; furthermore, some of them advanced Israeli masculinities linked with diasporic Jewish life and the Self-Evaluative masculine tradition that were more attuned to their sense of Israeliness. Through these efforts, they paved the way for subsequent writers such as Oz.

Hanoch Bartov's autographical novel *Pitze Bagrut* (The brigade, 1965) points to the significance of World War II military service and subsequent confrontation with the Holocaust and its implications in the immediate postwar period for many native-born Palestinian Jews and youth immigrants.[14] *The Brigade* constitutes one of four interlocking autographical novels covering a native-born Palestinian Jew's life from his birth in the 1920s until his golden years, and this initial installment focuses on a brief period in the protagonist's life beginning toward the end of World War II and concluding shortly after the war's conclusion. While minor discrepancies exist between the texts and the author refers to the protagonist as Nachman Shpiegler in two volumes and as Elisha Kruk in the others, the novels combine to produce an in-depth portrayal of an authorial alter ego's interior world.[15] Thus, a traumatic experience portrayed in *Shel mi atah, yeled*

(Whose little boy are you?, 1970), the novelistic installment covering the protagonist's life from his earliest memories to his bar mitzvah succinctly conveys a native-born Palestinian Jew's youthful perception of diasporic Jewish religion and the drive to uproot its traces that unconsciously propel him. Ultimately, however, war and postwar experiences described in *The Brigade* neutralize this drive. They push the protagonist toward reluctant embrace of elements he had long struggled to overcome, and initiate an intellectual shift from negation of diasporic Jewishness to its preservation.

In *Whose Little Boy Are You?*, financial difficulties force Nachman Shpiegler's father to take a teaching position at a Talmud Torah school in the early 1930s. Although an observant Jew, his new position compels him to increase his ritual observance and assume a more conservative mien. Thus, he removes his son from the secular Zionist kindergarten where he was learning to enroll him in the Talmud Torah. Rather than religious observance, lack of parental means and inability to gain admission to other schools underlie other children's enrollment in the small-town school; the young students, who see their religious education at odds with their inchoate lives in Palestine, resent the teachers and the purported suffering they impose on them. Nachman's father becomes the object of student ridicule, and the male students regard him as feminine.

His classmates' antipathy toward his father soon spreads to Nachman. They attack him in an alleged effort to clarify his seemingly ambiguous gender identity. Their ridicule and physical abuse drive a wedge between Nachman and his father:

> "Why don't we examine him ourselves," said Ozer, "and then we can tell him what he is." The idea was received enthusiastically, and the whole gang tackled him at once. Ozer grabbed his elbows while another boy reached for his pants. Just as on the first day of kindergarten, Nachman was seized by a blind impulse to break through the circle of humiliation, to run from it all so as not to hear his father mocked any longer or suffer disgrace for his sake. As on that day in kindergarten, he sprang forward with his head hunched between his shoulders and his fists leading the way, biting and scratching and butting at the solid wall around him. But the wall wouldn't give. Hands grabbed his wrists and ankles and heavy bodies sat on him. He was flat on the ground, powerful fingers pressing on his throat, threatening to choke him. Nachman twisted his head and his chin met an unidentified hand. He lifted his neck and sunk his teeth into it. There was a shout of pain from Ozer Lichtig. His throat was free now, but his hands and feet were still pinned by the bullies. Ozer got hold of his head and forced it to one side, grinding it into the dirt. Now they were all sitting on him and he had ceased to exist, except that he could hear them talking.

"He hits with his hands open, like a girl. Ha, ha, ha."

"He bites, he scratches, he's just like a girl."

"He's got to be a girl. Look at his nails, just like Adon Shpigeleh's."

"Come on, let's have a look!"

In vain Nachman squirmed and writhed like a worm, his mouth, nose, and eyes in the dirt. Hands unbuttoned his pants and pulled them down over his knees. Nachman said a prayer with the last of his strength, but he still couldn't move. Now, when it was already too late, he shouted papa, papa, into the dirt, but the sound was stillborn. His shame was complete. He was beyond human help.[16]

Nachman keeps this traumatic experience to himself. Yet his sense that internalization of the diasporic Jewish religiosity that his father embodies will feminize him and make him a wormlike creature forced to writhe in the dirt never leaves him. Thus, he progressively jettisons his patrimony. Then, when an accident leaves his father partially crippled and unable to do construction work, his desire to distance himself from his father's impotence rises to the surface. He disregards his father's contribution to Zionist state building through his work as a plasterer, overlooks the challenges his father's disability poses, and fails to assist him. Instead, Nachman spends his time trying to achieve a different and more viable masculine identity that his native-born Palestinian Jewish male contemporaries will appreciate.

Nachman's desire for his contemporaries' acceptance leads him to fantasize about various masculinities from a young age. These imaginative flights begin with a neighbor's playful assertion. If he accepts the claim that his dark skin and curly hair reveal him as a local Bedouin child adopted by his parents, he can envision a more compelling masculine pedigree. As his teenage years approach, Nachman's experimentation intensifies. His uncle, a murdered watchman, presents him with two attractive emulative models. The martial and self-sacrificial masculine models Rifael embodies seem attainable, and, as Nachman's embrace of Rifael's bicycle hints, they offer Nachman social mobility. Subsequently, contemporary socialist and communist literatures' valorization of the proletarian male's masculine verve produces further role play. Nachman trains as a welder and takes a factory job. Then, when infatuation with this masculine form wanes, Nachman embraces sex as a highly pleasurable way to voice his masculinity.

Performance of these various roles provides Nachman with a superficial sense of masculine vigor. Nevertheless, he remains tied to the Jewish morality his father inculcated in him; left unaddressed, this lingering connection to his father leaves him feeling emasculated. Thus, feelings of sinfulness overwhelm him when he commits adultery and negate the pleasure of the sexual act. Nachman still feels feminized and cut off from his Palestinian Jewish male peers.

When the prospect of serving in the Jewish Brigade presents itself, Nachman seizes hold of it as a way to finally jettison his Jewish religious heritage and emerge a man. As before, his military service fails to make him the type of man he thought he wanted to be. Instead, it pushes him to become the type of man he feels he should be. Presented with a chance to act in opposition to his paternal legacy and express his rejection of it, Nachman forgoes the opportunity and ceases to chase after his native-born Palestinian Jewish male peers' approval. Instead, he embraces moral tenets drawn from diasporic Jewish religiosity and strives to give mature expression to a masculine identity incorporating elements of his paternal legacy.

Initially, when Elisha (the name assigned Nachman in *The Brigade*) arrives in Europe, he closely resembles the units' other Palestinian-born soldiers. Like them, he views himself as superior to Diaspora Jews. Yet Italians, Germans, and sundry refugee groups that he and his fellows encounter fail to differentiate between them and Diaspora Jews. Like Leyzi, a native-born Palestinian Jew, who turns to his comrades and asks, "That's how they see us?" when confronted by the fading image of "a hunchbacked Jew with a wispy beard, wearing a gabardine gown, hauling Uncle Sam on a leash, bent beneath a sack of dollars," Elisha finds the Europeans' confusion disturbing.[17] Unprepared to actively confront the diasporic Jewish experience and associated antisemitic tropes, Elisha and the other young Hebrews look for a way to liberate themselves from the unpleasant feelings their surroundings arouse.

When allegations concerning the attempted rape of two German women by two members of the Jewish Brigade prompt a debate about vengeance, the debate externalizes ideas about the possibility of transcending diasporic Jewishness and the discomfort that it arouses swirling around in Elisha's mind. Thus, when one of the young Hebrews advances vengeance as the best way for the soldiers to unburden themselves of diasporic Jewishness's tainted legacy and move on, he voices Elisha's desire to erase his paternal legacy, assume a masculinity anathema to his father, and gain his peer group's acceptance: "We want one day of wild revenge. Murder for its own sake, just as they did to us, rape for rape. Looting for looting. Innocent victims for innocent victims. Only then, only after we cleanse ourselves of this canker, this rot, this nightmare of helplessness—only then, clean and at peace with ourselves can we take our place in human society once more."[18] The vengeance called for here constitutes a perverse reworking of the biblical law of retaliation. While it proves enticing and seems an effective way to overcome troubling feelings of impotence, Elisha's lingering connection to his father is voiced by a Diaspora-born soldier who questions such action. The soldier points out that vengeance will merely mimic Nazi action without severing the soldiers' connection to diasporic Jewish weakness. Thus, he calls instead for this connection's exploration. When this debate occurs, Elisha proves unprepared to address the implications of vengeance. Therefore, he tries to forget everything that is said.[19]

When Elisha meets his uncle Pinik in Italy, his ongoing efforts to erase his paternal legacy and emerge reborn alongside his peers force their way to the surface. A distant relation of Elisha's mother, Pinik enters Elisha's life just prior to his bar mitzvah, and Elisha's developing connection with him voices his growing rebelliousness. Elisha's devout disabled petit bourgeois father looks askance at Pinik, a young attractive tref-eating secular Jew with an epicurean streak, who avows socialist ideas and puts them into practice through his labor. Nonetheless, Elisha sees Pinik ushering "all that was joyous, daring, and reckless" onto the family property; he recalls Pinik as "the god of [his] childhood," who set off "a revolution in [his] life."[20] Thus, Elisha aspires to "be like Pinik. The exact opposite of Father."[21]

When Pinik finds Elisha in Venice and offers him the chance to realize his childhood wish, Elisha surprises himself by forgoing this opportunity and consciously renewing his connection to his father. Initially, however, Pinik draws Elisha in. Thus, while luxuriating in one of the gigantic bathtubs in Pinik's palatial Venetian apartment, Elisha feels himself "turning into another man."[22] Then he dresses in gaudy clothing provided by Pinik that transforms his appearance. Next, he sits down to a bountiful meal alongside Pinik, two other soldiers dressed in ostentatious civilian clothing, and three attractive well-dressed prostitutes. As he plies Elisha with food and drink, Pinik pushes Elisha to follow him without hesitation. Finally, when Pinik places an inebriated Elisha in bed alongside his naked and voluptuous paramour Felicia, Pinik's efforts reach their culmination. By sleeping with a willing Felicia, Elisha can realize his childhood dream and cement his union with Pinik. Pinik spurs him on, and as Elisha passes out, he delivers the following coup de grâce: "'Everything's gutted,' he said. 'The world's one black market and Europe's on her back with her legs wide open. So why not me? Why shouldn't I have a house in the Lido, why shouldn't

204 | *From Schlemiel to Sabra*

a woman warm my bed, why shouldn't I have money in my pocket? Don't tell me what I used to preach to you, Elisha. I told you what others told me. Forget it all, Elisha, forget it. Forget it.'"[23] In this exchange, Pinik hints at the questionable behavior that has enabled him to take on a lover with whom he shares a deluxe love nest. While the Allies struggle to defeat the Nazis and then work to rebuild Europe and lessen the plight of millions of homeless and hungry people, Pinik exploits his job to line his pockets. He steals war materials and sells them to black marketeers. Pinik now thinks solely about himself. He pushes Elisha to participate in the rape of a feminine Europe without considering its immorality, or the immorality of rape more generally. All Elisha needs to do to gain Pinik's comradeship is accept the gift of Felicia's body. By treating her like a meaningless piece of flesh and disregarding the traumatic events that likely led her to take up with Pinik, Elisha can cease acting like his father and renounce his patrimony. Elisha initially fails to understand what compels him to abandon Felicia's arms, but his desire to be like Pinik runs its course.

Regardless of Elisha's conscious desire to retain moral tenets of diasporic Jewish religiosity, he still harbors a hope for rebirth and his peers' unquestioned acceptance. It will take him years to accept that he cannot reconcile this hope with the moral tenets he strives to uphold. His encounters with Holocaust survivors points to his lack of the maturity necessary to forgo this hope and move toward development of a Jewish masculine form capable of integrating diasporic Jewishness's complicated legacy. Elisha, whose parents have told him of their lives in Europe and their relatives there, searches among the survivors for a relative and eventually finds a distant in-law. Through development of a homosocial bond with him, he looks to build a positive tie to Diaspora Jewry to complement his connection to its moral tenets. These efforts, however, go awry when his newfound in-law reveals that he survived Auschwitz by serving in a Sonderkommando.[24] Unsophisticated in his understanding of what transpired, Elisha proves unable to perceive Krochmal's actions as anything other than selfish and immoral collaboration with the enemy. Viewing realization of his vow to aid his "relative" as an admission of a similarly dishonorable character, Elisha lies to Krochmal and tries to abandon him and purge him from his memory:

> How I struggled to rid my mind of that memory. But all the years have not dimmed it or in any way changed its grotesqueness—except for this one difference: now I'm strong enough to admit what I was trying to hide from myself then. But even today, in the still silence of my soul, I am not free of the terror,

confusion, and shame that gripped me when I heard that relative, whom I had just adopted, say so plainly and matter-of-factly,

"In the crematorium."

More than anything else I was filled with revulsion at the thought of being connected to him. That feeling was more powerful than the terror and nausea. If only I could get out of there quickly, not remember the jumpy puppet. Not look into his eyes. Not breathe the air around him. And he had even said, "You wouldn't see me here today." Who wants to see you, goddamn it! Not me, that's for sure. Enough searching for family. I didn't want to ask questions or get answers, didn't want to be there at all, not see, not hear, not remember, not judge. I was looking for relatives—I found a relative.[25]

Initially, Krochmal's crematorium work repels Elisha. Yet his sense that in similar circumstances he would likely have taken similar steps to survive is what really bothers him. Rather than addressing this unflattering insight and working to avoid shame-inducing behavior, Elisha prefers to avert his thought from his character's abject features. Converting Krochmal into a diasporic Other, existing at an unbridgeable distance, serves his avoidance strategy. Yet as Elisha's subsequent encounter with Pinik reveals, even in Krochmal's absence, his ignominious features exist just beneath the surface waiting to express themselves.

Elisha's fear of painful introspection proves costly. It prevents him from appreciating his renewed connection with a positive strand of diasporic Jewish masculinity embodied by his father and his advancement of a native-born Palestinian Jewish identity integrating the best of the diasporic past and working to overcome its worst manifestations. Following his Venetian trial, Elisha and his unit travel to Germany. Bivouacking in a German suburb, Elisha and his comrade Brodsky aggressively requisition a place to sleep in an absent SS officer's home. Their forcible entrance into the home against the wishes of the officer's wife and daughters evokes the previously mentioned attempt by Jewish Brigade soldiers to rape German women in an act of vengeance. Yet neither man attempts to rape the women. On the contrary, when members of their unit break into the house with the intention to commit rape, Elisha prevents it. Finding one soldier holding down the arms of the teenage daughter and another kneeling between her legs ready to penetrate her, an armed Elisha threatens to kill his comrades if they don't stop. Elisha recognizes that vengeance will not differentiate the Hebrew soldiers from Diaspora Jews; he actively promotes a Jewish moral vision, upheld by Diaspora Jews for two thousand years, worthy of identification. Yet Elisha views his actions as a sign of embarrassing weakness.

Regardless of how youthful Elisha construes these events, neither the mature Elisha, who narrates what transpired twenty years earlier during his British military service, nor the implied author share his interpretation. By foiling their plans and threatening their lives, Elisha seriously embarrasses the would-be rapists; one of them seeks to take his revenge on Elisha. If the diasporic Jewish morality that leads Elisha to act was indeed a manifestation of feminine weakness, one would expect an individual identified with a vengeful and strong native-born Hebrew masculinity, free of diasporic traces, to easily vanquish him and voice his identity's superiority. Yet the mature narrator and Bartov push us to an alternative conclusion through a scene evocative of the abovementioned one from *Whose Little Boy Are You?*:

> "Prick!"
> The cry hit me suddenly along with the blow beneath my ear. As I bent over and raised my hand, I was kicked in the rear and fell forward. I recognized the voice; it was one of the three men I had chased away, rifle in hand.
> "Fuckin' nurse, gonna protect German girls, huh?"
> Again his boot landed on me, but now my head was clear, every muscle tense. I had nothing to protect myself with and I didn't want to expose my face. Pretending I was terrified I shielded my head with my hands, looking all the while at his legs. He made the predictable mistake of circling me, hoping to kick me where it would hurt most. The minute I saw him raise his left boot I sprang for it with all my might. While he struggled to regain his balance with my body wrapped around his right leg, I freed my right hand and with a swift upward thrust slammed my fist into his groin. He screamed in agony. As he doubled over to protect himself, I sprang to my feet and rammed my head into his face the way I learned to do as a kid from the Yemenites at the edge of our neighborhood. I was furious, mad enough to kill just like years before in school when I had to defend myself against kids bigger than me.[26]

Unlike the young child humiliated by his peers for his perceived divergence from native-born sabra masculinity and the youth striving to erase all evidence of his connection to diasporic masculinity, Elisha stands up for the positive moral vision his father brought from the Diaspora. He does so, however, through use of a combat technique learned from his hometown's rooted Yemenite Jews, whose regional ties purportedly reach back to the days of Solomon. Elisha merely feigns weakness and fear, and he appears ready to stand apart and promote an alternative form of Israeli masculinity.

As long as Elisha represses painful and defining moments like this, he will not be able to appreciate their significance—his ability to fearlessly assert a divergent masculine standard. Nonetheless, these incidents offer him no rest. His memory repeatedly returns him to Europe, and when he composes *The Brigade*, he starts processing them. It helps him mature and come to terms with the gender identity he voices in this fight.

Sibling Dissent and Brotherhood's Fracture

Despite *The Brigade*'s ability to demarcate the mid-1940s as the point at which native-born Palestinian Jews began to display discomfort with sabra masculinity and yearn for an alternative model of identity, other members of Bartov's generation paved the way for the challenge to sabra identity his novel mounted. While earlier discussion of *With His Own Hands* elucidated how the text advanced key elements of sabra masculinity, Holtzman's call for a more nuanced reading of Palmach-generation writing compels us to reexamine Moshe Shamir's fiction. It reveals that he numbered among the first native-born Palestinian Jewish writers who voiced discomfort with sabra masculinity and paved the way for subsequent writers to express similar reticence.

Awareness that *With His Own Hands* doubles as a biography of Shamir's brother Eliahu, whose life shares many details with Elik's life, helps one comprehend that this text offers an indirect but candid glimpse of Moshe Shamir's own self-perception through its portrayal of Elik's brother; it thereby points to Shamir's questioning of the masculine ideal that his text consciously promotes.[27] Prior to the partition plan's approval, Shamir had written *Hu halakh ba-sadot* (He walked in the fields, 1948), one of the Palmach generation's central texts, and had thereby contributed to the spread of the masculine norms Elik advances in *With His Own Hands*. Nonetheless, he failed to fully identify with these norms.

Shamir's use of gender in his short story "'Ad or ha-boker" (Until daybreak, 1952) further illustrates this incomplete identification.[28] The story features a female figure named Edna, who fights for art education and art's necessary place within the kibbutz. Her kibbutz secretary husband, who eliminates art instruction from kibbutz life in favor of a body-centered masculinity embodied by a winnower-operating farmhand, opposes her. The gendered nature of this struggle hints that Shamir internalized the negative perception of his literary efforts as an insignificant feminine endeavor. Nonetheless, like Edna, who leaves the kibbutz in an effort to force her husband and the kibbutz to reverse their decision, Shamir believed that art and artists were integral to Israeli society's spiritual health. Thus, he continued to devote his life to art, even if those around him considered it unworthy of his time.

Shamir's short story "Petihah le-sipur" (Opening to a story, 1953) offers a similar critique of the newly dominant masculine norm. Here, Shamir assumes the persona of a bereaved father to further question his promotion of a body-centered self-sacrificial form of Israeli masculinity.[29] Two of the father's primary points of contention with what his son, who fell in the 1948 war, represents are his son's dismissal of introspection and interpersonal connection. His decision to cease writing poetry voices his disdain for self-examination and his callous refusal to embrace fatherhood points to his disregard for interpersonal connections. Impregnating three different women, the son coerces them all into terminating their pregnancies. He thereby repudiates ties with them and the opportunity to foster a new generation. Unable to fully conceptualize a clear alternative to advance in lieu of the hegemonic body-centered self-sacrificial masculine ideal, Shamir nonetheless recognized its limitations and implicitly called for greater freedom for expression of Israeli masculinity. At an impasse, he long produced Janus-faced fiction simultaneously promoting and undermining the dominant masculine norm.[30]

While slightly older than Shamir, S. Yizhar stood alongside him as one of the foremost writers of the New Yishuv's first native-born generation, and his fiction deservedly found a prominent position in the *A Generation in the Land* anthology. Despite the widespread view of him as a partisan advocate of native-born culture, however, Yizhar, like Shamir, stood at a distance from those promoting Zionist masculinities grounded in self-sacrifice, violence, and physical development. Indeed, his fiction displays his strong connection to the Land of Israel and his awe-inspiring ability to convey its landscape through language. Yet exploration of his mature fiction's relationship to the writings of turn-of-the-century immigrant Palestinian Hebrew writers and their diasporic contemporaries proves more fruitful than its comparison with that of his contemporaries.[31] In fact, his depictions of uprooted fictional protagonists, evocative of those of his literary forebears, point to his identification with Self-Evaluative masculinity's tenets.[32]

In his early stories, one finds protagonists enamored by a masculine identity embodied by a strongly rooted, vital, and uncomplicated male figure redolent of the noble savage.[33] Sometimes these protagonists even act in accordance with this ideal. Thus, Reuven, the protagonist of "Laylah beli yeriot" (A night without fire, 1939), dreams about changing his life through participation in nighttime Palmach attacks; he thinks about how "wide horizons will be revealed and opened with one pull" of the trigger.[34] He then goes on to imagine that by "waving a bayonet and inserting it with a single complete drive below the ribs, turning it over and with a good kick to the stomach, painted a famous red, extracting it, and wiping it in the grass," he will encounter the sublime.[35]

In a firefight, Avner, the protagonist of "Mish'olim ba-sadot" (Pathways in the fields, 1938), actually experiences the type of sublime moment that Reuven subsequently dreams about:

"Yet when he freed the bolt to expel the bullet casing, his fear turned into a type of raging, excited, incomprehensible rejoicing, and he inadvertently caught a type of song gurgling forth from his throat. What refreshing powers coursed within him and the instinct of ancient times sang: I don't love anything on this earth, other than myself alone. Now I am alive."[36] As the protagonist sets his primitive instincts free and allows them to burst forth in song during battle, he feels reborn. Culture seems little more than a constraining force that must be put aside to truly live; Palestine appears to be a place where Jewish men can live free of such constraints.

Yizhar's subsequent fiction displayed the author's movement in a new direction that set him off from peers who unquestioningly glorified native-born youth and their normative values.[37] Like their author, Yizhar's narrator-protagonists stand at a distance from those around them and the values they embodied. The seminal 1949 works "ha-Shavui" (The prisoner) and "Khirbet Khizeh," where Yizhar voices his filiation with Self-Evaluative masculinity's earlier twentieth-century advocates, best exemplify this. In contrast with Reuven and Avner, these works' uprooted narrator-protagonists prove reticent to embrace sadism and violence as enviable expressions of masculinity or communal aspirations. Furthermore, they display a pacifistic outlook and, over time, come to terms with their *tlishut*. Thus, they assist Yizhar advance a masculine form he considered superior and more in line with the ideals he wanted the new Israeli state to embody.

Both "The Prisoner" and "Khirbet Khizeh" depict operational military units to illuminate an action-oriented male ideal's limitations. Extended deployments and the conditions of war desensitize the male soldiers, including the narrators, and make it easier for them to act and complete their assignments. Yet such desensitization disengages their moral faculties, pushes them to immoral action, committed both independently and in fulfillment of orders, and inhibits their derivation of pleasure from their actions. While both narrators find this process problematic and struggle intellectually with resultant actions and their moral implications, homo-social bonds initially prevent them from breaking with their fellows. Consequently, when their fellows' actions transgress their personal beliefs, the narrator-protagonists don't stand up for them. Nonetheless, they refuse to accede to a violent body-centered self-sacrificing masculinity's ascendency or necessity.

Prior to their presumed composition of the two works, the narrator-protagonists suffer from feelings of uprootedness tied to their inability to act according to their beliefs during military operations. Alienated from their fellows and lacking a male community maintaining alternative masculine standards in greater harmony with their personal beliefs, the narrators, like Oved 'Etzot in *mi-Kan umi-kan*, take up their pens. They too hope to build a community committed to introspection and joint pursuit of moral action serving the collective's best interest. Initially, the experiencing Is display a sense of inferiority to their fellows, whom they perceive as inhabiting a "world of courageous and energetic virility" during military activities.[38] Subsequently, however, the narrating Is take pride in their ability to process painful experiences and achieve a sense of superiority through self-improvement. It elevates them above their fellow soldiers who inhabit "the world of the insensitive and crude."[39]

Despite the literary and moral power of "The Prisoner" and "Khirbet Khizeh," they failed to generate a male community grounded in introspection and the struggle to square the Jewish tradition's historically high ethical standards with modern statecraft's demands. Moreover, "Khirbet Khizeh" and the expulsion of indigenous Palestinian Arabs during the State of Israel's establishment that it portrays were subject to an act of "collective forgetting."[40] Many Israelis considered sabra masculinity to have proven itself on the battlefield during the Independence War. Comrades and families of fallen native-born soldiers and the general population proved reticent to challenge it or memorial culture's use of native-born soldiers' death to promote it in the early state period.[41]

Filial Embrace and Alterity's Expression

Ultimately, a different member of Shamir, Yizhar, and Bartov's biological generation played a key role in undermining sabra masculinity's early state period predominance. When his poems were anthologized alongside the literary works of others born in Palestine and abroad that the *A Generation in the Land* anthology's editors saw firmly grounded in local experience, Yehuda Amichai did not seem to be someone who would go on to fulfill this function. His British military service, Independence War combat experience, and published poetry collection treating the theme of military service and featuring Israeli landscape depictions obscured how his mind-set diverged from those of others affiliated with the Palmach literary generation.[42]

Amichai was, in fact, already moving in an alternative direction.[43] This nonconformity became apparent as he increasingly drew on his and his family's diasporic connections to assert a Jewish masculinity he considered better able to fulfill Israeli society's protective, procreative, and provisioning needs than the predominant sabra model.[44] It has been convincingly argued that assertion of this divergent Israeli masculine form and the alternative vision of Israeliness that it promoted enhanced his literary status and contributed to his emergence as one of Israel's most prominent poets.[45]

Initially, Amichai's representations of war experiences served as a key indicator of his presence outside the mainstream, because they offered him a platform for expressing his discomfort with sabra masculinity and his sense of alienation from unselfconscious promoters of it. Like Yizhar, he did not turn to literature to promote a warrior-like culture of self-sacrifice. Instead, he referenced his Independence War experiences to undercut efforts to valorize male soldiers and their battlefield sacrifices for political purposes.[46] Thus, in contrast with Shamir's employment of Elik's death to sanctify his lived values, Amichai's "Geshem bi-sdeh krav" (Rain on a battlefield, 1955) refuses to ventriloquize the dead to advance an agenda. While the speaker's living friends use blankets to shield their heads from the rain, his dead friends cannot act, and their bodies get soaked. Hence, one cannot cross the impermeable barrier of death to confirm a dead man's virtue or the principles he upheld.

Furthermore, as Amichai's speaker in "Ani rotzeh lamut 'al mitati" (I want to die in my bed, 1958) asserts, the domestic sphere, rather than the battlefield, proves to be man's true measure. Thus, the soldier-speaker downplays the glory of military service. While contemporary Israeli soldiers were offered the mantle of the biblical hero Samson, who was renowned for his physical prowess, the speaker renounces it. He lacks the long hair that underlies Samson's strength anyway. It was shaved off when he mobilized for service, and his close-cropped hair reveals his plain appearance and average strength. Indeed, he consents to serve as a soldier in the "killing fields" and endanger his life like Joshua's Israelite soldiers during the Land of Israel's conquest, but he does not do this because he wants to die a heroic death or get tucked in tightly beneath the battlefield earth's "warp and woof."[47] Even as he heads out to battle, he yearns to return home to his wife's embrace and the textured feel of their conjugal bed's sheets and blankets.

The speaker's priorities might inhibit his and his fellows' ability to strike a death blow to opposing armies and ensure a period of peace and security for their people, but the speaker does not view them as unmanly or as a betrayal of the war dead. Perhaps the enemy will kill his wife and capture and torture him, but to ensure his homecoming, the speaker will risk this. The future proves uncertain and one should live life like the individual standing on the edge of a precipice.[48]

Through valorization of acknowledgment and acceptance of one's vulnerability and need for others as signs of masculine strength, the speaker in "I Want to Die in My Bed" shifts attention back to the domestic sphere and the roles that men need to perform there for their society to thrive. Thus, promotion of masculinity's provisioning and procreative components in Amichai's "Otobiografiyah bi-shnat 1952" (Autobiography in the year 1952, 1955) makes it an important corollary to this poem. As the poem's speaker explains, life lived in accordance with military norms proves unsatisfying, and homosocial fellowship forged during wartime fails to compensate. Life seems banal and purposeless. Thus, the way the speaker plods through it parallels "the movement of many slaves rowing a ship."[49] Escape from this monotony, rather than a desire to protect his community or display his heroic character, motivate the speaker's contemplation of the release offered by battlefield death. As he explains, his blood "wanted to escape in many wars, and through many openings."[50]

Adopting an alternative masculinity with different priorities than those typifying his peer group's militaristic masculinity offers the speaker a way out of his personal crisis. When he observes that the spring brings more birds than departed last winter and his thoughts shift to procreation and provision, the speaker finds a renewed desire to live. Linked to the blood surging through his pregnant wife's heavy body and nourishing their unborn child, the arterial blood he contemplates freeing through suicide or battlefield death assumes new meaning. This blood's passion sparks the conception of new life, and its preservation offers the speaker the chance to nurture another human being. Indeed, he might bequeath this child a tempestuous world with future challenges. Yet like the mother whose womb encompasses the fetus and allows her to nurture it, protect it, and meet life's earliest challenges, he can shelter his child from initial threats following its birth, foster it, and gradually teach it how to independently address life's challenges. Behold, this is what the speaker's father did. As the speaker recalls, "My father built a great worry around me like a dry dock."[51] Like a dry dock surrounding a ship during construction, the father's great worry encompassed the speaker, gave him a sense of stability that ships at sea are denied, and helped him mature.

Although dry dock–like worry parallels the maternal womb, the nurturing role it concretizes is advanced as a preferable masculine alternative to reckless endangerment on the battlefield. Connection to his father only makes this model more attractive to the speaker. Having gone to sea before his father socialized him to the masculinity he embodied, the speaker mistakenly assumed that no alternative existed besides the masculine norms of his peers. Yet on the verge of fatherhood, when his peers' norms push him to contemplate suicide, examination and embrace of his deceased father's example offers the speaker renewed life.

Despite his assertion of an alternative masculinity through a father's depiction, Amichai initially failed to stress this model's diasporic origins.[52] This changed, however, with publication of *Lo me-'akhshav lo mi-kan* (Not of this time, not of this place, 1963). The novel advances a form of Israeli masculinity explicitly linked with diasporic Jewish life and evocative of the Self-Evaluative masculine tradition. Like the speaker in "Autobiography in the Year 1952," the novel's protagonist suffers a midlife crisis, and sabra masculine norms prove incapable of extricating him from it. Amichai communicates this crisis through his protagonist's doubling. One Joel remains in Jerusalem, and a second Joel travels to his German hometown.[53] When Jerusalem Joel treads on a landmine and dies, the crisis resolves itself. Native Israeli identity produced through Diaspora experience's denial dies a symbolic death, and Joel becomes synonymous with the individual who moves forward after returning to Germany and addressing issues tied to his diasporic past.

Confrontation with his desire to play Judah Maccabee in a school play and his perceived betrayal of his childhood friend Ruth propel German Joel's psychological advance.[54] Young Joel wants to assume the Judah Maccabee role, because the "elephants and the battles" of the Hanukkah drama enamor him and the other Jewish schoolboys.[55] They want to be warriors like Judah, just as they previously wanted to be Native American or classical

Greek heroes; their desire to possess the military grandeur of combative masculine figures even leaves them willing to play the Seleucid king Antiochus IV Epiphanes and his general Nicanor, the Hanukkah drama's villains.[56]

Regardless of the age-appropriate nature of Joel's attraction to Judah Maccabee's martial characteristics, however, his obstinate refusal to cede this role is directly linked to feelings of insecurity and "feminization" that assert themselves following Hitler's rise to power. This Jewish role will aid Joel in keeping these feelings at bay. Joel feels that Siegfried, the principal's red-haired son, whose name evokes the *Nibelungenlied*'s dragon-slaying hero and whose red hair, redolent of the biblical he-man Esau, communicates a combative non-Jewish masculinity, has a less serious need for this role. Thus, he considers it unfair that he should be denied it. Ruth, who fails to grasp his underlying motivation, finds his stubbornness off-putting. Unable to change his mind, she bicycles off in a huff and gets into an accident.[57] Her leg's subsequent amputation foreshadows a worsening in her existential condition. After Joel immigrates to Palestine, she is murdered in a death camp. Thus, Joel's uncompromising desire to assume a warrior-like masculinity masks his feelings of Jewish impotence and his sense of guilt for having abandoned Ruth and left her to face the burden of their shared powerlessness alone.

The school Hanukkah play gets canceled after Ruth's accident, and Joel never plays Judah Maccabee. Yet, following his immigration to Palestine, he assumes the warrior role he dreamed of assuming in his childhood. As he recalls,

> I especially loved to play various heroes' roles. Especially enchanting to my imagination were Greek heroes like Achilles and his friend Patroclus. I'd perform the protracted anger of the beautiful and awesome Achilles in his tent, until the battle noise and storming enemy took me out of my tent and I would burst out in lion roars with the round shield in my left and the short-bladed Greek sword in my right. It was the anger of a theater prima donna. I especially loved to play war games where the enemy seemingly achieved the upper hand. I'd be pushed to the last corner, to the last wall, and I'd even lie on my back when the enemy army would surround me, and in the truly last minute I'd recover and defeat them all. The unreliability of fate entranced me. From the high wall to the deep well and back again. I got drunk on the intoxication of the sudden turning point, the last-minute salvation.[58]

Joel imagines the strong homosocial bond shared by Patroclus and Achilles mimicked by his tie with his comrades during the Independence War.

Consequently, he happily performs his military role, as he earlier performed the role of Achilles. Joel's military performance and his homosocial ties help him become a successful Israeli archaeologist and a member of the Israeli elite.

Unfortunately, Joel's warrior role and his prioritization of homosocial ties undermine his efforts to maintain a successful monogamous relationship. Discovery of what it is about them that leads him astray can help Joel right the course of his life. Repeated encounter with the physical landscape of his childhood gets this process started. Strolls through Weinberg's Hofgarten make him aware of the fear, shame, and guilt that weigh him down: "Later a boy from the Hitler Youth kicked Ruth cruelly, and the echo of those kicks beats in my head and my blood. Since that time, I have heard many violent collisions between bodies, iron striking earth, metal striking metal, iron striking stone, stone colliding with stone, steel with flesh, flesh with flesh. All those sounds dimmed in my memory. But the sound of the brown-shirted boy's foot striking Ruth's crippled body has grown stronger instead of dimming, until it has become the thunder in my life."[59] Years earlier, while strolling through the Hofgarten with Ruth, Hitler Youth attacked them. While two youths held Joel down and forced him to watch, others beat Ruth mercilessly. His inability to live up to his pledge to care for Ruth and protect her makes Joel feel guilty and ashamed. Yet what turns this traumatic experience into the "thunder in [his] life" is the damage it does to Joel's sense of masculinity. As his bar mitzvah approaches, the masculine warrior role assumed when he plays Achilles is shown to be no more than an act. Rather than recovering at the last minute, after his enemies pin him to the ground, Joel remains immobilized. Like Ruth, whose missing leg is revealed when a brown-shirted boy kicks her prosthesis, Joel has his impotence exposed. He has spent his subsequent life trying to hide it.

Consequently, Joel also elides the frightful circumstances behind his nuclear family's immigration to Palestine. After Nazis beat a local Jew to death, Joel's father, who prepares the corpse for burial, concludes that Jewish life in Germany is no longer tenable and flees with his family. To conceal these circumstances and the feelings of impotence, fear, and femininity he associates with them, Joel employs Zionist convention and presents his family's immigration to Palestine as a form of ascent, or ʿaliyah. Yet this cuts Joel off from his German past and any potentially heroic or positive association he can draw from it. Furthermore, it prevents him from arriving at a mature understanding of his father's motivations and his relationship with Ruth.

When Joel returns to Weinberg, repressed memories resurface and offer him a way to fix his marriage and overcome the impasse in his life brought on by his rigid adherence to a warrior role and the homosocial ties that help maintain it. Rather than becoming overwhelmed by these memories, Joel reveals the strength necessary to confront them. Through consideration of his connection with Ruth as well as his father's decision to leave Germany, he locates an alternative masculinity that aids him in moving forward with his life. He comes to see that feelings of vulnerability and weakness, like those he experienced during Ruth's beating, constitute unavoidable aspects of mortal existence and there is nothing shameful about them. As Ruth and his father understood, the individual's response to such feelings, rather than the existence of such feelings, defines him or her. Thus, after her accident, Ruth does not complain or make excuses. Instead, she works to best live her life with the limited resources available to her. Such behavior requires that she do what she sees best and disregard others' judgments. Similarly, his father's desire to protect his family trumps any embarrassment he might feel about others viewing him as cowardly and "feminine" for fleeing Germany.

Nonetheless, Joel's adoption of an alternative gender identity more attuned to Ruth and his father's example is circumscribed by the homosocial ties he maintains. But when his visit provokes consideration of his relationship with his childhood companion Heinz, Joel comes to recognize that not all such ties are beneficial and it is sometimes best to renounce those that inhibit individual development. A "pretty and pampered boy," Heinz was picked on by other boys.[60] Joel protects him, but neither friendship nor virtue guides him. Instead, he "protected him . . . so that he would become [his] slave and property."[61] In fact, his homoerotic attraction to Heinz and his love for him outweigh his love for Ruth:

> It was now clear that I had loved Heinz. I was always with Ruth, but I loved Heinz. . . . We used to wrestle frequently on the large soft carpet in his mother's house. He begged me to wrestle with him even when I told him to choose someone not as strong as I was, for it was not pleasurable for me to always win. . . . He would not answer and only pleaded with his brown eyes, and I could not resist him and again we rolled around on the carpet and held tightly to each other.[62]

Military service and Joel's homosocial ties with his fellow soldiers offer Joel an outlet for his homoerotic desire and his sadomasochistic tendencies that previously animated his relationship with Heinz. Consequently, they constitute important elements attracting him to martial masculinity and combat opportunities. Joel satisfies his desire for sadomasochistic pleasure through combat and exploitation of the unequal power relations characterizing his homosocial ties with his fellow soldiers. Simultaneously, however, these homosocial bonds prevent him from developing relationships grounded in empathy for the vulnerable and weak.

Rather than disappearing following Joel's completion of active military service, his sadomasochism searches for alternative expression. It leads him to distance himself from his wife, Ruth, whose name and character evoke his childhood friend, and invest heavily in an extramarital affair with the American doctor Patricia. Joel grasps this following exploration of his relationship with Heinz. As he notes, "the same long lashes, the dark skin and long nose, and almond eyes" link Patricia with Heinz.[63]

Consideration of Joel's relationships with Heinz and Patricia reveals that national commitment and soldierly homosocial bonds are not actually the primary motivations for his adoption of sabra masculinity and his participation in military activities. Recognition of this finally allows Joel to slough off this masculinity and its antidiasporic foundation. Subsequent adoption of a masculine identity more accepting of his weakness and vulnerability resolves his personal crisis. This identity only demands that he do his best to deploy his limited resources to meet personal and communal needs. Thus, Jerusalem Joel, who embodies a warrior-like sabra masculinity, meets his death, and the other Joel, who advances a Diaspora-inspired Jewish masculine form, remains on stage unopposed. In this way, Amichai directly challenges sabra masculinity's early state period primacy.

Subsequent literary works, such as *The Brigade*, show Israeli writers operating in the cultural space that Amichai developed. His pioneering fiction and poetry expanded the possibilities for Israeli masculinity's legitimate expression. But before diasporic Jewish masculinity would find mainstream acceptance as the basis for varied forms of Israeli masculinity, it would take decades and the work of scores of writers and cultural activists. It is here that our discussion arrives at Amos Oz's work.

Amos Oz and Collective Reclamation of Diasporic Patrimony

Israeli autobiography serves an important cultural role by negotiating the relationship between individuals and a national community looking to impose its cultural standards on its members. In this way, it "has been instrumental in the shaping of contemporary Israeli selves."[64] Thus, Amos Oz's autobiography *A Tale of Love and Darkness* proved able to permanently alter the possibilities for Israeli masculinity's legitimate expression by stressing diasporic Jewish masculinity's capacity to enrich Israeli masculinity and improve Israeli men's lives.

Over the course of Oz's long career, Israelis had come to closely identify him with Israeliness, and his autobiography's measured deconstruction of his public persona contributed significantly to its tremendous sway:

> When he emerged onto the Israeli literary scene in the 1960s, Amos Oz typified the ideal Sabra. His piercing blue eyes, mane of blond hair, and ease with Israeli Hebrew made him everything that the Jewish state wanted to be—the very antithesis of Diaspora Jewry. Oz, the kibbutznik, like the Jaffa Orange or the soldiers crying at the Western Wall in 1967, was the image that Israel sought to show to the rest of the world—the sum of everything that the Zionist project stood for: strength, vitality, and resolve that is also contemplative and open to self-doubt.[65]

Based on their familiarity with this public persona, readers expected that Oz's autobiography would provide a linear narrative detailing the triumphant process whereby an Israeli youth assumed sabra masculinity and rose to fame. Such a narrative, evocative of Shamir's *With His Own Hands*, would have offered Israeli readers a way to reconnect with sabra values and rededicate themselves to their expression through alignment of their lives with the autobiographical narrator's life course. Yet Oz chose not to fulfill his readers' expectations. Instead, he introduced a long-obscured figure who ushered in a masculine form grounded in the balancing of sabra Israeliness with a Jewishness that challenged its norms.

Given the name Amos Klausner at birth, Oz's public persona emerged when he was fourteen. As Oz explains, "a couple of years after my mother's death, I killed my father and the whole of Jerusalem, changed my name, and went on my own to Kibbutz Hulda to live there over the ruins."[66] Oz only committed an act of metaphoric parricide. Nonetheless, he intentionally dissociated himself from his father (and dead mother) in his quest for the masculine strength alluded to by his new Hebrew surname, as well as the vigor and resolve that became hallmarks of his public persona. Left behind, a teenage Oz assumed, was a diasporic heritage he saw forced upon him against his will.

While Oz retrospectively infuses humor into his narration of Amos Klausner's childhood efforts to cultivate a garden in the compacted and shaded soil of his family's backyard, this episode epitomizes the child's crushing disappointment with his bookish father. Yehudah Klausner cannot grant Amos access to the new Zionist world emerging "beyond the mountains of darkness" that he yearns to inhabit.[67] Furthermore, loyalty to Yehudah distances Amos from the "new, suntanned Jews" armed with shovels, pitchforks, and hoes, who bring forth "bread from the earth"; he and his father, who are "pale as two sheets of paper" and sport a covering of sunscreen as thick as Velveeta, struggle to successfully farm.[68] Consequently, the seedlings they plant quickly "bowed their heads and . . . started looking as sickly and weak as persecuted Diaspora Jews," and never yield nourishment.[69]

In contrast, the heroic Oz, who escapes paternity's chains, successfully crosses the imagined mountains of darkness. He joins a kibbutz, the locus classicus of Zionist realization; he successfully farms the land and sustains those around him. Furthermore, as the following anaphora-laden quotation captures, the youthful Oz believes that Zionist collective settlements will foster his masculinity's full expression: "There's where the land is being built and the world is being reformed, where a new society is forged. They are stamping their mark on the landscape and on history, they are plowing fields and planting vineyards, they are writing a new song, they pick up their guns, mount their horses, and shoot back at the Arab marauders: they take our miserable human clay and mold it into a fighting nation."[70] Here, he could emerge as "the resplendent new Hebrew youth at the height of his powers, making everyone who sees him tremble at his roar: like a lion among lions," that his father's tutelage had prevented him from becoming.[71]

In fact, Amos Oz neither self-actualizes in accordance with his plan nor acquires true brothers on Kibbutz Hulda. As his reference to efforts to "live over the ruins" alludes, the opposition between Jerusalem and the northern settlements, upon which Oz tries to construct a new life, proves illusory, and in an effort to cope with his disappointment, he starts writing. Consequently, one finds personal disappointment and anger concealed just beneath his early stories' surface—something that informs the dual role landscape plays in these largely kibbutz-set tales. They feature two separate and conflicting maps—an official upper map extolling the achievements of Israeli civilization realized through reason's employment and a lower map voicing "the emotions, desires, and drives that the official upper map conceals."[72] Furthermore, the kibbutz's topography parallels Oz's later autobiographical portrayal of his father, Yehudah—an individual whose smug hyper-rationalism hides his impotent inability to cope with his wife's emotions, desires, and drives and prevents him from building a successful marriage with her. When Oz allows the collection's narrators to pierce the upper map to reveal what is hidden below, he voices his paternal critique and Jerusalem's continuing influence on his psyche.

As long as Oz held firm to his public persona, he did not produce a fictional world that reconciled the upper map's rational and seemingly impotent "masculinity" with the lower map's emotional and highly volatile "femininity." Thus, *Mikha'el sheli* (My Michael, 1968) revolves around a talented geologist, who, ironically, proves unable to grasp his wife's subterranean psychic world. When she loses touch with reality, he proves unable to intervene in a timely fashion, because he only understands her superficially. Consequently, she descends into a fantasy world of her own creation.

Ultimately, Oz relaxed his hold on his public persona following Yehudah's death in 1970. He began to explore, rather than just represent, the gender dynamics animating his psyche and his fictional world, and he worked toward reconciliation with the masculine model his father represented. His largely unremarkable portrayal of the night of November 29, 1947, aids in comprehension of his changing worldview. It employs numerous details found in other depictions of that night. Thus, Oz describes a huge crowd listening to the United Nations partition vote on one of the few available radios, and the spontaneous songs, dancing, and drinking of the revelers after partition's approval. Yet a strange family bonding moment stands out:

> My very cultured, polite father was standing there shouting at the top of his voice, not words or wordplay or Zionist slogans, not even cries of joy, but one long naked shout like before words were invented.
>
> Others were singing now, everyone was singing, but my father, who couldn't sing and didn't know the words of popular songs, did not stop but went on with his long shout *aaaahhh*, and when he ran out of breath, he inhaled like a drowning man and went on shouting, this man who wanted to be a famous professor and deserved to become one, but now he was just *aaahhhh*.[73]

A Jewish state's seemingly inevitable establishment allows Oz's father to more fully express his long-circumscribed masculinity. Abandoning his cultured, polite demeanor, he unconsciously unleashes a long-pent-up primal scream and draws in his family. In a rare moment of physical affection, Fania caresses her husband. Amos is not embarrassed by his father's behavior either. As he recalls, "I might unawares have been helping my father shout."[74] In fact, by modeling his behavior on that of his father, he realizes his previously expressed desire to roar "like a lion among lions."

Rather than marking a transformative moment, after which he goes on to effectively till the soil, take up arms, or sacrifice himself for the nation, Yehudah's roar confirms a sense of masculinity that he had long doubted. This confirmation enables him to act on his long-repressed feelings. Thus, Yehudah tries to strengthen his bond with his young son by wordlessly expressing his love. As he puts Amos to sleep, he employs his inexperienced fingers to uncharacteristically and tenderly caress him, just as his wife caressed him hours before. Noting a previously undetected aspect of his father's personality, Oz comments that it was "as though in this darkness my father had turned into my mother."[75]

In fact, Yehudah derives pleasure from expression of his love for his son and engagement with what he perceives as his feminine side, and he feels compelled to explain what led him to embrace Zionism and eventually repress characteristics he perceived as feminine:

> He told me in a whisper . . . what some Gentile boys did to him at his Polish school in Vilna, and the girls joined in too, and the next day, when his father, Grandpa Alexander, came to the school to register a complaint, the bullies refused to return the torn trousers but attacked his father, Grandpa, in front of his eyes, forced him down onto the paving stones in the middle of the playground and removed his trousers too, and the girls laughed and made dirty jokes, saying that the Jews were all so-and-sos, while the teachers watched and said nothing, or maybe they were laughing too.[76]

Like Nachman's playground experience in *Whose Little Boy Are You?* and Joel's encounter with the Hitler Youth in *Not of This Time, Not of This Place*, the degradation Yehudah and his father endure leads him to question his and his people's masculine character and burden him with tremendous shame. Yehudah becomes a Zionist and immigrates to Palestine in an attempt to free himself of it. But absent the type of male homosocial community the Self-Evaluative writers looked to create, this shame festers. To not let it debilitate him, Yehudah adopts a rigid rationalist approach to rein in his drives, emotions, and desires. Yet when Jewish sovereignty draws near and Yehuda senses that he has ensured that his son will never face such humiliation for being a Jew, the intensity of his shame wanes and Yehudah proves able to temporarily disregard his ingrained rationalism. Consequently, he is able to engage his emotions and the world of the irrational for constructive purposes—the forging of a stronger tie with his son and instructing his son on the need to remain open to one's seemingly feminine emotional side.

Jewish sovereignty's effect persists, but it proves insufficient for Yehudah to effectively inculcate his values to his son or forge stronger ties with his wife or his son. In their absence, Fania commits suicide, and Oz leaves Yehudah for dead. In his later years, Oz recognizes Yehudah's changed tastes and his newfound appreciation of Yiddish literature, whose magic, supernaturalism, and emotionalism had previously deterred him. Yet in his youth, Oz fails to notice his father's character transforming. Instead, he interprets Yehudah's ineffective response to Fania's mental illness and his subsequent inability to independently work through his wife's suicide as signs of weakness.

This self-serving interpretation enables Oz to bury feelings of impotence and guilt resulting from his failure to save his mother, justify his abandonment of his father, and assume a public persona of invincibility. By concealing his shame and sense of "feminine" weakness, as Yehudah did before he confessed them to his son, Oz forgoes the opportunity to commune with his father over their shared failure and work through it together.

Oz's mature narrator progressively recognizes that his behavior closely resembles his father's earlier behavior. Rather than continue to hide this resemblance behind his public persona, Amos accepts that he too failed to fully confront his irrational side and give timely voice to his masculine potential. Jettisoning a public persona distant from his current self-perception, Oz forges a productive tie with his father through effective introspection. Yehudah's schlemiel-like inability to cultivate the soil and his ignorance of proper firearm use had previously been given disproportionate attention. Yet the mature narrator sees that these things are not that relevant. In contrast, the masculine model that Yehudah presented in 1947, with its openness to love and emotional expression, now appears strikingly germane. Consequently, the mature narrator embraces aspects of it, even if others might view them as diasporic and feminine.

When Oz lovingly presents what he views as the essence of Yehudah's pioneering spirit, his reconciliation with him proves evident:

> In Galilee and the Plains, in the Beth Shean Valley and the Valley of Jezreel, in the Sharon and the Hefer Valley, in the Judean lowlands, the Negev and the wilderness around the Dead Sea, pioneers are tilling the land, muscular, silent, brave, and bronzed. And meanwhile he the earnest student from Vilna plows his own furrow here.

One fine day he too would be a professor on Mount Scopus, he would help push back the frontiers of knowledge and drain the swamps of exile in the people's hearts. Just as the pioneers in Galilee and the Valleys made the desert bloom, so he too would labor with all his strength, with enthusiasm and dedication, to plow the furrows of the national spirit and make the new Hebrew culture bloom.[77]

Earlier in Oz's autobiography, his narrator accentuated the distance separating Yehuda from Zionist pioneers to diminish him. Here, the narrator's laudatory intentions underlie Yehuda's similarity to more conventional pioneers and the parallel nature of their activities. Yehuda's commitment to Hebrew culture's cultivation proves analogous to that of pioneers who endeavor to make the desert bloom. Yehuda never actually became a professor at the Hebrew University, but his ceaseless efforts to attain an academic position that would allow him to best aid in Hebrew culture's development reflected his commitment. Sadly, when he earned just such a position in Beer Sheva, he died before he assumed it. Nonetheless, the narrator promotes the pioneering role Yehuda strove to assume as worthy of emulation.

Whether consciously or not, when Oz assumed a professorship of literature at Ben Gurion University, the world-class institution that developed out of the institute where his father had been offered a position, he did emulate the model his father placed before him. This act, as the autobiography carefully details, breaks down geographic boundaries and bridges time to link Oz to a golden chain of Klausner men who dedicated themselves to nurturing the Hebrew spirit. Consequently, Oz's mature narrator traces his lineage back to his forebear Rabbi Alexander Ziskind of Horodno (?–1794), and gives his great uncle Yosef Klausner (1874–1958), a renowned Hebrew literary scholar, a prominent place in his narrative.[78]

Despite the changes wrought by Zionism and his inseverable ties to them, Oz stresses continuity and his equally important connection to diasporic Jewishness. Thereby, he legitimized diasporic Jewish masculinity as a source for varied expressions of Israeli Jewish masculinity. This constituted a monumental act. As Gershon Shaked emphatically noted, "The author-narrator-son that brings to life his fathers' traditions on one hand and his new life on the kibbutz on the other, and this book's readers, who absorb this complex and carefully designed world, are already 500 parasangs from the ideal of the 'New Hebrew' severed from his past."[79]

Readers' responses to Oz's autobiography and the huge number of people who engaged with it confirm Shaked's assertion concerning its impact.

Four hundred fan letters sent to Oz point to the sense of many readers that he burst a wall blocking them from their childhood pasts and the past of their parents and grandparents. It was as if he exorcised the demons from this Diaspora-infused world.[80] Efforts to conform to the dominant sabra prototype had previously rendered elements of these readers' pasts inaccessible. Now they could fully engage their memories, recoup them, and reimagine themselves. Simultaneously, hundreds of thousands of Israeli readers who were less directly affected by the autobiography, as well as viewers of its 2015 screen adaptation, came face-to-face with a new understanding of the past grounded in its synthesis of native Israeliness and diasporic Jewishness.[81] Sabra masculinity's unquestioned hegemony had come to an end and contemporary Israeli society proved progressively more willing to engage with variant forms of masculine expression reflective of its complex and frequently contradictory nature.

Self-Evaluative Masculinity's Scholarly Implications

An influential group of literary critics has arisen that aspires to study Modern Hebrew literature as part of a more diffuse phenomenon—modern Jewish literature and culture.[82] Taking multilingualism and cosmopolitanism as their work's starting point, they have transformed Modern Hebrew literary studies. Comparative examination of Hebrew and Yiddish literatures in the context of broader transnational developments in world literature has helped Hebrew and Yiddish literary studies transcend the ideological tunnel vision that previously characterized them.[83] Consequently, this scholarship has energized Jewish literary studies and catalyzed a productive reexamination of periodization, nomenclature, and literary canon.[84]

Even with the important insights made possible by directing attention to transnational modernism and cosmopolitan multilingualism, the scholars promoting these phenomena as keys to understanding Modern Hebrew literature have limited their findings' value. Instead of considering the prominent roles Zionism and efforts to establish the State of Israel played in the development of early twentieth-century Hebrew literature addressed in this book, they unduly discount their influence. Thus, they portray its writers as a loosely linked group of stateless individuals lacking a territorial home and even a modern sense of national belonging.[85] This description overstates these writers' rootlessness and their very real desire for social connection. Consequently, these scholars obscure how this desire drove Self-Evaluative Hebrew writers to employ literary representations of gender and sexuality to foster national ties between Jewish men in Palestine. Furthermore, their repudiation of Hebrew writers' ability to simultaneously affiliate with national and transnational communities runs counter to broader trends in scholarship on transnationalism.[86] This scholarship increasingly recognizes the coexistence of national and transnational elements in modernist writers' thought and work. As critic Sonita Sarker succinctly puts it, "trans is only partially post."[87] Therefore, those endeavoring to better understand early twentieth-century Hebrew literature must still take its complex and seemingly paradoxical relationship to Zionist history and culture into consideration.

Indeed, as those employing a transnational approach assert, early twentieth-century Hebrew literature written by writers dispersed across the globe had a high degree of internal coherence. Nevertheless, historical developments, geographic locations, and political conditions still influenced individual writers and influenced the work they produced. Therefore, these contextual elements that distinguish between authors are worthy of more serious consideration.

Prior to the late eighteenth century, the majority of world Jewry resided in the Polish-Lithuanian kingdom and participated in a trilingual Jewish culture employing Hebrew, Yiddish, and Aramaic.[88] Even after the kingdom's late eighteenth-century breakup, language, culture, and geographic proximity bound East European Jews to one another for almost a hundred years, but Jewish society was atomizing.[89] East European Jewish men, who perceived their society's dissolution as something that "feminized" them individually and collectively, struggled with their chaotic environment. They spearheaded the development of variant forms of secular Jewish culture intended to respond to this chaos and "remasculinize" the Jewish people. Ideology, geography, class, and language constituted important factors influencing how divergent Jewish cultures and divergent Jewish communities responded to modernity's challenges as they competed with non-Jewish cultural forms and communities for Jewish hearts and minds. Consequently, by the early twentieth century, differences begin to outweigh the commonalities binding East European–bred Ashkenazic Jewry together, and one can begin to talk about Soviet Jews, American Jews, and Palestinian Jews as distinct groups.

Advocates of the transnational approach to Hebrew literature soft-pedal the powerful centrifugal forces at play. Thus, they assert the existence of "diasporic communities of readers and writers . . . separated by vast distances and opposing ideologies, as well as by class and gender, [who] at the same time . . . were united by their shared cultural allegiances."[90] Even though the youth of these disparate Jewish diasporic communities were no longer universally socialized into trilingual Jewish culture, these scholars argue that devotion to literary modernism and opposition to myriad forms of territorial nationalism unified them.

Similarly, the divergent trajectories of Hebrew and Yiddish cultures in these diasporic communities are deemphasized. While bilingual Hebrew-Yiddish writers remained active throughout the twentieth century and select Hebrew and Yiddish writers remained abreast of developments in both literatures, the interaction between writers working in these two languages should not be overemphasized or advanced as central to literary innovation.[91] It seems highly unlikely that Yiddish poets living in the Soviet Union, where publication of Hebrew books was banned, devoted time to keeping abreast of innovative Hebrew verse produced by American Hebrew poets such as Gabriel Preil (1911–93).

Affiliation with the Hebrew literary community and the broader Jewish literary community provided writers with an important sense of community, but it did not insulate them or their writing from the effects of their physical surroundings. In the United States, Hebrew writers were granted citizenship rights and faced strong assimilatory forces. Thus, their lives and works contrasted sharply with Hebrew writers' lives and works in the Russian Empire.[92] Similarly, immersion in London's rough and tumble street life did not affect Hebrew writers or their work in the same way that Tel Aviv's developing Hebrew public culture did. Therefore, it seems dubious to portray early twentieth-century Hebrew writers as existentially secure "resident aliens."[93] As they pursued their literary craft, they did not pass unaffected through multiple geographical spaces. They were interested in the comforts of home, and they desired the domestic and extraterritorial rights of citizens.

The denial of the important and unique effects of immigration to Palestine by advocates of the transnational approach proves a central corollary of the previous point. The possibility that Jaffa–Tel Aviv and Jerusalem, Pre-State Palestine's primary developing cities, could foster literary development through service as culturally diverse and dynamic urban centers offering Hebrew authors a comparable experience to that offered by European cities is never engaged. Instead, Hebrew writers are portrayed as imaginatively mapping Europe onto Palestine.[94] As these scholars would have it, immigration to Palestine did not significantly affect Hebrew writers whose work displayed similar preoccupations before and after immigration to Palestine.[95] Yet, for Hebrew writers raised in traditional Jewish society, where they imbibed Jerusalem's unique position within a great messianic drama, physical presence in Palestine/Zion demanded confrontation with this myth.[96] If Israel had no messiah, as Brenner asserted, Palestinian Jews had to employ progressive means if they wanted to bring about a better Jewish future. Thus, proponents of Self-Evaluative masculinity turned to literature to advance norms that they believed would help Jewish men harness their inner strength to pursue it. Composition of such literature involved the forgoing of potentially rich avenues for aesthetic development that these writers might have otherwise pursued. In the case of Arieli, it meant abandonment of a rich symbolist style that produced "Hagadat ha-mavet" (The death tale, 1912) and "Metim me-heled" (Mortals, 1913).[97] Thus, scholars would be best served to consider the effects of presence in Palestine on Hebrew writers' work.

Just as this book advocates for the introduction of politics into the study of early twentieth-century Hebrew literature, it encourages the integration of Hebrew literature into the study of Zionism and Israeli history. Not only can Hebrew literature supply important insights about Israeli society and culture's early twentieth-century development, but it can also contribute to more effective understanding of subsequent Israeli developments.

First, attention to Hebrew literature challenges claims about the centrality of a pioneering immigrant nucleus's physical encounter with the Land of Israel to Israeli culture from 1900 to the 1970s.[98] Many forms of Israeliness, including the one promoted by the advocates of Self-Evaluative masculinity, placed greater value on individual Israelis' interconnectedness than they did on individual connection to the soil. Furthermore, Palestinian Hebrew culture was developed through an ongoing process involving competition between disparate groups within the wider population promoting and campaigning for different ideas and approaches.[99] The adoption, rejection, combination, and reformulation of various early twentieth-century elements produced normative Israeli culture. Closer examination of this complex evolutionary process offers a more nuanced understanding of Israeli culture and its ongoing development.

Second, consideration of Hebrew literature's early twentieth-century role helps account for the prominent role of Hebrew literature and its authors in Israeli culture well into the state period. The Land of Israel failed to fulfill its promise of redemption, and arrival in Palestine did not radically transform Jewish immigrants.[100] While their Zionist beliefs and attitudes were not wholly divorced from their prior worldviews, the Palestinian immigrant experience, including these immigrants' encounter with early twentieth-century Ottoman Palestine's nonredemptive character, played a central role in identity formation and reformulation. The difficult conditions immigrants encountered created or accentuated spiritual and metaphysical needs; the ability of variant streams of Zionism to respond to these needs proved critical to their recruitment efforts. While scholars have pointed to the important role played by newly invented rituals in translating the ideas and discourse of Zionism into action and supplying direction to immigrants and the native-born, early twentieth-century Hebrew literature constituted the primary address for immigrants looking to satisfy metaphysical needs. Its ability to satisfy this need through the act of reading garnered Hebrew literature a prominent role that would endure into the state period. Israeli historians would do well to remember this prominent role and engage Hebrew literature to see what it can teach them.

Notes

1. Yosef Hayyim Brenner, "Ha'arakhat 'atzmenu bi-shloshat ha-kerakhim," in *Ketavim* (Tel Aviv: ha-Kibutz ha-Me'uhad, 1978–85), 4:1223–96.

2. The Palmach was the largest Pre-State Palestinian Jewish self-defense organization.

3. Moshe Shamir, *be-Mo yadav: pirke Elik* (Tel Aviv: 'Am 'Oved, 1973), 221; Moshe Shamir, *With His Own Hands*, trans. Joseph Shachter (Jerusalem: Israeli Universities Press, 1970), 215.

4. Shamir, *be-Mo Yadav*, 219; Shamir, *With His Own Hands*, 213.

5. Shamir, *be-Mo yadav*, 220; Shamir, *With His Own Hands*, 214.

6. Shamir, *be-Mo yadav*, 220; Shamir, *With His Own Hands*, 214.

7. See Yael Zerubavel, *Recovered Roots: Collective Memory and the Making of Israeli National Tradition* (Chicago: University of Chicago Press, 1995).

8. Oz Almog, *The Sabra: The Creation of the New Jew*, trans. Haim Watzman (Berkeley: University of California Press, 2000), 2.

9. Almog, *The Sabra*, 3.

10. Almog, *The Sabra*, 123.

11. On the role Oz's novel played in Israeli society's movement out of a conceptual crisis that had long plagued it, see Yig'al Shvartz, *Pulhan ha-sofer ve-dat ha-medinah* (Or Yehudah: Dvir, 2011), 143–84.

12. 'Azriel Ukhmani, Moshe Shamir, and Shlomo Tanny, eds., *Dor ba-aretz: antologiyah shel sifrut Yisre'elit* (Tel Aviv: Sifriyat Po'alim, 1958), 7; Anita Shapira, "'Dor ba-aretz,'" *Alpayim* 2 (1990): 178–203; Tom Segev, *1949: The First Israelis*, ed. Arlen Weinstein (New York:

Henry Holt, 1998), 290. For a discussion of the term *Palmach generation* as well as other names assigned to the foremost young writers of the early state period, see Reuven Kritz, *ha-Siporet shel dor ha-ma'avak le-'atzma'ut* (Tel Aviv: Pura, 1978), 9–10.

13. Avner Holtzman, *Mafteah ha-lev: omanut ha-sipur shel Hanokh Bartov* (Jerusalem: Mosad Bialik, 2015), 15–38.

14. *The Brigade* appeared after the Eichmann trial catalyzed widespread changes in Israel society and culture's relationship to the diasporic past. By this time, as will be subsequently addressed, other Israeli writers had taken important steps to dislodge sabra masculinity from its perch and replace it with alternatives more receptive to positive features of the diasporic Jewish heritage. Nonetheless, I believe that Bartov's autobiographic novels accurately convey a feeling extent among native-born Palestinian Jews, even before statehood, that sabra masculinity proved overly restrictive and failed to reflect their self-perception. For brief discussion of the Eichmann trial's impact on Israeli culture, see Alan Mintz, *Hurban: Responses to Catastrophe in Hebrew Literature* (Syracuse, NY: Syracuse University Press, 1996), 240–44.

15. The reading of the autobiographical novels *Pitze bagrut*, *Shel mi atah yeled*, *Regel ahat ba-hutz*, and *mi-Tom 'ad tom* as one overarching text has previously been promoted by critics Gershon Shaked and Avner Holtzman. Gershon Shaked, "Matzevah le-avot ve-siman le-vanim: otobiografiyot Yisraeliyot mi-shnot ha-shmonim ve-'ad le-reshit ha-me'ah ha-'esrim ve-ahat," in *Temunah kvutzatit: hebetim be-sifrut Yisrael uve-tarbutah* (Or Yehudah: Dvir, 2009), 295–310; Holtzman, *Mafteah ha-lev*, 85–147.

16. Hanokh Bartov, *Shel mi atah yeled* (Bnai Brak: ha-Kibutz ha-Me'uhad, 2010), 101; Hanoch Bartov, *Whose Little Boy Are You?* trans. Hillel Halkin (Philadelphia: Jewish Publication Society, 1978), 122–23.

17. Hanokh Bartov, *Pitze bagrut* (Tel Aviv: 'Am 'Oved, 1965), 64; Hanoch Bartov, *The Brigade*, trans. David Segal (Philadelphia: Jewish Publication Society, 1967), 67.

18. Bartov, *Pitze bagrut*, 109; Bartov, *The Brigade*, 119–20.

19. Bartov, *Pitze bagrut*, 118; Bartov, *The Brigade*, 127.

20. Bartov, *Pitze bagrut*, 164; Bartov, *The Brigade*, 177–78.

21. Bartov, *Pitze bagrut*, 166; Bartov, *The Brigade*, 180.

22. Bartov, *Pitze bagrut*, 172; Bartov, *The Brigade*, 187.

23. Bartov, *Pitze bagrut*, 203; Bartov, *The Brigade*, 221.

24. Sonderkommandos were work units composed of prisoners in Nazi death camps who disposed of the bodies of gas chamber victims.

25. Bartov, *Pitze bagrut*, 148; Bartov, *The Brigade*, 161.

26. Bartov, *Pitze bagrut*, 223; Bartov, *The Brigade*, 243.

27. Dan Miron, *Arba' panim ba-sifrut ha-'Ivrit bat-yemenu* (Jerusalem: Schocken:, 1962), 362–65. On the problem of *With His Own Hands*'s generic classification, see Philip Hollander, "Beyond Martyrdom: Rereading Moshe Shamir's *With His Own Hands*," *Hebrew Studies* 49 (2008): 262–64.

28. Moshe Shamir, *Nashim mehakot ba-hutz* (Merhavyah: Sifriyat Po'alim, 1952), 7–32.

29. Originally published in *Masa* in 1953. Moshe Shamir, "Petihah le-sipur," in *Hamishim shanah, hamishim sipurim*, ed. Zisi Stavi (Tel Aviv: Yedi'ot Ahronot, 1998), 114–20.

30. This Janus-faced relationship to hegemonic masculine norms in Hebrew literature has been previously noted. Mikha'el Gluzman, *ha-Guf ha-Tzioni: le'umiut, migdar u-miniut ba-sifrut ha-'Ivrit ha-hadashah* (Tel Aviv: ha-Kibutz ha-Me'uhad, 2007), 28.

31. Miron, *Arba' panim*, 192–200.

32. For more on Yizhar and other Palmach-generation writers' incorporation of uprooted figures into their fiction to distance themselves from the dominant norms of their biological generation, see Hedi Shayit, "Lo 'margish ayzen': ha-tzabar ha-talush ba-siporet ha-mukdemet shel 'Dor ba-Aretz' al pi yetzirot shel S. Yizhar, Moshe Shamir, ve-Hanokh Bartov," *mi-Kan* 9 (2008): 159.

33. For further discussion of Yizhar's flirtation with this ideal, see Dan Miron, *Arba' panim*, 221–26.

34. S. Yizhar, *ha-Hurshah ba-giv'ah* (Merhavyah: Sifriyat Po'alim, 1947), 328.

35. S. Yizhar, *ha-Hurshah ba-giv'ah*, 328; Miron, *Arba' panim*, 224.

36. S. Yizhar, "Mish'olim ba-sadot," *Gilyonot* 7, nos. 5–6 (1938): 393.

37. This development was obscured by important works depicting collective experience. For example, in "ha-Hurshah ba-giv'ah" (The grove on the hill, 1947), Yizhar blurs the boundaries of individual consciousness to portray the collective experience of a group struggling to defend its position against enemy advance. On Yizhar's "collective" novellas, see Miron, *Arba' panim*, 248–64. Similarly, his novella *Shayarah shel hatzot* (Midnight convoy, 1950) focalizes around a protagonist who defers introspection to fully immerse himself in the task of getting a convoy with needed supplies safely to its destination.

38. Dan Miron, afterword to *Midnight Convoy and Other Stories*, by S. Yizhar, trans. Misha Louvish, Miriam Arad, and Reuven Ben-Yosef (Jerusalem: Israeli Universities Press, 1969), 265.

39. Miron, afterword to *Midnight Convoy and Other Stories*, 265.

40. Anita Shapira, "Hirbet Hiza: Between Remembrance and Forgetting," *Jewish Social Studies* 7, no. 1 (2000): 1–62.

41. Emmanuel Sivan, *Dor tashah: mitos, deyokan ve-zikaron* (Tel Aviv: Ma'arakhot, 1991), 55–72; Almog, *The Sabra*, 69, 252.

42. Ukhmani, Shamir, and Tanny, *Dor ba-aretz*, 8; Dan Miron, *Mul ha-ah ha-shotek: 'iyunim be-shirat Milhemet ha-'Atzma'ut* (Jerusalem: Keter, 1992), 276.

43. Chana Kronfeld views alterity as central to this alternative direction: "Amichai's oeuvre . . . offers an unrelenting critique of the dominant ideology of its time." Chana Kronfeld, *The Full Severity of Compassion: The Poetry of Yehuda Amichai* (Stanford, CA: Stanford University Press, 2016), 2.

44. On the centrality of diasporic experience to Amichai's work, see Nili Gold, *Yehuda Amichai: The Making of Israel's National Poet* (Waltham, MA: Brandeis University Press, 2008). Although Kronfeld disagrees with Gold about diasporic experience's centrality, she too sees Amichai drawing on a diasporic masculine model based on his father to challenge sabra masculinity: "The figuration of the father provides the poetry with a decidedly diasporic ideal of an alternative, 'soft' masculinity that is very different from the normative Israeli one." Kronfeld, *The Full Severity of Compassion*, 13.

45. Dan Miron, "A Good Boy Full of Love," *ha-Aretz*, October 3, 2005, 4.

46. Such politically motivated valorization was a key feature in the work of poet Natan Alterman who wielded tremendous influence on Palmach-generation writers. See Miron, *Mul ha-ah ha-shotek*, 202–3.

47. Yehuda Amichai, *Shirim, 1948–1962* (Jerusalem: Schocken, 1977), 95; Yehuda Amichai, *Yehuda Amichai: A Life of Poetry, 1948–1994*, trans. Benjamin and Barbara Harshav (New York: Harper Collins, 1994), 37; Gold, *Yehuda Amichai*, 286–88, 308.

48. This interpretation is based on Chana Kronfeld's reading of the phrase "To live in the lion's maw" (*liheyot be-lo'a ha-aryeh*). She explains that "it was an idiomatic expression

in 1950s and 1960s Hebrew for life in Israel; the meaning is roughly equivalent to that of the English idiom, 'life in the shadow of a volcano.'" See Chana Kronfeld, "Beyond Thematicism in the Historiography of Post-1948 Political Poetry," *Jewish Social Studies* 18, no. 3 (2012): 196.

49. Amichai, *Shirim, 1948–1962*, 15; Amichai, *A Life of Poetry*, 7.

50. Amichai, *Shirim, 1948–1962*, 15.

51. Amichai, *Shirim, 1948–1962*, 15; Amichai, *A Life of Poetry*, 7.

52. Gold asserts that Amichai camouflaged his origins in his poetry for many years. Gold, *Yehuda Amichai*, 11–15; cf. Kronfeld, *The Full Severity of Compassion*, 301.

53. On the novel's dual hero, see Glenda Abramson, *The Writing of Yehuda Amichai: A Thematic Approach* (Albany: State University of New York Press, 1989), 151–58.

54. Gold, *Yehuda Amichai*, 62–88.

55. Yehuda Amichai, *Lo me-ʿakhshav lo mi-kan* (Tel Aviv: Schocken, 1975), 399.

56. Amichai, *Lo me-ʿakhshav lo mi-kan*, 399.

57. As Gold notes, Joel presents conflicting versions of the disagreement, and I have selected the version above as more in accordance with the psychological and gender issues addressed by the novel. Gold, *Yehuda Amichai*, 79.

58. Amichai, *Lo me-ʿakhshav lo mi-kan*, 559.

59. Yehuda Amichai, *Not of This Time, Not of This Place*, trans. Shlomo Katz (New York: Harper and Row, 1968), 81; Amichai, *Lo me-ʿakhshav lo mi-kan*, 126.

60. Amichai, *Not of This Time, Not of This Place*, 73; Amichai, *Lo me-ʿakhshav lo mi-kan*, 109.

61. Amichai, *Not of This Time, Not of This Place*, 73; Amichai, *Lo me-ʿakhshav lo mi-kan*, 109.

62. Amichai, *Not of This Time, Not of This Place*, 73–74; Amichai, *Lo me-ʿakhshav lo mi-kan*, 110.

63. Amichai, *Not of This Time, Not of This Place*, 212; Amichai, *Lo me-ʿakhshav lo mi-kan*, 349.

64. Tamar Hess, *Self as Nation: Contemporary Hebrew Autobiography* (Waltham, MA: Brandeis University Press, 2016), 1.

65. Eran Kaplan, "Amos Oz's *A Tale of Love and Darkness* and the Sabra Myth," *Jewish Social Studies* 14, no. 1 (2007): 119–20; for a fuller discussion of Oz's assumption of this position and the factors underlying this persona's successful reception, see Shvartz, *Pulhan ha-sofer ve-dat ha-medinah.*

66. Amos Oz, *Sipur ʿal ahavah ve-hoshekh* (Jerusalem: Keter, 2002), 516; Amos Oz, *A Tale of Love and Darkness*, trans. Nicholas de Lange (Orlando, FL: Harcourt, 2004), 464.

67. Oz, *Sipur ʿal ahavah ve-hoshekh*, 271.

68. Oz, *Sipur ʿal ahavah ve-hoshekh*, 271–72; Oz, *A Tale of Love and Darkness*, 234.

69. Oz, *Sipur ʿal ahavah ve-hoshekh*, 280; Oz, *A Tale of Love and Darkness*, 242.

70. Oz, *Sipur ʿal ahavah ve-hoshekh*, 9–10; Oz, *A Tale of Love and Darkness*, 9.

71. Oz, *Sipur ʿal ahavah ve-hoshekh*, 372; Oz, *A Tale of Love and Darkness*, 327.

72. Yigal Schwartz, *Zionist Paradox: Hebrew Literature and Israeli Identity* (Waltham, MA: Brandeis University Press, 2014), 230.

73. Oz, *Sipur ʿal ahavah ve-hoshekh*, 403; Oz, *A Tale of Love and Darkness*, 356–57.

74. Oz, *Sipur ʿal ahavah ve-hoshekh*, 403; Oz, *A Tale of Love and Darkness*, 357.

75. Oz, *Sipur ʿal ahavah ve-hoshekh*, 405; Oz, *A Tale of Love and Darkness*, 359.

76. Oz, *Sipur ʿal ahavah ve-hoshekh*, 405; Oz, *A Tale of Love and Darkness*, 359.

77. Oz, *Sipur ʿal ahavah ve-hoshekh*, 152; Oz, *A Tale of Love and Darkness*, 126.

78. Dan Laor, "bi-Mehozot ha-zikaron: biografiyah, ide'ologiyah, ve-sipur bi-ketivato shel Amos Oz," *Yisrael* 7 (2005): 29.

79. Shaked, "Matzevah le-avot ve-siman le-vanim," 366.

80. For full discussion of these letters, see Shvartz, *Pulhan ha-sofer ve-dat ha-medinah*, 143–84.

81. More than 150,000 copies of the autobiography were sold. Taking library copies and shared copies into account, it is fair to assume that readers of the autobiography numbered in the hundreds of thousands—a remarkable number for a society with only 2.5 million adult readers literate in Hebrew. Shvartz, *Pulhan ha-sofer ve-dat ha-medinah*, 143.

82. David Shneer and Robert Adler-Peckerar, "The Berkeley School of Jewish Literature," *Journal of Jewish Identities* 7, no. 1 (2014): 1–7.

83. These scholars' ideas cross-fertilized with those of like-minded researchers in modernist studies stressing transnational exchange's importance to literary modernism. On this broader trend within literary studies, see Douglas Mao and Rebecca Walkowitz, "The New Modernist Studies," *PMLA* 123, no. 3 (2008): 737–48.

84. Important examples of this scholarship include Chana Kronfeld, *On the Margins of Modernism: Decentering Literary Dynamic* (Berkeley: University of California Press, 1996); Shachar Pinsker, *Literary Passports: The Making of Modernist Hebrew Fiction in Europe* (Stanford, CA: Stanford University Press, 2011); Allison Schachter, *Diasporic Modernisms: Hebrew and Yiddish Literature in the Twentieth Century* (New York: Oxford University Press, 2012). Noteworthy reexaminations of the Hebrew canon this scholarship helped spark include Naomi Seidman, *A Marriage Made in Heaven: The Sexual Politics of Hebrew and Yiddish* (Berkeley: University of California Press, 1993); Robert Alter, "Fogel and the Forging of the Hebrew Self," *Prooftexts* 13, no. 1 (1993): 3–14; Michael Gluzman, "Unmasking the Politics of Simplicity in Modernist Hebrew Poetry," *Prooftexts* 13, no. 1 (1993): 21–44; Sheila Jelen, *Intimations of Difference: Dvora Baron in the Modern Hebrew Renaissance* (Syracuse, NY: Syracuse University Press, 2007).

85. Pinsker, *Literary Passports*, 7; for similar positions, see Chana Kronfeld, *On the Margins of Modernism*, 57–70.

86. As Benjamin Harshav, a pioneering figure behind the use of a transnational approach for the study of Hebrew and Yiddish literatures, reminds us, "it is hard to imagine . . . a Jewish literature without the achievements of the revolutionary secular period." Benjamin Harshav, *Language in Time of Revolution* (Berkeley: University of California Press, 1993), 77.

87. Sonita Sarker, "Modernism in Our Image . . . Always, Partially," *Modernism/Modernity* 13, no. 3 (2006): 562.

88. Benjamin Harshav, *The Meaning of Yiddish* (Berkeley: University of California Press, 1990), 3–26. It should be remembered that full participation in this culture was restricted to an educated male elite fully conversant in Hebrew and Aramaic religious texts.

89. Israel Bartal, *The Jews of Eastern Europe, 1772–1881* (Philadelphia: University of Pennsylvania Press, 2002).

90. Schachter, *Diasporic Modernisms*, 17.

91. For an insightful discussion of Hebrew-Yiddish bilingualism and writers who continued to write in both languages well into the twentieth century, see Naomi Brenner, *Lingering Bilingualism: Modern Hebrew and Yiddish Literature in Contact* (Syracuse, NY: Syracuse University Press, 2016).

92. Attention to the significance of geography and its effects on Hebrew literary production underlies the important reevaluation of American Hebrew literature that

has occurred in the last decade. See Alan Mintz, *Sanctuary in the Wilderness: A Critical Introduction to American Hebrew Poetry* (Stanford, CA: Stanford University Press, 2012); Michael Weingrad, *American Hebrew Literature: Writing Jewish National Identity in the United States* (Syracuse, NY: Syracuse University Press, 2011); Stephen Katz, *Red, Black, and Jew: New Frontiers in Hebrew Literature* (Austin: University of Texas Press, 2009).

93. Pinsker, *Literary Passports*, 7.

94. Pinsker, *Literary Passports*, 401; Schachter, *Diasporic Modernisms*, 7.

95. Pinsker, *Literary Passports*, 393–94; Schachter, *Diaspora Modernisms*, 63.

96. Dan Miron, "Depictions of Jerusalem in Modern Hebrew Literature," in *City of the Great King: Jerusalem from David to the Present*, ed. Nitza Rosovsky (Cambridge, MA: Harvard University Press, 1996), 241–78; cf. Pinsker, *Literary Passports*, 393.

97. For more on these texts, see Natanel Segal, "A Study of Two Enigmatic Stories by L. A. Arieli: 'Mortals' and 'The Death Tale'" (PhD diss., New York University, 1991).

98. Bo'az Neumann, *Land and Desire in Early Zionism*, trans. Haim Watzman (Waltham, MA: Brandeis University Press, 2011).

99. My conclusion concurs with earlier scholarship. Saposnik, *Becoming Hebrew: The Creation of a Jewish National Culture in Ottoman Palestine* (New York: Oxford University Press, 2008), 254.

100. On the origins of this redemptive promise in traditional Jewish thought, see Gershon Cohen, "Zion in Rabbinic Literature," in *Zion in Jewish Literature*, ed. Abraham Halkin (New York: Herzl, 1961), 38–64; for a detailed historical presentation of the Land of Israel's failure to redeem immigrants' lives, see Gur Alroey, *An Unpromising Land: Jewish Migration to Palestine in the Early Twentieth Century* (Stanford, CA: Stanford University Press, 2014), 163–233.

SELECTED BIBLIOGRAPHY

Newspapers and Periodicals

ba-Mahaneh
Davar
Do'ar ha-yom
ha-Aretz
ha-Do'ar
ha-Mitzpeh
ha-Po'el ha-tza'ir
ha-Shiloah
Literarishe Bleter
Zemanim

Primary Sources

Abramovitz, Shalom Ya'akov. *Kol kitve Mendeleh Mokher Sefarim.* Tel Aviv: Dvir, 1958.

Agnon, Shai. "Avram Leybush u-vanav." In *Shai Agnon: mehkarim u-te'udot,* edited by Rafa'el Vayzer and Gershon Shaked, 30–33. Jerusalem: Mosad Bialik, 1978.

——. "Be'erah shel Miryam o kta'im me-haye enosh." In *Kovetz Agnon 2,* edited by Emunah Yaron, Rafa'el Vayzer, Dan Laor, and Reuven Mirkin, 11–42. Jerusalem: Magnes, 2000.

——. *See also* Agnon, Shmu'el Yosef; Agnon, S. Y.

Agnon, Shmu'el Yosef. *Shira.* Tel Aviv: Schocken, 1974.

——. *Yiddishe Verk.* Jerusalem: Hebreisher Universitet in Yerusholaim, Yidish-Eptaylung, 1977.

——. "Yosef Hayyim Brenner be-hayyav, uve-moto." In *Y. H. Brenner: mivhar divre-zikhronot,* edited by Mordehai Kushnir, 119–54. Tel Aviv: ha-Kibutz ha-Me'uhad, 1971.

——. *See also* Agnon, Shai; Agnon, S. Y.

Agnon, S. Y. *Shira.* Translated by Zeva Shapiro. New York: Schocken, 1989.

——. "Tishre." *Gazit* 33, nos. 9–12 (1977): 87–99.

——. *See also* Agnon, Shai; Agnon, Shmu'el Yosef.

Ahad ha-'Am. *Kol kitve Ahad ha-'Am.* Tel Aviv: Dvir, 1956.

Aleykhem, Sholem. *Ale Verk Fun Sholem Aleykhem.* 28 vols. New York: Sholem Aleykhem Folksfond Oysgabe, 1923.

Amichai, Yehuda. *Lo me-'akhshav lo mi-kan.* Tel Aviv: Schocken, 1975.

——. *Not of This Time, Not of This Place.* Translated by Shlomo Katz. New York: Harper and Row, 1968.

——. *Shirim, 1948–1962.* Jerusalem: Schocken, 1977.

——. *Yehuda Amichai: A Life of Poetry, 1948–1994.* Translated by Benjamin and Barbara Harshav. New York: HarperCollins, 1994.

Arieli, Levi Aryeh. *Kitve L. A. Arieli: sipurim, mahazot, hagadot, ma'amarim, igrot.* 2 vols. Edited by Mikha'el Arfa. Tel Aviv: Dvir, 1999.

———. "Yeshimon." *ha-Adamah* 1, no. 3 (Tishrei-Adar 1920): 253–73.

———. "Yeshimon." *ha-Adamah* 1, no. 7 (Iyar 1920): 2–17.

———. "Yeshimon." In *Dapim (kovetz rishon)*, edited by Dov Kimhi, 4–18. Jerusalem: Defus Y. Helperin, 1922.

———. *See also* Orlof, L. A.

Bartov, Hanoch. *Pitze bagrut*. Tel Aviv: 'Am 'Oved, 1965.

———. *Shel mi atah yeled*. Bnai Brak: ha-Kibutz ha-Me'uhad, 2010.

———. *The Brigade*. Translated by David Segal. Philadelphia: Jewish Publication Society, 1967.

———. *Whose Little Boy Are You?* Translated by Hillel Halkin. Philadelphia: Jewish Publication Society, 1978.

Birnbaum, Philip, trans. *High Holiday Prayer Book*. New York: Hebrew Publishing Company, 1951.

Brenner, Binyamin. *Gedolah haytah ha-bedidut*. Tel Aviv: 'Am 'Oved, 1978.

Brenner, Yosef Hayyim. *Ketavim*. 4 vols. Edited by Menahem Dorman and Yitzhak Kafkafi. Tel Aviv: ha-Kibutz ha-Me'uhad, 1978–85.

———. *Kol Kitve Y. H. Brenner*. 3 vols. Edited by Menahem Poznanski. Tel Aviv: ha-Kibutz ha-Me'uhad, 1955–67.

———. "Me'ever la-gevulin." In vol. 1, *Ketavim*, edited by Menahem Dorman and Yitzhak Kafkafi, 725–826. Tel Aviv: ha-Kibutz ha-Me'uhad, 1978.

———. "Reshimato ha-genuzah shel Brenner al 'Be'erah shel Miryam' me-et Agnon." In *Gam ahavtem gam sene'tem*, edited by Hayyim Be'er, 363–65. Tel Aviv: 'Am 'Oved, 2002.

Brody, Heinrich, ed. *Selected Poems of Jehudah Halevi*. Translated by Nina Salaman. Philadelphia: Jewish Publication Society, 1974.

Gnessin, Menachem. "Tehilato shel ha-te'atron ha-'Ivri." In *'Al Y. H. Brenner: od zikhronot*, edited by Yitzhak Kafkafi and Uri Brenner, 65–68. Tel Aviv: ha-Kibutz ha-Me'uhad, 1991.

Gordin, Jacob. "God, Man, and Devil." In *God, Man, and Devil: Yiddish Plays in Translation*, edited and translated by Nahma Sandrow, 29–95. Syracuse, NY: Syracuse University Press, 1999.

Gutman, Nahum. *Ben holot u-khehol shamayim*. Tel Aviv: Yavneh, 2001.

Hauptmann, Gerhart. *The Dramatic Works of Gerhart Hauptmann*. Edited by Ludwig Lewisohn. 9 vols. New York: B. W. Huebsch, 1912–29.

Mishpahat Brenner, "Halifat-mikhtavim ben Yosef Hayyim Brenner, ra'yato Hayah Broyda u-vnam Uri." In *Mahbarot Brenner 3–4*, edited by Menahem Dorman and Uzi Shavit, 9–91. Tel Aviv: ha-Kibutz ha-Me'uhad and Tel Aviv University, 1984.

Orlof, L. A. "'Allah Karim!" *ha-Shiloah* 27 (1912): 51–65, 107–19, 204–21, 323–36, 401–11, 501–8.

———. *See also* Arieli, Levi Aryeh.

Oz, Amos. "A Monologue: Behind the Sound and Fury." *Tikkun* 13, no. 2 (March–April 1998): 57–59.

———. *Sipur al ahavah ve-hoshekh*. Jerusalem: Keter, 2002.

———. *A Tale of Love and Darkness*. Translated by Nicholas de Lange. Orlando: Harcourt, 2004.

Pinski, Dovid. *Yenkel der Shmied [Yankele the Blacksmith]*. In vol. 4, *Dramen*, 7–122. Nyu-York: Poyle Tsien, 1918.

Re'uveni, Aharon. *'Ad-Yerushalayim*. Edited by Yig'al Shvartz. Jerusalem: Keter, 1987.

———. "Be-reshit ha-mevukhah." *ha-Adamah* 1 (1919–20): 11–30, 141–59, 338–43, 392–415, 501–23.

———. *ha-'Oniyot ha-ahronot*. Warsaw: Shtibel, 1923.

————. *Shamot*. Warsaw: Shtibel, 1925.

Shamir, Moshe. *be-Mo yadav: Pirke Elik*. Tel Aviv: 'Am 'Oved, 1973.

————. *Nashim mehakot ba-hutz*. Merhavyah: Sifriyat Po'alim, 1952.

————. "Petihah le-sipur." In *Hamishim shanah, hamishim sipurim*, edited by Zisi Stavi, 114–20. Tel Aviv: Yedi'ot Ahronot, 1998.

————. *With His Own Hands*. Translated by Joseph Shachter. Jerusalem: Israeli Universities Press, 1970.

Shimoni, David. *Idylls*. Jerusalem: Youth and Hechaluz Department of the Zionist Organization, 1957.

Ukhmani, 'Azriel, Moshe Shamir, and Shlomo Tanai, eds. *Dor ba-aretz: antologiyah shel sifrut Yisraelit*. Tel Aviv: Sifriyat Po'alim, 1958.

Weininger, Otto. *Sex and Character: An Investigation of Fundamental Principles*. Edited by Daniel Steuer and Laura Marcus. Translated by Ladislaus Löb. Bloomington: Indiana University Press, 2005.

Yardeni, Galyah. *Tet-zayin sihot 'im sofrim*. Tel Aviv: ha-Kibutz ha-Me'uhad, 1962.

Yavni'eli, Sh. "Divre ha-mehayevim." In *'Al ha-saf: kovetz le-'inyane ha-hayyim vela-sifrut*, 10–15. Jerusalem: Mifleget Po'ale Tziyon be-'Eretz Yisra'el, 1918.

Yizhar, S. *ha-Hurshah ba-giv'ah*. Merhavyah: Sifriyat Po'alim, 1947.

————. "Mish'olim ba-sadot." *Gilyonot* 7, nos. 5–6 (1938): 362–406.

Secondary Sources

Abramson, Glenda. "Haim Nahmias and the Labour Battalions: A Diary of Two Years in the First World War." *Jewish History and Culture* 14, no. 1 (2013): 18–32.

————. *Hebrew Writing of the First World War*. London: Valentine-Mitchell, 2008.

————. "'Perhaps We'll Meet Again'—Moshe Sharett's Military Service." *Israel Studies* 20, no. 3 (Fall 2015): 18–38.

————. *The Writing of Yehuda Amichai: A Thematic Approach*. Albany, NY: State University of New York Press, 1989.

Abramson, Glenda, and Tudor Parfitt, eds. *The Great Transition: The Recovery of the Lost Centers of Modern Hebrew Literature*. Totowa, NJ: Rowman and Allenhald, 1985.

Almog, Oz. *The Sabra: The Creation of the New Jew*. Translated by Haim Watzman. Berkeley: University of California Press, 2000.

Alro'ey, Gur. *Imigrantim: ha-hagirah ha-Yehudit le-Eretz-Yisrael be-reshit ha-me'ah ha-'esrim*. Jerusalem: Yad Yitzhak Ben-Tzvi, 2004.

————. "Mesharte ha-moshavah o rodanim gase ruah?—me'ah shanah le-agudat 'ha-Shomer'—perspektivah historit." *Katedra* 133 (2009): 77–104.

————. *See also* Alroey, Gur.

Alroey, Gur. "'Olim' or Immigrants: The Jewish Migration to Palestine in the Early Twentieth Century." Lecture, Arizona State University, Tempe, February 5, 2006.

————. *An Unpromising Land: Jewish Migration to Palestine in the Early Twentieth Century*. Stanford: Stanford University Press, 2014.

————. *See also* Alro'ey, Gur.

Alter, Robert. Afterword to *Shira* by S. Y. Agnon, 573–85. New York: Schocken, 1989.

————. "Fogel and the Forging of the Hebrew Self." *Prooftexts* 13, no. 1 (1993): 3–14.

Anderson, Benedict. *Imagined Communities: Reflections on the Origins and Spread of Nationalism*. New York: Verso, 2006.

Arbel, Michal. *Katuv 'al 'oro shel ha-kelev: 'al tefisat ha-yetzirah etzel Shai Agnon.* Jerusalem: Keter, 2006.

Aron, Lewis, and Karen Starr. "Freud and Ferenczi: Wandering Jews in Palermo." In *The Legacy of Sandor Ferenczi: From Ghost to Ancestor.* Edited by Adrienne Harris and Steven Kuchuck, 150–68. New York: Routledge, 2015.

'Arpali, Bo'az. *ha-'Ikar ha-shlilit.* Tel Aviv: ha-Kibutz ha-Me'uhad, 1992.

Aschheim, Steven. *Brothers and Strangers: The East European Jew in German and German Jewish Consciousness, 1800–1923.* Madison: University of Wisconsin Press, 1982.

Attia, Ali. *The Hebrew Periodical ha-Shiloah (1896–1919): Its Role in the Development of Modern Hebrew Literature.* Jerusalem: Magnes, 1991.

Avigur, Sha'ul, Yitzhak Ben-Tzvi, Eli'ezer Galili, Yisra'el Galili, Yehuda Slutzky, and Ben Tzion Dinur, eds. *Me-hitgonenut le-haganah.* Vol. 1 of *Sefer toldot ha-Haganah.* Jerusalem: ha-Sifriyah ha-Tzionit, 1956.

Bakon, Yitzhak. *Agnon ha-tza'ir.* Be'er Sheva: Singer Chair in Yiddish Studies, 1989.

——, ed. *Yosef Hayyim Brenner: mivhar ma'amare bikoret 'al yetzirato ha-sipurit.* Tel Aviv: 'Am 'Oved, 1972.

Band, Arnold. *Nostalgia and Nightmare: A Study in the Fiction of S. Y. Agnon.* Berkeley: University of California Press, 1968.

——. *See also* Band, Avraham.

Band, Avraham. "Agnon lifne hayoto Agnon: sipurav ha-'Ivriyim shel Shai Tshatshkes." *Molad* 175–76 (1963): 54–63.

——. *See also* Band, Arnold.

Bartal, Israel. *The Jews of Eastern Europe, 1772–1881.* Philadelphia, University of Pennsylvania Press, 2002.

——. *See also* Bartal, Yisra'el.

Bartal, Yisra'el. *Kozak u-bedvi: "am" ve-"eretz" ba-le'umiut ha-Yehudit.* Tel Aviv: 'Am 'Oved, 2007.

——. "'Yishuv hadash' ve-'yishuv yashan'—ha-dimui veha-metzi'ut." Chap. 5 in *Galut ba-aretz: Yishuv Eretz-Yisra'el be-terem Tzionut,* 74–89. Jerusalem: ha-Sifriyah ha-tzionit, 1995.

——. *See also* Bartal, Israel.

Bar-Yosef, Hamutal. *Maga'im shel dekadens: Bialik, Berdichevski, Brenner.* Be'er Sheva: Hotza'at ha-sefarim shel Universitat Ben-Guryon ba-Negev, 1997.

Be'er, Hayyim. *Gam ahavtem gam sene'tem.* Tel Aviv: 'Am 'Oved, 2002.

Ben-Ari, Nitsa. *Suppression of the Erotic in Modern Hebrew Literature.* Ottawa: Ottawa University Press, 2006.

Ben 'Ezer, Ehud. "'Eynayim lahem ve-lo yir'u oznayim." *Moznayim* 68, no. 1 (1993): 24–25.

Berkowitz, Michael. *Zionist Culture and Western Jewry before the First World War.* Chapel Hill: University of North Carolina Press, 1996.

Berlovitz, Yaffa. *Lehamtzi' eretz lehamtzi' 'am: tashtiot sifrut ve-tarbut bi-yetzirah shel ha-'aliyah ha-rishonah.* Tel Aviv: ha-Kibutz ha-Me'uhad, 1996.

Bernheimer, Charles. *Decadent Subjects.* Baltimore: Johns Hopkins University Press, 2002.

Bersani, Leo. "Is the Rectum a Grave?" In *Is the Rectum a Grave? and Other Essays,* 3–30. Chicago: University of Chicago Press, 2010.

Biale, David. *Eros and the Jews: From Biblical Israel to Contemporary America.* Berkeley: University of California Press, 1997.

Blackbourn, David. "Politics as Theatre: Metaphors of the Stage in German History, 1848–1933." *Transactions of the Royal Historical Society,* 5th Series, 37 (1987): 149–67.

Boele, Otto. *Erotic Nihilism in Late Imperial Russia: The Case of Mikhail Artsybashev's Sanin.* Madison: University of Wisconsin Press, 2009.

Boyarin, Daniel. *Unheroic Conduct: The Rise of Heterosexuality and the Invention of the Modern Jewish Man.* Berkeley: University of California Press, 1997.

Brenner, Naomi. *Lingering Bilingualism: Modern Hebrew and Yiddish Literature in Contact.* Syracuse, NY: Syracuse University Press, 2016.

Brenner, Yosef Hayyim. "Ha'arakhat 'atzmenu bi-shloshat ha-kerakhim" [Self-Evaluation in three volumes]. In vol. 4, *Ketavim*, edited by Menahem Dorman and Yitzhak Kafkafi (Tel Aviv: ha-Kibutz ha-Me'uhad, 1978–85), 1223–96. First published 1914.

Brinker, Menahem. *'Ad ha-simtah ha-tveryanit.* Tel Aviv: 'Am 'Oved, 1990.

Brod, Harry. "Of Mice and Supermen." In *Gender and Judaism*, edited by Tamar Rudavsky, 279–93. New York: New York University Press, 1994.

Brooks, Peter. *The Melodramatic Imagination: Balzac, Henry James, Melodrama, and the Mode of Excess.* New Haven, CT: Yale University Press, 1995.

Calhoun, Craig, ed. *Habermas and the Public Sphere.* Cambridge, MA: MIT Press, 1992.

———. "Introduction: Habermas and the Public Sphere." In *Habermas and the Public Sphere*, edited by Craig Calhoun, 1–50. Cambridge, MA: MIT Press, 1992.

Campos, Michelle. *Ottoman Brothers: Muslims, Christians, and Jews in Early Twentieth Century Palestine.* Stanford, CA: Stanford University Press, 2011.

Chances, Ellen. "The Superfluous Man in Russian Literature." In *The Routledge Companion to Russian Literature*, edited by Neil Cornwell, 111–22. London: Routledge, 2002.

Cohen, Gershon. "Zion in Rabbinic Literature." In *Zion in Jewish Literature*, edited by Abraham Halkin, 38–64. New York: Herzl, 1961.

Connell, Raewyn C., and James Messerschmidt. "Hegemonic Masculinity: Rethinking the Concept." *Gender and Society* 19, no. 6 (2005): 829–59.

Culler, Jonathan. "Anderson and the Novel." In *Grounds of Comparison: Around the Work of Benedict Anderson*, edited by Pheng Cheah and Jonathan Culler, 29–52. New York: Routledge, 2003.

Dekel, Mikhal. *The Universal Jew: Masculinity, Modernity, and the Zionist Movement.* Evanston, IL: Northwestern University Press, 2011.

Diamond, James. *Homeland or Holy Land? The "Canaanite" Critique of Israel.* Bloomington: Indiana University Press, 1986.

Efron, John. *Defenders of the Race: Jewish Doctors and Race Science in Fin-de-Siècle Europe.* New Haven, CT: Yale University Press, 1994.

Eley, Geoff, and Ronald Suny, eds. *Becoming National: A Reader.* New York: Oxford University Press, 1996.

Engelstein, Laura. *The Keys to Happiness: Sex and the Search for Modernity in Fin-de-Siècle Russia.* Ithaca, NY: Cornell University Press, 1992.

Feiner, Shmuel. *The Jewish Enlightenment.* Translated by Chaya Naor. Philadelphia: University of Pennsylvania Press, 2004.

Feldman, Yael. *Glory and Agony: Isaac's Sacrifice and National Narrative.* Stanford, CA: Stanford University Press, 2010.

Frankel, Jonathan. *Prophecy and Politics: Socialism, Nationalism, and the Russian Jews, 1862–1917.* New York: Cambridge University Press, 1984.

———. "The 'Yizkor' Book of 1911: A Note on National Myths in the Second Aliya." Chap. 8 in *Crisis, Revolution, and Russian Jews*, 183–215. New York: Cambridge University Press, 2009.

Freud, Sigmund. *The Standard Edition of the Complete Psychological Works of Sigmund Freud.* Translated and edited by James Strachey. 24 vols. London: Hogarth, 1956–74.

———. *Three Essays on the Theory of Sexuality.* Translated by James Strachey. New York: Basic Books, 1975.

Gilman, Sander. *Franz Kafka, the Jewish Patient.* New York: Routledge, 1995.

———. *Jewish Self-Hatred: Anti-Semitism and the Hidden Language of the Jews.* Baltimore: Johns Hopkins University Press, 1992.

———. *The Jew's Body.* New York: Routledge, 1991.

Gilmore, David. *Manhood in the Making: Cultural Concepts of Masculinity.* New Haven, CT: Yale University Press, 1990.

Gluzman, Michael. "Unmasking the Politics of Simplicity in Modernist Hebrew Poetry." *Prooftexts* 13, no. 1 (1993): 21–44.

———. *See also* Gluzman, Mikha'el.

Gluzman, Mikha'el. *ha-Guf ha-Tzioni: le'umiut, migdar u-miniut ba-sifrut ha-'Ivrit ha-hadashah.* Tel Aviv: ha-Kibutz ha-Me'uhad, 2007.

———. *See also* Gluzman, Michael.

Gold, Nili. *Yehuda Amichai: The Making of Israel's National Poet.* Waltham, MA: Brandeis University Press, 2008.

Goldstein, Yaakov. *From Fighters to Soldiers: How the Israeli Defense Forces Began.* Portland, OR: Sussex Academic Press, 1998.

Govrin, Nurit. *Alienation and Regeneration.* Tel Aviv: Mod Books, 1989.

———. *'Me'ora' Brenner': ha-ma'avak 'al hofesh ha-bitui (1911–1913).* Jerusalem: Yad Ben Tzvi, 1985.

Habas, Brakhah, ed. *Sefer ha-'aliyah ha-shniyah.* Tel Aviv: 'Am 'Oved, 1947.

Habermas, Jürgen. "The Public Sphere: An Encyclopedia Article (1964)." *New German Critique* 3 (Autumn 1974): 49–55.

———. *The Structural Transformation of the Public Sphere: An Inquiry into a Category of Bourgeois Society.* Translated by Thomas Burger. Cambridge, MA: MIT Press, 1996.

Halevi-Zwick, Judith. *'Agnon be-ma'agalotav: 'iyunim be-omanut ha-sipur shel 'Agnon.* Tel Aviv: Papyrus, 1989.

———. *Reshitah shel bikoret 'Agnon: 5669–5692.* Haifa: Haifa University Press, 1984.

Halkin, Shimon. *Mavo la-siporet ha-'Ivrit.* Edited by Tsofiyah Hillel. Jerusalem: Akademon, 1958.

Halper, Shaun. "Mordechai Langer (1894–1943) and the Birth of the Modern Jewish Homosexual." PhD diss., University of California, Berkeley, 2013.

Halperin, Liora. *Babel in Zion: Jews, Nationalism, and Language Diversity in Palestine, 1920–1948.* New Haven, CT: Yale University Press, 2015.

Harshav, Benjamin. *Language in Time of Revolution.* Berkeley: University of California Press, 1993.

———. *The Meaning of Yiddish.* Berkeley: University of California Press, 1990.

Hart, Mitchell. *Social Science and the Politics of Modern Jewish Identity.* Stanford, CA: Stanford University Press, 2000.

Haver, Yael. *What Must Be Forgotten: The Survival of Yiddish in Zionist Palestine.* Syracuse, NY: Syracuse University Press, 2004.

Hertzberg, Arthur. *The Zionist Idea: A Historical Analysis and Reader.* Philadelphia: Jewish Publication Society, 1997.

Hess, Tamar. *Self as Nation: Contemporary Hebrew Autobiography*. Waltham, MA: Brandeis University Press, 2016.

———. "'Tzarikh lenashek lah—dimui feministi bi-'Shekhol ve-khishalon' le-Y. H. Brenner." *Mehkere Yerushalayim be-sifrut 'Ivrit* 15 (1995): 197–221.

Hever, Hannan. "Poetry and Messianism in Palestine between the Two World Wars." *Studies in Contemporary Jewry* 7 (1991): 128–58.

———. Review of *Becoming Hebrew: The Creation of Jewish National Culture in Ottoman Palestine*, by Arieh Saposnik. *Studies in Contemporary Jewry* 25 (2011): 220–26.

Hirshfeld, Ariel. "Deyokan 'atzmi o ha-deyokan ba-derekh el 'atzmi.'" *Helikon* 5 (Winter 1992): 30–54.

Hollander, Philip. "Between Decadence and Rebirth: The Fiction of Levi Aryeh Arieli." PhD diss., Columbia University, 2004.

———. "Beyond Martyrdom: Rereading Moshe Shamir's *With His Own Hands*." *Hebrew Studies* 49 (2008): 259–77.

Holtzman, Avner. *Ahavat Tzion*. Jerusalem: Carmel, 2006.

———. *Mafteah ha-lev: omanut ha-sipur shel Hanokh Bartov*. Jerusalem: Mosad Bialik, 2015.

———. "Poetics, Ideology, Biography, Myth: The Scholarship on J. H. Brenner, 1971–1996." *Prooftexts* 18, no. 1 (1998): 82–94.

———. *Temunah le-neged 'eynay*. Tel Aviv: 'Am 'Oved, 2002.

Holtzman, Avner, Gid'on Katz, and Shalom Ratzabi, eds. *mi-Saviv la-nekudah: mehkarim hadashim 'al M. Y. Berdich'evski, Y. H. Brenner, ve-A. D. Gordon*. Kiryat Sede-Boker: Mekhon Ben-Guryon le-heker Yisra'el veha-Tzionut, Universitat Ben Guryon ba-Negev, 2008.

Iser, Wolfgang. *The Act of Reading*. Baltimore: Johns Hopkins University Press, 1980.

Jacobson, Abigail. *From Empire to Empire: Jerusalem between Ottoman and British Rule*. Syracuse, NY: Syracuse University Press, 2011.

Jelen, Sheila. *Intimations of Difference: Dvora Baron in the Modern Hebrew Renaissance*. Syracuse, NY: Syracuse University Press, 2007.

Kabak, Aharon A. *Masot ve-divre bikoret*. Jerusalem: Shalem, 1978.

Kaplan, Eran. "Amos Oz's *A Tale of Love and Darkness* and the Sabra Myth." *Jewish Social Studies* 14, no. 1 (2007): 119–43.

Katz, Stephen. *Red, Black, and Jew: New Frontiers in Hebrew Literature*. Austin: University of Texas Press, 2009.

Katzman, Roman. "Mahvot be-sifrut: tihalukh kognitivi ve-semiozis tarbuti bi-shne mikre mivhan: 'Ahot' ve-'Ma'agale tzedek' me-et Shai Agnon." *Mehkere Yerushalayim be-sifrut 'Ivrit* 22 (2008): 407–36.

Keshet, Yeshurun. "'Al A. Re'uveni." In *Aharon Re'uveni: mivhar ma'amare bikoret 'al yetzirato*, edited by Yig'al Shvartz, 86–104. Tel Aviv: ha-Kibutz ha-Me'uhad, 1992.

———. *Omadot*. Jerusalem: Hotza'at Shalem, 1970.

Kressel, Getzel. *Leksikon ha-sifrut ha-'Ivrit ba-dorot ha-ahronim*. 2 vols. Merhavyah: Sifriyat ha-Po'alim, 1967.

Kritz, Reuven. *ha-Siporet shel dor ha-ma'avak le-'atzma'ut*. Tel Aviv: Pura, 1978.

Kronfeld, Chana. "Beyond Thematicism in the Historiography of Post-1948 Political Poetry." *Jewish Social Studies* 18, no. 3 (2012): 180–96.

———. *The Full Severity of Compassion: The Poetry of Yehuda Amichai*. Stanford, CA: Stanford University Press, 2016.

————. *On the Margins of Modernism: Decentering Literary Dynamics.* Berkeley: University of California Press, 1996.

Kurtzveil, Barukh. "Shorashav ha-nafshiyim veha-metafisiyim shel ha-yesod ha-idili." Chap. 7 in *Sifrutenu ha-hadashah—hemshekh o mahpekhah?*, 301–28. Tel Aviv: Schocken, 1960.

Laor, Dan. "bi-Mehozot ha-zikaron: biografiyah, ide'ologiyah, ve-sipur bi-ketivato shel Amos Oz." *Yisrael* 7 (2005): 25–40.

————. *Haye Agnon.* Jerusalem: Schocken, 1998.

————. *"Ve-Haya he-Akov le-Mishor":* A Century Later." Lecture, Association for Jewish Studies Conference, Chicago, December 18, 2012.

Laplanche, Jean, and Jean-Bertrand Pontalis. *The Language of Psycho-analysis.* Translated by Donald Nicholson-Smith. New York: Norton, 1973.

Lederhandler, Eli. *Road to Modern Jewish Politics.* New York: Oxford University Press, 1989.

Lev-Ari, Shimon. "Hitpathut ha-te'atronim." In *Toldot ha-yishuv ha-Yehudi be-Eretz-Yisrael me-az ha-'aliyah ha-rishonah: beniyatah shel tarbut 'Ivrit be-Eretz-Yisrael*, edited by Zohar Shavit, 343–66. Jerusalem: Mosad Bialik, 2002.

Mandel, Neville. *The Arabs and Zionism before World War I.* Berkeley: University of California Press, 1976.

Mao, Douglas, and Rebecca Walkowitz. "The New Modernist Studies." *PMLA* 123, no. 3 (2008): 737–48.

Melman, Bili. "Min ha-shulayim el ha-historiyah shel migdar ve-Eretz Yisra'eliyut (1890–1920)." *Tzion* 62, no. 3 (1997): 243–78.

Mendes-Flohr, Paul, and Jehuda Reinharz, eds. *The Jew in the Modern World.* New York: Oxford University Press, 1980.

Michels, Tony. *A Fire in Their Hearts: Yiddish Socialists in New York.* Cambridge, MA: Harvard University Press, 2005.

Miller, D. A. *The Novel and the Police.* Berkeley: University of California Press, 1988.

Miller, Karl. *Doubles: Studies in Literary History.* London: Oxford University Press, 1985.

Milner, Iris. "Yosef Hayyim Brenner's *Mikan umikan:* The Telling of Trauma." *Prooftexts* 32 (2012): 33–62.

Mintz, Alan. "Agnon in Jaffa: The Myth of the Artist as a Young Man." *Prooftexts* 1, no. 1 (1981): 62–83.

————. *Banished from Their Father's Table: Loss of Faith and Hebrew Autobiography.* Bloomington: Indiana University Press, 1989.

————. *Hurban: Responses to Catastrophe in Hebrew Literature.* Syracuse, NY: Syracuse University Press, 1996.

————. *Sanctuary in the Wilderness: A Critical Introduction to American Hebrew Poetry.* Stanford, CA: Stanford University Press, 2012.

Miron, Dan. Afterword in *Midnight Convoy and Other Stories*, by S. Yizhar, 257–72. Translated by Misha Louvish, Miriam Arad, and Reuven Ben-Yosef. Jerusalem: Israeli University Press, 1969.

————. *Arba' panim ba-sifrut ha-'Ivrit bat-yemenu.* Jerusalem: Schocken, 1962.

————. *Bodedim be-mo'adam: li-deyoknah shel ha-republikah ha-sifrutit ha-'Ivrit bi-thilat ha-me'ah ha-'esrim.* Tel Aviv: 'Am 'Oved, 1987.

————. "Depictions of Jerusalem in Modern Hebrew Literature." In *City of the Great King: Jerusalem from David to the Present*, edited by Nitza Rosovsky, 241–78. Cambridge, MA: Harvard University Press, 1996.

———. *From Continuity to Contiguity: Towards a New Jewish Literary Thinking*. Stanford, CA: Stanford University Press, 2010.

———. *The Image of the Shtetl and Other Studies of Modern Jewish Literary Imagination*. Syracuse: Syracuse University Press, 2000.

———. *Im lo tihyeh Yerushalayim*. Tel Aviv: ha-Kibutz ha-Me'uhad, 1987.

———. *Kivun orot: tahanot ba-siporet ha-'Ivrit ha-modernit*. Jerusalem: Keter, 1979.

———. "me-Yotzrim ve-bonim li-vnei bli bayit." Chap. 1 in *Im lo tihyeh Yerushalayim*, 11–89. Tel Aviv: ha-Kibutz ha-Me'uhad, 1987.

———. *Mul ha-ah ha-shotek: 'iyunim be-shirat Milhemet ha-'Atzma'ut*. Jerusalem: Keter, 1992.

———. *The Prophetic Mode in Modern Hebrew Poetry*. Milford, CT: Toby, 2010.

Mosse, George. *Fallen Soldiers: Reshaping the Memory of the World Wars*. New York: Oxford University Press, 1990.

———. *The Image of Man*. New York: Oxford University Press, 1996.

———. *Nationalism and Sexuality: Middle-Class Morality and Sexual Norms in Modern Europe*. Madison: University of Wisconsin Press, 1985.

Nagel, Joane. "Masculinity and Nationalism: Gender and Sexuality in the Making of Nations." *Ethnic and Racial Studies* 21, no. 2 (1998): 242–69.

Naveh, Hannah. "Migdar ve-hazon ha-gavriut ha-'Ivrit." In *Zeman Yehudi hadash: tarbut Yehudit be-'idan hiloni; mabat entziklopedi*, edited by Yirmiyahu Yovel, 3:1117–23. Jerusalem: Keter, 2007.

Neumann, Bo'az. *Land and Desire in Early Zionism*. Translated by Haim Watzman. Waltham, MA: Brandeis University Press, 2011.

———. *Teshukat ha-halutzim*. Tel Aviv: 'Am 'Oved, 2009.

'Ofrat, Gid'on. *Adamah, adam, dam: mitos he-halutz u-fulhan ha-adamah be-mahazot ha-hityashvut*. Tel Aviv: Ts'erikover, 1980.

Olmert, Dana. "Miniut ve-merhav be-'ba-Horef' le-Y. H. Brenner—he'arot ahadot." In *Rega' shel huledet: mehkarim be-sifrut 'Ivrit uve-sifrut Yidish li-khevod Dan Miron*, edited by Hannan Hever, 387–401. Jerusalem: Mosad Bialik, 2007.

———. "Shama halo lo po: kri'ah bi-shne sipurim mukdamim shel Yosef Hayyim Brenner." *Mehkere Yerushalayim be-sifrut 'Ivrit* 19 (2003): 123–41.

Openhaimer, Yohai. *Me'ever la-gader: yitzug ha-'Aravim ba-siporet ha-'Ivrit veha-Yisra'elit (1906–2005)*. Tel Aviv: 'Am 'Oved, 2008.

Oz, Amos. *Shtikat ha-shamayim: Agnon mishtomem 'al elohim*. Jerusalem: Keter, 1993.

Parush, Iris. *Reading Jewish Women*. Translated by Saadyah Sternberg. Waltham, MA: Brandeis University Press, 2004.

Peleg, Yaron. *Derekh gever: siporet homoerotit ba-sifrut ha-'Ivrit ha-hadashah, 1880–2000*. Tel Aviv: Shufra le-sifrut yafah, 2003.

———. "Heroic Conduct: Homoeroticism and the Creation of Modern, Jewish Masculinities." *Jewish Social Studies: History, Culture, Society* 13, no. 1 (Fall 2006): 31–58.

———. *Orientalism and the Hebrew Imagination*. Ithaca, NY: Cornell University Press, 2005.

———. "Reinterpreting the East: Orientalism in Hebrew Literature, 1890–1930." PhD diss., Brandeis University, 2000.

Penslar, Derek. *Jews and the Military: A History*. Princeton, NJ: Princeton University Press, 2013.

———. *Shylock's Children: Economics and Jewish Identity in Modern Jewish Europe*. Berkeley: University of California Press, 2001.

Pilovsky, Aryeh. Introduction to *Gezamlte dertzeylungen*, by Aharon Re'uveni, vii–xl. Jerusalem: Hotza'at Magnes, 1991.

Pinsker, Sanford. *The Schlemiel as Metaphor: Studies in Yiddish and American Jewish Fiction.* Carbondale: Southern Illinois University Press, 1991.

Pinsker, Shachar. "Imagining the Beloved: Gender and Nation Building in Early Twentieth-Century Hebrew Literature." *Gender and History* 20, no. 1 (April 2008): 105–27.

———. *Literary Passports: The Making of Modernist Hebrew Fiction in Europe.* Stanford, CA: Stanford University Press, 2011.

Presner, Todd. *Muscular Judaism: The Jewish Body and the Politics of Regeneration.* New York: Routledge, 2007.

Ramraz-Ra'ukh, Gila. *L. A. Arieli (Orlof): hayyav ve-yetzirato.* Tel Aviv: Papirus, 1992.

Reeser, Todd. *Masculinities in Theory: An Introduction.* Malden, MA: Wiley-Blackwell, 2010.

Roskies, David. *Against the Apocalypse.* Cambridge, MA: Harvard University Press, 1984.

Sadan, Dov. *'Al Shai Agnon: masah 'iyun ve-heker.* Tel Aviv: ha-Kibutz ha-Me'uhad, 1959.

———. "Le-sugyah: Shlomi'el." *Orlogin* 1 (1950): 198–203.

Sadan-Loebenstein, Nili. *Aharon Re'uveni: Monografiyah.* Tel Aviv: Sifriyat Po'alim, 1994.

———. "Magemot dekadentiot be-siporet ha-mehagrim bi-shnot ha-'esrim be-Eretz-Yisrael." PhD diss., Bar Ilan University, 1976.

Saposnik, Arieh. *Becoming Hebrew: The Creation of a Jewish National Culture in Ottoman Palestine.* New York: Oxford University Press, 2008.

———. "Exorcising the 'Angel of National Death'—Nation and Individual Death (and Rebirth) in Zionist Palestine." *Jewish Quarterly Review* 95, no. 3 (2005): 557–78.

Sarker, Sonita. "Modernism in Our Image . . . Always, Partially." *Modernism/Modernity* 13, no. 3 (2006): 561–66.

Schachter, Allison. *Diasporic Modernisms: Hebrew and Yiddish Literature in the Twentieth Century.* New York: Oxford University Press, 2012.

Schwartz, Yigal. *The Zionist Paradox: Hebrew Literature and Israeli Identity.* Waltham, MA: Brandeis University Press, 2014.

———. *See also* Shvartz, Yig'al.

Sedgwick, Eve. *Between Men: English Literature and Male Homosocial Desire.* New York: Columbia University Press, 1985.

———. *Epistemology of the Closet.* Berkeley: University of California Press, 1990.

———. "Nationalism and Sexualities: As Opposed to What?" Chap. 8 in *Tendencies*, 143–153. Durham, NC: Duke University Press, 1993.

Segal, Natanel. "A Study of Two Enigmatic Stories by L. A. Arieli: 'Mortals' and 'The Death Tale.'" PhD diss., New York University, 1991.

Segev, Tom. *1949: The First Israelis.* Edited by Arlen Weinstein. New York: Henry Holt, 1998.

Seidman, Naomi. *A Marriage Made in Heaven: The Sexual Politics of Hebrew and Yiddish.* Berkeley: University of California Press, 1993.

Shaked, Gershon. *ha-Siporet ha-'Ivrit, 1880–1980.* 5 vols. Tel Aviv: ha-Kibutz ha-Me'uhad, 1977–98.

———. "Ha-te'om she-yarad—'al yetzirato shel L. A. Arieli-Orlof." *Siman Kri'ah* 5 (February 1976): 481–91.

———. "Matzevah le-avot ve-siman le-vanim: otobiografiyot Yisraeliyot mi-shnot ha-shmonim ve-'ad le-reshit ha-me'ah ha-'esrim ve-ehat." Chap. 15 in *Temunah Kevutzatit: Hebetim be-sifrut Yisrael uve-tarbutah*, 288–367. Or Yehudah: Dvir, 2009.

———. *Omanut ha-sipur shel Agnon.* Tel Aviv: Sifriyat ha-Po'alim, 1973.

Shapira, Anita. *Brenner: Sipur hayyim.* Tel Aviv: 'Am 'Oved, 2008.

———. "'Dor ba-aretz.'" *Alpayim* 2 (1990): 178–203.

———. "ha-Mitos shel ha-Yehudi ha-hadash." Chap. 6 in *Yehudim hadashim Yehudim yeshanim*, 155–74. Tel Aviv: 'Am 'Oved, 1997.

———. "Hirbet Hiza: Between Remembrance and Forgetting." *Jewish Social Studies* 7, no. 1 (2000): 1–62.

———. *Land and Power: The Zionist Resort to Force, 1881–1948*. Translated by William Templer. Stanford, CA: Stanford University Press, 1992.

———. "Le'an halkhah shlilat ha-galut." Chap. 2 in *Yehudim, Tzionim, u-mah she-benehem*, 63–110. Tel Aviv: 'Am 'Oved, 2007.

Shavit, Zohar. *ha-Hayyim ha-sifrutiyim be-Eretz Yisrael, 1910–1933*. Tel Aviv: ha-Kibutz ha-Me'uhad, 1982.

———. "Mavo." In *Toldot ha-yishuv ha-Yehudi be-Eretz-Yisrael me-az ha-'aliyah ha-rishonah: beniyatah shel tarbut 'Ivrit be-Eretz-Yisrael*, edited by Zohar Shavit, 1–7. Jerusalem: Mosad Bialik, 2002.

Shayit, Hedi. "Lo 'margish ayzen': ha-tzabar ha-talush ba-siporet ha-mukdemet shel 'Dor ba-Aretz' al pi yetzirot shel S. Yizhar, Moshe Shamir, ve-Hanokh Bartov." *mi-Kan* 9 (2008): 158–82.

Shmeruk, Khone. *ha-Kri'ah le-navi: mehkere historiyah ve-sifrut*. Edited by Yisra'el Bartal. Jerusalem: Merkaz Zalman Shazar, 1999.

Shneer, David, and Robert Adler-Peckerar. "The Berkeley School of Jewish Literature." *Journal of Jewish Identities* 7, no. 1 (2014): 1–7.

Shomer Organization. *Kovetz ha-Shomer: te'udot zikhronot ve-divre ha'arakhah ketuvim bi-yede vatike "ha-Shomer."* Tel Aviv: Arkhiyon ha-'Avodah, 1937.

Shvartz, Yig'al, ed. *Aharon Re'uveni: mivhar ma'amare bikoret 'al yetzirato*. Tel Aviv: ha-Kibutz ha-Me'uhad, 1992.

———. *Li-heyot ke-de li-heyot: Aharon Re'uveni—monografiyah*. Jerusalem: Hotza'at Magnes, 1993.

———. *Mah she-ro'im mi-kan*. Or Yehudah: Dvir, 2005.

———. *Pulhan ha-sofer ve-dat ha-medinah*. Or Yehudah: Dvir, 2011.

———. *See also* Schwartz, Yigal.

Siegel, Andrea. "Rape and the 'Arab Question' in L. A. Arieli's *Allah Karim!* and Aharon Reuveni's *Devastation*." *Nashim* 23, no. 1 (2012): 110–28.

Sivan, Emmanuel. *Dor tashah: mitos, deyokan ve-zikaron*. Tel Aviv: Ma'arakhot, 1991.

Tidhar, David. *Entziklopedyah le-halutze ha-Yishuv u-vonav*. 19 vols. Tel Aviv: Sifriyat Rishonim, 1947–71.

Tzemah, 'Adi. "Min ve-ofi le'umi: tzemed nos'im be-'Yeshimon' shel L. A. Arieli." *Moznayim*, 53, nos. 5–6 (1982): 371–83.

Tzuker, Shlomo. "Sipure Tshatskes ve-tikkune Agnon." In *Shai Agnon: mehkarim u-te'udot*, edited by Rafa'el Vayzer and Gershon Shaked, 11–38. Jerusalem: Mosad Bialik, 1978.

Ury, Scott. *Barricades and Banners: The Revolution of 1905 and the Transformation of Warsaw Jewry*. Stanford, CA: Stanford University Press, 2012.

———. "The Generation of 1905 and the Politics of Despair: Alienation, Friendship, Community." In *The Revolution of 1905 and Russia's Jews*, edited by Stefani Hoffman and Ezra Mendelsohn, 96–110. Philadelphia: University of Pennsylvania Press, 2008.

Veidlinger, Jeffrey. *Jewish Public Culture in Later Imperial Russia*. Bloomington: Indiana University Press, 2009.

Verses, Shmu'el. "Ben tokhehah le-apologetikah: 'be-'ir ha-haregah' shel Bialik umi-saviv lah." In *bi-Mevo'e 'ir ha-haregah: mivhar ma'amrim 'al shiro shel Bialik*, edited by Uzi Shavit and Ziva Shamir, 23–54. Tel Aviv: ha-Kibutz ha-Me'uhad, 1994.

Weingrad, Michael. *American Hebrew Literature: Writing Jewish National Identity in the United States.* Syracuse, NY: Syracuse University Press, 2011.

Wisse, Ruth. *The Schlemiel as Modern Hero.* Chicago: University of Chicago Press, 1971.

Zakh, Natan. "Omanut ha-sipur shel A. Re'uveni." In *Aharon Re'uveni: mivhar ma'amare bikoret 'al yetzirato*, edited by Yig'al Shvartz, 105–114. Tel Aviv: ha-Kibutz ha-Me'uhad, 1992.

Zerubavel, Yael. "Memory, the Rebirth of the Native, and the 'Hebrew Bedouin' Identity." *Social Research* 75, no. 1 (2008): 315–52.

———. *Recovered Roots: Collective Memory and the Making of Israeli National Tradition.* Chicago: University of Chicago Press, 1995.

Zipperstein, Steven. *Elusive Prophet: Ahad Ha'am and the Origins of Zionism.* Berkeley: University of California Press, 1993.

GENERAL INDEX

Numbers in italics refer to illustrations.

Abramovitsh, Sholem Yankev, 12, 15, 34, 146
adultery, 35, 166, 173–74, 190n75, 202, 217
Agnon, Shmuel Yosef: antisemitism and,
    28, 103; Austrian progressivism and,
    27–28; didacticism and, 4, 9, 11, 16–17,
    37–46, 51, 63–65; 100, 103, 184–85; Eastern
    European social reality and, 6, 38; gender
    and, 2, 9, 17, 36, 38, 49–55, 61–65, 184;
    German fluency and, 27–29, 132; literary
    aspirations and, 6, 25–29, 65n7; Nobel
    Prize for Literature and, 29; poetry of, 40,
    43, 46; Scandinavian impressionism and,
    28; secularism and, 28–29, 37–38, 42–44,
    63–64; sexual mores and, 9, 37–38, 48–54,
    58, 61, 71, 75, 131–32, 185. *See also characters
    and specific works by title in Index of
    Cited Works*
agricultural labor, 30, 35, 65n1, 81–82, 84, 88,
    91, 101, 110–11, 113–14, 121, 132, 196–98
Aharonowitz, Yosef, 1, 10
Aleichem, Sholem, 39. *See also specific works
    by title*
'aliyah, 215
Amichai, Yehuda, 194, 199, 211–13, 217,
    230n44. *See also specific works by title*
Anokhi, Zalman Yitzhok, 71
antidiasporic, 217
anti-intellectual, 46, 110
antisemitism, 12, 28, 58, 7, 84, 90, 94n8, 99,
    103, 108, 110, 127n42, 172, 180, 202
anti-Zionism, 4
apostasy, 99
Aramaic, 225, 232n88
Arieli, Levi Aryeh: American immigration
    and, 130; apolitical reputation and, 29–32;
    feminine egoism and, 16–18, 94, 112–13,
    123, 142; mentorship of Yosef Hayyim
    Brenner and, 102, 133; military service
    and, 18, 26, 30, 139–45, 157, 166; modernity

and, 112, 123, 165–66; Palestinian immi-
    gration and, 16, 20n4, 30–32, 100, 124, 165,
    227; political activism and, 4, 7, 9, 29–30,
    47, 99–103, 143, 153, 184; portrayal of Pal-
    estinian Arabs and, 102–5, 111–12, 139–41;
    reputation as decadent and, 18–19, 165–67,
    184; secular education and, 29, 119–21. *See
    also characters and specific works by title
    in Index of Cited Works*
Aronsohn. *See Anokhi, Zalman Yitzhok*
Artsybashev, Mikhail, 112
Aryan male ideals, 156n17, 167, 189n38
Ashkenazim, 89, 225
Auschwitz, 204

ba'al guf (physically developed Jew), 80
Bader, Gershon, 28
Balfour Declaration, the, 117, 154, 160–61
Bar-Giora, 109, 128n44
Bar Kochba revolt, the, 197
Bartov, Hanoch, 199, 206, 210. *See also specif-
    ic works by title*
battle of Tel Hai (1920), 165, 197
Bedouins, 79, 110, 146–47, 201
Ben-Gurion, David, 169–70
Ben-Zvi, Yitzhak, 31, 169, *170*
Berdichevsky, Mikhah Yosef, 24, 104
Bernheimer, Charles, 164–66
Biale, David, 1–2
Bialik, Hayyim Nahman, 24, 42–43, 62, 109
Białystok pogrom of 1906, 43
Blowstein, Rachel, 32
Bnei Moshe, 30
Bolshevik Revolution, the, 108, 160
Borochov, Ber, 31
Brenner, Yosef Hayyim: gender theory and,
    2–11, 16–17, 49, 65, 72–73, 79, 91–93, 164, 180,
    184–86; homosocial relations and, 17–18, 49,
    65, 69–75, 92–94, 101–3, 180, 185; influence

INDEX OF CITED WORKS

PHILIP HOLLANDER is Assistant Professor of Israeli Literature and Culture at the University of Wisconsin–Madison. He has published numerous articles dealing with Hebrew, Jewish, and Israeli literature, film, and culture. This is his first book.